Transformable Race

Transformable Race

Surprising Metamorphoses in the Literature of Early America

Katy L. Chiles

OXFORD
UNIVERSITY PRESS

OXFORD
UNIVERSITY PRESS

Oxford University Press is a department of the University of Oxford.
It furthers the University's objective of excellence in research, scholarship,
and education by publishing worldwide.

Oxford New York
Auckland Cape Town Dar es Salaam Hong Kong Karachi
Kuala Lumpur Madrid Melbourne Mexico City Nairobi
New Delhi Shanghai Taipei Toronto

With offices in
Argentina Austria Brazil Chile Czech Republic France Greece
Guatemala Hungary Italy Japan Poland Portugal Singapore
South Korea Switzerland Thailand Turkey Ukraine Vietnam

Oxford is a registered trade mark of Oxford University Press
in the UK and certain other countries.

Published in the United States of America by
Oxford University Press
198 Madison Avenue, New York, NY 10016

Library of Congress Cataloging-in-Publication Data
Chiles, Katy L.
Transformable race : surprising metamorphoses in the literature of early America / Katy L. Chiles.
p.   cm.
Includes bibliographical references and index.
ISBN 978-0-19-931350-1
1. American literature—18th century—History and criticism. 2. Race in literature.
3. Race awareness in literature. 4. Race relations in literature. 5. Human skin color in literature.
6. Blacks—Race identity—United States—History—18th century. 7. Indians of North
America—Race identity—History—18th century. 8. Whites—Race identity—United
States—History—18th century. I. Title.
PS195.R32C55 2014
810.9'3529—dc23
2013019945

9780199313501

1 3 5 7 9 8 6 4 2

Printed in the United States of America on acid-free paper

For Darrin and Grant

{ CONTENTS }

{ ACKNOWLEDGMENTS }

One of the joys of finishing a book is the opportunity it affords a writer to thank all of those who contributed to her thinking and writing along the way. This project took initial shape at Northwestern University under the direction of Betsy Erkkilä. Betsy demonstrates what it means to be a professional scholar, an engaging teacher, and a departmental citizen; she is also a dear friend. I have benefited enormously as well from my other mentors: Jennifer Brody taught me to question my own presuppositions; Jay Grossman posed the kind of rigorous queries about my work that I could only begin to answer years later and that made it (and me) much better for it; and Julia Stern's vivaciousness and searing intellect drew me to Evanston in the first place, inspired me while there, and influences me yet. My debt to each of them is substantial; my appreciation and admiration of them runs deep. Much earlier, Steven Weisenburger, Nikky Finney, and Kelly Ellis guided my first thinking on race and literature. Raymond Betts taught me to think harder and to live deeper; his memory shapes me still.

I owe particular debts of gratitude to others who contributed to my training at Northwestern, including Kevin Bell, Brian Edwards, Christopher Lane, Jeffrey Masten, Carl Smith, Shannon Steen, and Alex Weheliye. I also enjoyed the company of extraordinary colleagues who significantly shaped my academic worldview, such as Marcy Dinius, Abram Van Engen, Ryan Friedman, Deana Greenfield, Christopher Hager, Hunt Howell, Bishupal Limbu, Wendy Roberts, and Janaka Bowman Smith. Among countless other things, Coleman Hutchison helped carry my books. In particular, Sarah Blackwood, Peter Jaros, and Sarah Mesle have been the intellectual midwives who have helped bring this book into being. One could not ask for better writing partners and friends.

I am also grateful for the intellectual engagement and support I have received from my colleagues at the University of Tennessee. I thank my department chairs, Chuck Maland and Stan Garner, for providing the kind of environment where one's teaching and scholarship can thrive. Heather Hirschfeld has been an ideal mentor. The UT Americanist Reading Group provided a key intellectual community, comprised of Dawn Coleman, Amy Elias, Martin Griffin, Mark Hulsether, Tom Haddox, Bill Hardwig, Ben Lee, Steve Pearson, and Katie Burnett. Mary Papke, Michelle Commander, Michael Lofaro, and Lisi Schoenbach gave me invaluable feedback on chapter drafts, and Misty Anderson, Allen Dunn, Tom Heffernan, Nancy Henry, La Vinia

Jennings, Lisa King, Gichingiri Ndigirigi, and Alan Rutenberg shaped my thinking in innumerable ways. Margaret Lazarus Dean and Chris Hebert have been beloved friends and fantastic life and publication coaches; Urmila Seshagiri has been an exemplarly model for me in so many ways. I also thank my colleagues in Africana Studies, especially Dawn Duke, Rosalind Hackett, Barbara Heath, Tricia Hepner, Josh Inwood, Bert Louis, Amadou Sall, Jorge Serrano, and Courtney Wright for engaging with and encouraging my work. I have benefitted from the Eighteenth-Century Studies research group organized by Mary McAlpin. Thanks to my research assistants, Adam Coombs and especially John Stromski, whose work was absolutely essential to bringing this book into its final form. Thanks also to my students, both at Northwestern and Tennessee, who helped bring these ideas to life in the classroom.

Countless others outside the halls of these institutions have contributed greatly to this work, and I am thrilled to thank in particular Eric Gary Anderson, Ralph Bauer, Steven Blevins, Joanna Brooks, Gina Caison, Jeff Clymer, Robert Gooding-Williams, Sandra Gustafson, Annette Kolodny, Bob Levine, Chris Looby, Dennis Moore, Sam Otter, Yvette Piggush, Cassander Smith, Susan Sleeper-Smith, Cristina Stanciu, Steven Thomas, Caroline Wigginton, Kelly Wisecup, and Hilary Wyss. I have benefitted greatly from Chris Castiglia's engagements with my work. Dana Nelson has long been an inspiration to me, providing models of professionalism and of scholarship. I hope both Chris and Dana know how thankful I am for all they have done for me.

I thank Melissa Tantaquidgeon Zobel, Mohegan Tribal Historian, for answering my questions about Samson Occom, giving me a tour of Mohegan land, and demonstrating to me that what for some people is research, for others is family. David Freeburg, Mohegan Tribal Archivist (and Faith Damon Davidson before him) helped me with the Mohegan archives, made my research available to tribal members, and sent me utterly amazing citations long after I left Mohegan. Dorothy Davids, Mohican Elder and past chair of the Mohican Nation Stockbridge-Munsee Band Historical Committee, took the time ten years ago to answer the questions of a graduate student about one of her ancestors. I appreciate Nathalee Kristiansen, Leah Miller, and Betty Groh for making my research on Hendrick Aupaumut at the Arvid E. Miller Library and Museum both possible and a pleasure. Cindy Jungenberg, past library specialist of the Mohican Nation Stockbridge-Munsee Band, also helped make my research available at the tribal archives. Sherry White, Historical Preservation Officer, has fielded my queries and encouraged me to speak on Aupaumut at the NAI Algonquian Peoples' Conference. I am also so grateful to former Tribal Council member Jo Ann Schedler for her research and for her interest in mine.

This project has been supported by the National Endowment for the Humanities, the American Philosophical Society, the Mellon Foundation, the US Department of Education, the Northwestern University English Department and Graduate School, and the University of Tennessee English Department, Hodges Better English Fund, and Office of Research (though any views, findings, conclusions, or recommendations expressed herein do not necessarily reflect those of these organizations). I thank each of these institutions for providing me the opportunity to conduct this research. I also thank the University of Tennessee Graduate School Professional Development Award program for funding the time I was able to spend at the Mohegan Nation and the Stockbridge-Munsee Band of the Mohican Nation. I am grateful to the librarians and staff members of the American Philosophical Society, the Newberry Library, Northwestern University Library, the Library Company of Philadelphia, the Historical Society of Pennsylvania, Cornell University Library, and University of Tennessee Library for their assistance with my research. The Northwestern University Center for African American History (particularly Darlene Clark Hine, Eric Gellman, Justin Behrend, Ebony Utley, and Tobin Shearer), the Newberry Library Seminar in Early American History and Culture (particularly Sandra Gustafson, Justine Murison, and Laura Keenan Spero), the CIC American Indian Studies Program (particularly Chadwick Allen, Phillip Round, Jill Doerfler, and Rochelle Zuck), the University of Minnesota-Morris African American Writers speaker series (especially Michael Lackey and Julie Eckerle), and the UT Humanities Center symposium on Heredity and Racial Theory (especially Mary McAlpin and Robert Bernasconi) provided fertile ground for the development of these ideas. At Oxford University Press, Brendan O'Neil has been the editor I have always wanted for this book. The extremely thoughtful feedback I received from two anonymous readers greatly helped me strengthen this book's argument and form. I also thank Marcia Youngman, Philo Antonie Michael, and the staff at OUP for their contributions to this book.

I would also like to acknowledge my family and friends for their support throughout the writing of this book. I thank Kirk and Dianne Chiles for everything and more, and Gene and Donna Travillian for their constant support. Mandy Stone, Lucianne Junker, Corrie Scott, Mandy Lewis, and Jamie Winders answered questions and offered encouragement. Mary Vyskocil cared for my son while I read, researched, and wrote. I wish Lindsey Powell Rensch could have seen the way she influenced the writing of these pages. Most of all, I want to thank Darrin Travillian for all he did, every day, to make this a reality. I could not have done this without him, nor would I have wanted to. And at the end of each day, I am most grateful to and for Darrin and Grant Raymond Chiles Travillian, who always cheer from the sidelines as loudly for me as I do for them.

I thank the Modern Language Association of America for permission to publish a revised version of Chapter 1, which first appeared as an essay in *PMLA* (123.5).

Transformable Race

Surprising Metamorphoses

Let us begin with the word *dye*. In late eighteenth-century British North America, *dye* traveled easily between different modes of discourse, from natural history to poetry and back. And the fact that it moved so fluidly between scientific and aesthetic realms speaks volumes about what we do not yet fully understand about race and literature in early America. Indeed, the *dye* metaphor tells us much about the way race was conceptualized in this period: that it was external, that it was something that happened to the surface of the body, that it developed over time, that it was related to the place where one lived, and that it could possibly change. For instance, as early as 1744, John Mitchell, a Virginia doctor, naturalist, and geographer used *dye* to clarify his ideas about race in his "Essay upon the Causes of the Different Colours of People in Different Climates." Mitchell argued that both "Blacks" and "Whites" were descended from "People of an intermediate tawny Colour; whose Posterity became more and more tawny, *i.e.* black, in the southern Regions, and less so, or white, in the northern Climes."[1] He also asserted that "all the different People in the World" descended from one, original, "tawny People," and that humans' colors could change, although more or less easily for certain groups: "As for the black People recovering, in the same manner [as white people], their primitive swarthy Colours of their Forefathers, by removing from their intemperate scorching Regions, it must be observed, that there is a great Difference in the different Ways of changing Colours to one another: Thus Dyers can very easily dye any white Cloth black, but cannot so easily discharge that Black, and bring it to its first Colour" ("ECDC" 148).

As literary scholars will immediately recognize, nearly thirty years later, Phillis Wheatley used the dye metaphor (in its now-obsolete spelling *die*) in her oft-quoted poem, "On Being Brought from Africa to America,"

Some view our sable race with scornful eye,
"Their colour is a diabolic die." (5–6)[2]

As I explore more fully in Chapter 1, Wheatley employed *die* in the same way Mitchell did: to denote the process through which a "race" acquired their current surface color, presumably different from another that they had previously. The *dye* metaphor rebounded back into natural historical discourse in *Essay on the Slavery and Commerce of the Human Species, Particularly the African*, written in 1786 by Thomas Clarkson, British abolitionist and reader of Phillis Wheatley.[3] Clarkson attacked the institution of slavery by claiming that humankind's many varieties of people formed one species, thus making it grossly immoral for any human of one certain color to claim right over a person of a different one: "It is evident, that if you travel from the equator to the northern pole, you will find a regular gradation of colour from black to white. Now if you can justly take him for your slave, who is of the deepest die, what hinders you from taking him also, who only differs from the former but by a shade. . . . But who are you, that thus take into slavery so many people? Where do you live yourself? Do you live in *Spain*, or in *France*, or in *Britain*? If in either of these countries, take care lest the *whiter natives of the north* should have a claim upon yourself" (*ESC* 185–86, emphasis in original). Five years later, Benjamin Banneker, an African American writer who produced an almanac and worked in mathematics and astronomy, famously sent a letter to another scientific thinker—then Secretary of State Thomas Jefferson—writing that "Sir, I freely and cheerfully acknowledge that I am of the African race, and in that color which is natural to them of the deepest dye."[4] Here, "deepest" performs double duty; it signifies the rich, dark hue of the purported dye *and* the degree of depth the dye reaches moving from the surface of the body towards its interior—significantly, not from the inside out. In this example, circulating from a natural historical treatise to poetry, back to natural historical discourse and into personal, scientific, and obviously political correspondence, the *dye* metaphor conveys a thinking about race quite at odds with our sense of it in the twenty-first century.

This means a great deal for the way we read early American literatures. As the term *dye* demonstrates, the late eighteenth-century discourses of literature and natural history were tightly interwoven, and this period's idea of race varies significantly from those that would follow it. Indeed, historians such as Winthrop Jordan and John Wood Sweet have established that racial thought at the close of the eighteenth century differed radically from that of the nineteenth century, when the concept of race as a fixed biological category would emerge.[5] Instead, figuring centrally in early American writing on race is a multifaceted concept that I refer to as *transformable race*. Drawing on natural historical thinking, early Americans largely considered race—exactly as the *dye* metaphor suggests—to be potentially mutable: it was thought to be an exterior bodily trait, incrementally produced by environmental factors (such as climate, food, and mode of living) and continuously subject to change. This prevailing view—agreeing with the biblical account that all peoples sprang from a single origin—held that humans transformed physically as they moved into and interacted with various parts of the world.[6] As I will detail below, while this way of thinking had its detractors, what Jordan has termed an "environmentalist" mode of thought held sway.[7] Not every early American thought that exposure to the hot sun would make a white person into a "Negro" over the course of time, and nativist Indians made a powerful argument for the separate creations of red, white, and black peoples. However, many subscribed to the idea that the body, its racial features, and racial identity itself were always in flux and had to be consistently maintained; this belief informed a broad cultural logic about racial construction. While historians have documented aspects of transformable race, literary scholars have yet to consider the far-reaching implications this concept has for our understanding of literature produced at the time of the nation's founding. If we know some aspects of the story of how race was conceived in eighteenth-century America, thus far we do not know fully the literary dimension of that story.

Transformable Race: Surprising Metamorphoses in the Literature of Early America, then, endeavors to identify how eighteenth-century racial thinking informs the figurative language in this crucial period's literature. In the following pages, I argue that the notion of transformable race structured how early American texts portrayed the formation of racial identity—that is, both the development of physical features and how those attributes were understood within emerging racial classification systems. This book examines constellations of texts produced by a broad swath of writers: Samson Occom and Phillis Wheatley; Benjamin Franklin and Hendrick Aupaumut; J. Hector St. John de Crèvecoeur, John Marrant, and Charles Brockden Brown; Olaudah Equiano and Hugh Henry Brackenridge; and Royall Tyler. Demonstrating how these authors used language emphasizing or questioning the potential malleability of physical features to explore the construction of racial categories, I examine how they drew upon, reworked, or questioned eighteenth-century ideas about race. This book, ultimately, strives to illustrate for us how early American authors imagined, contributed to, and challenged the ways that one's racial identity could be formed in the late colonial and early national moment.

Thinking Race in Early America

When a man named Henry Moss arrived in Philadelphia in 1796, he appeared to be undergoing what Sweet calls "one of the strangest metamorphoses possible in eighteenth-century America" (*BP* 271).[8] A black man who had lived most of his life in Virginia, Moss appeared to be turning white. The way that his dark skin seemed to be giving way to light splotches fascinated some of the most significant figures in early American science and politics: George Washington,

Thomas Jefferson, Samuel Stanhope Smith, Benjamin Smith Barton, and Benjamin Rush, among others. As I explore more fully in Chapter 4, over the course of approximately twenty years, Moss was subjected to experiments such as the blistering of his skin to determine where his "color" resided. He also put himself on display in various US cities, where onlookers flocked to get a firsthand peek at the black man who was becoming white. Benjamin Rush took detailed notes about Moss's condition and even pasted a broadside describing Moss as "A Great Curiosity" into his commonplace book (Fig. 1.1).[9] In this image we see visually what the following pages take up in great detail—that on the topic of transformable race, different types of writing intersected, overlapped, and interacted with one another. Here, we see two pieces of paper literally overlaid, where the advertisement of Moss's display and attestation of his history is interpolated into Rush's natural historical notes.

Both the textual intercalation of the Henry Moss announcement into Rush's commonplace book and the route that the *dye* metaphor takes through both natural historical and literary texts illustrate the way that *Transformable Race* conceives of the relationship between scientific and aesthetic discourses about race in the late eighteenth century: namely, that they existed in a productive, sometimes problematic, and always active intertextual conversation. Indeed, as this book strives to demonstrate, notions of transformable race were produced in a dialectical movement between scientific and literary discourses. Because much scholarship on early America has focused mostly on one side of this conversation, as early American historiographies have shown how transformable race functioned in natural historical thought,[10] this study seeks to restore the literary side of this dialogue. *Transformable Race* turns our attention to the literature not because it conceives of literature as the foreground that simply reflects the background science; rather, it starts with what we have already learned about scientific thinking to help us tune our ears to what the literature is saying. In this respect, *Transformable Race* joins other studies of early American literary culture such as those by Ralph Bauer, Susan Scott Parrish, Ian Finseth, and Cristobal Silva that focus on the important relationship between literary and scientific thinking.[11] But, like these texts, even as *Transformable Race* takes up both scientific and literary discourses, it keeps a "distinction, rough and incomplete as it necessarily must be" between the two, as George Levine says, where one can conceive of "'science'" as "the disciplines of investigating the way the natural world is in as systematic a way as possible," and of "'literature'" as "the works of the human imagination as it creates its often brilliant, exploratory, and moving fictions."[12] It is my hope, then, that this approach will give us much greater insight into the thematic and formal features of the literary texts themselves *and* the particular ways that their aesthetic forms articulated, evaluated, and circulated notions of transformable race throughout early America. We will gain not just a diachronic sense of how subsequent scientific hypotheses about race displace

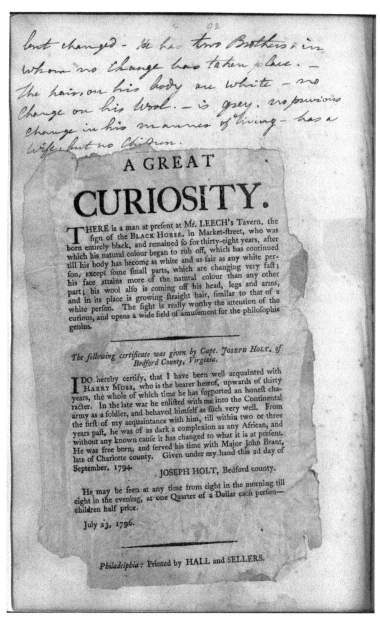

FIGURE I.1 *Benjamin Rush's Commonplace Book*
Courtesy of the American Philosophical Society.

earlier ones but also a synchronic sense of the complex process by which powerful ideas about race in this period are formed. Indeed, a focus on and a knowledge of only the science might lead us to believe that a full understanding of the idea of race or an answer to many of the problems caused by it will be provided by (yet) another advancement in scientific thinking. But as even the most recent developments in science involving DNA and the mapping of the human genome—and the debates they engender—make clear, part of this understanding must come from a much broader, extra-scientific focus on the formation of racial identity.[13] Thus, by listening to the literary side of this conversation, we come to understand more about the literature in and of itself, how the literature contributes to the way racial identities form and function in the material world of early America, and, thus, much more about the broad cultural logic of transformable race in this important historical moment.

To that end, in the next few pages, I describe in detail several (sometimes overlapping) systems of thought—such as natural-historical, nativist, environmentalist, and theories of social influence—that circulated in the United States during the late eighteenth-century, and here I take the time to delve into particular points because these ideas inform the close readings of literary texts that constitute the subsequent chapters. After first introducing how debates about the possible mutability of the physical body circulated through early American society, I describe how natural historians and those who are now referred to as "nativist" Indians offered conflicting accounts of the creation of humankind and, therefore, explanations of racial difference. Then I discuss how natural-historical ideas influenced the ways US leaders discussed racial identity around the time of the Revolution, specifically their theories of environmentalism and social influence. These ways of thinking are usually only studied in isolation; this book brings them together, incongruous though they may seem to be, juxtaposing them to provide a newer and much richer understanding of the multifaceted rhetorics early American writers used in their depictions of racial identity.[14]

   To return our focus to natural history, we must note that Henry Moss was not the only person during the late eighteenth century to draw the attention of natural philosophers. In 1789, John Bobey, a West Indian who was relocated to London as a child in the 1770s, captured public attention because of his striking multihued appearance. A portrait of Bobey was sent to the Library Company of Philadelphia (Fig. 1.2), and German natural historian Johann Friedrich Blumenbach commented on him in his 1795 *On the Natural Variety of Mankind*. Still earlier, Maria Sabine captured the imagination of natural philosophers. Born in 1736 in New Spain, she too had light patches on her dark skin, and Georges-Louis Leclerc, Comte de Buffon, included her case and portrait in his 1777 *Histoire Naturelle* (Fig. 1.3).[15]

   By the early nineteenth century people such as Moss, Bobey, and Sabine would be considered fabulous anomalies rather than legitimate objects of scientific inquiry and debate. But in the eighteenth century they were seen as what historian Joanne Pope Melish calls "products of systematic transformation that

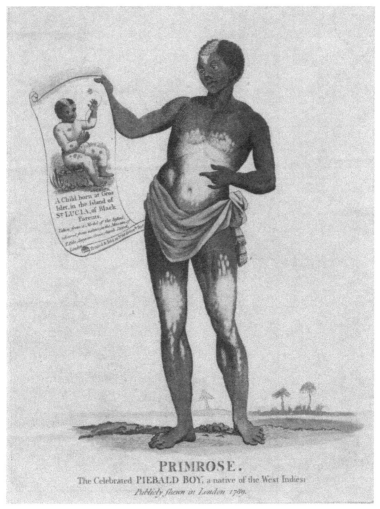

PRIMROSE.

The Celebrated PIEBALD BOY, a native of the West Indies:

Publicly shewn in London 1789.

FIGURE I.2 *"Primrose: The Celebrated Piebald Boy."*
Courtesy of The Library Company of Philadelphia.

could be explained and reliably replicated."[16] At the close of the eighteenth century, the "phenomenon of people of color who seemed to be turning white became a matter of intellectual concern and public interest," and attention to them had been increasing for several years (*BP* 274). Examples abounded in colonial newspapers, as did explanations to account for them and even political tracts parodying them.[17] Philadelphia physician Charles Caldwell over fifty years later reflected on the public's fascination with Henry Moss, claiming that his name "was almost as familiar to the readers of newspapers and other periodicals (so frequently was it recorded in them) as was that of John Adams, Thomas Jefferson, or James Madison."[18] As Sweet points out about Maria

FIGURE I.3 *"Piebald* nègre.*" From Georges-Louis Leclerc de Buffon,* Histoire Naturelle, gènèrale et particulière: Supplèment *(1777)*

Courtesy of the Watkinson Library, Trinity College, Hartford, Connecticut.

Sabine, her case helped lead to Buffon's famous analysis "that this remarkable birth might be due to the degenerative effects of the American climate on African bodies," and, moreover, "that if there were cases of blacks becoming white, it was only logical to assume that there were whites becoming black" (*BP* 276). While Buffon stopped short of specifically applying his theory of degeneration to Europeans relocated to the so-called New World, Abbé Guillaume-Thomas Raynal, an especially fervent adherent to Buffon's propositions, extended the theory and made the explicit claim.[19]

In so doing, Buffon and Raynal fanned the flame of the debate over how the many "varieties" of the one "species" of humankind came into existence—a discussion made all the more pressing for colonists and their creole descendants, who had not only immigrated to America but also recently had broken political ties with the mother country.[20] In the midst of declaring independence, fighting the Revolutionary War, and penning the Constitution, many founding fathers also debated how Africans and Native Americans came to look the way they did. They also wondered whether or not these peoples would ever, in the American environment or with the assistance of European cultural practices, become white. Implicitly, if secondarily, they also troubled over what effect the New World environment might have on themselves and other white settlers.[21] Several issues were at stake in this broad-ranging debate taken up by both ordinary persons and members of the highly esteemed American Philosophical Society (APS). Foremost, how *did* humankind's different "varieties" come into being? If all humans shared an identical origin and environmental factors over time influenced their external characteristics, what would happen when people from different geographic areas began to migrate *en masse* to new locations? Specifically, if the New World influenced the appearance of indigenous peoples of America and if transported Africans might become white, would it be possible that whites might become something else? And—most urgently—under what conditions could a person of one race *transform* into another? In the Revolutionary and early national periods, Americans hotly debated these issues and considered them among the most pressing concerns of their day.

In discussing these unfamiliar, complex, and often irreconcilable aspects of race thinking in the eighteenth century, I choose to employ the term *race*, and this choice has both drawbacks and advantages.[22] In *The Making of Racial Sentiment*, Ezra Tawil makes a compelling argument for using terms like *human variety* for eighteenth-century senses of human diversity and reserving the term *race* for specifically biologically essentialized notions of race that took hold in the nineteenth century. Drawing upon salient points made by both Colete Guillaumin and Ivan Hannaford that "the idea of race in its modern sense" arises at a specific point in history and that we should not assume "race" exits outside that history,[23] Tawil writes that in the eighteenth century, "it was a social-symbolic rather than a biophysical category, and hence was absolutely distinct from the modern notion of race as an essential and immutable biological property."[24] Roxann Wheeler makes a similar choice, using the terms *human variety* or *human difference* to "underscore eighteenth-century sensibility, which did not always register the sense of difference that the term *race* does today" (*CR* 303).[25] For both Tawil and Wheeler, using this terminology helps highlight the diverging conceptions of human difference between the eighteenth and nineteenth centuries, a methodology to which this book is both indebted and in sympathy.

Nevertheless, employing the term *race* also has its benefits: first, it follows how some eighteenth-century writers did use the term; second, it requires a defamiliarization of the term *race* to emphasize its specific eighteenth-century connotations; and third, it demands a similar kind of historical defamiliarization for *whenever* the term is used—the eighteenth, nineteenth, twentieth, or twenty-first centuries. Although writers indeed employed terms such as *human variety* in the late eighteenth-century, other writers ranging from Wheatley and Banneker to Immanuel Kant, Samuel Stanhope Smith, Timothy Dwight, and Gordon Turnbull used the term *race*,[26] illustrating Nicholas Hudson's point about the way that *race* increasingly became used to describe distinctions among humans over the course of the eighteenth century. As Hudson writes about this gradual change,

> Not all authors adopted the new terminology with the same alacrity or consistency. Yet over the period of a century, 'race' gradually mutated from its original sense of a people or single nation, linked by origin, to its later sense of a biological subdivision of the human species. . . . 'Race' [in the mid-nineteenth century] meant more than just a 'lineage' or even a variation of the human species induced by climate or custom [as it had in the eighteenth century]. It meant an innate and fixed disparity in the physical and intellectual make-up of different peoples.[27]

Indeed, for the eighteenth century, Hudson points out, "we might also note that the associated meanings of 'race' were conveniently ambivalent," and he remarks that even within the corpus of one thinker such as Buffon, the "terminology is maddeningly inconsistent."[28] Because the word *race* was used—inconsistently, ambiguously—in eighteenth-century writing and because, as Tawil and Wheeler note, when used it denoted such a radically different set of conceptions than it would later in the nineteenth century, this work seeks to denaturalize what we might assume the term means. Thus, I emphasize how the concepts that the word *race* signified changed—from one of exterior physical difference in the eighteenth century to one of internal difference in the nineteenth—rather than jettisoning the term itself. As will become clear, eighteenth-century writers used *race* to denote a sense of human somatic difference (albeit, and indeed, one that could change) influenced by environmental factors, not one in the blood. Although in the nineteenth century, conceptions of race crystallized around biologized notions of the body, in the eighteenth century, it could be used in conjunction with "variety" or other terms like "people" or "stock."[29] I emphasize the shifts in its understanding in part because we should not presuppose that the term always signified internally fixed difference. Indeed, conceptions of race have continued to change up to our present moment, so I hope my troubling of this term (to bring it closer to coincide with its eighteenth-century meaning) will remind us to problematize it each and every time we employ it, even today. Hoping to simplify my terms but complicate the terms' meanings, I choose to retain the word *race* where fitting and emphasize its incoherence, multiple meanings, contrasting usages, and modulations over time.

We can begin to do this by examining how throughout the eighteenth century, natural philosophers sought to categorize all plant and animal life; classifying external characteristics, they subdivided the human species into different varieties and then debated the causes of these varieties.[30] During this time, two hugely important and popular works of natural history reoriented how Europeans and Anglo-Americans thought about differences among humans. In 1735, Swedish naturalist Carl von Linné (Linnaeus) first published *Systema Naturae*, one of the earliest attempts to classify nature. *Systema Naturae* drew upon similarities in appearance in plants, animals, and humans to impose taxonomic order on all of visible life. Linnaeus viewed people as mutable according to their environment or interbreeding; while species were fixed, varieties developed over time due to the forces of climate, temperature, and other geographic factors. Compatible with the Biblical monogenetic story of Adam and Eve, Linnaeus's account attributed differences among varieties to these external factors.[31]

Building upon but also countering aspects of Linnaeus's work, in 1749 Buffon began publishing his *Histoire Naturelle*. Buffon's work is remembered in the United States most famously for claiming that the New World's cold and unhealthy environment could sustain only underdeveloped savages while the Old World nourished Europe's rich and civilized culture. While basing his differently classified system on reproduction, Buffon generally agreed with Linnaeus that the differences among the varieties of persons could be attributed to the effects that the environment had on the human form over time.[32] In addition to food, soil, air, and geography, Buffon claimed that climate was the most significant cause of bodily difference; he also believed that a group's cultural habits and customs could affect their physical body.[33] As Buffon wrote,

> From every circumstance may we obtain a proof, that mankind are not composed of species essentially different from each other; that, on the contrary, there was originally but one species, which, after being multiplied and diffused over the whole surface of the earth, underwent divers changes from the influence of the climate, food, mode of living, epidemical distempers, and the intermixture of individuals, more or less resembling each other. (4:351)

Both Linnaeus and Buffon and their burgeoning field of thought, staying true to the Judeo-Christian creation story, attributed surface distinctions among men to external forces that acted *upon* bodies, rather than only to inherent and fixed differences lodged *within* bodies.[34] The transformation of varieties of men from the commonly assumed original whiteness resulted from surface changes to the body. As Andrew Curran notes specifically in reference to Africans, "Buffon's degeneration theory ultimately encouraged more, as opposed to less, speculation regarding the corporeal specificities of the African 'variety.' Indeed, his compelling narrative of racial transformation—from white to tan, tan to brown, and from brown to black—prompted anatomists to 'flesh out' the story of degeneration."[35]

Analyzing racial classification in England in the 1700s, Roxann Wheeler has elaborated how this natural-historical thinking influenced Britons' "racialization of the body politic." According to Wheeler, during the last part of the century, four-stages theory (which differentiated among peoples according to their "states of civilization") was being replaced by natural-historical understandings of the racialized body as the main way to delimit variances among humans.[36] Arguing that "humoral/climate theory" influenced both four-stages thinking and natural history, Wheeler emphasizes the particularly "elastic conception of race" (*CR* 7) at this time, which for her mainly refers to the "several registers" used to demarcate difference among humans (*CR* 2).[37] As she explains, most Britons conceptualized Adam and Eve as white. Thus, if they followed monogenetic thought, they reasoned that all other peoples on the globe transformed physically as they moved to different parts of the world and interacted with various climates. Only in the "last quarter of the eighteenth century," did skin color in Britain become "the primary signifier of human difference" (*CR* 7). Wheeler tells us that

> climate theory was the secular rationale for various skin colors, behaviors, and abilities. The linchpin to understanding most eighteenth-century pronouncements about the body's appearance is climate. Positing that all bodies (minds, emotions, and the like) responded similarly to the environment, climate theory also suggested that some environments were better than others for enabling humans to fulfill their potential. . . . Comprehending the profound respect Europeans granted climate accounts for their superficial and malleable beliefs about skin color and race during the eighteenth century. (*CR* 21)

Classical humoral theory conceived of the body as porous, acted upon by the four humors (blood, bile, phlegm, and choler) that influenced the body's "complexion," a term indicating both skin color and temperament or disposition. Furthermore, the work of Buffon and Linnaeus helped establish complexion as "a significant visible human difference" (*CR* 30).

Natural historians like Buffon and Linnaeus clearly shaped the thought of colonists such as John Mitchell who (as I explore later in more depth because two of his interlocutors included both Benjamin Franklin and Olaudah Equiano) claimed that blacks and whites did not constitute separate species; rather, their differences in appearance came from the fact that they had different degrees of thickness of skin. For Mitchell, whites had a thin "Epidermis" which transmitted the color of the "*Cutis*" under it; blacks had a thicker skin which did not allow their (similarly light-colored) "*Cutis*" to show through. Mitchell mainly wanted to dispute the idea that blackness resulted from a raising of the humors, but he agreed with general natural historical thinking that these variations in color resulted from differences in the environment. He was somewhat of an outlier in that he did not see whiteness as the original human form from which all the others over time deviated. "For there is no Doubt," he avowed, "but that *Noah* and his Sons were of a Complexion suitable to the Climate where they resided, as well as all the rest of Mankind; which is the Colour of the southern *Tartars* of *Asia,* or northern *Chinese,* at this Day perhaps, which is a dark swarthy, a Medium betwixt Black and White: From which primitive Colour the *Europeans* degenerated as much on one hand, as the *Africans* did on the other . . ." ("ECDC" 146–47). Although he disagreed on the shade of the "primitive Colour," Mitchell concurred with Linnaeus and Buffon that surface differences among humankind arose over time.

Enlightenment natural philosophers, however, were not alone in positing truths regarding the creation of humankind and the distinctions among red, black, and white peoples. Indeed, the indigenous peoples of America were just as engaged in understanding human difference. Whereas natural philosophy posited the body's change in appearance over time, those who historian Gregory Dowd has termed "nativist" Indians claimed original difference that resulted from separate creations. Describing what he calls "the Indians' Great Awakening" from 1745 through 1775, Dowd contends that this "militant, pan-Indian religious movement" was "a widespread, often divisive, yet intertribal movement . . . spreading the truly radical message that Indians were one people" (*SR* 19, xix).[38]

Amongst the tribes of the Susquehanna and Ohio Valley regions, various Native Americans reported learning from the Master of Life that Natives, whites, and Africans were created separately. They also became aware that they should practice entirely discrete religions: Christianity was for Europeans exclusively, since God did not give the Bible to the Indian or to the black man. Of the many separatist spiritual leaders detailing this type of vision, the Delaware prophet Neolin became the one most recognized by British colonists by the 1760s. Neolin's message had several implications: Indians should not partake of European culture (including alcohol and religion), they should evict white settlers from their lands, and they should return to their own traditional Native customs.[39]

Neolin's teachings and the larger nativist movement also articulated what Dowd calls a "new theory of polygenesis" that emphasized Indian unity and Anglo-American impurity. While not a "science" in the way we have come to use that term, nativist thinking—along with Judeo-Christian religions—posited origin stories that have racial implications. This "Indian theory of the separate creation" demanded that Natives eschew all European practices to maintain sacred power and the balance of the universe (*SR* 21). Historian Daniel Richter contends that nativist thought implied that the Bible with its accounts of creation and salvation were "true," but only for the Europeans for whom it was intended; that Native creation stories and modes of spirituality were equally true and revealed what the Master of Life expected of them; that the mixing of European and Indian ways was the source of Native peoples' current problems; and—the key insight above all—that Indians were a single people with common interests that transcended national rivalries. Thus, in the same period that diverse colonists of varied European backgrounds were discovering in North America their first glimmerings of a "White" racial identity, nativist Indians perhaps even more compellingly discovered that they were "Red."[40]

As Dowd claims, "there was no single Indian outlook but at least two major contending viewpoints" at this time (*SR* xxiii). Nativist Indians greatly differed from what he terms "accommodationist" Indians, those who "often cooperated with, although they were only rarely controlled by, the imperial powers" (*SR* xxi). Dowd explains that the "notion of the separate creation gave legitimacy to the Indians' way of life" (*SR* 30). Thus, when accommodationist Indians would convert to Christianity or maintain close relationships with Anglo-Americans, nativist Indians would accuse them of "abomination."

Mohegan minister Samson Occom and Mohican leader Hendrick Aupaumut were two such Christianized Indians that nativist Indians would have seen in this light, and it is crucially important to remember, as historian David Silverman demonstrates, that not all Native peoples held a "nativist" viewpoint.[41] For example, as I discuss in Chapter 1, in his 1784 sermon, "To All the Indians in this Boundless Continent," Occom claimed that there is "but one, Great ^good^ Supream and Indepantent Spirit above, he is the only Living and True God," who created "this World." Occom also attested that God created Adam and Eve, whom Occom called "the Father and Mother of all Nations of the Whole World."[42] Aupaumut used similar rhetoric in an 1819 letter that he addressed to "our great Father, the President and to his great Council, the Congress of the United States." He opened his letter: "We your red Brethren, Chiefs and principal men of the Muhheakannuk or Stockbridge Nation desire you to listen to us, We are all descended from one father, and, with our white Brethren, acknowledge and worship one GOD. . . ."[43] After using paternal rhetoric to address US President James Monroe, Aupaumut immediately switched to fraternal rhetoric to emphasize the shared creation and thus equality of Native peoples.[44] The letter continued to ask for assistance in securing promised lands. Both Occom and Aupaumut endorsed the biblical creation story, the idea that all races descended (and developed differently amongst themselves) from this single creation, and that, therefore, Indians should be seen as equals and "brothers" with the white man. They do not, however, ever characterize Adam and Eve as white; perhaps, like Mitchell, they thought of this original pair as "tawny," thus positioning whites as more degenerate than Indians.[45] Christianity did not displace Occom's and Aupaumut's respective foci on their tribes; on the contrary, both Native leaders practiced Christianity in a way that enabled them to advance the sovereignty of their respective indigenous nations.[46] Nevertheless, although both Occom and Aupaumut shared with nativist tribes an investment in tribal sovereignty, they clearly differed from them in their religious claims, their account for racial difference, and their strategies of leveraging both of those things against whites and for Native rights. As I explore in more depth in Chapters 1 and 2, the writings of both Occom and Aupaumut have to be understood within the context of the differences of thought within Indian Country. Indeed, as we shall see, although nativist thought was most prominent in the Susquehanna and Ohio Valley areas, its powerful and much-circulated argument for separate creations impacted how Native Americans anywhere in Indian Country could discuss racial difference.

The whites who would come to establish the US nation-state also faced a similar context. By the time of the American Revolution, natural-historical and nativist thinking, which offered two fairly well-established explanations of racial difference explained above, framed how American colonists confronted the issue of race in the New World. Perhaps it is not surprising that the natural-historical theories of Linnaeus and Buffon influenced many Anglo-Americans. Indeed, in *White over Black*, Jordan explains how environmentalist thinking arose in tandem with revolutionary and republican politics of the late eighteenth century, and he outlines the implications for debates about race's potential changeability. Environmentalism—a manner of thinking that conceived all men as essentially equal but affected by their different environments—became "an engine in the hands of republicans asserting their independence from the Old World" (*WOB* 270). Jordan and Sweet see environmentalist thinking in its broadest sense as being part and parcel with revolutionary ideology and with the social and political upheavals around the time of the Revolution. As I explore in Chapter 3, Benedict Anderson points to the environment as part of the reason those in cosmopolitan centers thought that those born in the Americas "were by nature different from, and inferior to, the metropolitans,"[47] leading to the metropole shunning the colonies, and the colonists developing a sense of nationalism. This, in turn, as Jordan sees it, influenced how Americans thought of themselves both in the New World and in relationship to folks residing in England. He writes that "as the political crisis mounted, they developed a more pressing interest in their habitat. Since they thought of themselves as colonial Englishmen and yet were undergoing an unwelcome estrangement from England, they were compelled to ask what made the child different from the parent, the New World different from the Old, the continent different from the island" (*WOB* 288). As colonists increasingly talked about the natural rights of man, environmentalism helped explain the differences among men.[48] Indeed, "the environmentalist mode of thought presupposed that the differences among men were circumstantial, that they were alterable, and that the core of human nature was everywhere, as Benjamin Rush put it, 'the same.' This postulation of quintessential human nature formed the critical point of contact between environmentalist thinking and the political ideology of the Revolution" (*WOB* 289). Particularly after the Revolution, Americans had to find a way to acknowledge their English heritage and also to assert that they were "not Englishmen."[49] The environment provided a perfect answer to this dilemma. US citizens had established a new government, but they also turned to their natural surroundings to argue for the exceptionalism of their new national identity. The American environment would make them truly different from their English ancestors, even if the Revolution had not done so fully. Henceforth, because of their location in the New World, they would eventually come to be particularly American, a fraught process that—as I explore more in Chapter 3—turns out to be quite complex, indeed.[50]

In this context, Buffon's claims about the New World helped prompt Thomas Jefferson's impassioned response about the continent's physical attributes in his *Notes on the State of Virginia* (circulated privately in manuscript before being published in France in 1784, in London in 1787, and in the United States in 1788).[51] In addition, Jefferson was one year old when Mitchell—a fellow Virginia naturalist—published his "Essay," so Jefferson's *Notes* must be read in light of multiple theories. Jefferson argued for the nurturing quality of the American environment by refuting Buffon's allegations about Native Americans. As scholars have noted, it is interesting because Jefferson seemed to agree with Buffon's supposition that the environment could affect humans—at least, for Jefferson, Native Americans (and perhaps whites)—but he vehemently disagreed with Buffon's claim about the quality of the New World environment and that, as Jefferson says, animals "degenerated in America" (*Notes* 78). When it came to blacks, Jefferson famously equivocated on whether they shared an original creation with whites and developed differently over time or if they were created separately. He advances his "suspicion only" that "the blacks, whether originally a distinct race, or made distinct by time and circumstances, are inferior to the whites in the endowments both of body and mind" (*Notes* 192–93).

Although often scholars rightly focus on the issues of race and slavery in Jefferson's writings, philosophy, and personal life, we would be gravely mistaken to allow his account of racial difference to stand in for the entirety of eighteenth-century natural-historical thought. Indeed, Jefferson's proto-polygeneticist proclivities lay outside mainstream thinking at the close of the eighteenth century.[52] As Peter Onuf explains, "Jefferson thought racial differences were fixed in nature, whatever their source and however they might be assessed. His comparative method focused on and therefore

exaggerated racial differences. Where other observers invoked environmental conditions and cultural constraints to explain racial distinctions,
Jefferson's approach worked in the opposite direction as 'time and circumstances' conspired with nature to produce a natural racial hierarchy."[53]
Indeed, Ralph Bauer brilliantly places Jefferson and his racial arguments in
a hemispheric and historical context:

> Jefferson's patriotic defense of creole (European American) character and
> culture is thus predicated on a particular rhetorical shift in which the
> eighteenth-century discourse about cultural creolization and degeneration
> is displaced by a modern discourse of "race." If the American environment
> did not have a degenerative influence on human culture (as his discussions
> of Native American and white creoles intend to demonstrate), but African
> American creoles were obviously (to Jefferson) inferior, it must be that Af-
> ricans had arrived in the New World already as a distinct "race," whose in-
> feriority must be seen as essential and independent of environmental and
> geographical factors or social "condition." Jefferson's *Notes* manifests thus
> not so much "the failure of anthropological method" as the emergent chal-
> lenge posed by a modern anthropological method that would ultimately
> shatter the Enlightenment discourse of natural history by rending its envi-
> ronmental contingencies asunder and by breaking up the study of "nature"
> into its discreet modern disciplines—geography, botany, zoology, anthro-
> pology, and so on.[54]

And, as Bauer points out, Benjamin Banneker was able to challenge Jefferson on his claim of black inferiority. Furthermore, Banneker baited Jefferson
not only on how he had penned the natural rights argument that "all men
were created equal" while slaves did not enjoy the same liberty, but also on
how surely Jefferson's "sentiments are concurrent with mine [Banneker's],
which are, that one universal Father hath given being to us all; and that he
hath not only made us all of one flesh, but that he hath also, without partiality, afforded us all the same sensations and endowed us all with the same
faculties; and that however variable we may be in society or religion, *however diversified in situation or color*, we are all of the same family, and stand
in the same relation to him."[55] Because Banneker knew he held the majority
(and Christian-endorsed) view on a single origin for humankind, he practically dared Jefferson to counter this claim on the shared creation among all
the races.

Indeed, this type of mainstream, monogenetic racial thinking reached its
apex in the 1787 address Samuel Stanhope Smith gave to the American Philosophical Society that contradicted much in Jefferson's thinking on racial difference. As I explore more fully in Chapters 2 and 4, Smith delivered the address and subsequently published *An Essay on the Causes of the Variety of
Complexion and Figure in the Human Species*, what Jordan calls "the first

major American study of the races of mankind."[56] Like Jefferson, Smith held
that transplanted Europeans would not degenerate in the New World. However, writing from a monogenetic Christian perspective, Smith explicitly
argued for the shared origin of *all* humankind and attributed changes in
humankind's countenance to the influences over time of both the climate and
what he called one's "state of society" (*EC* 43). For Smith, "the state of society
comprehends diet, clothing, lodging, manners, habits, face of the country, objects of science, religion, interests, passions and ideas of all kinds, infinite in
number and variety. If each of these causes be admitted to make, as undoubtedly they do, a small variation on the human countenance, the different com-
binations and results of the whole must necessarily be very great; and combined with the effects of climate will be adequate to account for all the varieties
we find among mankind" (*EC* 62–63).

Smith's inclusion of physical environs as an influence on race was not new.
However, his emphasis on civilization specifically responded to the racial
questions posed by the mass immigration to the Americas. Contemporaries
largely understood Smith to claim that if Africans displaced to the New World
were put in favorable conditions, they would eventually come to resemble
whites (*WOB* 515). Although Smith felt that facial features were more malleable than skin tone, Jordan explains that "he never closed the door on the
possibility that America was going to whiten black men" (*WOB* 516). Not all
American natural historians were convinced, but Smith's theses profoundly
influenced the likes of Benjamin Rush and others. While there was much
debate over Smith's assertion, "the notion that environmental influences
could cause Negroes gradually to become less Negroid was by no means ridiculous or scientifically disreputable" (*WOB* 516). The natural historians who
explored these lines of thinking, furthermore, did not limit their conversations to Africans and applied these environmentalist claims to Native Americans. Ever since the first contact between whites and Natives, colonists had to
account for what they felt was the radical difference between themselves and
various indigenous groups. Late eighteenth-century environmentalism provided a counterintuitive way to account for that distinction: fundamentally
similar to whites, North American Indians were different only because of the
circumstances in which they had lived.[57] Unlike Africans, however, whom
some Anglo-Americans felt would "whiten up" as a result of climatic and
other environmental changes, Indians were generally expected to become
more like whites specifically through their adoption of white social practices
and cultural habits.[58]

Smith's ideas take shape in Timothy Dwight's *Travels in New England and
New York* (written throughout 1790–1817 and published posthumously in
1821–1822), a text of crucial importance here because of the way it brings together environmentalist thinking about red, white, and black peoples in an
interesting and comparative fashion. President of Yale College, Dwight had

also been fascinated with Henry Moss, announcing himself "an eyewitness" who hosted and conversed with Moss in Dwight's New Haven home in 1796.[59] In *Travels*, Dwight's interest in Moss is connected to his "strong inclination to see civilized Indian life, i.e. Indian life in the most advanced state of civilization in which it is found in this country" (*T* 124). As he relates it, Dwight therefore decides to travel to Brothertown, "to a collection of Indians who left Connecticut for this place under the conduct of the Rev. Samson Occom" (*T* 124). Dwight then outlines what Smith would have called the Native Americans' "modes of living," detailing that while they have taken up Anglo agricultural practices, their "fences are indifferent, and their meadows and arable grounds are imperfectly cleared" (*T* 125). He then asks of his imagined "English gentleman" addressee, "You will excuse me for giving you this sketch of civilized Indian life because it presents to you one feature in the character of man rarely seen by persons really civilized, and hitherto untouched by the pens of others" (*T* 125). He then inserts a letter sent to him by "one of [his] pupils, Mr. Hart, now the minister at Stonington," that describes in detail the physical change that has taken place in Elijah Wampey, Jr., Andrew Carrycomb, Ephraim Pharaoh, and Samuel Adams, all members of Native groups that had removed from Connecticut to New York.

Worth quoting at length, in his letter to Dwight, Hart writes the following:

> Among these Indians, I observed the following singular facts, viz., four men whose skin in different parts of their body has turned white. Where the skin is not exposed to the sun, and the change has been of long standing, it has completely lost its natural color and become entirely white. . . .
>
> But the most remarkable instance is Samuel Adams, aged fifty-seven. He is almost become a white man. He gave me the following account.
>
> That fourteen years since his skin began in a number of places to change its color, that it changed gradually until it reached its present degree of whiteness, that no pain whatever attended the change, ...
>
> The hair on his head still retains its original Indian color, excepting a part which has the same appearance as the gray hair of aged white people. The appearance of the skin on the parts changed is different. Where it has been exposed to the sun, it appears of a darkish color. Where it has not been exposed, it appears tender and delicately white. The skin lately changed appears like that of a child, and through the apparent stages of changing advances gradually from infancy to full age. . . .
>
> So little attention has been paid to these extraordinary facts that persons who have been for years intimately acquainted with these Indians have not taken pains to examine them. (*T* 126)

Dwight immediately turns from Hart's letter to his own epistle to his implied reader, by declaring, "From this account, the accuracy as well as the truth of which may be relied on with perfect confidence, it is evident that a change in several of the race of red men, by which in every instance they have become in some degree, and in one almost absolutely, white men, has actually taken place under the eye of indubitable testimony" (*T* 126).

Dwight closes out his letter with nine numbered "observations" that he "derive[s]" from the "accounts" of both Moss's self-report and Hart's third-person description. Dwight's "observations" includes statements such as "the change of the hair was intimately connected with the change of the skin, less strikingly in the red men, but with the fullest evidence in the black man" (*T* 128). Practically offering as pithy a condensation of eighteenth-century environmentalism as one could get, he also notes that "From these facts I infer also that the external appearances of the complexion and hair on the human body are not original, nor at all essential to the nature of the body. All these men continued in every other particular the same in body and mind, while they were yet entirely changed in complexion to a considerable extent. . . . These appearances, therefore, were not essential, but incidental; not original, but superinduced upon the human constitution. In other words, men are not red, black, nor white, necessarily, but merely as incidental circumstances direct" (*T* 128). All of this—Dwight's description of his own trip to Brother-town, the details of Hart's included report, and the first eight of Dwight's observations—bring him to his culminating, particularly striking observation:

> Hence I conclude that the varieties observed in the complexion and hair of the human species furnish no probable argument that they sprang from different original stocks. The three great varieties are white, black, and red. On the last two classes these changes have here taken place, and on one of each they have been almost completed. A black man in one instance, and a red man in another, have become almost entirely white men, ... Of white men, therefore, others may have become red or black men, with changes equally unessential. That this has really taken place is fairly presumable from the facts here recounted. The ordinary course of Providence, operating agreeably to natural and established laws, has wrought the change here. A similar course of Providence is therefore justly concluded to have wrought the change from white to red and to black, or what is perhaps more probable from red to white on the one hand, and from red to black on the other. The change here, so far as it has existed, has been accomplished in a few years. How easily, as well as how imperceptibly, may it have been accomplished during the lapse of ages. (*T* 128)

For Dwight, racial change has happened for a few individuals within their lifetimes, and it follows the "course of Providence" that "white, black, and red" peoples may change into something else.

The implication of these competing claims about the changeability of Africans and Native Americans, of course, caused white natural historians to ponder what might happen to European bodies in the new American environment.[60]

While the concept of degeneration certainly included aspects that were not necessarily racialized, many natural historians used and understood the term to be racial in its eighteenth-century sense.[61] As historian Kariann Yokota argues, "aware of this close identification with the 'colored' people among them, white Americans imagined a need for a distinction between the white, civilized Americans and the 'savage' Americans. Defenses against the theory of New World degeneration differed in strategies of counterattack. What unified them all, however, was a reliance on the link between American 'whiteness' and the materiality of civilization."[62] Samuel Stanhope Smith argued that Americans kept from degenerating *not* because of a favorable New World climate *but rather* because, as Yokota puts it, of "their advanced degree of civilization."[63] While most natural historians had stressed the role of climate in developing lighter or darker races, Smith emphasized that physical features also were impacted by such things as manners, language, and civilization. While climate theory implied that European whites migrating to the New World might become savage and perhaps darker, Smith claimed that cultural practices would help them maintain their civilized status and ostensibly lighter skin tone. In other words, even if relocated Europeans could not transport their Old World climate and natural surroundings with them to the New World, they could take their culture. Smith also hypothesized that even if whites were to degenerate, they would never completely resemble the Indian in physical appearance because of their civilization and because their "features" were originally formed in the climate of Europe. As Yokota points out, Smith worked to assuage his audience's anxieties, fears, and uncertainties about living in a new environment among people of color.

The way that some Americans emphasized the state of society as an agent in the production of physical racialized features differs from the way Britons understood society to function in relationship to racialization in Britain for much of the eighteenth century. Wheeler documents how British culture largely measured differences between humans through beliefs about *either* physical characteristics (which were coming to be read as signifying "race") *or* the state of society. However, toward the end of the century and particularly in the United States, physicality and society were complexly linked in terms of producing and/or signifying "race."[64] The British four-stages theory viewed "civilization" mainly as a way to delineate human difference. But for Anglo-Americans trying to establish a nation-state while living in the same geographic environment as Native Americans, "civilization" and society came to be considered an agent in—either a cause of or a safeguard against—the process of degeneration.[65] Thus, early Americans understood society at times to be an active agent in the production—rather than mainly in the description—of human difference. Furthermore, it came to occupy a paradoxical place in the cultural imaginary. It was thought *to influence* physical characteristics as an environmental factor itself and simultaneously *to be influenced by* environmental factors (such as climate and geography) in the same way as physical characteristics. Therefore, society could become both the cause of one's degeneration and the resulting proof of it.[66]

Trying to think about race in these ways—the ways that eighteenth-century Americans thought about it—can be strange and unfamiliar. Moreover, from our vantage point of the twenty-first century, we can see how these ideas have been discounted by changes in scientific thinking, and we can easily cast a wary eye at the outlandishness of many of these notions (as author Hugh Henry Brackenridge actually did at the close of the eighteenth century). But even as we might tend to dismiss and possibly mock these seemingly fantastical ideas, thinking about race in these ways makes us more aware of the means that science uses to *imagine* race. It uses language to call into being categories of racial difference, and it advances narratives about how features of the human form came to be what they are. And, at its most basic level, how these ways of thinking tell stories and use language (no matter what particular theory might be advanced) is exactly what makes them so important to consider alongside the literature produced in the same moment.

Early American Literary Articulations of Race

Having laid out the contours of eighteenth-century scientific racial thought, we now turn our attention to the literature. Much like the realm of science, literature occupies a place that is both *a part of* and *apart from* social reality. In terms of late eighteenth-century science, these earlier ways of thinking about race often existed in paradoxical tension with the lived experiences of early Americans. For instance, as Occom's writings demonstrate, even if whites accepted prevalent natural-historical accounts (supported by the Judeo-Christian creation story) and therefore their shared genealogy with Native peoples, many of them nevertheless denied Natives their tribal sovereignty, acquired their ancestral lands, and behaved toward them dissimilarly than they did toward fellow whites. In addition, as Equiano makes clear, a belief in natural-historical explanations of the development of racial difference from a shared creation did not compel many whites to treat blacks fairly, economically or legally. Native Americans and African Americans were treated differently from whites in early America, even as Anglo natural philosophers were investigating the ways various peoples were originally the same but developed into different races. Early American literature could record and respond to this differential treatment *and* (much like science) provide an experimental space where these racial ideas were explored, tested, theorized, or altered. While not necessarily producing what were considered the scientific "facts" of the day per se, the literature of this time period helped create the thinking around this topic of transformable race. These ideas about race structured early American literature, but early American literature also helped constitute (both in concert with and in challenge to) this broad configuration of ideas. This book attempts, then, to analyze how scientific thought informs literary texts *and* the work these texts do at the cultural level of impacting how race is constructed. Attending to both these things not only helps us better appreciate the nuanced relationship between race and early American literature; it also gives us an enriched understanding of early American literature more broadly.

Transformable Race: Surprising Metamorphoses in the Literature of Early America thus develops multiple lines of inquiry in two major fields in American literary scholarship: early American studies and critical race theory. Unlike when the field of early American literary studies first began with its focus on Puritan New England, more recently scholars have been addressing the topic of race. The work of scholars such as Dana Nelson, Philip Gould, Jared Gardner, and Joanna Brooks have all demonstrated that the concept of race is important to our knowledge about early American literature.[67] Further, focusing on sentiment and post-colonial relationships, Julia Stern, David Kazanjian, and Andy Doolen have illustrated the ways that period texts enact the establishment of the "white nation" on the exclusion of African Americans, Native Americans, and others.[68] Thanks to the groundbreaking work of these scholars, early American studies has increasingly turned its attention to racialized dynamics in literature. Adding to that scholarship but differing from it significantly, this study shows that the way earlier notions about race have been replaced by subsequent beliefs obscure our view of earlier American texts; therefore, it focuses on how the specifically eighteenth-century ideas about race inform the period's literature. Thus, contributing a new and important dimension to early American scholarship, this book interprets this literature in relationship to its own racial epistemology of the late eighteenth-century—the very one through which these early American writers both knew and wrote their world.

It has not been easy for early Americanists to talk about race. As Robert Levine recently noted, race "remains a problematic term in early American studies," and because it is far from being resolved, this present study aims at examining the particular problematics of race thinking in early America.[69] On the one hand, *Transformable Race: Surprising Metamorphoses in the Literature of Early America* argues strongly that the notions regarding the formation of racial categories of the eighteenth century differed dramatically from those of the nineteenth—and that the ways in which they were different *really matter* to how we read and interpret the literature written in the late eighteenth-century moment. On the other hand, this book also attends to how divergent notions regarding the formation of racial categories often *did not affect* the daily lives of many writers of color, mainly because it examines how several of the minority writers included herein make this clear (as the examples of Occom and Equiano included above indicate). It also examines how the oppressive ideological ends to which those racial categories were put to use sadly remain relatively consistent from the eighteenth century into the nineteenth and beyond. So, for example, although Samuel Stanhope Smith and Benjamin Rush tried to harness aspects of environmentalist thinking in order to argue against slavery and although many people wondered whether and how black peoples would eventually become white, slavery still existed. Furthermore, as I hope to make clear, even as notions of transformable race might explain how a person of a certain race developed *into* that race or might explore how she could potentially change *from one race into another*, it was not always necessarily utopic or liberating thinking. Some early American writers such as Phillis Wheatley used it that way, but others certainly did not. And while these racial categories were not "essential" (in the way contemporary scholarship uses that term), there were character traits that were often assumed to correlate strictly with certain racialized physical features. For example, blacks were not believed to have essential traits such as "laziness," but it was largely thought that prolonged residence in the environment of the African continent necessarily produced the human attributes of black skin and lethargy in the same people. To put it another way, it was not thought that because one was black, one was indolent; but rather that because one was in the sun, one was both black and indolent. To say that the racialized body was believed to be malleable is to say that race was not essentialized in the same way that it would be in the nineteenth century; it is not to say that characteristics were not assigned to bodies understood as a particular race. We must also remember, as I expand upon in Chapter 2, that aspects of this thinking informed federal Indian policy aimed at making Indians white, including later relocations of Native children from their homes to boarding schools where they were taught "white" ways, an insidious attempt at Indian decimation. Taking into consideration these complex historical nuances of race in this period, this book both speaks to the ongoing discussion in regard to race in early American literature and breaks new scholarly ground by trying to account for how the specific late eighteenth-century notions about race imbue this literary writing.

This book builds on earlier scholarship by scholars such as Gould and Wheeler that has made us aware of how peoples in different time periods and locations use various paradigms to delineate racial difference. Indeed, I take what Wheeler calls "the fluid articulation of human variety" (*CR* 6–7) to refer to various epistemological rubrics—such as sentiment, economics, religion, stages of development—used to delineate what has come to be known as racial difference. This study likewise draws attention to change over time between different ways to conceptualize race. But this book departs from this earlier work because in addition to predicating its analysis on what we might think of as the somewhat sequential fluidity of conceptual frameworks about race,

Transformable Race tries to grapple with the very serious eighteenth-century beliefs about the fluidity of the racial body itself.[70] It also answers many questions raised by important scholarship on the literature and culture of nineteenth-century and twentieth-century America. For instance, Nelson, Tawil, and Robyn Wiegman all demonstrate that the sciences of comparative anatomy, biology, and gynecology of the nineteenth century shifted away from eighteenth-century natural history, but they focus their attention on what happened during and after that shift, leaving unarticulated what that specific discourse of early American natural philosophy meant for the literature of its own moment.[71] Thus, *Transformable Race: Surprising Metamorphoses in the Literature of Early America* is distinctive in the way it reads the literature of both the historical period and geographic location of early America.

This book also aims to help us understand the literatures of early America anew by bringing understudied minority writers to the fore and by showing us new layers to texts we already know so well. Featuring the voices of African American, Native American, and Anglo American writers together, *Transformable Race* gives a kaleidoscopic picture of how early Americans wrote about race. Assembling various groupings of these authors writing in a vast range of genres and from radically different subject positions while trying to maintain the historical and cultural specificity for each, this study shows that these writers do not always agree and that racial thinking does not necessarily line up according to racial groupings. In addition, using the methodology of what has been called the "New Early Native American Studies," this book focuses on the specific tribal contexts of Samson Occom and Hendrick Aupaumut.[72] For all the texts studied here, attention to understanding *how* each of them uses ideas of transformable race gives us a much richer, more complete, and increasingly complex understanding of them *and* what they say about topics as varied as religion, aesthetics, the process of acculturation, Native tribal sovereignty, national identity, textuality, and sentiment.

In the field of critical race studies, this study replaces prevailing critical race frameworks particular to later periods with one that is apt for early America. Field-establishing critical race studies of nineteenth- and twentieth-century American culture by Toni Morrison, Eric Lott, and David Roediger provide us with a significant understanding of nineteenth- and twentieth-century racial formation in the United States, but we are left with very little knowledge about how it operates in the eighteenth century. These scholars aptly show how racial identities in those periods develop in contraposition to one another.[73] In contrast, my study of this earlier literature examines how such identities take form through *one's potential to transform from one race into another*. For example, in *Playing in the Dark: Whiteness and the Literary Imagination*, Morrison demonstrates how "whiteness" formed by being contrasted to what it was not (i.e., "blackness"), what she calls "the process of organizing American coherence through a distancing Africanism."[74] As Morrison writes, "black slavery enriched the country's creative possibilities. For in that construction of blackness *and* enslavement could be found not only the not-free but also, with the dramatic polarity created by skin color, the projection of the not-me."[75] By contrast, in the late eighteenth century, one would have been understood to be a certain race right now only in an ever oscillating relationship to how near or far—in physical appearance and/or in developmental time—to another race that she once had been *or* was in the process of becoming. To say this yet another way, if we have understood nineteenth-century and later racial logic to be "white is white because it is not black," we should understand the eighteenth-century racial logic to run closer along the lines of "white is white for now because it is no longer nor not yet black." I hope to convey this kind of thinking in my use of the word *transformable*, (trans/form/able), to describe that which is capable of taking form by moving across. To prevent scholars from anachronistically reading later understandings of race back onto these earlier texts, I posit a historically specific, transformational model of critical race theory that refigures our understanding of racialization in early American literatures and advances a new paradigm that offers critical race studies a fresh way of understanding racial formation. Conceiving of race in an earlier, transformable way rather than a later one typifies, I want to suggest, Sandra Gustafson's claim that early American studies can examine "the disjunction between an established theoretical model and the archive offered by colonial America" with "the potential to create new paradigms."[76] Making clear the distinction between eighteenth-century and later processes of racialization operative in American literatures, this book develops a new theory of racial formation to help us interpret those cultural productions.

Challenging unexamined tenets on which critical race theory has operated in literary studies, *Transformable Race: Surprising Metamorphoses in the Literature of Early America* demonstrates that we have been using temporal perspectives that we have not yet understood to be temporal. While it is embedded with the historical contextualization of late eighteenth-century racial thought, this transformational model presents critical race studies with a new way of conceptualizing racial formation. If literary scholars have come to think of the constitution of identities in part as the reiteration of recognizable acts, we must also understand that those acts can vary widely over time. This not only changes the way we read and study early American literature. As I detail most explicitly in Chapter 3, it also demands that we rethink axiomatic angles of analysis in critical race studies, such as passing, iteration, and performance. Furthermore, although critical race studies has importantly pried apart scientific from social conceptions of race, this book illustrates and analyzes the ways that scientific and cultural understandings of race develop in tandem.

Many of the sophisticated rhetorical practices of the writers examined here have long gone unnoticed because we have not yet analyzed how each of them engaged with and contributed to different aspects of the notion of transformable race. As I explore in the following chapters, writers responded to and impacted in various ways these contemporaneous ideas about what might influence characteristics that were coming to be read as race. By highlighting these engagements, *Transformable Race* intervenes in some of the most central scholarly debates about each author's work. In the first chapter, "Becoming Colored in Occom and Wheatley's Early America," I show how Protestant religious thinking about the body and about the distinctions among humankind's varieties informs these writers' portrayals of racialization. Drawing upon certain aspects of natural history that validated Christian monogenesis, Occom and Wheatley represent the process of "becoming colored" as part of a divine plan, one that establishes both universality and particularity throughout humankind. I argue that Occom's "Short Narrative" and *A Sermon, Preached at the Execution of Moses Paul, An Indian* use contemporaneous beliefs about the status of the "red" Indian body to take issue with the contradictions in colonialists' religious viewpoints and that his "To All the Indians in this Boundless Continent" draws upon transformable race to assert tribal sovereignty. I then show how Wheatley's *Poems on Various Subjects, Religious and Moral* combines mythological with natural-historical beliefs about the generation of poetic genius and skin pigmentation to characterize the black poet not as a surprising oddity but rather as an expected likelihood. Both Occom and Wheatley explore aspects of transformable race that—in concert with Christian thinking—try to account for the development of racial differences since the single creation.

Benjamin Franklin and Hendrick Aupaumut, however, are much less concerned with religious aspects of transformable race and much more interested in what ideas of transformable race might mean politically. "The Political Bodies of Benjamin Franklin and Hendrick Aupaumut," the book's second chapter, demonstrates how the narratives of Franklin and Aupaumut coupled natural-historical thinking with more explicitly political thinking related to the notion of transformable race. Both diplomats employed by the US government, Franklin traveled to Europe to negotiate Revolutionary War alliances; Aupaumut, a Mohican veteran of the Revolutionary War, journeyed past the western border of the new nation-state to negotiate with hostile Native American tribes. Both Franklin and Aupaumut present their own textual and physical bodies for their multiple audiences to consider in relationship to the notion of transformable race and in relationship to how political bodies might be constituted out of identical or dissimilar physical bodies. As both men composed their texts, various groups debated the extent to which race was influenced by the environment, and Native Americans held divergent views on the explanation of the different varieties of mankind. In part because of their diplomatic positions, neither Franklin nor Aupaumut adamantly advance a theory of how the races originated, but the topic of race plays a structuring role in their texts, one we come to understand first by reading Franklin's implicit and explicit evocations of natural-historical texts published as he composed the *Autobiography*; and then by analyzing how Aupaumut's strategic use of the term "color" intervenes in Native American discussions about race.

If Franklin and Aupaumut's concerns center on political engagements of the moment, the writers considered in Chapter 3 try to look forward in time to explore the prospective implications of transformable race. "Transforming into the Native: Crèvecoeur, Marrant, and Brown on Becoming Indian," examines how Crèvecoeur's *Letters from an American Farmer*, Marrant's *A Narrative of the Lord's Wonderful Dealings with John Marrant, A Black*, and Brown's *Edgar Huntly* take up the natural-historical idea that race was a condition one managed to sustain rather than an immutable bodily fact. These texts explore the possibilities of racial transformation by featuring the protagonists' journey among American Indian tribes. If Wheatley and Occom draw upon the aspect of transformable race that held that any given race gradually developed into what they were at the present moment, these writers place their texts in the middle of debates over what might happen to any given person's race *in the future*. Understanding how *Letters* examines both the positive and negative potential of whites altering racially in the New World provides a new understanding of what Crèvecoeur's "American" is. I take this book's subtitle from Crèvecoeur, who describes the "surprising metamorphosis" Americans undergo, as I will demonstrate, as a racial transformation. Marrant's *Narrative* offers up a picture of an African American "becoming" Native American. Brown's *Edgar Huntly* explores, first, what might happen to creole whites by depicting the strange transformation Edgar undergoes, a process that begins years before the novel opens and, second, what that transformation might mean for whether the nation-state project might work. All these texts demand a reconsideration of the notions of racial masquerade and "playing Indian." This chapter argues that the concept of passing as we currently understand it is not a sufficient way to comprehend these scenes of transformation. A conceptualization of how the external body could possibly fail to display one's "true" race would not have been fully meaningful at this time. Rather, the concept of racial transformation underpins these literary depictions of how one's race begins to change into that of another, as these scenes of racial metamorphosis imagine instances not where characters "pass as" Natives, but rather where they "transform into" Natives.

In a manner unlike any of the preceding authors, Olaudah Equiano and Hugh Henry Brackenridge question the limits of what some saw as the beneficial aspects of transformable race. Chapter 4, "Doubting Transformable Race: Equiano, Brackenridge, and the Textuality of Natural History," discusses how Equiano's *Interesting Narrative* (a slave autobiography) and Brackenridge's *Modern Chivalry* (a burlesque novel) perform this questioning and, moreover, express remarkable reservations about not only natural-historical texts but also textuality more generally. Equiano endorses specific natural histories but remains cynical about the fulfillment of their implicit promises of equality. Unlike Wheatley, for example, whose work made much of the notion that differences in color among people were mere "dyes" applied to God's single creation of humankind and thus should be celebrated, Equiano witnesses the promises of transformable race going unfulfilled. In addition, the *Narrative* demonstrates that written texts have only limited power to ensure the states of being that they supposedly call into being. Brackenridge's *Modern Chivalry* criticizes the American Philosophical Society, the institutional location of major debates over racial production. More widely, by emphasizing the gothic nature and the textuality and narrativity of natural history, *Modern Chivalry* does not just parody one natural-philosophical theory but rather all theories. Drawing attention to how these theorems are discursively created, *Modern Chivalry* hints at the impossibility of ever articulating a definitive truth. In these ways, both texts highlight the relationship between literary writing and scientific writing. They evidence that we should not assume that literary texts simply or exclusively drew upon scientific facts but rather that literature and natural history existed as intertwined discourses. In this way, because these two books show how they—like natural histories—create, circulate, and constitute these ideas in discourse, they make us aware that literary pieces and scientific works were both attempts to narrate the world. Thus, both the *Narrative* and *Modern Chivalry* demonstrate the interactive engagement between literature and natural history.

Taking us to the end of the eighteenth century, the epilogue, "Interiorizing Racial Metamorphosis: *The Algerine Captive*'s Language of Sympathy," shows how Royall Tyler's novel marks the slow shift from eighteenth-century conceptions of an external, flexible race to later beliefs about internal and fixed racial differences. This fictional Barbary captivity story chronicles the story of Dr. Updike Underhill who travels through the recently-formed United States, to England and West Africa as a surgeon on a slave ship, to Algiers as a slave himself, and back to the United States as a free man. I show how *The Algerine Captive* uses eighteenth-century theories of sentiment to depict racial difference moving "inside" the body. While working as a physician on a slave ship, Dr. Underhill's profound sympathetic identification with African slaves "blackens" his soul in a metaphorical interior racial metamorphosis. Because his cross-racial sympathy is closely linked to his enslavement, Underhill represses that identification upon his return to the United States in order to reinstate his citizenship status. The narrative depicts that the white citizen can transform into the rhetorically internally raced slave; however, it simultaneously denies white-black affective identification and the abolitionist sentiment to which it gives rise. Reading Tyler's scenes of vexed racial transformation provides a vantage point from which to reflect on the racial epistemologies of the eighteenth century and to begin to analyze the change to those of the

nineteenth. Furthermore, it gives occasion to think about the ongoing endeavor to comprehend the relationship between science and culture. In our
present moment, as we vigorously debate what kinds of claims contemporary
genetic science might make about one's racial background, literary scholars
should continue to be involved in trying to understand racial identity, the
ways it is constructed, and what we take those constructions to mean. If we
develop a better sense of how science and literature interacted in the definition
of early American racial categories *and* how this interaction has changed over
time, we will have a better sense of how to think about our own conceptions of
race, right now.

Becoming Colored in Occom and Wheatley's Early America

In the preface material to Phillis Wheatley's 1773 *Poems on Various Subjects, Religious and Moral,* her owner John Wheatley attests to his slave's prodigious literacy by referring to a 1765 letter she sent to Native American minister Samson Occom. "As to her Writing," John states, "her own curiosity led her to it; and this she learnt in so short a Time, that in the Year 1765, she wrote a Letter to the Rev. Mr. Occom, the *Indian* Minister. . . ."[1] John Wheatley's statement launched a two-centuries-old critical tradition of often referring to—but seldom examining—the literary affiliation between "America's two most famous nonwhites [of the] time."[2] Indeed, Wheatley's famous diatribe against slavery in her 1774 letter to Occom has become a cornerstone of Wheatley scholarship that illustrates her poetry's antislavery sentiment. However, even as Wheatley and Occom scholars frequently cite Wheatley's caustic statement—"How well the cry for Liberty, and the reverse Disposition for the exercise of oppressive Power over others agree,—I humbly think it does not require the Penetration of a Philosopher to determine"[3]—very few juxtapose the work of these key early American writers of color. In contrast, this chapter compares how they conceptualized the process of "becoming colored" in colonial America.

In what follows, I argue that these writers engage with contemporaneous debates about how environmental factors alter the surface of the human body and that they do so to depict the production of racial difference—*both* the formation of professedly impressionable physical features *and* the ways those attributes signify in systems of racialization. Drawing upon the idea that racial characteristics were produced over time since the original creation, Occom and Wheatley use language emphasizing the ostensible malleability of racial characteristics—what I call a symbolics of metamorphosis—to explore the construction of racial categories in ways particular to early America. Transformable race, a sense of the external mutability of the racialized body, figures centrally in how Occom and Wheatley characterize racial formation.

For Occom, the beliefs his Anglo and Native American contemporaries held about the status of the "red" Indian enable him to challenge colonial society's contradictory Christian epistemology in his 1768 "A Short Narrative of my Life" and his 1772 *A Sermon, Preached at the Execution of Moses Paul, An Indian.* Then, in his 1784 "To All the Indians in this Boundless Continent," Occom uses notions of transformable race to assert Mohegan tribal sovereignty. In *Poems*, Wheatley fuses ancient mythological beliefs and natural-historical axioms about the production of poetic genius and dark skin to characterize the black poet as an inevitable outcome rather than an anomalous exception. Furthermore, she points to how the practice of slavery mobilizes blackness as a category of identity in order to underwrite its own system of forced labor.

Protestant religious thinking about the body and about the distinctions among humankind's varieties informs how these writers portray racialization. Marshaling certain aspects of monogenetic natural history that validated Christian creationism, Occom and Wheatley represent the process of "becoming colored" as a God-inspired design. It is one that establishes universality throughout and simultaneously variegates beautifully the vast diversity of humankind. Thus, to misread the variation of God's peoples as a signifier of irreparable difference is to sin.

However, while they rely upon religious doctrine to portray the constitution of racial identities, their engagements with processes of racialization diverge from one another. Able to travel extensively and sermonize authoritatively among multiple Native tribes, Occom and his writings are necessarily contextualized by the widely diverse indigenous religious traditions and practices with which he came in contact—both Christian beliefs and what we now term "nativist" beliefs (as I shall explain below, those that emphasized a return to indigenous customs, religious practices, and a belief in separate creations).[4] He demonstrates that how both Christian and nativist customs account for racial difference force religious whites to evaluate their epistemological worldview, and he advances a particular kind of indigenized Christianity and Native sovereignty. Although also drawing on a Christian and natural-historical understanding of racial difference, Wheatley—infamously forced to prove that a female black slave could indeed write poetry[5]—utilizes changing beliefs about the effect of the African climate to intervene in debates about race, science, and aesthetics. Recovering these distinctions unearths the breadth of approaches to theorizing racial difference that Native and African Americans in 1770s British North America could and did take.

To Make Samson Occom "So"

While many Occom biographies have focused on his position within colonial missions, this chapter follows the groundbreaking work of scholars such as Lisa Brooks (Abenaki), who thoroughly situates Occom specifically in his Mohegan tribal context.[6] Taking what Joanna Brooks calls an "indigenist" perspective,[7] it attends to the differences between white and Native worlds *and* to the diversities within late eighteenth-century Indian Country, and it recognizes how other historical occurrences affected his life and work. Situating Occom's history within Native American worldviews and the discipline of natural history demonstrates how debates about the potential transformation of the Indian body pervaded Native American and British colonial culture.[8] Given the fairly recent "discoveries" made by natural historians who invented and then classified the species of "man" into different varieties, great tensions existed between the orthodox Christian origin story of Adam and Eve so recently underwritten by this "natural" history and what have come to be called "nativist" beliefs about *separate* red-white creations. Occom's narrative and sermons intervene in these debates, not by posing an alternate theory, but by considering the implications of competing ways to account for racial difference. Occom's work explores how the Indian body comes to be seen as and considered "red."

Occom was born on an unknown day in 1723 into the Mohegan tribe in southeastern Connecticut. And although later Occom would lead many Mohegan to relocate to Brothertown, New York, and some of the descendants of those people subsequently relocated to Wisconsin, the federally recognized Mohegan nation prospers today in Uncasville, Connecticut, where Mohegan tribal historian Melissa (Fawcett) Tantaquidgeon Zobel and Mohegan tribal archivist David Freeburg keep Occom's history alive.[9] Believed to be a descendant of the famous chief Uncas, Occom experienced what LaVonne Brown Ruoff terms a "traditional" Mohegan upbringing.[10] Growing up in a wigwam, Occom remained largely unaffected by British society until he converted to Christianity during the Great Awakening.[11] After his conversion, Occom remained active in tribal life; in 1742, sachem Ben Uncas II appointed Occom one of twelve Mohegan councilors. Occom later studied under Congregationalist Eleazar Wheelock and spent 1761–1763 intermittently preaching to the Oneida tribe of the Iroquois Confederacy.[12]

However, the Christian Great Awakening was not the only spiritual revival sweeping Indian Country in the eighteenth century to which Occom was exposed. Indeed, the nativist spiritual movement also inevitably inflected Occom's missionary work among the easternmost Iroquois tribe, although most biographical studies of Occom do not draw an explicit connection between Occom's Christian ministry and nativism. As I explained in the introduction, "the Indians' Great Awakening" taught that Natives, whites, and Africans were created separately (*SR* 21). Nativist thought implied a pan-Indian identity. If Europeans were coming to think of themselves as "'White,'" nativist Indians conceived of themselves as "'Red.'"[13]

The nativist "doctrine of separate creations" of the Indians' Great Awakening underwrote what is now known as Pontiac's War.[14] While the majority of this violence took place within the Ohio Valley, the effect of nativism and the war spread into the Great Lakes region, affecting the six tribes of the Iroquois Confederacy, including the Oneidas with whom Occom worked during this time.[15] Panic caused by the rebellion reached areas located between the Oneidas of New York and the Mohegans of Connecticut.[16] The news of Pontiac's rebellion spread through both Indian Country and British colonial territory.

From 1761 to 1763, Occom made three trips to the Oneidas during the beginning of the rapid spread of nativist thought. Although Occom's diaries say frustratingly little about the tribes he visited, his notoriety among the Six Nations and his periodic unease among the confederacy are well recorded.[17] Occom's missionary work among the Oneida finally ended in 1763 as a result of the outbreak of the Pontiac War.[18] Furthermore, as Mohegan tribal historian Melissa (Fawcett) Tantaquidgeon Zobel attests, the widespread anti-Indian sentiment resulting from Pontiac's rebellion contributed to the decision that Occom should raise missionary funds abroad rather than in the colonies.[19] Scholars such as Lisa Brooks, David Silverman, and Caroline Wigginton have shown us the extensive interaction Occom had with the Oneida, and Occom certainly would have been attuned to various religious movements throughout Indian Country as a context for his missionary efforts.[20] Thus, when Occom left Oneida, we can assume he would have understood the tenets of this non Christian indigenous religious movement.[21] While the war effort eventually collapsed, prophetic nativism remained alive and well (*SR* 36).

As I outlined in the introduction, Enlightenment natural philosophy, like nativism, also advanced theories about humankind's creation and different "varieties." By the time Occom raised money throughout England for the Moor Indian Charity School, both Linnaeus and Buffon had attributed flexible surface characteristics among men to external factors (such as climate, temperature, food, and mode of living) that acted *upon*—rather than fixed differences lodged *within*—one's body.[22] These natural histories were influenced by Biblical monogenism (*CR* 14–33). While nativism claimed that separate creations caused racial difference, natural philosophy attributed the development of humankind's varieties to surface changes to the body, a theorem on which both Occom and Wheatley drew.

Just as natural history considered how literal bodily transformation produced Natives' "human difference," Occom's teacher, Eleazar Wheelock, conceptualized Native American conversion as a metaphorical bodily transformation. Wheelock thought that his students' conversion process necessarily involved making them culturally white and therefore suitable for becoming proper British subjects. Ethnohistorian James Axtell writes that Wheelock entered into his Christianizing mission "with a driving vision of tawny souls blanched by the Bible."[23] If Wheelock saw the conversion process as metaphorically whitening Indians, some Christians believed in its literal effects. Many New England whites debated whether religious conversion would cause racial transformation and "so strongly associated Christianity with whiteness that they imagined Indian and African converts physically changing color."[24] Thus, Occom lived in a world infused with possibilities of physical or figural metamorphoses of the Indian body—a topic that structures Occom's work in heretofore unacknowledged ways.

When Occom returned home from England, he entered what biographer William Love calls the "Dark Days at Mohegan."[25] Despite his promises, Wheelock had neglected Occom's family in his absence, had decided to move the Indian School from Connecticut to New Hampshire, and had chosen to educate more white than Indian students. Occom's relationship with Wheelock began its famous deterioration. The Boston Commissioners, one of the missionary societies that had supported Occom's ministry, began to spread rumors contesting his "authenticity" as an Indian and recent Christian convert.[26] To respond to this hearsay and to protest the fact that he had received less funds than white missionaries engaged in identical work, Occom sat down on September 17, 1768, to pen an appropriate response in what has come to be known as his "Short Narrative."[27] Recontextualizing Occom's text within this much wider history, we find Occom hinging his entire narrative on its last word: so.

During the Great Awakening, evangelicals like George Whitefield and Jonathan Edwards converted large numbers of Africans and Native Americans, ostensibly following Christian theology's primary concern with the state of one's soul, despite the supposed status of one's racialized body.[28] Occom's "Short Narrative," however, unlike many religious autobiographies, emphasizes the link between physicality and spirituality.[29] It also shows that while Christian missionaries might have professed to care only about the Indian's soul, how they registered inherent difference in the body undermined their own beliefs, especially in the validity of their Biblical creation story and its implied theories of "racial" difference. Occom's "Short Narrative" queries how "Indianness" comes to be displayed on the body and how this characteristic begins to be read as "race." If Occom in part composed his narrative to dispute the Boston Commissioners' accusations of Indian "inauthenticity," he counters these reports less by detailing autobiographical facts and more by querying what it means to be an "authentic" Indian.

At a key point in his narrative, Occom points out that although the Boston Commissioners begrudgingly grant him money to sustain his mission a bit longer, he receives less than his missionary peers. He claims that "these Same Gentlemen, gave a young Missionary, a Single man *one Hundred Pounds* for one year, and fifty Pounds for an Interpreter, and thirty Pounds for an Introducer; so it Cost them one Hundred & Eighty Pounds in one Single Year, and they Sent too where there was no Need of a Missionary."[30] Using what

Kimberly Roppolo (Cherokee, Choctaw, and Creek) conceptualizes as the Native rhetoric of indirect discourse,[31] Occom contrasts this with his own tasks: "Now You See What difference they made between ^me^ and other Missionaries; they gave me 180 Pounds for 12 years Service, which they gave for one years Service in another Mission—In my Service (I speak like a fool, but I am Constraind) I was my own Interpreter. I was both a School master, and Minister to the Indians, yea I was their Ear, Eye & Hand, as Well Mouth" ("SN" 58).[32] Occom then poses the rhetorical question, "what can be the Reason? that they used me after ^this^ manner. . . ." He answers his own question by relating a short anecdote:

> I Cant think of any thing, but this as a Poor Indian Boy Said, Who was Bound out to an English Family, and he Usd to Drive Plow for a young man, and he Whipt and Beat him allmost every Day, and the young man found fault with him, and Complaind of him to his master and the poor Boy was Calld to answere for him^self^ before his master,—and he was askd, what it was he did, that he was So Complaind of and beat almost every Day; he Said, he did not know, but he Supposd it was because he could not ^drive^ any better; but says he, I Drive as well as I know ^how^; and at other Times he Beats me, because he is mind to beat me, but Says he, ^I believe^ he Beats for the most of the Time, because I am an Indian. ("SN" 58)

After Occom uses this story to show that whites base their actions toward the boy (and, by implication, Occom himself) on the fact that he is an Indian, he concludes his "Short Narrative":

> So I am ready to Say, they have usd thus, because I Cant Instruct the Indi-ans so well as other Missionaries, but I Can asure *them* I have endeavourd to teach them as well as I how—but I must Say, I believe it is because I am poor Indian. I Can't help that God has made me So; I did not make my self So. ("SN" 58)

Occom draws the distinction between what he is "ready to Say"—that the com-missioners treat him differently because they suspect that he cannot draw as many converts as other missionaries—and what he "must Say"—that he endures discrimination from the white Boston Commissioners because he is an Indian.[33] The closing paragraph then shifts the emphasis from Occom's own stated suspi-cions about why he receives this treatment to the Boston Commissioners' unde-cidability about what to do with an Indian and what an Indian, exactly, *is*.

Here, Occom draws attention to the contradictory nature of the Boston Commissioners' beliefs about the Indian, especially in light of how nativist doctrine, Christian creation theology, and natural history account for the pro-duction of radical difference. The phrase "God has made me so" raises many questions, since the very issue of God's creation of the Indian was one of the most hotly debated topics of the period. Occom's use of *so* instead of *one*, underscores not the *fact* of the Indian (e.g., I am poor Indian; God has made me *one*) but rather the *condition* of the Indian (e.g., I am poor Indian; God has made me *so*).[34] The phrase states that God created him, but its construction begs the question: what exactly is *the condition* of the "poor Indian" that God has made? Is the state of the Indian, on the one hand, that of a body that carries inherent difference since creation or, on the other hand, is it a body that mutates and changes over time? To ask the question a different way, is the Indian body able to undergo various types of transformative processes that produce what then becomes read as "difference"?

How the commissioners define "so," according to what they believe about the status of the Indian, necessarily dictates one of two implications for their religious epistemology. If one follows the Biblical creation story, where all humankind descends from Adam and Eve, then one must understand the Indian body as changeable and attribute any contrasts among humans, as most natural historians did, to changes wrought by the environment. However, if one believes that the Indian is unchangeable, then he must have been irreparably different since his creation. If one holds this belief about Indian distinction (as the actions of the Boston Commissioners seem to suggest), then one's stance resonates with radical nativism and early white polygenists that claimed separate Indian-white creations. By posing this choice, Occom's narrative not only highlights the hypocrisy of the Boston Commissioners paying a white missionary more money for less work; it demonstrates that if the commission treats Indians as inherently different when its espoused religion claims that they share the same creation, it compromises its entire belief system and values.

By juxtaposing "God has made me So" with "I did not make my self so," Occom's narrative implies that his treatment from the Boston Commissioners results less from what he has done in his life than from what they believe about how God created him. If the commissioners think that Indian bodies cannot and have not transformed over time from their initial shared creation with whites, then what Occom has done in converting to Christianity and abandoning his "heathenistic" ways matters very little, along with, by implication, the work that the Boston Commissioners support among the Indians. Occom's final paragraph places as much emphasis on white belief about the Indian body. Therefore, the rhetorical structure of the "Short Narrative" performs exactly the same engagement with white readers that Occom describes with the Boston Commissioners: what he actually does matters only insofar as how it is interpreted through their beliefs about the creation of the Indian.[35] This does not privilege white thought above all else but, rather, muses on the processes of signification and interpretation of the racialized body within Christian discourse. Unashamed of being an Indian, Occom demonstrates that the problem centers on how the Boston Commissioners must decide on and act accordingly upon what they think *being an Indian means.*

Therefore, when Occom says "Now You See What difference they made between ^me^ and other Missionaries" ("SN" 58), he does not just discuss "making *a* difference" in terms of discrepancies in pay. He alludes to the way that the Boston Commissioners choose to interpret the signification of the body. In other words, the "difference they made" has less to do with how surface characteristics come to be on the body and more to do with how the commissioners choose to interpret these traits—their power works to "produce" signs (skin color, physical features) that they then believe signify in a certain way. It is not just that they made "a" difference by treating dissimilarly the Indian and the white missionaries. It is that they *made difference*, by producing on their own a certain kind of distinction.[36] Occom not only queries the various explanations for how red people "became red" (how the Indian body has transformed since its Adamic creation), but also how difference itself (how those "changes" might signify) is made.[37] Occom shows how the Boston British Commissioners' entire Christian faith and racial ideological system are implicated in the beliefs they hold about the status of the Indian body.

DIS-FIGURING THE IMAGE OF GOD

The issue of the Indian body recurs as a central concern for Occom four years later when he gave what would become one of the era's most famous sermons.[38] In June 1772, Moses Paul, a Native American recently convicted of murdering the white Moses Cook after being thrown out of a tavern for being drunk, solicited Occom to "preach to me upon [the execution]." Paul cited the fact that "we are of the same nation."[39] Occom agreed, and by the time he stood in front of the congregation a little over a month later, the atmosphere was a racialized one: Occom was the first American Indian to deliver the execution sermon of another Native American *and* the details of Paul's crime and trial made racial difference the key component.

Moses Paul protested his conviction by arguing that the jurors' preconceived assumptions about drunken Indians caused them to misinterpret the evidence presented about that night, including his claim that he acted in self-defense. Because all British subjects were guaranteed equal treatment before the law, the court "ignored Paul's status as a racial subject" by relegating difference to the private sphere and constituting him "as a legal subject only."[40] However, when convicted of capital murder, Paul's appeal petition asked the judges to consider if the court's refusal to recognize racial difference publicly could actually ensure justice. As Ava Chamberlain claims, Paul "propose[d] that racial difference may have created the gap between the testimony of the witnesses and the conclusions of the jury."[41] Paul contended that because he acted in self-defense, he should be charged with manslaughter, not capital murder. Chamberlain sums up the importance of the jurors' preconceptions: "If the court attributed to Paul not agency but savagery, however, the circumstances of the killing would be irrelevant, for degrees of intentionality apply only to rational beings. If all Indians are savages, then all killings of whites by Indians are savage murders—despite extenuating factors."[42] Paul pointed to how the jurors' views, particularly shaped by racial ideology, held more sway that what he considered the factual evidence of the case.

When Occom then delivered Moses Paul's execution sermon on a blustery September day, it had all the trappings of a noteworthy event.[43] Additionally, the fact that a few years earlier Wheelock had charged Occom with drunkenness himself made Indian drinking a tricky topic for Occom to negotiate.[44] A teeming audience of local clergymen, British colonists, Native Americans, and the convicted murderer himself packed into New Haven's First Congregational Church.[45] Before Occom could even draw breath to preach in a situation equally momentous and delicate, many questions hung in the air. How would the internationally famous Indian preacher address the convicted Wampanoag Indian and the racially mixed crowd? Would he chastise his fellow Natives for their savage and drunken nature or denounce the enduring nativist movement? Would Wheelock's past accusation of Occom's own rumored intemperance affect how he could address inebriation? And perhaps most importantly for the condemned Moses Paul on the last morning of his life, would Occom allude to Paul's opinion that white-held assumptions about "drunken Indians" influenced the judgment against him?

In the sermon, Occom quotes Dr. Isaac Watts' *The Psalms of David Imitated in the Language of the New Testament*:

> *See the vain race of mortals move,*
> *Like shadows o'er the plain,*
> *They rage and strive, desire and love,*
> *But all the noise is vain.*[46]

Here, the only "race" of which Watts and Occom speak is that "of mortals," not whites, Indians, or Africans.[47] How "race" becomes a defining feature between rather than of mortals suffuses the rest of the sermon. Occom considers bodily transformations related to religious experience. Also, by implicitly exploring the question of how Native Americans "became red" since their original creation—as Wheatley will examine the process of "becoming black"—the sermon considers the implications of potential answers.[48]

Occom begins by stressing the universally transformative qualities of sin— rather than contemplating how Christian conversion might "whiten" Native Americans—and emphasizing the separation of the soul from the body. However, near the sermon's conclusion, he uses physical metaphorics to emphasize the status of the Indian body. As we shall see, arguing that alcohol makes Indians irrational and "dis-figures" men from the "image of God," he makes the production of racial difference a spiritual issue. By reframing debates on the Indian's "degeneration," Occom leads his audience to consider the

compatibility of Christian thinking with belief in the drunken Indian stereotype and implies that Paul's sentencing might be wrong.

In the sermon, Occom emphasizes how sin identically affects every person.[49]
He claims that "as long as sin is cherished, death is chosen; and this seems to be
the woful case of mankind of all nations, . . . vice and immorality, and floods
of iniquity are abounding every where amongst all nations, and all orders and
ranks of men, and in every sect of people" (S 7). Occom also intimates that all
men are cursed because of their link to Adam.

> And it seems all the enjoyments of men in this world are also poisoned with
> sin: for God said to Adam after he had sinned, "Cursed is the ground for thy
> sake, in sorrow shalt thou eat of it all the days of thy life." By this we plainly
> see that every thing that grows out of the ground is cursed, and all creatures
> that God hath made for man are cursed also; and whatever God curses is a
> cursed thing indeed. (S 11–12)

The natural-historical theory that the New World's feeble environment led
to the degeneration of the red man is incidental to Occom's claim that *all*
men who live on *all* ground are cursed specifically because of their Adamic
ancestry.[50] Occom uses and reworks the language of natural history and its
environmentalist claims, here to emphasize original sin. Any "degeneration"
that might have happened to the Native American in the New World environment pales in comparison to man's feeding on the cursed ground's harvests.

In contrast to nativists, Occom stresses commonality among all earthly
men. Occom explicitly talks about the length of eternity as "the same unex-
hausted duration" that "must be the unavoidable portion of all impenitent
sinners, . . . Negroes, Indians, English, or of what nation soever, all that die
in their sins, must go to hell together; for the wages of sin is death" (S 17).
Regardless of what surface physical changes the environment might have
wrought since Adam's day, Occom envisions a world created at once by a
single God; when one dies, he ascends or descends into the afterlife according
only to his salvation status.[51]

In Occom's sermon, religious corporeal transformation is no longer something exclusively wrought on red bodies. If many whites focus on how religious conversion might—metaphorically or literally—lighten red Indians,
Occom shows how sin transforms all humankind by becoming an agent of
bodily transformation. He declares that "it was sin that transformed the very
angels in heaven, into devils. . . . If it had not been for sin, there never would
have been such a thing as hell or devil, death or misery" (S 8). He here implies
that each body, including those of angels, holds the potential to mutate. Even
if natural-philosophical theories of degeneration argue that Native Americans did worsen from their "original state" as white, sin renders more intense
change. Occom claims that

man is a most unruly and ungovernable creature, and is become as the wild
ass's colt . . . he is more like the devil than any creature we can think of: and
I think it is not going beyond the word of God, to say, man is the most devilish creature in the world. . . . Thus every unconverted soul is a child of the
devil, sin has made them so. (*S* 11)

As a transformative cause, sin turns man into beast. "Sin has made him beastly
and devilish; yea he is sunk beneath the beasts, and is worse than the ravenous
beasts of the wilderness" (*S* 10). Therefore, Indians are not "naturally" devils;
devils are men (or even angels) made so by sin.

In addition to articulating how sin affects all humankind, Occom discusses
death, or the "separation between soul and body" (*S* 15). At the "cessation
of natural life, there is an end of all the enjoyments of this life; there is no
more joy nor sorrow; no more hope nor fear, as to the body" (*S* 15). However, he adds, "the poor departed soul must take up its lodging in sorrow,
wo and misery, . . . where a multitude of frightful deformed devils dwell, and
the damned ghosts of Adam's race; . . . where poor guilty naked souls will
be tormented with exquisite torments . . ." (*S* 16). Because one is of "Adam's
race," the soul departs for heaven or hell, regardless of earthly racial categories. Rearticulating the way "poor" and "naked" were "terms essential to New
England's racial discourse," Occom uses them to describe all damned souls—
not just Indian ones.[52]

Given Occom's sermonizing on the universality of souls and the soul's
split from the body, why does the sermon then radically shift to emphasizing
physicality? After articulating the equality of souls, why does Occom address
Paul and his fellow Indians "according to the flesh" (*S* 28)? I'd like to suggest
that this switch to bodily metaphorics—not incompatible with the preaching
on the state of one's soul—enables Occom to render the status of the Indian
and the production of racial difference specifically religious concerns and to
dispute the drunken Indian stereotype Moses Paul felt so detrimentally informed his conviction.

Occom, referring to his fellow Indians as "my brethren and kindred according to the flesh" (*S* 28), uses a phrase with a seemingly paradoxical signification. His metaphors of the flesh mark his simultaneous inclusion within
both a Christian metaphysical brotherhood and an Indian physical brotherhood. This expression states that the commonality among his fellow Natives
is located not in the soul but simply in the body. However, this language also
signifies his membership in the metaphysical body of Christ, partly because
it paraphrases the Biblical Apostle Paul's recurring employment of the same
phrase. Occom's use of this Pauline construction calls attention to Paul's position in his own cross-cultural ministry, which necessarily inflects Occom's
own.[53] In Romans 9:2–5, Paul's letter to the Jewish-gentile congregation in
Rome laments the fate of his unconverted Jewish brethren: "I have great

heaviness and continual sorrow in my heart. For I could wish that myself were accursed from Christ for my brethren, my kinsmen according to the flesh: Who are Israelites; . . . Whose are the fathers, and of whom as concerning the flesh Christ came . . ."[54] Like Occom, Paul uses the phrase to accentuate his relationship with both fellow Jews (expressed as being "of the flesh") and fellow Christian believers (Jews *and* gentiles joined together "in the spirit"). This metaphor demonstrates simultaneously Occom's physical relation with Indians as opposed to whites and his spiritual relationship with all "varieties" of Christians.[55]

Addressing Moses Paul directly, Occom refocuses the sermon from individuals' souls to the specificity of his and Moses Paul's bodies and ambiguously mediates between Christian and nativist thought.[56] Occom says, "*My poor unhappy Brother* MOSES; As it was your own desire that I should preach to you this last discourse, so I shall speak plainly to you.—You are the bone of my bone, and flesh of my flesh. You are an Indian, a despised creature; but you have despised yourself; yea you have despised God more. . . ." (*S* 21). By quoting Genesis 2:23 ("you are the bone of my bone, and flesh of my flesh"), Occom marks his simultaneous inclusion within the Christian community and also his exclusive bodily relationship to other Indians. His use of the familiar locution from the Adam and Eve story is conspicuously ambiguous. Its origin in Genesis authorizes the monogenetic creation story. However, because it emphasizes a shared, exclusive Indian origin by signaling the uniqueness of *Indian* flesh, it simultaneously resonates with nativism. This "one flesh" status of Indians poses for Occom's audience one of two mutually exclusive interpretations. In one, the radically nativist idea claims a separate Indian creation. Alternately, Occom's phrase alludes to how the Apostle Paul addresses the Jews as "brethren according to the flesh," thus emphasizing a spiritual brotherhood with everyone while retaining a special kinship with Indians.

However, given the conflicted status of Indian "flesh" in natural-historical and nativist thought at the eighteenth century's end, Occom's employment of bodily metaphorics reverberates through religious and scientific discourses in a way that Paul's did not. The sermon's audience could indeed take the phrase to mean that Indians have a completely separate flesh from whites, thus endorsing nativist thought. However, if one follows the Biblical creation story, one must attribute human difference to changes wrought by the environment—as most natural historians did. In this case, Occom's use of "flesh" denotes a specific type of relation but not an inherent distinction. Holding that Indians and whites do share the same creation, Occom's sermon suggests that physical differences among people must arise from environmental factors. The characteristics of Indian flesh reflect this influence on the body rather than signify God-ordained difference. Occom's uncanny quotation begs the creation question and requires his audience members to contemplate, according to their religious beliefs, to what degree they are all bones of one another's bones and flesh of one another's flesh.[57]

Occom then depicts a heaven where converted Indian souls exist with those of other believers, regardless of earthbound differences. Occom tells Moses Paul that

> O, what a joyful day would it be if you would now openly believe in and re-
> ceive the Lord Jesus Christ; . . . it would cause the angels to come down from
> the realms above, and wait hovering about your gallows, ready to convey
> your soul to the heavenly mansions, there to . . . join the heavenly choirs in
> singing the songs of Moses and the Lamb: there to set down forever with
> Abraham, Isaac and Jacob in the kingdom of God's glory; . . . and there shall
> you forever admire the astonishing and amazing and infinite mercy of God
> in Christ Jesus. . . . (S 25–26)

Occom clearly depicts a heaven where converted Indian souls exist with those of all other believers who have gone before. If the convicted murderer so chooses, he can that day reside among several Judeo-Christian forebears: Moses, Abraham, Isaac, Jacob, and Jesus himself. For Occom, there is no sep-arate creation and no irreparable difference when it comes to peoples' souls.

In the last portion of the sermon Occom chastises "the Indians, my breth-eren and kindred according to the flesh" (S 28)—who were likely seated in the church gallery[58]—for being susceptible to "the sin of drunkenness." Here he highlights how alcohol *makes* them exhibit the traits that Paul's jurors assume are natural: drunkenness, irrationality, and brutality. He declares that "it is this sin . . . that has stript us of every desirable comfort in this life; by this we are poor, miserable and wretched; by this sin we have no name nor credit in the world among polite nations; for this sin we are despised in the world. . . ." (S 28–29). Occom argues that the Indians' inherent nature does not make them bad; rather, "by" this sin of alcohol, Indians have become irrational and savage. Occom continues, "when we are intoxicated with strong drink, we drown our rational powers, by which we are distinguished from the brutal creation. . . ." (S 29). Occom points out that Indian drinkers "have brought [them]selves" into this "miserable condition" (S 31).[59]

Furthermore, the Indian becomes the drunken savage as a result of a trans-formation that happens to *all* God-created men when they drink.

> My poor kindred, do consider what a dreadful abominable sin drunk-
> enness is. God made us men, and we chuse to be beasts and devils; God
> made us rational creatures, and we chuse to be fools. Do consider further,
> and behold a drunkard, and see how he looks, when he has drowned his
> reason; how deformed and shameful does he appear? He dis-figures every
> part of him, both soul and body, which was made after the image of God.
> (S 29–30)

Created in the "image of God," man—both Indian and white—disfigures his soul and body by drinking. For Occom, all men have degenerated from God's perfect form. Any bodily difference, racial or otherwise, occurs after creation. With this example, Occom reframes transformation in natural history from theories of Indian degeneration to the degeneration of all. He reconceptualizes corporeal transformation in religious thought from conversion's "whitening" of Indians to sin's disfiguration of everyone.[60]

While Occom's sermon functions in a disciplinary capacity by chastising Indian drinking habits, it also criticizes whites engaged in similar behaviors. Suggesting that Cook bears some responsibility for the drunken brawl, Occom gives theological validity to Paul's contention regarding the stereotype of the drunken Indian:

> Again, a man in drunkenness is in all manner of dangers, he may be kill'd by his fellow-men, by wild beasts, and tame beasts; he may fall into the fire, into the water, or into a ditch; or he may fall down as he walks along, and break his bones or his neck; he may cut himself with edge-tools. . . .
>
> *I believe you know the truth of what I have just now said*, many of you, by sad experience; yet you will go on still in your drunkenness. (*S* 30, emphasis added)

In this striking quotation, Occom demonstrates that drinking alcohol turns one *not* into a murderer *but rather* into a murder victim. "A man in drunkenness" might be killed or may cause his own demise. Given Paul's claim that the drunk Cook instigated the fight, Occom intimates that Cook may have had much to do with his own death. Like the ambiguity arising from the coincidence of the perpetrator's and victim's identical first names, this passage's subtle shift in agency leaves the question unanswered: to which drunken Moses does Occom allude?

Following this daring potential reassignment of blame, Occom blasts that "we find in sacred writ, a wo denounced against men, who put their bottles to their neighbours mouth to make them drunk, that they may see their nakedness: and no doubt there are such devilish men now in our day" (*S* 31). While alcohol may "drown the rational powers" of the Indian and have the potential to "disfigure" him, these devilish figures are white men who distribute alcohol to their Indian neighbors. Occom does not limit the potential and danger of transformation to the Indian. Here, white men's own metamorphoses into devils lead to Indian drinking, Cook's demise, and Paul's immediately impending execution.

Furthermore, Occom gives degeneration a new twist: if Indians have degenerated, they have fallen not from Adamic whiteness but from the perfect "image of God," and whites have played a crucial role in this process. One of the most pressing issues of the late eighteenth-century concerned why Indians had not "progressed" to high civilizations. Natural history attributed this to environmental influences.[61] Thus, it is not only important, as scholars point out, that Occom relates Indian drinking to white distribution.[62] If alcohol is one of the substances believed by many to affect bodily change, then liquor from whites actually helps *cause* this degeneration. If white Christians follow natural history's monogenetic explanation for the Indian's bodily difference (and then contradictorily insist on reading ontological distinction from that difference), then they must accept their own role in this transformative disfiguration of the Indian.

How Occom's sermon makes the Indian body one of its focal points is both ingenious and grotesque. With all attention focused on Paul's body hanging from the pillory, whites and Indians alike had to consider not only Paul's corpse but also—because of Occom's sermon—the way that ideologies about the Indian body might have contributed to his death. Following Christian doctrine, Native Americans have a valid ancestral claim to Adam and Eve. Therefore, God did make them rational; if not, then nativism's claim of separate red-white creations must be correct. Occom rhetorically leads his audience members to make a strategic choice: if they claim that Christianity holds true, then the drunken Indian stereotype is wrong; conversely, if the stereotype is right, then Christian theology is untrue. Occom puts his audience of Christian believers in a position to question this stereotype and the role it played in Paul's trial. By raising the question of the status of the Indian body, noting how whites contribute to the "dis-figured" state of the drunken Indian, and implying that Paul might not be guilty of the specific crime of which he was convicted, Occom's sermon opens up spaces of contestation that complicate its disciplinary function.

SAMSON OCCOM'S ORIGINS

As both the "Short Narrative" and the *Sermon* show, Occom often had to account for his "origins," either his own personal origin (i.e., "I was Born a Heathen and Brought up in In Heathenism till I was between 16 & 17 Years of age, at a Place Calld Mohegan in New London Connecticut, in New England" ["SN" 52]) or that of all peoples (i.e., from Adam and his cursed ground [S 11–12]). But he addresses this issue most directly in his understudied 1784 sermon "To all the Indians in this Boundless Continent," a text—written to Native Americans and not a white audience—that tells of the creation of "all Nations," including Indians, as the Biblical story of Adam and Eve.[63] Considering that Occom traveled extensively in what Lisa Brooks calls the "Native space of the northeast" and that he penned this sermon right before reinitiating the Mohegan migration from their ancestral homes to Oneida lands, where the tribes of the Iroquois Nation had been exposed to nativist thinking, we find that Occom writes this sermon with attention to where he started and where he was going; or, in other words, it is written with attention to both Occom's connection to his indigenous home and his travels across many physical places. In this sermon, Occom's use of the Adam and Eve framework enabled him to continue to argue for both a specific kind of Indian difference from *and also* Indian equality with the white race because of how he draws upon ideas of transformable race. Furthermore, given the historical context of the then-upcoming removal to Iroquoia, this sermon proposes an alternate Native religiosity than that propagated by nativists, and it advances Mohegan tribal and intellectual sovereignty.[64]

Occom begins his sermon: "To all the Indians in this Boundless Continent,— I am an Indian also, your Brother and you are my Brethren the Bone of my Bone and Flesh of my Flesh, I live at Mohegan or M^m^oyanhegunnuck. . . ." ("BC" 196). Perhaps better thought of as an epistle than a sermon, this text then goes on to chronicle the beginning of the world.

> There is but one, Great ^good^ Supream and Indepentant Spirit above, . . . And this God made Heaven and Earth and all things and all Creatures therein— . . . in Six Days he Made all things and all Creatures, and on the Six^th^ Day, on the last Day of the Creation, he made one man, and after wards he Caused ~~woman~~ a Deep Sleep to fall upon the man, and God took out one of his Ribs and made a woman for him, and they were Beautiful, Excellent and Glorious above all Creatures in this World they were made in the Image & Likeness of their Creator. . . . ("BC" 196)

This man and this woman ("Adam" and "Eve," Occom later calls them) resided in a garden where "there was one Tree planted in the midst of the Garden, that was Gods Tree, and the man and woman were forbid to meddle with it, and it was Call'd the Tree of Kno^w^ledge of good and Evel, and god told them in the Day they eat of the Fruit of the Tree they should surely die . . ." ("BC" 196). The text then relays how the woman and the man were convinced by "the Devil and Serpent" to eat of this fruit, such that "now their Eyes were opened only to See their Misery, . . . and they now see and know, that they have lost all, they have lost the Blessed Image and Likeness of God, they have lost their Beauty, Excellence, Holiness, and glory, . . . and Contracted the Image of the Devil and all his Likeness" ("BC" 197).

There are very particular effects of Occom's choice to tell the story in this way.[65] The idea of transformable race was not simply compatible with the Adam and Eve origin story; for many, it scientifically justified the biblical account that all peoples sprang from a single origin. This view stands in contrast to the ideas about creation espoused by the nativist spiritual movement, and as David Silverman's work makes clear, Occom's indigenous Christianity contrasted sharply with that of the nativist movement that spread through Indian Country.[66]

Occom uses the Adam and Eve story, and implicitly the idea of transformable race with which it is closely associated during this period, to argue strongly for a kind of singularity for Indians and also a communal equality among all peoples. He opens his letter by saying, "I am an Indian also, your Brother and you are my Brethren the Bone of my Bone and Flesh of my Flesh" (196). Just as in the *Sermon*, Occom's wording here marks his concurrent participation within both a Christian metaphysical brotherhood and an Indian physical brotherhood. This expression states that the commonality among his fellow Natives is not a soulful—but rather a bodily—difference arising not from a separate origin (as both nativists and polygenists would have it) but rather from the body's response to the environment. At the same time, this language also signifies his inclusion in the metaphysical body of Christ, partly because, like his *Sermon*, it draws upon Paul's use of the same wording. As in the *Sermon*, this metaphor marks Occom's physical kinship with Indians as opposed to whites and simultaneously demonstrates his spiritual affiliation with all Christians.

And even while preserving this special relationship with other Indians, Occom's text posits a radical equality among all people *because of* their shared origin. In Occom's sermon, Adam and Eve were the progenitors not just of the white race but of all races: "Now this one man and Woman, is the Father and Mother of all Nations of the Whole World" ("BC" 197). According to ideas about transformable race, each "race" developed its distinctive racial characteristics over time, but all peoples shared a common origin. Occom extends this line of thinking to include that Indians also shared a common equality with others because they all descended from the same, original pair. In addition, while some natural historians emphasize this "change over time" as a kind of degeneration, a movement away from an assumed primary and superior "whiteness," Occom's sermon emphasizes instead how *all peoples* change from being like God to resembling Satan as the consequence of Adam and Eve's sin: "Now their Eyes were opened only to See their Misery . . . that they have lost all, they have lost the *Blessed Image and Likeness of God*, they have lost their Beauty, Excellence, Holiness, and glory, they have lost the Sweet Fellowship, Communion and Enjoyment of God, and *Contracted the Image of the Devil and all his Likeness*" ("BC" 197, emphasis added). As in his earlier work, Occom reframes transformation in natural history from theories of Indian "degeneration" to the equal degeneration of all. Indians are not characterized as devils; *all* of fallen humankind "in Stead of being Gods they are Devils" ("BC" 197).

Drawing upon the Adam and Eve creation story, Occom used the most prevalent understanding of racial difference circulating at that time. And he did not use this origin story to spread a kind of colonizing Christianity to Indians but rather to indigenize Christianity and to argue for the radical equality of "*all* Nations of the *Whole* World" ("BC" 197, emphasis added).[67] Occom's sermon takes part in a larger debate about the origin of humankind, the cause of racial difference, and the commonality of all peoples; but it does so for the sake of "all the *Indians* in this Boundless Continent" ("BC" 196, emphasis added).

Clearly, Occom's sermon is not only engaging in a conversation that includes white natural historians and ministers, in part because here his comments are directed *specifically* toward a Native audience, one we can think of, on the one hand, as "*all* the Indians in this Boundless Continent" ("BC" 196, emphasis added) and, on the other, perhaps the Oneida Indians onto whose lands Occom was getting ready to relocate in 1784. Given this context, Occom's sermon offers a specific indigenized Christianity as an alternative to the nativist outlook sweeping Indian Country, and it argues for native sovereignty in an act of what Jace Weaver (Cherokee) calls "communitism," that which joins together both "community" and "activism."[68] Occom had already made several missionary trips to Oneida in the 1760s, and since then, he and the Mohegan leadership had been planning on removing there. The Oneida were open to Christian missionizing, but this placed them in a tense relationship with the rest of the Iroquois Confederacy tribes that leaned more toward nativism.[69] Here, by framing his origin story as something of particular importance to Indians *from an Indian preacher*, Occom offers up a different kind of Native religious worldview that Oneidas could embrace; he presents not an Anglo creation story told by an Indian but rather an Indian creation story, one that counters those told by nativists. One does not have to subscribe to the nativists' account of separate origins for the red, black, and white races in order to articulate a specific kind of relationship among "all" Indians or to argue for equality with the white race.

Furthermore, it is important that Occom here emphasizes this "Boundless Continent" as Indian Country. As Joanna Brooks points out, "the trope of America as a 'boundless continent' also appears in petitions coauthored by Occom and the Montaukett and Brotherton tribes in 1785. It invokes a powerful sense of North America as indivisibly and inalienably indigenous territory" (196). Indeed, in the "Brotherton Tribe to United States Congress" petition, the "aboriginal Nations of this Great Indian World" tell "The Congress of the Thirteen United States, in this Boundless Western New World," that "The Most Great, The Good and The Supream ^Spirit above^ Saw fit to Creat This World, and all Creatures and all things therein; and the Children of man to Inhabit the Earth and to enjoy."[70] Furthermore, the "Great ^govr^ of the Worlds,—Saw fit in his good pleasure, to Divide this World by the Great Waters, and he fenced this great Continent by the Mighty Waters, all around, and it pleased him, to Plant our fore Fathers here first, and he gave them this Boundless Continent" ("BT" 149). Here, Occom claims that God— the ultimate authority both spiritual ("Supream ^Spirit above^") *and* political ("Great ^govr^ of the Worlds")—created the "Boundless Continent" and *gave it to Native peoples first*. Only later, after the "aboriginal Nations of this Great Indian World" were clearly established, did "in Process of Time, The great

Sovereign of the Universe," allow whites to leave Europe and to establish themselves on native lands. This was a time when this "Sovereign"

> Saw fit to permit the [word crossed out] ∧Brethren∧ of your fore Fathers to rise up against them for their maintaining the pure Religion of Jesus Christ, and they killd many of them, and a few of them fled from the Face of their Cruel Bre[thr] en and the good Spirit above Directed their Course to the West, [an] d he brought them over into this Country, and here the Good Spirit made Room for them ∧and here your Fathers found us very poor and Wild and Ignorant∧ and others of their Brethren Soon Come after them, and Settle with them, and Soon Multiplied, and our fore Father Sold them Lands for little or nothing our Fathers knew not the Value of Lands. . . . ("BT" 149)

And it was this error, this selling of the lands, that became "a mistake for now we find our selves Stript of all our *Natural Priviledges*" ("BT" 149, emphasis added). Thus, in this petition and others, Occom strongly articulates an argument for tribal sovereignty bestowed upon Native peoples by "The great Sovereign of the Universe" who placed the "aboriginal Nations of this Great Indian World" on this "Boundless Continent" *first* ("BT" 149).[71] Therefore, in his sermon "To all the Indians in this Boundless Continent," when Occom notes that "I live at Mohegan or M∧m∧oyanhegunnuck," but that he is preparing to leave his homeland to establish a community elsewhere, he casts *anywhere* he might live in North America as always already Indian Country. Although he is preparing to leave the physical location of Mohegan, he considers where he is going as *also* Native land. Occom figures the upcoming relocation not as a concession to white land grabs but rather as a relocation to a different place, a space that is already "Native space." He and his fellow Mohegans will not be giving up their sovereignty when they relocate; they will simply take it with them. Their sovereignty is with them both in Mohegan and also wherever in the "Boundless Continent" that they might choose to go.

"To Make a Poet Black"

Samson Occom was not the only Christian of color in the early 1770s whose writings addressed the production of racial difference by concentrating on the status of raced bodies. Beginning with its frontispiece, Wheatley's *Poems* (Fig. 1.1) brings together changeable bodies with issues of race and poetic inspiration.[72] Analyzing the poet's left hand raised thoughtfully to her cheek and her darkened visage, literary critic Astrid Franke locates the famous Wheatley portrait within the "iconography of melancholy," because it displays "a mournful reflexivity proceeding from the insights of the religious

FIGURE 1.1 *Frontispiece of Phillis Wheatley,* Poems on Various Subjects, Religious and Moral. *London: A. Bell, 1773*
Courtesy of the Library of Congress.

convert and the poetic genius."[73] However, Franke contends, unlike other melancholic poet figures depicted with faces darkened by strategically drawn shadows,

> [Wheatley's] darkness invokes the traditional physiological under-standing that a melancholy temperament was caused by an excess of black bile. Giving a figurative meaning a surprising literal turn, then, the portrait and the portrayed are at once part of a long and vital history and yet also something entirely novel. To put it another way, the unprecedented public

depiction of a black female poet is moderated by familiar iconographic elements that encourage Wheatley's readers to view her within a longstanding cultural tradition.[74]

This African poet was not only mournfully contemplative but also "really" darkened as a corollary to her "melanchol(ic) temperament;"[75] Wheatley's "literal" darkness connects poetic inspiration and the production of black skin—crucially (but unremarked upon by Franke) because of natural-historical conceptions of a malleable body made darker through extended exposure to the sun.[76] The visual depiction of a poet physiologically blackened and made melancholic by an excess of black bile therefore asks: what exactly is the linkage between blackness and poetic inspiration? Furthermore, given the suggestive frontispiece, how does Wheatley's poetry depict this specific relation?

A 1774 *London Monthly Review* anonymous review of *Poems* addresses these issues:[77]

> If we believed, with the ancient mythologists, that genius is the offspring of the sun, we should rather wonder that the sable race have not yet been more distinguished by it, than express our surprize at a single instance. The experience of the world, however, has left to this part of mythology but little probability for its support; and indeed, it appears to be wrong in its first principles. A proximity to the sun, far from heightening the powers of the mind, appears to enfeeble them, in proportion as it enervates the faculties of the body. Thus we find the topical [sic] regions remarkable for nothing but the sloth and languor of their inhabitants, their lascivious dispositions and deadness to invention. The country that gave birth to Alexander and Aristotle . . . was Macedonia, naturally a cold and ungenial region. Homer and Hesiod breathed the cool and temperate air of the Meles, and the poets and heroes of Greece and Rome had no very intimate commerce with the sun.
>
> The poems written by this young negro bear no endemial marks of solar fire or spirit. They are merely imitative; and, indeed, most of these people have a turn for imitation, though they have little or none for invention.[78]

Prefacing a generally positive review, this author attempts to disprove the "ancient mythology" that the sun produces artistic genius by drawing upon eighteenth-century environmentalist beliefs that the hot African climate resulted in the undesirable characteristics of the "Negro," including the enervation of his/her mind.[79] For this reviewer, the sun produces "sloth" and "imitation" in the "topical regions" rather than genius; Alexander, Aristotle, Homer, Hesiod, and Greco-Roman poets all hailed from "cold and ungenial" locales.

That the reviewer calls upon eighteenth-century natural history to disprove the classical correlation between the sun and poetic genius might seem odd to twenty-first-century readers, but it clearly carried cultural resonance for contemporaneous ones. As Eric Slauter notes, unlike other literary reviews that were indexed by author's name or book's title, the *London Monthly Review* listed this as "MIND, the powers of, not enlightened in those climates that are most exposed to the action of the sun."[80] What the reviewer feels is the irreconcilable tension between these two historically successive logics culminates in his central claim: that "the poems written by this young negro bear no endemial marks of solar fire or spirit." While eighteenth-century climate theory claimed exactly that Africans received their blackness from extended subjection to the sun and *Poems'* frontispiece depicted a black African poet clearly bearing a "mark" precisely endemic of this exposure, for the reviewer, her poetry itself *did not* bear any kind of similar "mark."

Poems, however, contradicts just that stance. If Occom discounts the association whites draw between whiteness and Christianity, Wheatley challenges the disassociation this reviewer makes between blackness and poetics. She draws upon beliefs about exposure to the sun from both ancient mythology and eighteenth-century natural philosophy to depict the existence of the black poet not as a surprising oddity but rather as an expected likelihood. Her poetry brings together two beliefs about the sun's influence: first, the mythological notion that the sun produces genius (emphasized by the association of poetic creation with Apollo, god of the sun, poetry, and music); and second, the natural-historical claim that the sun triggered the body to exhibit blackness on the skin.[81] Wheatley praises blackness as one of God's providential works and links her race with poesy, even though environmentalism desired to separate them. She draws upon the accepted theorem that the sun causes blackness while eschewing its negative associations; she thus recouples the association ancients held among the sun, blackness, and creativity while retaining the eighteenth-century scientific validity of sun-produced darkness.[82] For Wheatley, blackness is one of many Godly colors spread throughout creation, not necessarily a binary opposite to whiteness. For her, it also is not an organizing factor in the way that slavery utilizes blackness as an ontological identity category in the social world. Wheatley's choice to write in a neoclassical vein—rather than being an "imitative" gesture—enables her to utilize this mythological belief in sun-inspired poetics.[83] Although Countee Cullen would marvel at why God would choose "To make a poet black, and bid him sing!" Wheatley's poetry intertwines mythology and natural history to render blackness and poetic genius as correlative results of the same solar cause.[84]

Wheatley's poetry actively engages eighteenth-century discourses on science, racialization, and poetics. From Thomas Jefferson to Henry Louis Gates, Jr., Wheatley's interlocutors have debated (and/or analyzed Wheatley's contemporaries' beliefs about) the incompatibility of blackness and poetic genius and then evaluated the degree to which the quality of Wheatley's poetry might be used to support either side in this argument.[85] This focus on the contested incompatibility of blackness and poetics has obscured a crucial point. Wheatley's poetry—not just an object of study—voices its own theoretical intervention in this aesthetic and scientific debate: the sun correlatively produces both poetic genius and dark skin tones, but when the slave trade renders blackness a racial category that then undergirds human bondage, it prohibits poetic production.[86] In this schema, the sun produces poetic genius and dark skin tones in harmonious tandem, but the use of blackness to undergird slavery results in a gothic nightmare.[87]

Like Occom, Wheatley rethinks how human difference—specifically blackness—is used to cohere an ontological identity category, here to justify slavery. For her, blackness is one of God's "beauteous dies" until the system of slavery makes it signify in an oppressively racialized way. As we shall see, Wheatley connects "excessive" sunlight to her "race['s]" "abhor[ed] life" under the "length'ned chain," suggesting that divinely bestowed blackness becomes problematic only when it is linked directly to slavery. Rejecting slave apologetics based upon the assumption that blacks could labor longest under the hot sun, Wheatley links only poetic production to the sun, not slave labor; furthermore, she reworks the implications of natural history to argue that the sun inspires—not enervates—the mind. Wheatley highlights the figuration of blackness as a racialized category and instead characterizes it as one of many colors spread throughout the natural world, depicting the process of "becoming colored" as part of God's plan to vary the progeny of a single creation.

DYEING SCENES

"To Maecenas" and "On Imagination" illustrate the poet's dependence on the sun for her poetry. Greek mythology, from which Wheatley and her neoclassical eighteenth-century predecessors such as Alexander Pope extensively drew, linked poetic genius with the sun in the figure of Phoebus Apollo.[88] As John Shields points out, allusions to the sun god and Aurora, the goddess of the dawn, "always [appear] . . . in close association with [Wheatley's] quest for poetic inspiration."[89]

In "To Maecenas," the piece that opens *Poems*, the poetic voice addresses the Roman patron of letters. Associating poetic inspiration with fire, the poet asks him, "What felt those poets but you feel the same? / Does not your soul possess the sacred flame?" (3–4). The poet laments, in seeming self-deprecation, her paucity of such inspiration:

> And the same ardors in my soul should burn:
> Then should my song in bolder notes arise,
> And all my numbers pleasingly surprize;
> But here I sit, and mourn a grov'ling mind
> That fain would mount, and ride upon the wind. (26–30)

While the poet notes that she lacks Maecenas' fire, she intimates that it certainly belongs to Terence, who Wheatley footnotes "was *African* by birth."[90]

The poet inquires why the Muses have shown "this partial grace, / To one alone of *Afric's* sable race;" (39–40), but then insinuates that she too shares in the poetic flame. As many scholars point out, following what must be interpreted as feigned modesty, the speaker characterizes herself appropriating the power to create verse: "While blooming wreaths around they temples spread, / I'll snatch a laurel from thine honour'd head, / While you indulgent smile upon the deed" (45–47).[91] The poem describes the scene of poetic creation: "While *Phoebus* reigns above the starry train, / While bright *Aurora* purples o'er the main" (50–51).[92] In the final couplet, the poet-persona characterizes Maecenas's own support of her poetry as a stream of sunlight: "Then grant, *Maecenas*, thy paternal rays, / Hear me propitious, and defend my lays" (54–55). Here, Wheatley characterizes poetic inspiration as fire, notes the presence of Apollo and Aurora at the site of poetic creation, and renders her own imaginary patron as a sun-figure himself.

Similarly, "On Imagination" connects the sun's heat with poetic creation by illustrating that imagination—even in producing a warm scene—itself necessitates heat to raise the poet's "fire." Imagination, "soaring through air to find the bright abode," seems to hold the power to overcome the coldest of weather:

> Though *Winter* frowns to *Fancy's* raptur'd eyes
> The fields may flourish, and gay scenes arise;
> The frozen deeps may break their iron bands,
> And bid their waters murmur o'er the sands.
> Fair *Flora* may resume her fragrant reign,
> And with her flow'ry riches deck the plain; (23–28)

Here, the heat of imagination can prevail over winter by envisioning a rejuvenated natural world, which overflows with water, flowers, and life. Later, the poet explicitly connects imagination with the sun:

> *Fancy* might now her silken pinions try
> To rise from earth, and sweep th' expanse on high;
> From *Tithon's* bed now might *Aurora* rise,
> Her cheeks all glowing with celestial dies,
> While a pure stream of light o'erflows the skies. (41–45)

The poet characterizes fancy as the goddess of the dawn, whose very cheeks are colored with "die" (a point to which I will return) when she rises to suffuse the sky with light.

However, toward the end of the poem, the poet reverses the thematic of imagination trumping cold weather:

> The monarch of the day I might behold,
> And all the mountains tipt with radiant gold,

> But I reluctant leave the pleasing views,
> Which *Fancy* dresses to delight the *Muse*;
> *Winter* austere forbids me to aspire,
> And northern tempests damp the rising fire;
> They chill the tides of *Fancy's* flowing sea,
> Cease then, my song, cease the unequal lay. (46–53)

Why would the speaker, after lauding imagination's power to picture a bountiful, warm earth, allow winter to be the final influence?[93] Emphasizing the effect winter—not necessarily imagination itself—has on the poet, these lines underscore the position of a writer whose poetic fire comes from the sun. While the imagination might be able to picture such a fecund, halcyon scene (indicated by the poem's many *may*'s), the poet finds herself "forbid[den]" by the austere winter from activating imagination to do so. Imagination and poetic inspiration, even with their ability to envision such heat, are predicated upon the poet being always already located *in* that very warmth.

A seeming aside Wheatley makes in "On Imagination" illustrates the link between the sun and blackness. The couplet "From *Tithon's* bed now might *Aurora* rise, / Her cheeks all glowing with celestial dies," (43–44) describes the goddess of the dawn rising from her lover's bed; the "dies" that glowingly color her cheeks are also the same "celestial" beams that radiate from her.[94] "Dies" attracts the reader's attention partly because of its significant placement: it ends the middle line in the only tercet embedded in a poem otherwise consisting of heroic couplets. While literary scholars have noted Wheatley's use of "die" (an obsolete form of *dye*) in "On Being Brought from Africa to America," they have paid virtually *no attention* to the racialized trope of "die" in other parts of her oeuvre. Wheatley uses *die* or *dye* elsewhere in *Poems*, explicitly praising the sun for producing so much "color" throughout God's works.

Like eighteenth-century natural historians, Wheatley portrays the human body as a malleable and amorphous mass to which God's influence gives shape, and she claims God's existence by pointing to his role in producing humankind's varieties.[95] Wheatley signifies on this idea in "On Being Brought" where the second half of the octave reads:

> Some view our sable race with scornful eye,
> "Their colour is a diabolic die."
> Remember, *Christians*, *Negros*, black as *Cain*,
> May be refin'd, and join th' angelic train. (5–8)

Numerous scholars aptly argue how Wheatley's final couplet ambiguously identifies "Christians" and "Negroes" as overlapping groups, both of whom are "black" with sin and might end up in a heaven together.[96] However, Wheatley also renders blackness specifically as a "die"—something that alters a preexisting state. Here, Wheatley's "sable race" *becomes* black through a dark dyeing. Reflecting environmentalist accounts of sun-produced skin pigmentation, Wheatley depicts race taking form through a God-ordained bodily transformation. Wheatley's quotation marks and mocking tone intimate that she does not view blackness as "diabolic."[97] Her use of the concept—so clearly racialized here—suggests this same connotation when she returns to the word elsewhere.[98] If whites understand blackness as a "die" of a specifically "diabolic" nature, Wheatley transvalues and celebrates the dyes bestowed throughout nature by God, which she then associates with the sun, blackness, and poetic inspiration.[99]

In "Thoughts on the Works of Providence," Wheatley ostensibly praises God's life-giving sun around which the earth travels, but a nightmare ruptures the poem's praise. It illustrates the racialization of blackness and calls forth but does not produce the unspeakable name of slavery. Wheatley lauds God's works by focusing on the sun's centrality:

> Ador'd for ever be the God unseen,
> Which round the sun revolves this vast machine,
> Though to his eye its mass a point appears:
> Ador'd the God that whirls surroundings spheres,
> Which first ordain'd that mighty *Sol* should reign
> The peerless monarch of th' ethereal train:
> Of miles twice forty millions is his height,
> And yet his radiance dazzles mortal sight
> So far beneath—from him th' extended earth
> Vigour derives, and ev'ry flow'ry birth: (11–20)

In this panegyric, the earth abounds with Providence's works as God actively rotates the universe around "mighty *Sol*."[100] In this last couplet, Wheatley's husbandry metaphor links "ev'ry flow'ry birth" to the "vigour" derived from the sun.

However, the next twelve-line stanza qualifies Wheatley's celebration of God, creation, solar influence, and the spread of celestial dyes. Here, an excess of light takes a gothic turn when sun-produced blackness leads to life in chains.

> Creation smiles in various beauty gay,
> While day to night, and night succeeds to day:
> That *Wisdom*, which attends *Jehovah's* ways,
> Shines most conspicuous in the solar rays:
> Without them, destitute of heat and light,
> This world would be the reign of endless night:
> In their excess how would our race complain,
> Abhorring life! how hate its length'ned chain! (29–36)

The poet renders a terrifying picture of the skewed balance of this sun-centered universe.[101] A single couplet signals the eternal darkness that would ensue without solar power. However, for six lines, the speaker paints a gothic picture filled *not* with dark shadows *but instead* with an overabundance of sunlight. "Our race," of course, signifies doubly here: not only would the "human race" suffer from extensive sunlight but also Wheatley's own "race," those that suffer under the "length'ned chain" would suffer because of their blackness. They endure said experience precisely because of this "excess" heat. Although the sun inspires poetic labor for Wheatley, slave apologists argued that Africans were best suited for agrarian slave labor in the hot sun, replacing more theologically based rationales.[102] Therein lies the delicate balance of the sun that should not be tipped to "excess"; what Wheatley uses to legitimize her own poetic creation, others use to justify slavery. For her, blackness—one of God's many "dies"—does not carry horrible connotations; rather, slavery diseases the land.[103]

> From air adust what num'rous ills would rise?
> What dire contagion taint the burning skies?
> What pestilential vapours, fraught with death,
> Would rise, and overspread the lands beneath? (37–40)

The sun-produced "dies," linked to skin, are lauded as God's works. But these "ills" arise from an atmosphere "adust," a word the *Oxford English Dictionary* (1989, second edition) defines as "Brown, as if scorched . . . by the sun" and "Applied to a supposed state of the body and its humours, . . . its alleged symptoms being dryness of the body, heat, thirst, black or burnt colour of the blood, . . . atrabilious or 'melancholic' complexion." This adjective serves as a conceptual nexus connecting the sun's surfeit, the body's reaction to its environment, melancholic complexion, and black bile. Blackness becomes problematic only when the excess of the sun is linked directly to "our race" and its hated life under the chain. The poem questions three times what the disease might be, but the answer of slavery itself remains unspoken.

The nightmare subsiding, the speaker finds equilibrium in a balanced world, where the sun spreads God-inspired color throughout the skies and earth below:

> Hail, smiling morn, that from the orient main
> Ascending dost adorn the heav'nly plain!
> So rich, so various are thy beauteous dies,
> That spread through all the circuit of the skies,
> That, full of thee, my soul in rapture soars,
> And thy great God, the cause of all adores. (41–46)

Drawing upon her earlier use of "die" to signify dark skin, Wheatley intimates that she herself is infused with the same kind of "die," since she is "full of thee," and soaring through God's beautifully tinted sky. Blackness here is one God-made color among many. This divine—rather than diabolic—die imbued throughout the poet herself makes her one of the "adored" "works of providence." Only in "excess," an interepellative system that racializes that very blackness by turning it into a principle of social organization, does it result in the nightmare of slavery.

The poem then points out, much in the vein of the natural-historical beliefs of Wheatley's day, that God's earth helps give rise to the different types of life that populate it:

> But see the sons of vegetation rise,
> And spread their leafy banners to the skies.
> All-wise Almighty providence we trace
> In trees, and plants, and all the flow'ry race;
> As clear as in the nobler frame of man,
> All lovely copies of the Maker's plan. (69–74)

Just as Occom emphasizes God's influence on Adam's descendants, here Wheatley echoes the theory of monogenism. What begins as an agrarian metaphor quickly becomes anthropomorphized. Vegetation becomes sons, and God's beauty throughout all the flora is just as "self-evident" in the "nobler frame of man." Every "copy" of God's "plan"—including the original Adam—is just as "lovely" as the other. Indeed, Wheatley quotes the Genesis origin story, depicting a simultaneous instantiation of light and God's creation, through which that light is diffused:[104]

> The pow'r the same that forms a ray of light,
> That call'd creation from eternal night.
> "Let there be light," he said: from his profound
> Old *Chaos* heard, and trembled at the sound:
> Swift as the word, inspir'd by pow'r divine,
> Behold the light around its maker shine,
> The first fair product of th' omnific God,
> And now through all his works diffus'd abroad. (75–82)

For Wheatley, God created light first, which is spread throughout and serves to diversify all of his "works" that sprang from an original, single creation.

Like "On the Works of Providence," "An Hymn to the Morning" begins and ends as an ostensible praise poem for the rising sun in the figure of Aurora. Each dawn, the sun comes up to bring the earth to life, inspiring both the poet and birds to sing songs of praise. However, the sun that produces both color and poetic fervor can become too strong, forcing the poet to seek refuge in the surrounding groves. The poet opens the ode with a standard invocation to the Muses:

> ATTEND my lays, ye ever honour'd nine,
> Assist my labours, and my strains refine;
> In smoothest numbers pour the notes along,
> For bright *Aurora* now demands my song. (1–4)

However, where the sun in other poems inspires poetic fervor, here Wheatley subtly shifts the tone of this relationship from one of inspiration to one of injunction.[105] As the poem progresses, the poet suddenly hides from the excess of the sun. Now a "demand[ing]" figure, Aurora short-circuits the poetic creation in what becomes—as in "Providence"—a scene of scorching light. The praise poem contains within it a problem of irresolvable difference. The ways that the sun produces both poetry and blackness manifest no tension in Wheatley's poetry. However, in these gothic scenes of extreme fluorescence, slavery forces blackness to signify within a racial system, thus becoming the defining feature of New World slavery.

In "Morning," Aurora simultaneously produces poetry and color, and in the second stanza, the sun commands the song not only of Wheatley but also of morning birds, suggesting their analogous positions:

> *Aurora* hail, and all the thousands dies,
> Which deck thy progress through the vaulted skies:
> The morn awakes, and wide extends her rays,
> On ev'ry leaf the gentle zephyr plays;
> Harmonious lays the feather'd race resume,
> Dart the bright eye, and shake the painted plume. (5–10)

Through this figure of the "painted" birds singing their "harmonious lays"— echoing the poet's own "lays" in the first stanza—Wheatley again addresses how the sun produces beautiful color throughout vegetation, animals, and humans. Abruptly, however, this scene gives way to another version of the bright nightmare;[106] the poet cries out:

> Ye shady groves, your verdant gloom display
> To shield your poet from the burning day:
> *Calliope* awake the sacred lyre,
> While thy fair sisters fan the pleasing fire:
> The bow'rs, the gales, the variegated skies
> In all their pleasures in my bosom rise. (11–16)

Within the gothic rupture, the poet seeks the balance for poetic creation. Even in the midst of the scorching sun, she calls out to Calliope, the muse of epic poetry, for her "pleasing fire" to color the "variegated skies" and to carry the poet to her song's end.

Mirroring the journey from freedom through the Middle Passage to slavery, in this move from inspired ode to coerced song, the poet's self-celebrated blackness becomes the burden that underwrites enslavement rather than the solar corollary to her own poesy. This shift from free poetic creation to forced labor terminates poetic inspiration:

> See in the east th' illustrious king of day!
> His rising radiance drives the shades away—
> But Oh! I feel his fervid beams too strong,
> And scarce begun, concludes th' abortive song. (17–20)

Unlike the poem "Providence," the poetic voice cannot find a restorative equilibrium. The poem stops, performing its own constitutive termination. Although Wheatley often does characterize the positive "light" of Christian knowledge driving the "shadows" of ignorance away, here the sun—the "illustrious king of day"—becomes a negative force that, like the fluorescent gothic scenes of slavery, "concludes th' abortive song."

However, of all Wheatley's poems, the epyllion, "Niobe in Distress for her Children slain by Apollo," most poignantly illustrates the tension resulting from both a beneficent and retributive figure of the sun. Describing the blessings and drawbacks of the sun, Wheatley's poem displays the paradox that while the sun produces blackness and poetic genius in tandem, blackness deployed as difference in a racialized system of slavery forecloses poetic production. Here, both the problems and promises of racial transformation condense around the metamorphosis of Niobe. In Wheatley's translation of Ovid, based in part on Wilson's painting (Fig. 1.2),[107] when Thebans worship the goddess Latona, Niobe brags that while Latona may have birthed Apollo and Artemis, Niobe herself deserves more praise for having fourteen children.[108] Different from Ovid's version, Wheatley's poem makes Niobe a sympathetic rebellious figure[109] and highlights Apollo as a vengeful force. The sun makes Niobe's daughters most beautiful (and makes the poet so lyrical) and ultimately kills them (and terminates the poetic process).

Wheatley describes the beauty of the children as an attribute of the sun's effect on them:

> Seven sprightly sons the royal bed adorn,
> Seven daughters beauteous as the op'ning morn,
> As when *Aurora* fills the ravish'd sight,
> And decks the orient realms with rosy light
> From their bright eyes the living splendors play,
> Nor can beholders bear the flashing ray. (23–28)

The sun imbues the children with their beauty, but—much as in the bright gothic scenes—others cannot witness their too-brilliant attractiveness.[110] Their sun-kissed beauty actually precipitates their demise:

> Wherever, *Niobe*, thou turn'st thine eyes,
> New beauties kindle, and new joys arise!

FIGURE 1.2 Niobe. *William Woollett, After a painting by Richard Wilson, Written by Ovid, Published by J. Boydell, Cheapside, London*

Courtesy of Philadelphia Museum of Art: The Muriel and Philip Berman Gift, acquired from the John S. Phillips bequest of 1876 to the Pennsylvania Academy of the Fine Arts, with funds contributed by Muriel and Philip Berman, gifts (by exchange) of Lisa Norris Elkins, Bryant W. Langston, Samuel S. White 3rd and Vera White, with additional funds contributed by John Howard McFadden, Jr., Thomas Skelton Harrison, and the Philip H. and A. S. W. Rosenbach Foundation, 1985.

> But thou had'st far the happier mother prov'd,
> If this fair offspring had been less belov'd:
> What if their charms exceed *Aurora's* teint,
> No words could tell them, and no pencil paint,
> Thy love too vehement hastens to destroy
> Each blooming maid, and each celestial boy. (29–36)

Niobe's love of them, which leads to her disastrous boast, causes their untimely death.[111]

In addition to associating the sun with beauty, Wheatley's revisions also emphasize Apollo's retaliatory role. While Ovid's Niobe story is only slightly demarcated from the rest of his epic, Wheatley's poem bears a title that emphasizes "Apollo('s)" slaying just as much as "Niobe('s)" distress. Once Niobe utters "What if indignant she decrease my train / More than *Latona's* number will remain?" (81–82), Latona orders her son Apollo, "'. . . Wrap her own sons for her blaspheming breath, / *Apollo!* wrap them in the shades of death'" (99–100). Furthermore, as Shields notes,[112] Wheatley adds the couplet, "With clouds incompass'd glorious *Phoebus* stands; / The feather'd vengeance quiv'ring in his hands" (107–8). Apollo's influence on the shade of the targeted bodies figures centrally in Wheatley's version. The painting also features this ambivalent rendering of sun figurations: while the sun breaks through the stormy clouds to shine down, it only highlights the massacre happening below. While the sun pushes through the clouds, Apollo stands to the side, dispensing his fatal arrows. One by one, Apollo shoots each of Niobe's sons. Afterward, "On each pale corse the wretched mother spread / Lay overwhelm'd with grief, and kiss'd her dead" (177–78). Seeing her sons' whitened dead bodies stretched across the ground, Niobe defiantly continues her boast: "Tho' I unhappy mourn these children slain, / Yet greater numbers to my lot remain" (187–88). As a result, Apollo kills each additional daughter.

Wheatley's poem ends with (and the painting depicts) Niobe surrounded by her dead children—or, one should note, it ends where *Poems* leads its readers to believe Wheatley intended to conclude. A final stanza is appended with the note that "This Verse to the End is the Work of another Hand" (59). Here, "another Hand" carries Ovid's version of the story to completion, and Niobe slowly turns into a white marble statue from which mournful tears flow. As a poem that continues Wheatley's meditation on the influence of the sun on both poetic genius and blackness and the sun's "excess" resulting in the disease of slavery and the termination of poetic creation, it makes perfect sense that the poem's ending should come under the most undecidable scrutiny.

We may never know whether Wheatley or someone else composed these final lines. But we do know that this possibility of collaboration was the precise concern that the signed prefatory material and John Wheatley's allusion to her Occom letter, both testimonials to Wheatley's authorial authenticity, attempted to assuage.[113] In this final (and unattributable) stanza, the vexed status of the poem's miscegenational authorial collaboration points toward the infamous "Attestation" and reference to Wheatley's Occom letter in *Poems*'s preface material. Likewise, the figure of Niobe, on the verge of metamorphosing into a frozen, white, ever-crying melancholic statue becomes an uncanny doppelgänger for the productive, blackened, writing melancholic Wheatley depicted in the frontispiece. Because Wheatley revises Ovid's version by *not* depicting Niobe as a stone statue, this pair of figures, with their potential to be stymied by the sun's "excesses," be it scorching heat or Apollo's wrath, suggests how Wheatley's entire volume dances on the verge—precisely where Wheatley leaves Niobe—of being made black and productive by the sun or of being entirely "frozen" by solar excesses. *Poems* characterizes race not as bodily truth but as a potentially dangerous process of transformation.

Thus, by using a symbolics of metamorphosis—by drawing upon contemporaneous religious and scientific beliefs about malleable physical attributes to explore how the body displays characteristics that are then read—Occom and Wheatley figure "race" as a transformable element. By mining Christian and natural-historical explanations for where color comes from, they are then able to refigure what "blackness" and "redness" might mean. Attention to how Occom and Wheatley depict these cultural processes of racialization reveals how they not only challenge the ontology of racial identities in their own ways, but also hold Christianity accountable for its monogenetic explanation of racial difference and assert indigenous sovereignty (for Occom) and theorize the relationship between color and aesthetics (for Wheatley). Thus, re-recognizing the notion of transformable race rewrites our interpretations of Occom and Wheatley's work and enables us to appreciate anew the process of becoming colored in their early America.

The Political Bodies of Benjamin Franklin and Hendrick Aupaumut

In the 1770s, Samson Occom and Phillis Wheatley drew upon complementary natural-historical and Protestant religious beliefs to depict racial identity coming into being. In contrast, Benjamin Franklin and Hendrick Aupaumut, two late eighteenth-century diplomats, coupled natural-historical thinking with more explicitly political thinking related to the notion of transformable race. Not as odd a pair as they may initially seem, these two men lived much of their lives away from the first US capital of Philadelphia and composed letter-narratives that they sent back there. Franklin and Aupaumut share striking similarities along with crucial differences: both men were emissaries employed by the fledgling US government in an attempt to stymie violent combat. One was sent east to the British colonial metropole to smooth over breaks in the imperial relationship and later to France to form a partnership with a bene-ficial ally; the other traveled west to negotiate with hostile Native American tribes confederated together to oppose the new nation-state. One—a white British colonial and then an American national—received citizenship status and self-consciously modeled American citizenship in his writings. The other, a Mohican Native American concerned only with citizenship in his own tribal nation, had to cajole the federal government to pay him for his military service. One's book, what we have come to know as Franklin's *Autobiography*, is canonical; the other's text, that which Aupaumut entitled "A Short narra-tion of my last Journey to the western Contry," was published through surrep-titious means without Aupaumut's knowledge and remains less well-known today.[1] At different times, both held treaty meetings with Ohio Valley Native Americans, but they give vastly different depictions of how those indigenous nations engage in diplomatic forums. Their two separate sets of negotiations with the same groups of tribes link these two historical and writerly figures. Reading Benjamin Franklin and Hendrick Aupaumut in relation to one an-other thus broadens the contextualization of both texts (not the least of which is to read an alternate, Native American view to one of the most unnerving scenes in Franklin's *Autobiography*) and, most importantly, gives insight into how both of their texts engage with discourses of transformable race.

Both writing in a moment when debates about racial identity had come to have political implications, Franklin and Aupaumut present their own textual and physical bodies for their multiple audiences to consider in relation to the notion of transformable race and in relation to how political bodies might be constituted out of a number of physical ones. As I explained in the introduction, various groups debated the extent to which race was influenced by environmental factors, including both climate and what natural historian Samuel Stanhope Smith called the "state of society." As we have seen, many natural philosophers discussed how the environment and "mode of living" could shape racial identity. In addition, Native Americans were also divided on their explanation of the different varieties of mankind. Generally, Christianized Indians shared the monogenetic view that humanity sprang from a unified origin and over time grew to display various racial characteristics, while nativist Indians claimed *separate* creations and races (*SR* 30).[2] Thus, although the belief in different origins specifically espoused by the militant nativist Indians in the Ohio Valley was a minority viewpoint among most Native Americans east of the Mississippi River, it became a powerful notion with which anyone discussing race in Indian Country would need to negotiate.[3]

Neither Franklin nor Aupaumut vociferously hold forth on how differences in race originated. However, as this chapter will show, the topic of race is a strong undercurrent in their texts, one we come to understand by reading Franklin's implicit and explicit evocations of natural-historical texts published as he composed the *Autobiography* (several of them presented at and/or published by his own American Philosophical Society), on the one hand; and by analyzing how Aupaumut's strategic use of the term "color" intervenes in Native American discussions about race, on the other. Both Franklin and Aupaumut responded to contemporaneous ideas about what might or might not produce characteristics that were coming to be read as "race." While, as I detailed in the introduction, many New World thinkers had an investment in thinking about society as an agent in producing "race," Franklin and Aupaumut troubled the idea that one's "mode of living" would help form racial characteristics and identity. This chapter argues that Franklin and Aupaumut tend to unlink strict relationships between various social practices and the production of race. Interestingly, while both diplomats who negotiate among these various disagreeing groups, neither Franklin nor Aupaumut *explicitly* argues whether the environment, modes of living, or separate creations cause the differences among races. Nevertheless, the discourse of transformable race structures how they could write about racial identity, even when they do not directly engage in the debates about its origin. Rather, both focus on race as a category in relationship to evolving political identities. For Franklin and Aupaumut, the formation of political bodies such as a nation-state or a pan-tribal confederacy connects complexly to the racialization of physical bodies. This chapter juxtaposes Franklin and Aupaumut—two writers who, in many senses, were outliers of mainstream racial thinking—to throw into relief the way each draws from and reconfigures various popular conceptions of race. I bring these two writers together not because they share a common background but because of their positions as diplomats; furthermore, this juxtaposition allows us to see, across racial divisions, how transformable race—even when not directly addressed—can shape even ostensibly different kinds of eighteenth-century texts and to see the ways that Franklin and Aupaumut write about bodies, both corporeal and corporate.

You Are What You Eat; or, Franklin's Practice Makes (Almost) Perfect

Benjamin Franklin seemed to be much less disturbed than Thomas Jefferson by the allegation of Georges-Louis Leclerc, comte de Buffon, that the American environment negatively impacted plant and animal life in the New World. Jefferson openly addressed Buffon's claims in *Notes on the State of Virginia*, and he arranged to have a large, North American moose sent across the Atlantic to Buffon in Paris.[4] By contrast, Benjamin Franklin was less aggressive about disproving Buffon's claim, later extended by the Abbé Raynal.[5] When Jefferson raised the subject years later with Franklin, Franklin shared a telling story. Jefferson recounted that story in an 1818 letter to Robert Walsh:

> [Franklin] had a party to dine with him one day at Passy, of whom one half were Americans, the other half French, and among the last was the Abbé [Raynal]. During the dinner he got on his favorite theory of the degeneracy of animals, and even of man, in America, and urged it with his usual eloquence. The Doctor at length noticing the accidental stature and position of his guests, at table, "Come," says he, "M. l'Abbé, let us try this question by the fact before us. We are here one half Americans, and one half French, and it happens that the Americans have placed themselves on one side of the table, and our French friends are on the other. Let both parties rise, and we will see on which side nature has degenerated." It happened that his American guests were . . . of the finest stature and form; while those of the other side were remarkably diminutive, and the Abbé himself particularly, was a mere shrimp. He parried the appeal, however, by a complimentary admission of exceptions, among which the Doctor himself was a conspicuous one.[6]

Franklin was not as preoccupied nor directly involved with the degeneration dispute as Jefferson, but this story provides a glimpse of his reaction to both Buffon and Raynal's claims. Indeed, the story of Franklin's dinner party should lead us to evaluate the odd way the *Autobiography* seems stubbornly silent on issues of racial science. In many ways, it doesn't make much sense. For instance, we know that Franklin was the foremost American natural philosopher in the Atlantic world. We know that he not only organized what would become the American Philosophical Society—in time, the institutional site of the most pressing, scholarly, and contentious debates about the production of racial difference—but also served as its president, continually, from 1769 to his death in 1790. We also know that Franklin wrote his life as one "fit to be imitated"[7] and as a how-to guide for new American citizens (at least, explicitly, parts 2, 3, and 4 addressed to a post-Revolution, US audience). Nevertheless, it seems that Franklin's *Autobiography* does not address the debate around how the actions taken by New World creoles might impact their racial status, and the related silence in Franklin scholarship concerning these issues appears to confirm this.[8] However, given Franklin's role as an esteemed scientist and the model American advanced in his narrative, we must ask: how can the *Autobiography* remain *altogether silent* about the debates over what might have caused the production of the various races in the past and what might impact one's race in the present and in the future? How can it have *nothing to say* about how the New World environment might impact white, British colonials who relocate there or about how one could defend the New World against the aspersions heaped upon it by Buffon and Raynal? Once we consider Franklin's notoriously sly rhetorical style, we find that the answers to these questions are, of course, that it isn't, and it doesn't.

On the contrary, Franklin's *Autobiography* is not silent but, rather, engages deeply with these raging debates over the production of racial difference. It may not necessarily advance its own particular theory of how racial categories developed in the way other, explicitly natural-historical texts do. Nevertheless, it has a great deal to say about these debates, in part because the *Autobiography* engages discourses relating to society, cultural practices, and the body that necessarily were racialized in this historical moment. The Franklin of Franklin's *Autobiography* is not only a protean figure, as many scholars have ably shown; he is also a protean *racial* figure. The *Autobiography*'s Franklin tries and then fails to maintain habits and characteristics racially coded as white in the eighteenth century and takes on the habits and characteristics of non-white racial groups, but, in the end, he remains white. Franklin validates aspects of natural-historical theories that claim that certain practices might influence one's race, but then he humorously—and sometimes ambiguously—qualifies them. Thus, he is able to mock the debate and the seriousness of those who take part in it but nevertheless make his own point.

In regards to the debates about racial change in the New World, Franklin's *Autobiography* functions much like his dinner party; both there and in the narrative, Franklin advances himself and/or a textual version of himself as the example to consider. Rather than directly refute Raynal, Franklin jovially invites his guests to stand to see how Raynal's scientific hypothesis might apply to his fellow diners. Likewise, in the *Autobiography*, Franklin's Franklin serves as the test case to which to apply these natural-historical theories. And, in like manner, he engages these debates in a lighthearted—rather than heavy-handed—manner.[9] For Franklin, "to *inform*" and "to *persuade*," one must also "*please*" (582). Franklin employed this rhetorical strategy throughout the 1771–1790 composition of his *Autobiography*. Thus, if we picture Jefferson frenziedly composing answers to the queries posed to him by François Barbé-Marbois for his *Notes on the State of Virginia*, we might think of Franklin as telling a series of amusing anecdotes. If we see Jefferson having animal carcasses hauled across the Atlantic Ocean to Buffon in Paris, we find Franklin offering an almost misleadingly entertaining narrative, one ostensibly about his rise from humble beginnings to international fame that nevertheless functions as a partial answer to Buffon's and Raynal's claims about the New World. Thinking of Franklin as oddly silent, when Jefferson was both vociferous and highly involved, is a fundamental misunderstanding of Benjamin Franklin, the *Autobiography*'s rhetorical strategy, and the "model America" advanced therein. At the Passy dinner party, while Raynal defended his position by suggesting "the Doctor himself" was a "conspicuous" exception to the rule that animate life degenerated in the New World, the *Autobiography*'s Franklin is anything but. The model American Franklin puts forth in his narrative is just that—a model, one "fit to be imitated" (*A* 567) in both the senses that it is worthy of imitation and also *is able to be imitated* by each American Everyman and one, moreover, that models American whiteness.[10] But, in order to see this, we must see how Franklin engages ideas of transformable race in his *Autobiography*.

YOU (MIGHT) BECOME WHAT YOU EAT; YOU (MIGHT) BECOME WHAT YOU DO

We can begin to do this by bringing together the scientific, political, and writerly aspects of Franklin's career. Franklin wrote the four parts of his autobiography in three different locations at four different times; he himself went from being a diplomat working to smooth over relationships with the crown to being a radical patriot wooing the French aristocracy's help in overthrowing British rule in the colonies. And, crucially, the *entire time* he did these things, he remained president of the American Philosophical Society, even when living abroad, removed from the Society's everyday workings.[11] When Franklin began writing his *Autobiography*, he was already a renowned scientist in the British Atlantic world. Partly because he had already won Buffon's praise for his work on electricity, he had broken into the highly exclusive world of French and British natural philosophers.[12] In 1744, he met John Mitchell, the Virginian whose "An Essay upon the Causes of the Different Colours of

People in Different Climates" had been recently discussed by the Royal Society and published in its *Philosophical Transactions*, as I outlined in the introduction and will discuss in greater detail in Chapter 4. Shortly after meeting Franklin that fall, Mitchell was elected—in part, one supposes, because of the international reception of his essay—to membership in Franklin's American Philosophical Society. In this first section, Franklin might have been depicting an early time in his life when he learned to write and strolled through the streets of Philadelphia, practically penniless with puffy rolls under each arm, but he had already become the established American colonial natural philosopher everyone knew him to be and one, moreover, exposed to the latest natural-historical racial theories.

In the first section of Franklin's *Autobiography*, written in 1771 ostensibly as a letter to his son, several anecdotes about Franklin's diet irreverently engage contemporaneous conversations about degeneration, complexion, and natural-historical classification schemes. Although it is unclear where Franklin came down in the discussions about what constituted the distinctions among white, black, and red peoples, several of his programs to regulate diet and habits are pertinent to and informed by contemporaneous debates about racial formation.[13] At this time, Franklin did not yet advocate a colonial split from Great Britain but, rather, worked to resolve tensions between the colonists and the crown. The narrative opens with a detailed genealogy of the Franklin family in England, leading Christopher Looby to note that Franklin's "mode of direct paternal address, and the pronounced emphasis on ancestry, together constituted an assertion of the power and value of genealogical continuity."[14] At this time, Franklin proudly considered himself an Englishman who just happened to live in America. Much to his dismay, despite the fact that immigration to the Americas had been taking place for over a century, many people in the metropole held tightly to misconceptions about life in the New World. They harbored fears that its climate would cause them to lose their Englishness and that Anglo-Americans had "dark skin, like Africans."[15] Numerous Americans protested this characterization, but Leo Lemay claims that "no colonial American objected so strongly or so often to the prejudice against America as Franklin."[16] Franklin clearly had a vested interest in showing that Englishmen could live in the New World while retaining their Englishness. Furthermore, when Franklin began writing his memoir at age sixty-five, he was viewed as an exemplary colonial—one who clearly had not degenerated since his youth.

In one of the most noted examples of Franklin's plans for improvement, he relates his endeavor and eventual failure to maintain a diet free of flesh and fish, and this scene reverberates with the seventeenth- and eighteenth-century emphasis on maintaining one's national constitution and natural complexion. Franklin declares that "when about 16 Years of Age, I happen'd to meet with a Book written by one Tryon, recommending a Vegetable Diet"

(*A* 580). Franklin began "refusing to eat Flesh" and became "acquainted with Tryon's Manner of preparing some of his Dishes, such as Boiling Potatoes, or Rice, making Hasty Pudding, & a few others" (*A* 580). Unlike the other pressmen, young Franklin appears to embody perfect "Temperance in Eating & Drinking" (*A* 581).

By no accident, Franklin draws—in a very particular manner—upon Thomas Tryon's 600-page *The Way to Health, Long Life and Happiness: Or, A Discourse of Temperance*, partially subtitled *And the Particular Nature of all Things requisite for the life of Man; As, All sorts of Meats, Drinks, Air, Exercise &c., with special Directions how to use each of them to the best Advantage of the Body and Mind.*[17] Well-known for his instructional writing, Tryon frames his popular treatise as an instruction manual on how to regulate what he calls "the four grand Qualities" from which "the four Complexions" proceed.[18] In outlining these complexions—"Cholerick," "Phlegmatick," "Sanguine," and "Melancholy"—Tryon describes what only after the eighteenth century came to be distinguished as the separate traits of physical characteristics and temperament (*CR* 2). Tryon details what persons of each complexion should do in order to enhance the desirable qualities of that complexion, which Tryon felt was mutable. The ends to Tryon's means have an explicitly national bias: God produces food in each geographic region that suits people in that location; Englishmen should therefore avoid aliment from other—and consequently, unsuitable— areas. That is, because Englishmen differ from "the People of [the East and West Indies] . . . in their *Complexions, Constitutions, Religions, Inclinations, Governments, Shapes* and *Languages*" (*Way* 161), people should eat food produced in their own locale.[19]

Tryon asserts that "Natives of [the East and West Indies]" sparingly eat their own fruit, spices, and wine, while Englishmen tend to overindulge, "which is one main cause why our *English* are so unhealthy when they travel and live in such hot Countries." This leads to a situation wherein "their Bodies and Natures do much alter and change, when they alter the Climate; and not only our *Bodies*, but also our *Dispositions* and *Inclinations* are thereby much changed. Therefore," he writes, "all People ought strictly to observe such degrees of *Temperance*" (*Way* 167). While Tryon's distinctions display a national rather than an explicitly racial predilection, he does state that "the *Salnitral and Seminary Virtues* of the Earth, varying also in the predominant Qualities from ours, there being a concurrence in all Countries and Climates between the Influences and Operations of the *heavenly Bodies*, and the *earthy*; whence it comes to pass, that the people of the *South* are *black*, and the *Northern white*; . . . Therefore the Herbs, Drugs and Fruits that are brought forth in those remoter Regions, are not *Homogenial* to our Bodies" (*Way* 425).

In Tryon's text, these complexions are mainly used to describe Englishmen, but by the time Franklin cited Tryon, the complexion had come to be considered a distinguishing characteristic between groups of people. In his

1751 "Observations Concerning the Increase of Mankind, Peopling of Countries, &c," Franklin asks, "Why should *Pennsylvania*, founded by the *English*, become a Colony of *Aliens*, who will shortly be so numerous as to Germanize us instead of our Anglifying them, and will never adopt our Language or Customs, any more than they can acquire *our Complexion*."[20] For Franklin, the Germans have "what we call a swarthy Complexion . . . the *Saxons* only excepted, who with the *English*, make the principal Body of White People on the Face of the Earth."[21] Englishmen in both Britain and America share this white complexion, something most Germans can never claim. While Franklin problematically wishes the number of "Blacks and Tawneys" in America would decrease to allow the increase of "the lovely White and Red," he also admits that "but perhaps I am partial to the Complexion of my Country, for such Kind of Partiality is natural to Mankind."[22]

Franklin's use of "complexion" as a term associated with divisions of humankind was part of a larger cultural shift, partly a result of Linnaeus's use of the four complexions to distinguish varieties of humankind, dividing the global population into, as Stephen J. Gould puts it, "four geographic regions, four humors, four races."[23] Under the Linnaean system, Europeans had the sanguine complexion; Native Americans were choleric; Asians, melancholic; and Africans, phlegmatic. For the sanguine complexion, Tryon advises that "a little Intemperance either in Meats, Drinks or Labour, will disorder them; therefore they ought *above all People* to observe and keep themselves within the bounds of Sobriety. . . . They are to forbear all sorts of Meats and Drinks" (*Way* 20, emphasis added). These "Meats and Drinks" are what Franklin most emphatically and, at the same time, sardonically addresses. In citing Tryon's diet guidelines, Franklin seems to endorse a program regulating one's diet in order to maintain his complexion, natural character, and—when read through eighteenth-century Linnaean categories—race.

But Franklin is rarely that straightforward. Later in the narrative, he tells how he failed to follow Tryon's instructions on his "first Voyage from Boston."[24] When the fishermen net a catch of cod, Franklin states that "hitherto I had stuck to my Resolution of not eating animal Food; and on this Occasion, I consider'd with my Master Tryon, the taking every Fish as a kind of unprovok'd Murder" (*A* 598). Tryon prohibits the eating of fish and flesh, claiming that "savages" take part in this violent process (*Way* 253). Franklin hesitates, but when he realizes that each fish's stomach holds another previously eaten fish, he rationalizes that he can be excused for joining the feast: "So I din'd upon Cod very heartily and continu'd to eat with other People, returning only now & then occasionally to a vegetable Diet. So convenient a thing it is to be a *reasonable Creature*, since it enables one to find or make a Reason for every thing one has a mind to do" (*A* 599). Scholars have aptly characterized this scene as "a contribution to the long history of the debate on reason versus the passions"[25] and as an example of where "Reason" and "Principle" "themselves become instruments of the appetitive body."[26] However, because Franklin evokes and then fails to keep Tryon's dietary program, the scene also enters into discussions about what maintains one's bodily complexion and national status.

Franklin's use of Tryon therefore cuts both ways: it cites Tryon's program as authoritative only to confound the associations Tryon draws between national (and later racial) character, wellness, and nutrition. Because Franklin's stature as an influential colonial scientist and diplomat was so well known at the time of his writing, the fact that he had not lost his national or racial status by living in the New World or by failing to keep Tryon's diet becomes part of the anecdotal humor. To say this another way, Franklin depicts himself following Tryon's prescriptions, leading his readers to believe that he subscribes to natural-historical thought that linked together diet and racial characteristics; however, by depicting himself *failing* to keep Tryon's diet, he demonstrates that he would probably have become what he is at the time of writing—a well-known, healthy, and white British national living in America—regardless of whether or not he had followed Tryon's regime. Nevertheless, while making fun of the debate, he makes his point: examining his case, one can see that white British American creoles do not degenerate in the New World.

Indeed, although Franklin's readers and Franklin himself surely chuckled over how the aroma of freshly fried fish cracked the young Franklin's resolve, discussion about food (and, furthermore, climate and geography) was far from a trifling matter to early Americans. When Franklin met John Mitchell in 1744, he undoubtedly read Mitchell's "Essay," which claims that the climate in which one lives affects the thickness of one's skin and, thus, how much the underlying whiteness every human Mitchell believed to possess is able to show through that skin. For Mitchell, "the thicker the Cuticle is, . . . the more the Light will be intercepted in passing them, and the more the Colour of the Skin will degenerate from the pure White of the Membranes below it" ("ECDC" 121). The African climate causes those who live there to develop a thicker cuticle that makes them appear degenerate and black, a sign that early Americans were coming to read as a racial distinction. One's color, however, is not *just* dependent on one's climate; habits play a part, too. Mitchell titles his Proposition VII: "The Influence of the Sun, in hot Countries, and the Ways of Life of the Inhabitants in them, are the remote Causes of the Colour of Negroes, Indians, &c. And the Ways of Living, in Use among most Nations of white People, make their Colours whiter, than they were originally, or would be naturally" ("ECDC" 131). For Mitchell, what people can do affect what they look like.

This interest in climate, cuisine, and habits does not fade over the next thirty years. Indeed, in the first volume of the American Philosophical Society's *Transactions*, a text published in 1771—the same year Franklin composed the first section of the *Autobiography*—and one that Franklin gave to Buffon, contained several pieces that directly addressed important concerns about the American climate and foodways that British creoles had adopted. The preface to *Transactions*, Vol. I, specifically concerns itself with the "tract of country now possessed by the *English* in *North-America*," where the "*Indians* who were natives of this country" failed to cultivate any crops besides "*Indian* corn." Upon colonization, however, the preface claims this soon changed: "The fruits, trees, plants and grain, introduced by the new inhabitants, are mostly such as were cultivated in *European* countries, from whence these inhabitants came."[27] To wit, although relocated to America, Europeans continued to eat mainly European food. The preface then goes on to detail the climate, latitude and longitude, soil condition, and crop production of the American landscape, even claiming that someday "with a little care and industry, *America* might produce Wine sufficient, not only for home consumption, but even for exportation" (*Transactions* I x). Indeed, correct management of American natural resources will "render us more useful to our Mother Country" (*Transactions* I xiii), something "this Society may, as far as in their power, contribute to the carrying such a Plan into execution" (*Transactions* I xv). This inaugural edition of *Transactions* also included several pieces submitted by Dr. Hugh Williamson, a natural philosopher who would become renowned for his work on climate and who, in later years, would point to the climate's role in producing the variety of racial appearances throughout humankind and, furthermore, would claim that Africans would become physically whiter by living in the American climate (*WOB* 449–51). Williamson effectively cuts through the debate about the results of the impact of the New World climate by claiming that the climate itself can be impacted by how one treats the land: "There are sundry other causes, from which the heat of the air may be increased or diminished, yet I cannot recollect a single instance of any remarkable change of climate, which may not be fairly deduced from the sole cultivation of the country."[28] As a part of his larger argument about the working of the land, Williamson invests those who live on the land with the power to shape that land and, thus, the land's purported power to shape those who live upon it. The upshot of all this is that—given the natural-historical epistemological world in which the natural-philosophical and writerly Franklin lived every day—the food that the young, textual Franklin eats and the habits he adopts have racialized aspects that inflect the narrative.

Ironically, given all this, instead of painting himself as the white colonial vigilantly adhering to Tryon's diet, Franklin metaphorically characterizes himself as a slave—with surprising results. Within the contemporaneous contexts of race-based slavery, relationships between parents and children, and connections between the mother country and its colonies, Franklin's story of running away from home and indenture to his brother becomes a site of conflicted racialized associations. Franklin identifies with runaway slaves and servants and also with those trying to establish an enduring political social order. Franklin's narration of his escape from his sibling's printing house in Boston collapses two allegorical readings popularized in the revolutionary rhetoric of America's early national period. First, because Franklin's father arranged for young Benjamin to serve as his brother's apprentice, Franklin's departure from his brother's print shop can be read as a story of a young man making a break from his family as he matures into his own authoritative agent. Franklin indicates, however, that his relationship with his brother could not be reduced to that between two siblings. He points out that "tho' a Brother, he considered himself as my Master, ... my Brother was passionate & had often beaten me, which I took extreamly amiss;* and thinking my Apprenticeship very tedious, I was continually wishing for some Opportunity of shortening it, which at length offered in a manner unexpected" (*A* 584).

This short anecdote also resembles that of a slave escaping from his master. As David Waldstreicher points out, when Franklin runs away from his brother's shop, the "stealing of his own labor" in order to "make the self-made man" resembles stories of other eighteenth-century runaways printed in fugitive slave advertisements.[29] Furthermore, in his 1770 "A Conversation on Slavery," a dialogue between an Englishman, an American, and a Scotsman about the inconsistency of slavery and the contemporary struggle for liberty in the colonies, Franklin contradictorily associates racialized slavery and non-racialized forced labor. He incriminates British and Scottish participation in various forms of slavery, giving a definition of *slavery* that closely resembles the *Autobiography*'s runaway. In order to implicate Scottish mine owners in slavery involving their "*own* [white] *Countrymen*," Franklin's American advances a race-free definition of slavery that includes one who is "stolen, taken by Force, or bought . . . compelled to serve the Taker . . . is bound to obey . . . is subject to severe Punishments for small Offences, to enormous Whippings, and even Death, for absconding from his Service, or for Disobedience to Orders. I imagine such a Man is a Slave to all Intents and Purposes."[30] Nevertheless, the American conjures up the notion of blackface to allege that the Scotsman's greatest sin is his enslavement of his own citizens, claiming that Scottish mine workers

> have no more Liberty to leave [the coal mines] than our Negroes have to leave their Master's Plantation. If having black Faces, indeed, subjected Men to the Condition of slavery, you might have some small Pretence for keeping the poor Colliers in that Condition: But remember, that under the Smut their Skin is *white*, that they are *honest good People*, and at the same Time are *your own countrymen*![31]

The American conjectures that perhaps "having a black Face" does not justify one's enslavement, but he never decides the issue. Instead, he implies that the whiteness of the Scottish mine workers should free them from occupying the subject positions of slaves. The logic implies that while not all persons with "black Face[s]" are slaves, all slaves are—or perhaps should be—black. Nevertheless, in his definition of slavery (which emphasizes the passivity of a body that is purchased, forced to work, and subject to beating), the issue of race drops out completely. For the American, even when race is not an integral component of his definition of *slavery*, stories of coerced labor can clearly signify blackness.

This short newspaper piece evinces Franklin's recognition that during a period when, as David Roediger points out, the labor of both black slaves and white servants was "virtually interchangeable," stories of forced servitude of white servants could resonate quite closely with that of black slaves.[32] Thus, for eighteenth-century readers, Franklin's short story of a young white laborer would register on several metaphorical levels—the child leaving the family, the colonies dissociating from the mother country, the apprentice fleeing the master, and the black slave escaping the slave owner.[33]

Instead of resolutely endorsing his break away from his family and apprenticeship, however, Franklin presents a conflicted account. On the one hand, Franklin adds this footnote to the description of his brother's "passionate" beatings: "*I fancy his harsh & tyrannical Treatment of me, might be a means of impressing me with that Aversion to arbitrary Power that has stuck to me thro' my whole Life" (*A* 584). Franklin apparently champions his youthful action "to assert [his] Freedom" (*A* 585) and makes indirect reference to the British Parliament that many colonists felt exercised a similar type of "arbitrary Power."

On the other hand, Franklin qualifies the action he took as a young man by positing that "it was not fair in me to take this Advantage, and this I therefore reckon one of the first Errata of my Life: But the Unfairness of it weigh'd little with me, when under the Impressions of Resentment, for the Blows his Passion too often urg'd him to bestow upon me. Tho' He was otherwise not an ill-natur'd Man: Perhaps I was too saucy & provoking.—" (*A* 585). While Franklin initially endorses his assertion of freedom against tyrannical power, he then tempers that recommendation by declaring his action a mistake.

Mostly written in 1771 when Franklin labored to reconcile the mounting tensions between Great Britain and the American colonies,[34] the story suggests not an unqualified aversion to colonialism as such but, rather, to the misuse of "arbitrary" power by Franklin's brother and, by extension, Great Britain. Franklin's editorial interjections complicate his revolutionary rhetoric, providing his readers with different potential readings of the allegorical story.[35] Indeed, both the footnote and the statement that "I therefore reckon [this] one of the first Errata of my Life" were roughly contemporaneous "columnar additions" in Franklin's double-bookkeeping style of his manuscript.[36] Franklin's impulse to footnote and reflect upon his anecdote registers his ambivalence over modifying existing social and political structures and determining when power, whether that of a slave master or royal monarch, is legitimate or merely "arbitrary." The short tale can be viewed as Franklin's first step toward becoming the model self-made man, but the scene can be read as both an inspirational escape narrative and also a morality tale to masters and royal sovereigns. Franklin depicts this scene both as a blunder and as the foundation for his later success.[37] Furthermore, despite being rhetorically linked with black slaves, the young Franklin becomes anything but one.

These ideas continue to contextualize and inflect the *Autobiography*, but by the time Franklin composed the short, second, and arguably most famous section of his narrative, much had changed. Perhaps most importantly, in 1774, Franklin underwent what has come to be known as the "Cockpit hearing," wherein the British Privy Council interrogated and humiliated Franklin over his role in the publication of private letters of public officials who wished to curtail colonial autonomy.[38] This, along with many other factors of much broader import, convinced Franklin that the colonies' best option was not, in fact, to remain a British holding but, rather, to separate from the Mother Country and establish their own nation-state. Thus, while Franklin wrote the first section of the *Autobiography* as a "British Whig factotum unsure where his career was heading," as Ed White puts it,[39] he composed the second section *after* the writing of the Declaration of Independence, the outbreak and resolution of the Revolutionary War, and the ratification of the Treaty of Paris, all events in which, of course, Franklin took large part. Also in the interlude between writing the first and second sections of the *Autobiography*, Franklin witnessed the Court of King's Bench hand down the decision in the famous 1772 *Somerset* case, wherein British colonial slaveholders were forbidden from taking their slaves back with them to the colonies, thereby outlawing slavery in England in practice, if not in fact.[40] In that same year and in recognition of his scientific career, Franklin was elected to the Academie Royale des Sciences and earned a considerable reputation among the French for his scientific knowledge. As Joyce Chaplin shows, in fact, Franklin accrued much political negotiating power in France in part because of his scientific reputation.[41] While in France, Raynal presented Franklin with a list of questions about North America, questions that Franklin forwarded to the APS, which subsequently decided "that Raynal's inquiries lay outside its proper field."[42] The Society, however, did take up the questions sent by the Marquis de Condorcet, which included the following:

4th. I should be glad to know if there are in the English Colonies, Negroes who having obtained their liberty, have lived without mixing with the white people? If their black Children born free and educated as such, have retained the genius and character of the Negroes, or have contracted the Character of Europeans? If Men of genius & parts have been observed among them?[43]

According to APS historian Whitfield Bell, we do not know if the committee appointed to answer Condorcet's questions did so.[44] Therefore, the Franklin who began writing his narrative's second portion in 1784 was writing not only to an enlarged audience of the recently declared US citizenry (thus giving the remainder of the *Autobiography* a new, shifted political import) but also to an Atlantic scientific community eager to ascertain what impact the New World would have on these "new" citizens and their race.[45] Thus, while the APS answers to these two sets of queries were either never written (in the case of Raynal) or remain unknown (in the case of Condorcet), Franklin's *Autobiography*'s second section should be read in part as a response to general European questions about the "Character" of the different races and whether or not that "Character" can be "contracted."

Franklin began the second portion of his narrative in Passy, France, and, at first glance, it seems to say little—much like the diplomat Franklin himself—about degeneration and race. Historian Gilbert Chinard conjectures that perhaps Franklin held a relative silence about the degeneracy debates while in France because of his ambassadorial endeavors, claiming that "it does not appear from any direct evidence that, before going to Paris, he was particularly disturbed by the aspersions thrown by Buffon on the climate of America, and he was too skillful a diplomat to engage in public discussions and controversies with the French philosophers. His long experience in dealing with public opinion had convinced him that positive affirmations are better than elaborate denials, and that facts spoke louder than theories."[46] Franklin's diplomatic position required that he engage these debates obliquely, which he does. The second section's emphasis on virtue, self-regulation, and perfection intersects with debates about degeneration and race, and Franklin burlesques the debate by mockingly taking part in it. Franklin again advances and then ironically undercuts a program for social habits that were understood, among other things, to maintain whiteness. Certainly, while his list of virtues, tables for maintaining them, and the speckled axe allegory are not exclusively about race, they have a racialized aspect (one we have yet to recognize) because they are also related to these larger conversations about what might make one white, civilized, or even American. Here Franklin shifts from writing to his own son to modeling the prototypical "American" for what Benjamin Vaughan's interpolated letter calls "*a rising* people" (*A* 634). Perhaps following Vaughan's advice to "invite all wise men to become like yourself" (*A* 635), Franklin lays out his "bold and arduous Project of arriving at moral Perfection" (*A* 643). Certainly, the virtues Franklin planned to embody— including silence, resolution, sincerity, and tranquility—encompass a broader schema of practices than those considered by dietary advisors and natural philosophers to affect complexion and "race." However, those such as temperance, industry, moderation, cleanliness, and chastity certainly do fall under that rubric. Franklin's table of virtues lies within a self-regulatory tradition that encompassed Tryon's *Way to Health*, early modern English and Scottish histories that connect "the causes and effects of shifts in national character" to "changes in diet, habitat, and climate,"[47] and the work of US natural historians who emphasized the "state of society" as a factor in influencing one's complexion and racial identity.

The similarities between Franklin's list of virtues and Benjamin Rush's 1786 "An Account of the Vices peculiar to the Savages of N. America" furthermore evidence the racialized nature of Franklin's proposed habits (Figs. 2.1 and 2.2).[48] Rush's ten vices are not a mirror image of Franklin's thirteen virtues, but each of them describes the inverse misdeed of Franklin's good deeds. While Rush chastises Indians for their "Drunkenness," Franklin practices "Temperance." Rush emphasizes Native "Idleness;" Franklin advises "Industry." Each of Rush's items pairs or groups with Franklin's: "Nastiness" (Rush) relates to "Cleanliness" (Franklin). "Cruelty," "Theft," and even what Rush calls "the infamy of the Indian character" (i.e., "the low rank to which they degrade their women") connects with Franklin's emphasis on "Justice: Wrong none, by doing Injuries or omitting the Benefits that are your Duty" (*A* 645). Franklin claims that he was undertaking "the bold and arduous Project of arriving at moral Perfection," (*A* 643), but he was simultaneously avoiding the habits— identified by his fellow American Philosophical Society officer—"peculiar" to Native Americans.

Franklin, though, admits his shortcomings in all thirteen categories, wearing out his "little Book" from marking and erasing his faults.[49] Nevertheless, Franklin depicts his relative victory of improving himself while not achieving perfection. He likens himself to the man who, wanting a bright axe but unwilling to expend the effort to make it so, decides that "*I think I like a speckled Axe best*" (*A* 650). Franklin regrets his imperfection but feels that "the Endeavour made a better and a happier Man than I otherwise should have been" (*A* 651). Writing of himself in the third person, Franklin asserts that "to *Temperance* he ascribes his long-continu'd Health, & what is still left to him of a good Constitution" (*A* 651). In this section, Franklin subtly satirizes French natural historians who claim that creoles degenerate because of the food and climate of the New World. But he also pokes fun at American natural philosophers who counter those assertions by positing a causal connection between social practices and racial identity. Furthermore, like his references to Tryon's prescribed diet, Franklin's tables gesture in two directions at once: the outlandishness of constantly keeping tables and vigilantly monitoring one's behaviors does indeed poke fun at those who connect cultural habits to the maintenance of national or racial character. At the same time, Franklin's attempts at his program make him into the model (white) American he presents to his readers.[50] By giving these practices at least some credit in maintaining his "Constitution," this entire parody is part and parcel of how Franklin proposes that new citizens who imitate his model "American" will maintain their American whiteness. Franklin satirizes the connection between habits and race only to suggest their

For *the* COLUMBIAN MAGAZINE. *An Account of the Vices peculiar to the Savages of N. America.*

IT has become fashionable of late years for the philosophers of Europe to celebrate the virtues of the savages of America.—Whether the design of their encomiums was to expose christianity, and depreciate the advantages of civilization, I know not; but they have evidently had those effects upon the minds of weak people. Without contradicting the accounts that have been published by those gentlemen, of the virtues of the Indians in North America, I shall briefly add an account of some of their vices, in order to complete their natural history. My information shall be taken from the travels of Charlevoix—Hennepin—Carver—and Romans, and from conversations with persons of veracity who have resided among them.

The first vice I shall name, that is universal among our savages, is UNCLEANNESS. They are, in general, strangers to the obligations both of morality and decency, as far as they relate to the marriage bed. — The exceptions to this remark, have been produced among those nations only, who have had an occasional intercourse with civilized nations.

2. NASTINESS is another Indian vice. This is exemplified in their food—drink —dress—persons—and above all, in their total disregard to decency in the *time—place—*and *manner* of their natural evacuations.

3. DRUNKENNESS is a more general vice among savages than among civilized nations.—Whole Indian tribes have been destroyed by it. Indeed they glory in their fondness for strong liquors, and consider it as a part of their character. A countryman who had dropt from his cart a keg of rum, rode back a few miles in hopes of finding it. On his way he met an Indian who lived in his neighbourhood, whom he asked if he had seen his keg of rum on the road? The Indian laughed in his face, and addressed him in the following words. "What a fool you are to "ask an Indian such a question. "Don't you see I am sober? Had I "met with your keg, you would "have found it empty on one side "of the road, and Indian Tom "drunk and asleep on the other."

4. GLUTTONY is very common among Indians. To this their long abstinence, produced by their idleness, naturally tempts them.—It is very common to see them stretch themselves on the ground after a full meal, and grunt there for several hours till they recover from the effects of their intemperance.

5. TREACHERY is another Indian vice. Who ever trusted to an Indian treaty?—They generally begin their wars with professions of peace and perpetual friendship.

6. The cruelty of Indians is well known. They are strangers to humanity. They even consider compassion as an act of effeminacy. Their treatment of their prisoners, shews them to possess a spirit of revenge, which places them upon a footing with infernal spirits.

7. IDLENESS is the universal vice of savages.—They are not only too lazy to work, but even to think. Nothing but the powerful stimulus of hunger or revenge is sufficient to rouse them into action.

8. THEFT is an Indian vice. The Indians not only steal from their civilized neighbours, but from each other. A horse—a gun—or spirits, have charms in the eyes of an Indian that no restraints can prevent their stealing, whenever they come in their way.

B 9. But

FIGURE 2.1 *"An Account of the Vices Peculiar to the Savages of North America,"* Benjamin Rush. The Columbian Magazine, *September 1786, vol. 1. page 9*

This article originally appeared in *The Columbian Magazine*, vol. 1, Sept. 1786, as part of ProQuest's American Periodicals Series. Reprinted with permission from digital images. produced by ProQuest LLC, Ann Arbor, MI 48106–1346. http://www.proquest.com.

9. But the infamy of the Indian character is completed by the low rank to which they degrade their women. It is well known that their women perform all their work. They not only prepare their victuals, but plant, hoe, and gather their corn and roots. They are seldom admitted to their feasts, or share in their conversation.—The men oblige them to lie at their feet, when they sleep *without* fire ; and at their backs, when they sleep *before* a fire.—They afford them no assistance in the toils of tending, feeding, and carrying their children. They are even insensible of the dangers to which their women are often exposed in travelling with them. A gentleman from Northumberland county, informed me, that he once saw a body of Indian men and women wading across the most easterly branch of the river Susquehannah. The men arrived first on the opposite shore, and pursued their journey along the river. The women, some of whom had children on their backs, upon coming to a deep and rapid current, suddenly cried out for help, and made signs for their husbands and fathers to come to their assistance. The men stood for a few minutes— and after attentively surveying their distress, burst out a-laughing, and then with a merry indifference walked from them along the shore.

This is a short nomenclature of the vices of the Indians of North America. If it were necessary, I would quote the chapters and pages of the authors who have established, by their observations, the truth of the character I have given of them. I am not disposed to enter into an examination of their virtues, but I cannot help supposing them to be rather the *qualities of necessity*, than the offspring of feel-

ing, or principle. Their hospitality—their friendships—their patience—and their fidelity to engagements, are the effects of necessity, and are as essential to their existence as honesty is to a band of associated robbers. Their politeness in never contradicting any person, I believe is the effect of indolence, for I know of nothing that lazy people dislike more than to dispute,even where truth is on their side, or where victory is certain.—Where is the man that in a lazy fit (to which all men at times are subject) has not heard false and absurd opinions advanced in company without contradicting them ?

The taciturnity of the Indians which has been so much celebrated, as a mark of their wisdom, is the effect of their want of ideas. Except in cases of extraordinary pride, I believe taciturnity, in nine cases out of ten in civilized company, is the effect of stupidity. I will make one more exception to this rule, and that is in favour of those people who are in the habits of communicating their thoughts by writing for the public, or by corresponding with their friends.—Ideas, whether acquired from books, or by reflection, produce a plethora in the mind, which can only be relieved by evacuations from the pen or tongue.

But what shall we say to the encomiums that have been lavished upon the love of liberty which characterizes our savage neighbours ? —Why—that they arise from an ignorance of the influence of property upon the human mind.—Property, and a regard for law, are born together in all societies. The passion for liberty in an Indian is as different from the passion for it in a civilized republican, as the impurity of lust is from the delicacy of love. There is a certain medium to be observed

FIGURE 2.2 *"An Account of the Vices Peculiar to the Savages of North America,"* Benjamin Rush. The Columbian Magazine, *September 1786, vol. 1. page 10*

This article originally appeared in *The Columbian Magazine*, vol. 1, Sept. 1786, as part of ProQuest's American Periodicals Series. Reprinted with permission from digital images produced by ProQuest LLC, Ann Arbor, MI 48106-1346. http://www.proquest.com.

connection at the same time. The larger point seems to be that the American political body be made up of consistently white physical bodies.

Thus, it makes sense that Franklin's Franklin possesses the ability to take up the habits of both African Americans and Native Americans and still remain white. Images of Franklin—those that made his face, as he claimed, "as well known as that of the moon"[51]—circulating in France as he was writing his second section emphasize this point. This image of Franklin in his fur cap circulated widely in France, indicating both Franklin's "Americaness" and the contact that, as a frontiersman, he would have had with Native Americans (Fig. 2.3).[52] Nevertheless, despite signifying this

FIGURE 2.3 *Augustin de Saint-Aubin,* Benjamin Franklin, *1777*

Courtesy of Harvard Art Museums/Fogg Museum, Gift of William Gray from the collection of Francis Calley Gray, G3526.

FIGURE 2.4 Au GENIE de FRANKLIN. *Marguerite Gérard (French, 1761–1837) after Jean-Honoré Fragonard (French, 1732–1806). To the Genius of Franklin (Au Génie de Franklin), 1779. Etching. Second of two states*

Friends of the Davison Art Center funds, 1996.24.1 (photo: R.J. Phil). Open Access Image from the Davison Art Center, Wesleyan University. http://www.wesleyan.edu/dac/openaccess.

geographic closeness to indigenous Americans, Franklin is simultaneously conceived of as a white, genius natural philosopher (Fig. 2.4). Franklin could live in America and wear the frontiersman hat—signaling his proximity with Native American tribes—but still remain the angelic natural philosopher that the French loved to love.

CONTAGION, DEGENERATION, AND CHANGE IN FRANKLIN'S COLONISTS-CUM-CITIZENS

But as much as Franklin enjoyed aspects of his stay in France, he returned to Philadelphia, his new nation-state, his domestic life, and his circle of American natural philosophers in 1785. He resumed his work with the American Philosophical Society, and that next year, the APS published Volume 2 of their *Transactions*, a volume Chaplin points out focused on "Franklin's career in the sciences."[53] Also included toward the end of the volume is Dr. John Morgan's "Some Account of a Motley Coloured, or Pye Negro Girl and Mulatto Boy, Exhibited before the Society in the Month of May, 1784, for Their Examination, by Dr. John Morgan, from the History Given of Them by Their Owner Mons. Le Vallois, Dentist of the King of France at Guadaloupe in the West Indies."[54] An article I discuss at length in Chapter 4, this piece describes Adelaide and Jean Pierre, two children whose skin displayed patches of white among those of black. Morgan dedicates most of his piece to describing in excruciating detail the physicality of these two children. However, at the conclusion, although he claims that "what causes have produced those surprising phænomena and alteration of the natural colour of their skin, are left for others to investigate and explain,"[55] he advances possible causes, including the maternal impression of a starry nighttime sky on Adelaide's mother and spilled milk on Jean Pierre's great grandmother. The very same natural-philosophical publication that touted Franklin's scientific genius thus also raised questions about why one's skin color might be and/or become white or black. Furthermore, this particular volume of the already highly-regarded *Transactions* was particularly well-circulated. APS records show that copies of Volume 2 were owned by François Barbé-Marbois, David Rittenhouse, Benjamin Rush, William Bartram, Charles Willson Peale, and, of course, Franklin himself,[56] and on July 21, 1786, the APS appointed Franklin, Vaughan, and Hopkinson "'to forward the sales of the Volume . . and send, in donations, any number not exceeding 20 copies, to such Societies and particular persons in Europe, as they shall think entitled to this respect.'"[57]

But even as we find Franklin linked to racial debates in the pages of the second volume of *Transactions*, his engagement with Samuel Stanhope Smith's theories of racial origin and development was much more pronounced. The APS invited Dr. Smith to give its annual oration, and on February 21, 1787, he gave the first version of what would become his *Essay on the Causes of the Variety of Complexion and Figure in the Human Species*. It was an auspicious occasion. The American Philosophical Society membership processed to "the Hall of the University."[58] There they heard Smith lay out his monogenetic thesis about how racial distinctions had emerged: namely, that after the single creation, peoples moved around the world and, over time, were impacted by the environments in which they lived. For Smith, the land's climate and state of society made a big difference, but one's practice of a given civilization could also impact one's physical structure. Extending Smith's line of thinking, one can see that if white European creoles continue to practice white, European civilization, they can mitigate the effects of living in the New World environment. To this same end, if one moved and adopted the practices of a given people, they could begin to acquire the physical traits of those people, or, as Smith says, "Not only their complexion, but their whole constitution seems to be changed" (*EC* 22). As strange as Smith's theorems may sound to us today, it nevertheless "was in fact a well-sustained statement of longstanding and widely held views on the question of race,"[59] and it garnered the praise and support of the philosophical society. It arranged to have 1,800 copies of his oration printed,[60] with several copies going to Franklin himself. Thus, after Franklin heard Smith's spoken oration and acquired copies of its printed version, he began the final parts of his *Autobiography*, two sections that continue to be marked by and in conversation with these circulating theories.

Issues concerning the contagion of blackness and nativeness occur in the final portions of Franklin's narrative, where the "new American" is a citizen somewhat connected to but still distinct from African Americans, Native Americans, and even the British.[61] Furthermore, inflected by contemporaneous theories of racial science, these scenes take up similar concerns about contagion, degeneration, and change, but here when the Franklinian character takes on traits of or is rhetorically associated with other races, he does not become them, a fact that has specifically political implications. For instance, in a scene in which Franklin dines at the home of Pennsylvania Governor Robert Morris,

> [Governor Morris] told us Jokingly that he much admir'd the Idea of Sancho Panza, who when it was propos'd to give him a Government, requested it might be a Government of *Blacks*, as then, if he could not agree with his People he might sell them. One of his Friends who sat next me, says, 'Franklin, why do you continue to side with these damn'd Quakers? had not you better sell them? the Proprietor would give you a good Price.' The Governor, says I, has not yet *black'd* them enough. He had indeed labour'd hard to blacken the Assembly in all his Messages, but they wip'd off his Colouring as fast as he laid it on, and plac'd it in return thick upon his own Face; so that finding he was likely to be negrify'd himself, he as well as Mr. Hamilton, grew tir'd of the Contest, and quitted the Government. (*A* 693)

This passage alludes to the antagonistic relationship between the Pennsylvania governor and the Quakers, who refused to fight in the Seven Years' War and who were often rhetorically associated with black slaves because of their abolitionist beliefs. It also refers to a passage in Cervantes' *Don Quixote* where Sancho Panza becomes aware that he can sell the "blacks" that he governs.[62]

Franklin blithely reprimands the governor and his friend for their reliance on rhetorics of blackness and servitude, but he does so in a manner that also depends upon those same problematics. Franklin's retort to the governor's friend relies upon the interconnections of rhetorical and figurative blackness, but it does not directly attend to its underlying logic. Instead, it addresses the dynamics of intra-Assembly negotiations. Here, Franklin proves himself agile in turning around a statement offensive to him because it castigates Pennsylvanians generally (and Quakers, more specifically) and because it implicitly endorses the institution of slavery.[63] The governor—by wishing for a "Government of *Blacks*" that he could sell rather than govern—associates physical blackness, slavery, and non-citizenship. The governor's friend then links rhetorical blackness to the Quakers. But Franklin even further plays upon how *blackness* signifies across the discourses of slavery, race, physicality, and morality when he links a blackened reputation ("the Governor . . . has not yet *black'd* them enough") with physical blackface ("wip'd off his Colouring"). Franklin ends the anecdote where the governor began the joke: when the governor subsequently found his own status blackened by the assembly ("negrify'd himself"), he "quit[s] the Government." Franklin's wit makes explicit the overlap between a blackened character and racial blackness to show how the governor's association with a racially blackened reputation led to his departure from governmental civic participation. Franklin here concerns himself with the fluidity of metaphorical blackness as it relates to one's political status. Like other early American scientists interested in the changeability of the color of one's skin, Franklin's anecdote shares with those scientific endeavors an interest in mutability. Morgan conjectured that one might attribute Adelaide and Jean Pierre's skin color to maternal impression; Franklin's linking of metaphorical blackening to rhetorical maneuvers oddly seems as simultaneously outlandish and plausible as Morgan's does. And, as Smith directly links one's climate and state of society to what appearance one has, Franklin likewise seems to suggest that what one does matters to how one appears. Like Morgan and Smith, Franklin is concerned with *not becoming black* here, but race science—even as it animates these concerns over changing racial status—is muted in relationship to the implication Franklin makes that the race of one's physical body has for the constitution of political bodies. It seems to be important for an American citizen, even when blackened physically or rhetorically, to stay white.

In the anecdote, despite critiquing his host and his associate, Franklin's own familiarity with the multiple rhetorical uses of blackness nevertheless depends upon the link between rhetorical and physical blackness and non-citizenship. He makes fun of Morris and his friend for using the metaphor of black slavery to denigrate the oppositional Quakers. Trumping the outlandishness of their metaphorical language by suggesting the governor himself subsequently became blackened and run out of state government, Franklin parodies their use of this type of language. This evinces Franklin's disapproval of their flippant comparison of slavery to governance, slaves to constituents, and governors to masters. But he does not challenge the implicit equation on which the entire anecdote turns: that one can be excluded from government if one is black.[64] Here blackness is equated with non-governmental status, and Franklin's retort thus both rebukes and invokes this way of thinking about and delineating white citizenship. And, indeed, while this scene in the 1730s is presented humorously, this was no laughing matter in 1788—just a year after Franklin and the rest of the Constitutional Convention wrote into law that African American slaves in the south each counted as three-fifths of a person for the purpose of representation and thus helped constitute the US body politic of whole, white bodies.[65]

Like blackness, nativeness also figures in Franklin's writing on citizenship in the *Autobiography*. Franklin aligns colonists with Indians and against the British, but he also contrasts Native Americans with the ideal American.[66] As Erkkilä suggests, the third section of the *Autobiography* can be seen in deep conversation with the events of the Constitutional founding and therefore has implications for Franklin's conceptualization of savage and unruly behavior in the new nation. This section recounts Franklin's involvement during the 1750s with Pennsylvania–Native American relations and the Seven Years' War. As a Pennsylvania representative, Franklin worked alongside the British to form strategic alliances with certain indigenous groups and to secure the western Pennsylvania border for white settlers against attacks. Franklin describes a crucial time in Indian-white affairs as both the French and British empires tried to deploy various tribes against one another in an attempt to acquire Native land.[67] And although Franklin narrated these 1750s events in 1788, the conflicts over the establishment of borders between whites and Native Americans and over the political formation of the new nation still remained to be fully settled. Given the historical context of its composition, the third section illustrates, then, some of Franklin's concerns over the establishment of the nation-state through his depictions of Native Americans.

At times, Franklin presents Native American practices as those to be emulated by white Americans in an effort to define themselves against the British.[68] Toward the end of his narrative, Franklin equivocally associates himself with Native Americans in the protection of white settlers. During the Seven Years' War, Franklin worked with British Major-General Edward Braddock, supplying him with wagons to use in his 1755 march against the French at Fort Duquesne. In the *Autobiography*, Franklin advises Braddock against his plans to hike to Duquesne and then to Niagara, arguing that an Indian ambush could surprise and fatally wound his ranks. Franklin writes that Braddock "smil'd at my Ignorance, & reply'd, 'These Savages may indeed be a formidable Enemy to your raw American Militia; but, upon the King's regular & disciplin'd Troops, Sir, it is impossible they should make any Impression'" (*A* 701). As

Erkkilä makes clear, Braddock's comments align Franklin and other white Americans with the Indians; ignorant, raw, irregular, and undisciplined, their bodies show no dissimilarity from that of the red man.[69] When the march ends in the slaughter of two-thirds of Braddock's men, Franklin comments ironically that "this whole Transaction gave us Americans the first suspicion that our exalted Ideas of the Prowess of British Regulars had not been well founded" (*A* 702).[70] In this scene, Franklin finds himself and his countrymen associated more with the Indians they purportedly fight against—since the British hold a unsavory opinion "of both Americans and Indians" (*A* 700)— than the British with whom they collaborate. Franklin's comment suggests that like "these Savages," the "raw American militia" could indeed defeat the British forces, enabling them to found the new nation. Importantly, Franklin's "savages" play a constitutive role here in the formation of American identity against that of the British.

However, in the same section, Franklin renders his most denigrating portraits of Native Americans, those whom rational, white citizens do *not* want to emulate. The scene is at Carlisle, Pennsylvania, where he and other elected representatives traveled in 1753 to negotiate a treaty with the Ohio Indians— many of the same groups with whom Aupaumut would negotiate nearly forty years later. The British previously had solicited them to join the coalition they already enjoyed with the Iroquois, because they suspected that if the Ohio Indians sided with the French, the Iroquois would soon follow. However, the British-Iroquois alliance failed to supply aid to the Ohio Indians when the French army attacked them at Pickawillany. Only when the French army began to advance toward the Ohio River did Pennsylvania belatedly provide support and offer condolences for the warriors lost in the attack by sending Franklin's delegation to Carlisle.[71]

Eliding this historical background, Franklin's account focuses on how the Indians get drunk on rum, and it notes how he and his other council members bribe them to stay sober during the treaty meetings with a promise of later alcohol distribution. After the treaty is reached, as Franklin notes, to "mutual Satisfaction," the agreed-upon rum is given to the Indians. That night,

> hearing a great Noise among them, the Commissioners walk'd out to see what was the Matter. We found they had made a great Bonfire in the Middle of the Square. They were all drunk Men and Women, quarrelling and fighting. Their dark-colour'd Bodies, half naked, seen only by the gloomy Light of the Bonfire, running after and beating one another with Firebrands, accompanied by their horrid Yellings, form'd a Scene the most resembling our Ideas of Hell that could well be imagin'd. There was no appeasing the Tumult, and we retired to our Lodging. At Midnight a Number of them came thundering at our Door, demanding more Rum; of which we took no Notice. (*A* 681–82)

The next day, three of the Indian elders make their apologies to Franklin's group, claiming the rum instigated their behavior. They declare that the "great Spirit" who created rum did so for the "INDIANS TO GET DRUNK WITH" (A 682).

In Franklin's passage, the Indians are worthy of official state negotiation, but they also evoke trepidation in rational whites because of their difficulty with alcohol.[72] In other interactions with state leaders, Franklin utilizes alcohol to assist in brokering an agreement. For instance, he secures eighteen cannons from New York Governor Clinton only after a dinner with "great Drinking of Madeira Wine" (A 672), and he advises the Presbyterian minister Mr. Beatty to administer rum to soldiers only after prayer meetings, in order to increase attendance (A 708–9). In relation to these two passages which bracket the rum-induced bonfire scene, Franklin implies that, like the governor of New York and the white soldiers, the Indians are just another group with whom bargaining talks can be productively lubricated with a bit of alcohol.

However, Franklin also adds that "indeed if it be the Design of Providence to extirpate these Savages in order to make room for Cultivators of the Earth, it seems not improbable that Rum may be the appointed Means. It has already annihilated all the Tribes who formerly inhabited the Seacoast" (A 682). Here, Franklin seems to claim that rum makes the Indian both like and unlike the white man, easing negotiations but still influencing the red man differently. Whereas Tryon wrote that alcohol most affected the sanguine complexion, Franklin paints a scene wherein it wreaks more havoc among Native tribes. The Native American body is radically different from that of the white men whom Franklin portrays drinking and, simultaneously, closely similar to the "sanguine" Anglo who, according to Tryon, is so susceptible to alcohol's effects.[73] For Franklin, rum not only turns Indians into demon-like creatures from hell. It also "annihilate[s]" tribes, and here Franklin displaces the blame for the annihilation of Indian tribes from the white settlers to the alcohol itself. As historian Richard White points out, when Franklin and his associates met with the Native Americans "to perform the necessary ceremonies of condolence," they were "bewildered by the necessary protocol."[74] This leads one to believe that this scene can be read less as an accurate anthropological account of Native American practices and more as Franklin's own perspective on the Indians' "tumultuous" behavior.[75] Ed White is even more skeptical of Franklin's attribution of the decrease of the Native population to drink:

> Franklin, as an erstwhile diplomat and publisher of Indian treaties, of course knew better, knew that the Delawares, Susquehannas, and Shawnees were not "annihilated" by drink but rather displaced by land fraud, Iroquois-Proprietary diplomacy, imperial warfare, and yeoman violence—in some of which he was implicated. Even as Franklin writes, the supposedly extirpated Delawares are uniting with the Shawnees and other Indians

from the Great Lakes to the Gulf of Mexico in an unprecedented effort to halt the American advance . . .⁷⁶

And, as White indicates, these tribes Franklin visits in 1753 and writes about in 1788 would by the late eighteenth century be building a powerful, anti-US, American Indian coalition in Ohio Country, one that Hendrick Aupaumut— Mohican Indian and US envoy—would visit and negotiate with in the 1790s. Franklin's 1788 composition describing his 1753 trip to Carlisle depicts Native Americans as "People . . . extreamly apt to get drunk" (*A* 681), those who "continue sober during the Treaty" merely "because they could get no Liquor," only to become rum-drunk, hell-like specters dancing around a bonfire at night once the treaty is complete. Indeed, Franklin's "dark-colour'd Bodies, half naked" resemble Rush's "Savages of North America" in their "Drunkenness" (Rush's Vice #3) as opposed to Franklin's Franklin who practices "Temperance" (Franklin's Virtue #1). In sharp contrast to Franklin's account, although it does mention a "great frolick, according to the old Custom of Shawannese," Aupaumut's narration offers us a record of highly intricate protocol and ritual, articulate and passionate arguments for various viewpoints, and the elaborate and tangled deliberation process that nearly fifteen different tribes undertook when weighing competing options of how best to proceed in their relationships with the new United States and its own unruly citizens living on its "border."⁷⁷ Despite these obvious differences between Franklin's and Aupaumut's texts, we come to understand both better when we understand how for both these men, their diplomacy and writing include negotiating between competing notions about race.

Hendrick Aupaumut's Own Color

Like Benjamin Franklin, Mohican Hendrick Aupaumut was hired as an emissary by the US government to negotiate with Native American tribes, and looking at the discourses of transformable race—particularly Aupaumut's use of the concept of color—gives further insight into his writings. In the fall of 1787, the year before Franklin began the third section of the *Autobiography* (the same time, of course, that the Constitutional Convention would take up issues of political membership and race), Aupaumut and eight other New Stockbridge Indians petitioned Samson Occom to be their permanent minister precisely because he was "red." Formerly of Massachusetts, these New Stockbridge Indians had decided to follow the lead of Occom's own Mohegan tribe by removing onto a tract of Oneida land.⁷⁸ The tribe relocated to New Stockbridge, six miles from the Mohegan Brothertown settlement in what would become upstate New York. The "Muhheacunnuk Tribes" declare to Occom that "we believe that this God has raised you up as an Ambassador

into this wilderness upon this purpose, that you might be the first instrument
or means to stir up your own Nation to try embrace the whole Religion. . . ."[79]
They claim that "a Number of us cheerfully agreed to begin to pursue what we
believe to be our Duty since we have felt and experience the great goodness
of God—for raising and fiting one of our own Collour—to be instrumental to
build up the Cause and the Kingdom of our Lord Jesus Christ—."[80] The language of the request—that their new minister be "one of our own Collour"—
places Aupaumut and his fellow Mohicans squarely within a number of
discursive formations. While Richard White notes that the phrase "loomed so
large in Indian speeches of the period,"[81] Aupaumut later uses it in a particularly contextualized instance—to a confederated alliance of both nativist and
accommodationist Indians, recorded in a journal to be sent to US government
officials—in a way that comments on the nature of racial identity and the constitution of political alliances.

Heeding the New Stockbridge request, Occom split his ministry between
Brothertown and New Stockbridge, where Aupaumut translated his sermons to other Mohicans. Mohican life at Oneida was unstable, however, as
white settlers continued to encroach upon Native lands, and the tense relationship between the Mohicans and their Oneida hosts began to worsen.
Aupaumut started seeking out ways to secure other areas where both the
Brothertown and New Stockbridge Indians could remove. Taking advantage of the opportunity to serve as a US emissary to the collection of Natives
forming in the Ohio Valley in opposition to the United States, Aupaumut
hoped to ingratiate the fledgling government to his tribe by delivering a
message of peace to the confederation and to secure a new Mohican home
by renewing ancient kinship ties with these western indigenous peoples. In
1792, he traveled to present-day Defiance, Ohio, to engage in treaty negotiations. His record of these travels, which he titled "A Short narration of my
last Journey to the western Contry," was sent to US government officials in
Philadelphia (and was published thirty-five years later in the 1827 edition of
the *Memoirs of the Historical Society of Pennsylvania*). Although, in the end,
Aupaumut's diplomatic mission did not follow his plans and his Mohican
tribe had to remove from Oneida to the White River area in present-day
Indiana in 1818, and eventually to what is now Wisconsin in the 1820s, his
descendants—the Stockbridge-Munsee Band of Mohican Indians—today
live, flourish, and keep alive the history of their people and Aupaumut's role
in that history.[82]

In analyzing Aupaumut's text, I consider the complexity of Aupaumut's
argument and the contested context of these 1792 negotiations in which he
had to make it. Like Franklin, Aupaumut occupied a fraught position as he
negotiated between and among various groups that held different beliefs
about the racialization of physical bodies, and Aupaumut's diplomatic mission was a particularly difficult one because of these competing ideas about

what influenced one's race and how that related to the constitution of political bodies. Indeed, as with Franklin, Aupaumut's own body came to be of
issue when he traveled between the two forming political bodies of the United
States and what Lisa Brooks calls the "United Indian Nations." When he went
to negotiate, the confederated Indians (comprised of Native Americans who
themselves disagreed about the origins of racial difference) cast a wary eye
on Aupaumut because of his adoption of Christianity, his taking on of many
"white ways," and his close affiliation with the US nation-state. US officials
also came to be suspicious; Aupaumut felt that in his written account of his
travels he had to dispel rumors about himself and justify his conduct to the
American governmental officials in Philadelphia. Like Franklin, Aupaumut
does not write a natural-historical text that explicitly advances its own particular race theory. Nevertheless, he writes in the midst of these debates and
engages deeply with them. In what follows, I examine Aupaumut's "Short
Narration" that chronicles his diplomatic journey and his "History (of the
Muh-he-ka-ne-ok Indians)," a text roughly contemporaneous with the "Short
Narration." I show how Aupaumut's presentation of and performance of the
idea of color in the "Short Narration" and his description of social practices in
his "History" challenge aspects of what *both* nativist Indians *and* many white,
natural historians thought about racial difference. Nativist Indians attributed
racial difference to separate creations, and natural historians posited a causal
connection between actions and bodily appearance, but Aupaumut—while
never directly refuting either claim—reworks both ways of thinking about
race held by these groups. On the one hand, this makes Aupaumut a fascinating figure for how he (similar to Benjamin Franklin) recasts major aspects
of eighteenth-century thinking about race and how various Native Americans
themselves conceived of racial difference. On the other, during his mission—
already hampered by mixed messages the United States was sending to the
United Indian Nations and the unrelenting advance of white, backwoods
settlers—it also becomes part of the reason why he was unable to earn the
trust of the confederated Natives and his diplomacy ultimately did not work
out the way he had envisioned.[83]

WHAT BEING RED MEANS

As a Mohican born at the Protestant Stockbridge Mission, Aupaumut was no
stranger to red-white interactions. Growing up in the community that had
been evangelized by Jonathan Sergeant, Aupaumut began to practice Christianity as a youth and, along with several other Mohicans, enlisted in the
Continental Army during the Revolutionary War. He was commended and
promoted to Captain by General George Washington. However, after the war,
the Mohican soldiers felt they did not receive appropriate compensation for
their service and continued to solicit the government for their wages.[84] When

encouraged by the New England tribes already in the process of removing to Oneida territory, the Stockbridge tribes followed suit.

As the Stockbridge Indians were making a life for themselves at New Stockbridge in the waning years of the eighteenth century, the new government was retooling its official policy toward Indian tribes to attempt to guarantee peaceful but steady white encroachment onto Native lands.[85] The 1783 Treaty of Paris negotiated between Franklin, John Adams, and John Jay and representatives of the British monarchy (but without input from Native Americans) brought an end to the Revolutionary War and established the Mississippi River as the new border between the United States and Indian Country. The subsequent way that the Americans treated the tribes allied with the British during the Revolution as subjugated peoples whose lands were ceded to the United States and the way that the Native Americans refused to be subject to a treaty in which they took no part—and to be considered conquered peoples as such—led to much bloody fighting on the "frontier" immediately following the war.[86] Thus, by the late 1780s, federal officials adopted a more coherent federal Indian policy to avoid what they felt would be a damaging Indian war and to curtail aggressive, advancing white backwoods settlers unlikely to follow federal dictates. At the same time, the government, believing that Native Americans held the capacity for change and would become more "white" if coerced into adopting white cultural practices, also sought to assimilate Natives into white society so that their land could be more easily obtained.[87]

Also during this period, a confederacy of a number of Native peoples led by the Miamis, Shawnees, and Delawares was forming in the Ohio Valley in explicit and possibly violent resistance to white backcountry settlers, as well as to the US government more generally.[88] Before and then again later after this brief time period, many of these western tribes (what Gregory Dowd has termed "nativist" in part because of their militant beliefs in separate red-white-black creations and a return to tribal practices) strongly disapproved of more "accommodationist" tribes (those more willing to adopt white cultural practices and to negotiate with whites themselves).[89] Although put to the side, disagreements still existed between nativists and accommodationists joined together in this delicate alliance. Moreover, tribes could be internally divided over various topics and—like the US government's vexed relations with its own backwoods settlers—struggled to control their more war-prone members. Nevertheless, in the 1790s, many of these groups came together to build a vibrant and threatening affront to the United States. As historian Colin Calloway states, "headed by the Miamis, the Shawnees, and the Delawares, the western confederacy continued to develop and . . . combined with the Six Nations and other tribes to present the United States with the most formidable array of Indian power mustered in united opposition."[90]

In this precarious moment, a most significant period in the history of white-Native relations, Aupaumut was one of several Native leaders to jockey for position as the main Native negotiator enjoined by the federal government to propose peace with the western confederacy. Captain Aupaumut strategized to ensure that his tribe would continue to be considered by the new government as the "front door" to Indian Country, a metaphor that denotes the tribe's prized role as intermediary between the more western Native tribes and the US government.[91] Shortly after Benjamin Franklin died, Aupaumut traveled to Philadelphia, where President George Washington selected him over the Mohawk leader Joseph Brant for this important position.[92] Once endorsed by the United States to carry the "message of peace" to the Indian confederacy, Aupaumut traveled to the "Glaize," the area of land where the confederacy met, with the future of Indian Country and the new US nation-state riding on his diplomacy.[93] Because of the present-day contentious debate about Native tribal sovereignty, the journal Aupaumut kept as record of the talks and sent back to the US government serves as a crucial piece of evidence. That is, by soliciting the confederacy to negotiate a peace treaty, the United States did engage with indigenous groups as independent *political* entities that, as Maureen Konkle has demonstrated, shows a recognition of Native tribes as sovereign nations.[94]

Aupaumut begins his detailed record of the intertribal treaty negotiations transcribed for US government officials by writing as follows:

> Having agreed with the great men of the United States, to take a tour, with their message of peace to the hostile nations—which enterprise some of the principal chiefs of the Five Nations did oppose—alledged that it would be folly for the United States to send me on that business. . . . But on my part, I have hitherto had a persuasion on my mind, that if the Western Nations could be rightly informed of the desires of the United States, they would comply for peace, and that the informer should be an Indian to whom they look upon as a true friend, who has never deceived or injuried [sic] them. ("N" 76)

Aupaumut sent his manuscript to Colonel Timothy Pickering to counteract rumors that he did not fulfill his duty when working with the Western Nations. The text, however, was not printed until 1827 when Philadelphia antiquarian Benjamin Coates obtained the manuscript, presented it to the Historical Society of Pennsylvania, and published it in the Society's *Memoirs*. While English-literate Aupaumut composed his manuscript without a transcriber, his text was published without his input, permission, or even knowledge. Furthermore, Aupaumut's text is doubly performative: it not only records the ceremonial aspect of the intricate nature of intertribal diplomacy; it also reperforms it, as a written speech act, for the white government officials in Philadelphia who eventually received this text.[95]

In his "Narration," Aupaumut uses the idea of color to identify himself with the confederated Natives despite their various differences as one racial group, but the very ground on which he bases his diplomacy is highly vexed: first, because among the confederated natives, there is no consensus on where "redness" comes from, nor what it exactly means; and second, because Aupaumut contradicts his own color logic when he describes differences among whites in his ultimate argument for peace. To see this, we must first understand how Aupaumut legitimates his engagement with the Western Confederacy by embodying and performing a specific type of Native identity. Citing what was coming to be considered at that time "racial" correspondence, Aupaumut repeatedly emphasizes the similarity between himself and the alliance by citing their "one colar" ("N" 77). But as straightforward as this assertion of commonality in "color" may seem to be, Aupaumut entered contested ground among these Native groups about what it meant to "be red" during this fraught time period. The Western Nations confederated in the Ohio Valley joined in a coalition with Indians who held widely different views on what it might mean to be an Indian. For instance, the Shawnee and Delaware tribes were largely "nativist" because of their adherence to "traditional" tribal customs and their eschewal of white cultural practices that they felt corrupted their people's Nativeness. Also believing that the Master of Life ordained separate red-white creations for the various races, nativists claimed distinct origins for red, white, and black peoples. Further, nativists felt "that Indians were a single people with common interests that transcended national rivalries."[96] While the nativist violence arising from what Dowd calls the "Indian Great Awakening" had subsided by Aupaumut's visit in the 1790s, many nativist groups still stridently held these beliefs.[97] During the late 1760s and 1770s nativists considered the mostly accommodationist-leaning Six Nations Iroquois as "Slaves of the White People" (quoted in Dowd, *SR* 43), but in the early 1790s, "accommodation and nativism worked together in the movement for Indian unity" (*SR* 21). Although they had fought bitterly in the past, accommodationists participated alongside the nativists against whites despite their differing rationales. "The cooperation of nativism and accommodation," Dowd writes, "rested upon a dual means to a mutual end: the united Indian defense of both land and political autonomy" (*SR* 91). Thus, these tribes put aside their differences to take a unified stand against the "Big Knives," the name they used for white frontier settlers who, ignoring the dictates of the fledgling federal government, continually pushed across the Ohio River into Indian Country.[98]

But even as nativists held differing views from accommodationist Indians, including parts of the Iroquois Confederacy and the (Catholic) Seven Nations of Canada[99] on the topic of where "redness" came from, tribes other than those identified strictly as "nativist" also saw literal body color as a way for them to self-identify during the late 1700s. Thus, clearly the diplomatic tactic of citing color helps establish commonality among Aupaumut, the relatively "accommodationist" tribes, and the nativist Shawnee and Delaware. Primarily analyzing the discourses of the Iroquois and Cherokee, Nancy Shoemaker writes that:

> Ideas about what constituted Indian and European identities hardened into a new reality in the eighteenth century as multiply diverse peoples sifted through and fixed on their own distinguishing characteristics as compared with others. The British may have enjoyed denigrating the French, but they also saw the French as fellow Europeans, Christians, and whites. The Iroquois and Cherokees may have spent much of the eighteenth century fighting each other, but by the century's end, they had come to see themselves as people with a common heritage and common interests, joined together primarily by their antagonism to Euro-Americans.[100]

Shoemaker claims that even before the 1740 publication of Linnaeus's *Systema Naturae*, Indians in the southeast "were claiming the category 'red' for themselves in the arena of Indian-European diplomacy."[101]

Therefore, by the time that Aupaumut arrived at the Western Nations and used the seemingly simplistic term "color," the various tribes agreed that it alluded to "redness" as an identifying common trait. But what being of the "same colar" actually *meant* to the diverse indigenous groups was anything but an uncomplicated issue. Most accommodationist Indians saw "color" as signifying a common "Indian" identity, but nativists went even further in considering "color" as evidence of separate red-white creations. By contrast, the Christianized Aupaumut, more aligned with the accommodationist tribes, most likely considered color as something that developed after what he believed was a single creation for humankind, the Adam and Eve origin story that Aupaumut himself professed.[102] In a later letter to "our great Father, the President and to his great Council, the Congress of the United States," Aupaumut wrote that "We are all descended from one father, and, with our white Brethren, acknowledge and worship one God. . . ."[103] Thus, holding that color was a sign of separate creations—as the nativist Indians did—directly contradicted Aupaumut's Christian beliefs.[104] Indeed, Aupaumut prepared a report to be sent back to Philadelphia where prominent white political leaders and men of science debated what produced bodily color and what that color then signified, but he also entered into *Native* debates over the cause and signification of color.

In addition, citing the "one colar" he shares with the western tribes in the 1790s is not the only sense in which Aupaumut embodies and performs a composite Indian identity. While visiting the western tribes, Aupaumut rehearses past tribal relationships between his tribe and those he visits.[105] Importantly, Alan Taylor contends that Aupaumut's tribe should rightfully be termed "Mohican" rather than "Mahican." Taylor points out that as a result of historical and political circumstances, the Mahican, Wappinger, and Housatonic tribes merged together, resulting in a "partially reinvented, culturally synthetic, and ethnically and geographically diverse people" of which Aupaumut considered himself a part.[106] As Taylor's analysis makes clear, Aupaumut's own specific tribal identity fused together various but related Native peoples, and this was the position from which he negotiated with the western tribes.

When making his journey toward the Western Nations, Aupaumut meets with various tribes along the way, including the Iroquoian Seneca nation, a group initially opposed to his carrying the message of peace before they could themselves travel to the summit. The Senecas then learn that two of their warriors have killed two Delaware, and despite their eagerness to lead the delegation to the west, they "are willing to let us [Aupaumut's party] go before them" ("N" 81). In addition to this, they send a message to the Delawares via Aupaumut, saying:

> Nephews of Delawares on Miamie, attend the words of your uncles the Five Nations—
> I am very sorry that some of my foolish young men have been led astray by the big knifes, consequently have killed two of their nephews.
> Nephew—
> Be assured, that we do not approve of this conduct, for we have no desire to take up hatchet against you, or any of our own color, but the fool when he is drinking strong liquor will go astray—I have calld all such to return home. ("N" 81)

The way that the Seneca use the term "color" and that Aupaumut represents it when he gets to the Delaware tribe is significant: despite language barriers (Senecas speak an Iroquian language; Aupaumut and the Delaware speak similar Algonquian languages), past intertribal warfare, and obvious fatal violence between members of their tribes, these two peoples share something in common, a "color" that is supposed to supersede any of the above differences. Furthermore, as Shoemaker makes clear, as a result of contact with white colonialists, "color" became a way for tribes to conceive of themselves as Native Americans in addition to specific tribal members.

When he reaches the Delaware—traditionally identified as the Mohicans' grandfather—Aupaumut delivers the requested "news from the east."[107] He opens his report with "my nation live in peace," thus immediately setting the stage for the reason for his visit, "—and that the great men of the United States wished to live in peace with all Indians" ("N" 89). But his report also mentions that "there is some wars among the great people over the great waters—and that negroes also have cut off many of their masters—," news that Aupaumut notes, perhaps surprisingly in a report to the US officials, that "the Indians glad to hear" ("N" 89). On the one hand, the Natives' response to what was probably news of the Haitian Revolution is quite logical, especially as these various tribes coming together in a collectively Native alliance against white encroachment seem to identify with the armed rebellion of another non-white group. On the other, the mention of it in Aupaumut's narration serves both as a gesture toward transparent recording and also as a subtle reminder to the United States about the very real threat the confederacy posed and the difficulty Aupaumut faced in negotiating with it on the behalf of the white Americans.

Just as the Senecas did in their message to the Delawares, Aupaumut very early in the treaty emphasizes the "colar" he shares with the confederated tribes. Performing part of the Iroquois condolence ritual aimed to acknowledge past deaths of tribal members and thereby to allow public discussion and debate, Aupaumut says to the "Shawannese, my younger brother," that "I set your heart aright, as it was fixed by our good forefathers in ancient days, that you may now understand both what is good and bad—and that you may contemplate the wellfare of our own colar—that our mornings may be lengthened" ("N" 90–91).[108]

After the protocol requirements have been met, Aupaumut begins to "faithfully deliver the message of the United States" ("N" 92). In his introductory speech, he claims that "Since the British and Amaricans lay down their hatchets, then my nation was forgotten. We never have had invitation to set in Council with the white people—not as the Five Nations and you are greatly regarded by the white people—but last winter was the first time I had invitation from the great man of the United States to attend Council in Philadelphia. According to that invitation I went—and after we arrived in Philadelphia, I find that the business was for the wellfare of all nations—and then I was asked whether I would carry a message of peace to you here" ("N" 92). Although Aupaumut's nation "was forgotten" when the United States decided it wanted to move toward peace, the government once again acknowledged the Stockbridge tribe by summoning him to this important mission. In the message from "the 15 sachems of the United States," the American government sends a "message of peace" that claims that "we the 15 Sachems have no desire to quarrel with you—but on the contrary we sincerely wish to have lasting peace established" ("N" 93–94). If the tribes accept, "the forts which stands on your Lands shall fall—and if you are disirous for peace, you must instantly call in all your war parties. With respect to the Big knifes, they are not to be compared to our least fingure. We will hold them fast, and they shall not stir until we let them lose" ("N" 94–95). The message makes great promises, of course, but includes within it a thinly veiled threat of what will happen if the terms are not accepted.

But although the US message itself emphasized that it sent the message via one of "your own colar" ("N" 93), the United States and Aupaumut were not the only parties making their argument by referring to a supposed commonality among the different native factions. Brant also uses the same phrase, but in order to argue for alliance with the British and against the Americans. Brant's nephew Tawalooth delivers his message:

My friends of the whole Confederate nations, who has one colar, attend—

I now send my voice to you, to let you know that I have wonderfully got thro from here to Congress and back again. I am much concernd for you but am lame and could not go at present—but will go and see you as soon as may be.

My friends—

I now tell you do not believe what Message the Muhheconneew [Aupaumut] brought to you, neither believe what he says, if you do you will be greatly deceived. I have myself seen Washington, and see his heart and bowels; and he declared that he claims from the mouth of Miamie to the head of it—thence to the head of Wabash river, and down the same to the mouth of it; and that he did take up dust, and did declare that he would not restore so much dust to the Indians, but he is willing to have peace with the Indians, &c. ("N" 112–13)

As Lisa Brooks makes clear, the competing visions of Brant and Aupaumut in part led to this intra-native competition over deciding what the United States really intended to do and what the confederacy's best option was.[109] More to the point here, Brant's message not only contradicts the message carried by Aupaumut but also shows that Aupaumut's claim to "one colar" does not necessarily make him a native who can be trusted. Indeed, what being of "one colar" actually *meant*—in terms of a Native alliance, in terms of race, in terms of a confederacy—was at the crux of the issue and remained, it seems, unresolved. As warrior Puckonchehluh puts it to the Iroquois: "Uncles—In our publick council you tell us, we whose are one colar, now have one heart and one head. If any Nation strikes us, we must all feel it. Now you must consider whether this is true what you told us" ("N" 117).

In addition, during the negotiations, the question of what being "white" meant would also arise. The Iroquois retell the story of what the US government would call the American Revolution:

When the white people first arrived in this country they were friendly to our ancestors, and they use to purchase land of them. At length they would demand so much land—and our forefathers used to grant it. At last these whites parted and quarrel. The Americans then advise us not to join either side, but set still mind our own affairs, and they then give us a caution that if we do contrary to this advise we shall forfeit our lands. But soon after this advise we put ourselves on the British side, and few days after, the English was thrown down. Then the Big knifes cut off our lands. ("N" 118)

Just as various tribes can confederate together as being of "one colar," those who are one color can also break apart.[110] Indeed, the Shawnee remain doubtful over whether they could or should meet with the United States to discuss peace. In a speech to the Iroquois, they say that "be it known to you that we could not speak to the Big knifes at the forts for in those places is blood. The United States have laid these troubles, and they can remove these troubles. And if they take away all their forts and move back to the ancient line, then we will believe that they mean to have peace, and that Washington is a great man—then we may meet the U.S. at Sandusky, or kausaumuhtuk, next spring" ("N" 121). To make matters for Aupaumut even worse, Tawalooth delivers another message from Brant: "I have seen the great men of the U.S.—they speak good words to Muhheconnuk, but they did not speak so well to the Five Nations, and they speak contrary to the Big knifes, that the Big knifes may prepare for war and fall upon the Indians unawares; and the Presidend of the U.S. did declare that he claim from the mouth of Miamie river on Lake Erie to its head from thence to the head of Wabash river, and down the same to the mouth of it, and that he will by no means restored to the Indians" ("N" 124–5). Indeed, rumors were spreading—and a few seem to have been true—that some whites were making preparations toward violent attack even as Aupaumut worked toward a treaty. Aupaumut tries to dispel these claims, but he also sends a message to General Putnam at Fort Jefferson to "lengthen his patience" ("N" 102). His narrative makes clear how the Big Knives continue to compromise his efforts:

> On the 14th of the inst. an Alarming Voice reached us that the Big knifes had come down, about one days walk, this side the fort, and have killed three of the Delawares.
>
> I was now obliged to use my utmost endeavours to convince the Chiefs respecting the morderation of the United States. ("N" 104)

At this intensely strained point in the negotiations when the natives were doubting the veracity of Aupaumut's message because of claims that whites were moving toward war, the ground from which Aupaumut performs his commonality with the Ohio tribes—a composite "Mohican" tribal identity in the first place, and a "color" identity held in common by all Indians, no matter what their differences, in the second—complicates the ultimate argument he makes for peace. The Indians contend that white people have stolen and will continue to steal Native lands, especially the "Big knifes" that the United States cannot control. Aupaumut replies that "it has been too much so, because these white people was governed by one Law, the Law of the great King of England; and by that Law they could hold our lands, in spite of our dissatisfaction; and we were to fond of their liquors. But now they have new Laws their own, and by these Laws Indians cannot be deceived as usual, &c" ("N" 126). He goes on to emphasize that "the great men of the United States" are not like frontier settlers of the past, "especially since they have their Liberty—they begin with new things" ("N" 127), different from the British who do not endeavor to assist the Native tribes. Aupaumut concludes his rationale:

the reason the Big knifes are so bad, is this because they have run away from
their own country of different States, because they were very mischivous,
such as thieves and robbers and murderes—and their laws are so strict these
people could not live there without being often punished; therefore they run
off in this contry and become lawless. They have lived such a distance from
the United States, that in these several years the Law could not reached them
because they would run in the woods, and no body could find them. But at
length the people of the United States settle among them, and the Law now
binds them. . . . ("N" 128)

Richard White characterizes Aupaumut's argument as part of a "struggle over
image" of the Americans as either compassionate like George Washington or,
conversely, marauding like the Big Knives.[111] However, the racialized aspects
of Aupaumut's argument make it more nuanced than what White suggests.
In his articulation, Aupaumut attributes the "white people['s]" deception of
the Native Americans to their governance by Great Britain and identifies the
process whereby whites, instead of being a coherent group, become metaphorically separated into the irresponsible British and benevolent Americans,
which, most importantly for him, carries vast implications for how they will
engage with tribal peoples. The grammatically incorrect clause "these white
people was" ("N" 126) raises the question of how the many former British subjects might be united as "one" people and answers it, counterintuitively: even
as whiteness is severed into two mutually exclusive groups of the British and
the Americans, it is precisely the whiteness that US citizens share that unites
them as a group. This is true not only in a cultural sense; the 1790 Naturalization Law, passed just two years before Aupaumut's mission, limited national
citizenship naturalization to "free white persons" and so reconstituted whiteness in a legal sense.

     Additionally, Aupaumut argues for *increased* white settlement close to the
Ohio River in order to enforce law on the Big Knives who had been living
"such a distance from the United States, that in these several years the Law
could not reached them because they would run in the woods . . ." ("N" 128).
Rather than argue that whites should withdraw, Aupaumut describes a critical mass of US citizens living on the frontier who transport this new national "Law" with them as they relocate. Paradoxically, Aupaumut intimates
that the more one kind of white settlers (law-abiding US citizens) relocate
closer, the less likely another set of white settlers (Big Knives) will continue
moving westward. However, Aupaumut himself had been the victim of Euro-
American settlers' deception, and his own tribe had been displaced by white
expansion. As Sandra Gustafson, Hilary Wyss, and Taylor have correctly
pointed out, Aupaumut was fully aware of his conflicted and complicit position
as an "intercultural broker" as he even comments in the text upon his own past
grievances with whites—which he withholds from telling the western tribes.[112]

Concurring with these readings, I see Aupaumut as neither fully "subversive" nor a "willing accommodationist."[113] Indeed, I read Aupaumut's bifurcation of "whiteness" into two nationalities not as a transparent and full description of what he knew to be true but, rather, an important and instructive speech act of his own. In other words, by making this argument—to the western Indians in their tribal councils and to the US government through his report—Aupaumut hopes to help create law-bound, US citizens who could possibly live with Native Americans in peace as they moved westward from Philadelphia. This was, of course, extraordinarily problematic for the confederated Indians who felt from their past experiences with the Big Knives that this was highly unlikely to happen.

Thus, despite trying to use "colar" rhetorically to legitimize himself and to establish a racial correspondence with the confederated tribes, Aupaumut argues that the new US nation necessitates significant differences among those whose shared "colar" is white—even as color is the unifying concept for both groups. The difference he draws between the Americans and the British necessarily complicates the logic of the "racial" identity and tribal relationships he embodies, performs, and cites in order to gain credence with the Western Nations. For Aupaumut, "whiteness" splits apart into two distinct political units while "redness" synthesizes not only Aupaumut's combined Mohican Stockbridge Indians but also the political alliance of the Western Nations. Nevertheless, it seems that the confederated natives found his argument unconvincing: they did not believe that now that the Big Knives were ostensibly "American" that they would behave differently than when they were British nor that Aupaumut's shared "colar" of redness made him similar enough to them to truly advocate for their best interest.

In addition to this, in terms of speaking to the confederated tribes, Aupaumut's use of "colar" points to the basis of the tribes' alliance while simultaneously suggesting a fundamental fracture that this performed racial identity seeks to cover over—namely, that not all Native Americans agreed with the nativists that their "red color" signaled their essential difference and separate creations from whites. Color may consolidate this group, but the difference in opinion over what that means is an unresolved tension ever waiting to rupture the delicate sense of Indian unity itself. If, at his dinner at Passy, Franklin raised but did not aggressively press the degeneration issue because of his diplomatic mission, Aupaumut also only gestures toward how the concept of color has the potential simultaneously to stabilize or to disrupt the grounds of pan-Indian discussion. That is, Aupaumut's reference to "colar" calls attention to an ostensibly shared physical characteristic with the nativists *and* to the fact that their opinions on the production and meaning of that characteristic were something that they did not share at all.[114] In many ways, then, this helps us understand the difficulty of his diplomacy and the part that racial thinking played in that difficulty.

Furthermore, Aupaumut's use of "colar" also complexly engages with contemporaneous natural-historical debates about the production of race and
its role in the structuring of political entities. While much of the natural-
historical belief in the US context claimed that social practices could influence
physical characteristics that then signified "race," Aupaumut dismisses this
causal connection. For him, while the establishment of the new US government divides whiteness into two collectives, both Americans and Britons are
still considered "white," especially since their race is the consolidating factor
for their nation-state. Likewise, despite radical differences in governmental
structure, social practices, and religious beliefs among himself and the various
tribes assembled at Defiance, they are still of the same "color." By intimating
that social factors and cultural practices do not influence racial characteristics
in a one-to-one relationship, Aupaumut's utilization of the logic of "color"
does not completely align with either nativist Indians or US officials hoping to
make the Native "more white" through cultural practice.[115]

Society may not influence racial characteristics for Aupaumut, but "color"
must be performed, maintained, and cited for it to be a cohesive element for
political alliance. For instance, the Americans were able to split off from the
British despite the fact that they are all of "one color," but that same reconstituted American whiteness binds the new US citizens together under the
"Law"—and once they settle among the Big Knives, they will be able to enforce the law on them, too. Indeed, when asked whether his "nation would
accept the plan of Union" ("N" 100) of the confederated tribes, Aupaumut
responds that he is actually "maintain[ing] a Union," an old one forged by
both tribes' ancestors. As Wyss points out, this assertion helps legitimate Aupaumut as already a part of the Native assembly instead of an outsider used by
the Americans,[116] especially since Aupaumut hoped to remove his own tribe
there someday. Significantly, too, it underscores how Aupaumut felt that race
and racial correspondence, rather than being a predetermining factor in how
political alliances might cohere, only sutures together various peoples into political entities if mobilized in such a manner. Indeed, toward the end of his
narration, Aupaumut emphasizes his frustration at negotiating from a position he wants the US government to realize was a very vexed one. He draws
attention to the key fact that would have strengthened his case that he was
quite similar to the Ohio Indians but that he had to withhold in an effort to
get them to listen to the US message of peace. "In all my arguments with these
Indians," he writes,

> I have as it were oblige to say nothing with regard of the conduct of York-
> ers, how they cheat my fathers, how they taken our lands Unjustly, and
> how my fathers were groaning as it were to their graves, in loseing their
> lands for nothing, although they were faithful friends to the Whites; and
> how the white people artfully got their Deeds confirm in their Laws, &c.

I say had I mention these things to the Indians, it would agravate their prejudices against all white people, &c. ("N" 128)

And it would not only "agravate their prejudices against all white people;" in so doing just that, it would go further against Aupaumut's claim that there are significant differences among these whites. As he comes toward the conclusion of his narration, he closes his illustration of his diplomacy and all the factors working against it: "I now have occasion to say that I have been endeavouring to do my best in the business of peace and according to my best knowledge with regard of the desires of the United States, I have press in the minds of friends in the westward repeatly" ("N" 130).

ALWAYS ALREADY MOHICAN

Around the same time that Aupaumut composed his "Narration," he also wrote a history of his own Muhheakunnuk Indian tribe that was reprinted in various versions in the early nineteenth century.[117] As Wyss notes, Aupaumut's "History" likely was written for a white audience since the preservation of tribal knowledge through oral transmission would not have necessitated a written record.[118] In his "History," Aupaumut surprisingly claims that his tribal ancestors practiced aspects of Christianity before encountering white missionaries, utilized certain Anglo-American farming techniques prior to having tools, and governed themselves by a "democratical" government before the establishment of the US nation-state. Scholars such as Rachel Wheeler, Taylor, Wyss, and Gustafson attribute what they view as "invented tradition"[119] into which Aupaumut projects Christianity as part of Aupaumut's efforts to frame "accommodation to European religion, education, and agriculture [as] the only avenue for native American survival."[120] For these scholars, in other words, Aupaumut rewrites Mohican history in such a way that white acculturation offers a return to Native practices, an enhancement—rather than a loss—of Mohican identity.

But Aupaumut's history also works on a broader level by unsettling natural-historical and even nativist beliefs about the relationship between cultural practices and the production of race. He writes a history in which Mohicans are already participating in practices generally coded as "white," but he presents the Mohicans as fully embodying a Native identity. In so doing, it is not so much that he recodes these practices as "Native" but, rather, that he strips them of their racialized tenor. Cultural critics who focus exclusively on how, in their view, Aupaumut encouraged Natives to "emulat[e] white ways"[121] neglect the way he recasts these practices in his history. If white natural historians wanted to claim that "civilizing" the Indians would make them culturally and physically more "white," Aupaumut shows that despite having participated in "white" cultural practices, the Mohicans remain Native. Aupaumut also responds to nativists who try to rid themselves physically of any "white ways": in Aupaumut's view, these ways do not make one any "less" of a Native. In these examples, Aupaumut—much like Franklin—unsettles the relationship many white scientists *and* militant nativists wanted to maintain between society, cultural practices, and race. The ancestral Mohican Indians in his "History" are not degenerated "savages," nor are they replicas of white Anglo colonists.

Aupaumut's historical Mohicans, then, take part in "white" cultural practices prior to being taught to do so by whites who "instead of taking Indian lives and Indian lands, then, . . . proposed to take Indian culture and Indian lands" by making Indians white.[122] These ancestors practice a religion that does not claim to be Christian, per se, but does worship a single God that Aupaumut links to Christianity: "Our ancestors, before they ever enjoyed Gospel revelation acknowledged one Supreme Being who dwells above, whom they styled Waun-theet Mon-nit-toow, or the Great, Good Spirit, the auther of all things in heaven and on earth and governs all events; and he is good to all his creatures" ("H" 18).

Furthermore, in addition to hunting, these ancestors utilize white agricultural practices before being cajoled to do so by whites: "As our fathers had no art of manufacturing any sort of metal, they had no implements of husbandry, therefore were not able to cultivate their lands but little—that of planting shammonon, or Indian corn, beans, and little squashes, which was chiefly left under the management of women, and old men who are incapable of hunting, and little boys" ("H" 15). Even this "but little" aspect of farming frustrates any acculturation project aimed at "civilizing" Natives in order to gain their lands: these Indians, Aupaumut demonstrates, already use these techniques and remain Indians nonetheless. (Aupaumut's reaction to US attempts at "civilizing" Indians differs from nativist leader Painted Pole, who did not take kindly to American efforts to make Indians place "'Hoes in ther hands to plant corn,' and would 'make them labour like their beasts, their oxen & their Packhorses'" [quoted in *SR* 105–6] and who identified this as a reason to go to war against the whites.)[123]

In addition to religious and agricultural issues, Aupaumut takes up the governmental structure of his tribe. He writes that:

> Our ancestors' Government was a Democratical. They had Wi-gow-wauw, or Chief Sachem, successively, as well as other nations had, chosen by the nation, whom they looked upon as conductor and promoter of their general welfare, and rendered him obedience as long as he behaved himself agreeably to the office of a Sachem. And this office was hereditary by the lineage of a female's offspring, but not on man's line, but on woman's part. That is—when Wi-gow-wauw is fallen by death, one of his Nephews, (if he has any) will be appointed to succeed his Uncle as a Sachem, and not any of his sons. ("H" 20)

Aupaumut's description of his tribe's governmental structure as "Democratical" has implications for how society works with race and evinces a keen understanding of the new US governmental structure. On the one hand, Aupaumut seeks to highlight the electoral aspect of Mohican politics, a process so prized by new US citizens. On the other, he does not obscure the fact that the "appointment" procedure is not free from considerations of heredity. By calling this electoral method "Democratical," clearly alluding to the structure of the US government, Aupaumut again suggests how two similar but not necessarily seamlessly compatible systems allude to each other. Nevertheless, the fact that some type of exclusive lineage—that of propertied white males—constituted the eligibility of political leaders makes the Americans' democracy oddly resemble that of the Mohicans. As opposed to the term *republican*, *democratic* at this time was still associated generally with the potential unruliness of the "mob." Thus, like the American democracy, the radicalism of the Mohican "democratical" government is tempered by the fact that only select individuals could hold its highest office.

Even as he outlines Mohican traditions such as passing communal values onto their children through daily lessons and keeping the "bag" and "pipe of peace," Aupaumut continues to imply likenesses between his ancestral Mohicans and the new Americans. Like the US President, the Mohican Sachem is advised by a council of elected "Counselors," "not gotten by hereditary," whose job it is to "consult with their Sachems in promoting peace and happiness for their people." Just as the US government consists of many states, the Nation is comprised of "three clans or tribes." For the Mohicans, the "Bear Tribe formerly considered as the head of the other tribes, and claims the title of hereditary office of Sachem. Yet," Aupaumut continues, "they ever united as one family" ("H" 22).

Aupaumut also relates that when the Mohicans defeated the Miami in war, they maintained a civil—not despotic—relationship with them. Although the conquered Miami nation "offered obedience" and "a large tract of land" to the Mohicans, Aupaumut attests that since "our forefathers loved not superiority over their fellow Indians, or using authority as tyrants over any nation, they only accepted the present given to them out of friendship, remembering that it may in time to come, our children some occasion or other would come and live there" ("H" 17). The Mohicans, like the Americans, loathe tyranny; they only accept the "present" of land to save it as an alternative homeland if they ever should, or—as Aupaumut's white readers would have known—when they did lose their land by "some occasion or other."

Ultimately, if whites seek to recreate the Mohican Indians in their own image, Aupaumut frustrates that project by presenting the Mohican tribe as an uncanny doppelgänger of the young nation-state, where what Anglos might consider "white" cultural practices *will not* make the Natives more "white," either culturally or physically.[124] Indeed, while Aupaumut notes the

"little" bit of "cultivat[ion of] lands" ("H" 15) in the Mohican past, Jeremy
Belknap and Jedidiah Morse in 1796 record that the "sachem Hendrick Aupaumut has a good field of wheat, Indian corn, potatoes, and grass, and we had
the pleasure of meeting him in the road driving his oxen team."[125] But while
many, including Belknap and Morse, no doubt applauded Aupaumut for
what appeared to be his taking up of the white man's ways, we can't help but
think of the young Franklin, pushing his wheelbarrow through the streets of
Philadelphia precisely because of the importance of "*Appearances*" (*A* 629).[126]
As Belknap and Morse note, in addition to wheat, potatoes, and grass, Aupaumut grows "Indian corn"—a staple that his "History" chronicles Mohicans
growing before meeting the white man. Despite what others may think, for
Aupaumut, these practices will only make the Mohicans be what they always
already have been.

***

Reading the work of Benjamin Franklin alongside Hendrick Aupaumut
points up a counterintuitive fact about early American discussions about
"race": supporters of various racial theories *do not* necessarily line up according to racial divisions. Instead, we find a number of surprising intellectual bedfellows. For instance, Jefferson—with his conjecture that blacks might
have sprung from separate creations—shares much in common with Neolin,
a militant nativist who preached separate creations to all Native Americans.
Likewise, Samson Occom and Samuel Stanhope Smith, two faithful Christian
apologists for monogenesis, suggest that the varieties of humankind sprung
from their species' shared origin. And while Franklin and Aupaumut were not
friends, acquaintances, or even interlocutors, they similarly challenged links
between modes of living and the production of race—be it Tryon's prescribed
diet or Washington's advocated agriculture—and instead focused on race as a
category in relationship to political identities.

Two emissaries who strategically measured their engagement with debates
over transformable race because of their diplomatic missions, both troubled
the necessarily racialized connotation to various practices. As we shall see,
their texts thus contrast with those considered in the next chapter—*Letters
from an American Farmer* by J. Hector St. John de Crèvecoeur, *A Narrative of
the Lord's Wonderful Dealings with John Marrant, a Black* by John Marrant,
and *Edgar Huntly or, Memoirs of a Sleep-Walker* by Charles Brockden Brown.
Working according to a different logic than either Franklin's *Autobiography*
or Aupaumut's "Short Narration," these texts explore how persons who take
on the cultural practices of another race transform into the racial "Other."

Transforming into Natives: Crèvecoeur, Marrant, and Brown on Becoming Indian

During the 1780s and 1790s, three vastly different texts—a series of fictional letters composed by a Frenchman who became a naturalized British subject, an Indian captivity narrative written by a black freeman, and a Gothic mystery penned by America's "first novelist"—explored what it might be like to live among Native Americans. J. Hector St. John de Crèvecoeur's *Letters from an American Farmer* (1782), John Marrant's *A Narrative of the Lord's Wonderful Dealings with John Marrant, a Black* (1785), and Charles Brockden Brown's *Edgar Huntly or, Memoirs of a Sleep-Walker* (1799) feature the main characters' actual or contemplated sojourn among American Indian tribes. In *Letters'* bleak final epistle, Crèvecoeur's narrator Farmer James considers how he might relocate his family among nearby Natives without his children becoming "perfectly Indianized."[1] In his autobiographical narrative, Marrant chronicles his captivity by the southeastern Cherokee tribe and how his adoption of Cherokee ways renders him unrecognizable to most of his family once he returns home. A similar thing happens to Edgar, Brown's main character, who fights, eats, and speaks like an Indian in the Pennsylvania wilderness. All these texts consider one of the most pressing questions of their day: what exactly would happen to non-Natives living in the "New World" among the peoples indigenous to the North American landscape? Because these protagonists become (or fear becoming) Indians from adopting a certain way of life, we must raise the following critical questions: if we unearth the mutable aspects of race as they were debated at the turn of the eighteenth century, how do we understand these texts anew? Furthermore, if these writers depict race as something transformable, how do we need to rework our hermeneutic models to understand better these scenes of "masquerade" and adaptation?

In what follows, I argue that Crèvecoeur's *Letters*, Marrant's *Narrative*, and Brown's *Edgar Huntly* take up the natural-historical idea that race was a condition one managed to sustain rather than a fixed or immutable bodily fact. These texts explore the possibilities of racial transformation by imagining the outcome of an extended stay among Indians. Often, the texts explore both the points of contact and points of friction between the notion of transformable race and other discourses, such as national affiliation, Native American epistemology, and other ways of conceiving race. Indeed, we will find that these points of confluence and conflict are closely related to the central concerns that arise in each text.

If Phillis Wheatley and Samson Occom drew upon the aspect of transformable race that held that any given race gradually developed into what they were at the present moment, these writers place their texts in the middle of debates over what might happen to any given person's race *in the future*. They consider these ideas and what they imagine could be the various ends—be they nightmarish, utopic, or somewhere in between—to these most interesting means through which race was believed to be produced. As I will show, *Letters* examines both the positive and negative potential of white bodies altering racially in the New World, a process Farmer James metaphorically associates with the caged Negro that he observes in Charleston, South Carolina. Understanding the way transformable race functions in *Letters* provides a new window into understanding what Crèvecoeur's "American" is. Marrant's *Narrative* offers up a picture of black transformation, not of an African American "becoming white" (as in the Henry Moss case discussed in the introduction and Chapter 4), but, rather, of a black man "becoming" Native American. Brown's *Edgar Huntly* explores, first, what might happen to creole whites by depicting the strange transformation Edgar undergoes—not, as we have assumed, initiated after he follows Clithero into the wilderness—but beginning years prior to the opening of the novel and, second, what that transformation might mean for the success of the nation-state project. All these works, moreover, consider how an adopted "mode of life" can affect one's racial identity, imagine Indian transformation to disidentify their main characters from an "American" national identity, and emphasize the temporal component inherent in early American understandings of race.

Thus, these texts necessitate a reworking of the way cultural critics currently understand notions of racial masquerade and what Philip Deloria calls "playing Indian." As I shall explain, the concept of passing as we currently understand it is not a sufficient way to comprehend these scenes of transformation. A conceptualization of how the external body might—or might not—display one's "true" race would not have been fully meaningful at this time. Rather, the concept of racial transformation underpins these literary depictions of how one's race begins to change into that of another, as these scenes of racial metamorphosis imagine the particular early American version of becoming the racial Other.

Passing as, Transforming Into

Eighteenth-century conceptions of race force us to reconsider how we traditionally think of "passing" as a way to understand the crossing of racial boundaries. The way we commonly use this term in discussing nineteenth- and
twentieth-century racial experience presumes ideas about race not dominant
in the early national moment. According to the *Oxford English Dictionary*,
the familiar definition of *passing* as "The fact of being accepted, or representing oneself successfully as, a member of a different ethnic, religious, or sexual
group" first appeared in print in Carl Van Vechten's *Nigger Heaven* (1926).
However, the term becomes more resonate for the early American moment
when we emphasize another, slightly varied meaning: "The action of going or
moving on, through, or by; an instance of this; the process or fact of changing
from one state to another. Also: movement, motion (obs.)." Richard Joseph
Sulivan's use of this meaning of *passing* in his 1794 *View of Nature* proves
quite telling: "The passing of a substance from a fluid into a solid state." It is
this sense of passing—of moving from one state into another, of occupying a
potentially temporary status, of transforming—that I want to restore to our
critical understanding of how race operates in eighteenth-century American
literature.

It is also important to note the nuances of the verb "to *pass*." The *OED* gives
the 43.a definition of *pass* as "to be taken for or to serve as (usually with the
implication of being something else); to be accepted or received as equivalent
to," a sense of the term that stretches back into the 1400s. Indeed, this sense
has existed concurrently with definition 33: "To change from one form or state
to another, esp. by regular or gradual transitions; to undergo chemical, miner-
alogical, structural, or other gradual conversion *into*" (emphasis in original).
Thus, on one hand, the term "to pass" was used, for instance, in early American runaway slave advertisements to refer to black slaves who adopted the
dress and habits associated with whites in order to escape to the North. On the
other hand, however, what we have forgotten and must restore to critical view
is that the adoption of that same manner of dress and habits could *also* be considered a means of changing one's body from one thing into something else.

To say this another way, nineteenth- and twentieth-century quotidian understandings of race deemed it an internal rather than an external phenomenon.[2] As a wealth of critical literature—in addition to famous passing scenes
in the fiction of Stowe, Chesnutt, Twain, and Larsen—attests, nineteenth- and
twentieth-century "passing" depends on both "an optical economy of identity" and a posited racial interior.[3] It only works in a system that simultaneously assumes a direct correspondence between exterior markings of race
and the inner, biologized "truth" about race *and also* conjectures that sometimes these external characteristics do not reliably indicate an individual's
interiority—a situation that Amy Robinson calls "the false promise of the

visible as an epistemological guarantee."[4] For example, when Clare Kendry passes for white in Nella Larsen's *Passing* (1929), society assumes that her appearance will signal what race she actually "is" (and this, of course, presupposes that what Clare actually "is" is defined legally—that any "black blood" renders one black, even if one also has, as Clare does, white ancestry). Clare passes, of course, because her skin does not indicate her "true" black race. In this framework, the exterior body ceases to signify its "interior" in a trusted, dependable way. In other words, people presume that one's body represents (or should represent) what one "really is" on the "inside."[5]

By contrast, in the late eighteenth century, one's appearance signals what one "is" at the moment—not internally but, rather, just "in fact." Within this way of thinking, for instance, if one lives in Africa and acquires dark skin from exposure to the sun, one "is" black. If one lives in America and develops a tawny complexion, then one "is" red. If one's light coloring forms from living in Europe, then one "is" white. While certainly these examples are oversimplified—as I discussed in the introduction, debates abounded on how exactly the varieties of humankind formed—the scientific belief that one's true race emanated from one's interior was far from a foregone conclusion at this historical moment. Instead, many people largely understood their race to be a reflection of their exterior circumstances (both of environment and of culture), and thus they considered race not an inner truth that might or might not be displayed faithfully on the body. Rather, most early Americans envisioned racial identity as a place one maintained on a spectrum of racial states.

Because one might morph from one status to another (in the sense of visible alterations of the exterior body), potential changeability constituted a central aspect of race. These examples point up a *temporal* component particular to racial formation in early America. Because of beliefs about the plasticity of one's body, race is less a statement about what one "is" internally (and how that might or might not be visible on the skin), but, rather, what one *remains*—for a shorter or longer period of time—externally. Rather than a "truth" that might or might not be displayed on the body, racial identity is a condition of the body that one manages to sustain. This accounts for the differentiation between later understandings of passing as a certain kind of misidentification of an unchanging racial identity versus an earlier one as a type of transforming into another racial identity.

Both these models of identity function performatively, but fundamentally different assumptions about the body and racial identity undergird these chronologically successive, but sometimes overlapping, frameworks. Thus, as I outlined above and as the work, for instance, of scholars such as Judith Butler and Elin Diamond have helped us understand, narratives of passing not only demonstrate how one's exterior does not signify one's interior in a trusted way (as nineteenth-century common conceptions of the body would have it).[6]

These narratives also show race itself to be performative because they illustrate how that supposed "racial interior" is itself a produced fiction of ontology.

But can we think a performative model of identity in different terms, under different circumstances, in different historical periods? And if so, how?[7] Butler has pointed to how citational models must be thought differently in various epochs, claiming that "regulatory schemas are not timeless structures, but historically revisable criteria of intelligibility which produce and vanquish bodies that matter."[8] To wit, then, if nineteenth-century science thought race to be "in the blood" whether or not it was indicated by the skin, performance theory has already helped us understand how certain acts produced an ontology of race residing on the "inside." Likewise, if eighteenth-century science largely thought race to be on the surface of the body, performance theory can now help us understand how certain acts produce another ontology of race—not "in" the body, but on the body's "outside." I want to look at the process of how various contemporaneous discourses constitute the materiality of the eighteenth-century body along the lines of citationality and also at the (intimately related, but not necessarily identical) process of how certain acts—such as living in a certain place, speaking in a particular manner, or practicing the culture of a specific group—were believed to physically alter that body.[9] Therefore, while both nineteenth-century and eighteenth-century examples of performing the Other are versions of "becoming" the Other, if we think of nineteenth-century instances as "passing as" the Other, we should think of eighteenth-century instances as "transforming into" the Other.

Thus, this particular notion of transformation in turn helps us rethink how we have understood acts of dressing as an Indian. In the influential accounts of Philip Deloria and Shari Huhndorf, one crosses a boundary line to pretend briefly to be the Other, while keeping, as Deloria says, the "*real* 'me' underneath" (7)—all in the service of constituting white American national identities.[10] However, as we shall see, Crèvecoeur, Marrant, and Brown depict a process wherein one does not cross over to try on another identity but, rather, engages in the means of *transforming into* an Indian. These authors explore, then, the understanding of one's racial identity through its possible bodily transformation into the Other, and it is this process that Farmer James calls the "surprising metamorphosis."

Crèvecoeur's American Race

Letters from an American Farmer presents a conflicted account of how racial formation might play out in early America.[11] The story of Farmer James advances a particular version of transformable race by depicting the racial metamorphosis of the European in the British colonies, but this notion of fluid race is at times coupled with a more internal—and, thus, contradictory—sense of race.[12] Farmer James subscribes to the tenet that one's environment impacts one's body and racial identity. When he describes the "new American" who undergoes a "surprising metamorphosis" (*L* 69) after his immigration, Crève-coeur's narrator depicts this alteration as specifically racialized. However, this concept of transformable race exists at times in uneasy tension with a sense of race as less flexible. Each time James revisits this notion of racial transforma-tion, he tempers his celebration of it, and he is terrified of his family's possible Indianization. On the one hand, James's letters explore how racial mutability might work, but, on the other, they seek some sort of stability of racial iden-tity. These two conflicts—how race forms and how James feels about that process—intensify other textual discords. His racial fear of becoming "savage" is linked to his political fear of a radical separation from Great Britain, and he suggests that the white man's potential to form a "new race" (*L* 70) in the Americas is predicated upon black slaves' blood and sweat, which literally saturate the ground that enables the white man's metamorphosis.

In this reading, we come to understand the "new American" as much more a racialized—and much less a nationalized—personage.[13] Indeed, in *Letters*, the "new American" is not a fully formed figure for an established nation-state, but is better understood as a racialized persona that, as Edward Larkin has persuasively argued, is a "type of British person" who, I contend, also should be seen only as a precondition for the formation of an American national identity.[14] The idea of a cultural melting pot so often attributed to Crèvecoeur does not only "melt" men into a new race[15]—this new race is also particularly nourished by the ground on which it resides. It is not at all incidental that James uses the term *race* to describe the "new American."[16] While European natural historians had already posed the question of what would happen to white immigrants in America, James refines the terms of this debate: if the white European must necessarily alter when he relocates to British America, James depicts this "surprising metamorphosis" as a change—not to American savagery—but to American whiteness. Interestingly, the most peculiar thing about this American identity is that while it results from a radical change, it *nevertheless* allows one to retain his Old World nationality, in part because James does not use the term "American" strictly as a national descriptor.[17] When we overemphasize the "melting pot" aspect of James's letters and si-multaneously overlook the text's exploration of transformable race, we are more likely to misread and underappreciate the surprising complexity of what James's "American" is.

Crèvecoeur's opening dedication to the Abbé Raynal frames *Letters from an American Farmer* as a fictional exploration of the natural-historical and racial claims that Raynal advanced about life in the Americas in his *Histoire Philosophique et Politique des Établissemens et du Commerce des Européens dans les deux Indes* (*Philosophical and Political History of the Settlements and Trade of the Europeans in the East and West Indies*, 1770).[18] This French natural historian, as I explored in the introduction, famously extended Buffon's thesis about the degeneration of animal species in the New World. Raynal's suggestion that whites would also degenerate and become savages in the American environment sparked international debate, prompting North American scientists to concern themselves with his theories. As *Letters'* 1782 British edition's advertisement claims, the letters "contain much authentic information little known on this side of the Atlantic: they cannot therefore fail of being highly interesting to the people of England at a time when everybody's attention is directed toward the affairs of America" (*L* 35).[19] Certainly, British readers were highly interested in the "affairs of America" at this time when the war with the colonies had not yet been formally resolved (as it would be with the Treaty of Paris in 1783). At the same time, given that *Letters'* early audience consisted mostly of European readers who largely assumed that the North American climate would degenerate white men and given that Raynal played a key role in that debate, Crèvecoeur's dedication also frames the text within the transatlantic debates about racialization in America.[20]

Crèvecoeur deals with Raynal's ideas about the Americas in a conflicted manner.[21] As much as Crèvecoeur might agree with the premise of Raynal's theories that the environment determines the man, his narrator at the outset advances an outcome much different from Raynal's. Initially, where Raynal envisions degeneration and savagery for the European in the New World, Farmer James imagines an idealized new race of Americans. But, as we shall see, this vision of one's white-American racial identity being influenced by his surroundings comes under enormous pressure late in the text when James dreads the very real possibility that he might become an Indian. In other words, despite repudiating Raynal's claims in the beginning, James rearticulates them in the end.[22]

Farmer James uses a natural-historical—more specifically, environmentalist—language throughout his text.[23] While past critics have attributed this language to either a belief in Lockean or physiocratic philosophy, I argue that placing it in the context of early American debates about how external factors can influence the body illustrates how Crèvecoeur theorizes race.[24] With feigned simplicity, James claims to be a "perfect stranger" to "scientific rules" (*L* 49), but his language leads us to believe otherwise. Describing the "back settlers," James claims that "it is with men as it is with the plants and animals that grow and live in the forests; they are entirely different from those that live in the plains" (*L* 76). In his ruminations on Nantucket, James writes that "if New Garden exceeds this settlement by the softness of its climate, the fecundity of its soil, and a greater variety of produce from less labour, it does not breed men equally hardy" (*L* 147). Furthermore, because different types of peoples are best suited for their indigenous habitats, Nantucketeers are not tempted to move to more "pleasing scenes" (*L* 148). As James writes, "the same magical power of habit and custom which makes the Laplander, the Siberian, the Hottentot, prefer their climates, their occupations, and their soil to more beneficial situations leads these good people to think that no other spot on the globe is so analogous to their inclinations as Nantucket" (*L* 148). This language echoes that of Buffon, with whom Crèvecoeur spent time with in 1782–1783 while in Paris, from *A Natural History, General and Particular*:

> The climate may be regarded as the chief cause of the different colours of men. But food, though it has less influence upon colour, greatly affects the form of our bodies. Coarse, unwholesome, and ill-prepared food, makes the human species degenerate. All those people who live miserably are ugly and ill made. Even in France the country people are not so beautiful as those who live in towns; and I have often remarked, that in those villages where the people are richer and better fed than in others, the men are likewise more handsome and have better countenances. The air and soil have great influences upon the figure of men, beasts, and plants. In the same province, the inhabitants of the elevated and hilly parts are more active, nimble, handsome, ingenious, and beautiful, than those who live in the plains, where the air is thick and less pure. In France, it is impossible to perpetuate the race of Spanish or Barbary horses: they degenerate even in the first generation, and in the third of fourth, unless the breed be crossed by the importation of fresh stallions, they become altogether French horses. The effects of climate and of food upon animals are so well known, that we need hardly mention them; and though their operation is slower and less apparent upon men; yet from analogy, we ought to conclude, that their effects are not less certain, and that they manifest themselves in all the varieties we find among the human species.[25]

Later in *Letters*, a Russian gentleman who visits famed botanist "John Bertram" (John Bartram) articulates a similar vision regarding the efficacy of the environment. He suggests that "either nature or the climate seems to be more favourable [in Pennsylvania] to the arts and sciences than to any other American province" (*L* 187). Although they do not mention racial classification specifically, the Russian and Mr. Bertram discuss the plant classification system of Carl von Linné. Linnaeus—not at all incidentally—was one of the first eighteenth-century natural historians to posit, as I discussed in the introduction, that the varieties of humankind arose from the way that different corners of the globe helped shape the corporeal surface.[26] While these examples may not speak directly of the environment's producing certain physical characteristics that are then read as one's "race," this discourse that links nature, climate, and surroundings is nevertheless coincident with the rhetoric used to describe how the environment impacts one's body and racial identity.[27]

Such sentiments are echoed when Farmer James declares in Letter III that "men are like plants" (*L* 71). James speaks in simile here, but natural historians considered and classified both men *and* vegetation in a similar manner. For them, just as plants are native to certain areas, particular types of people are formed through their interaction with specific geographic regions. Migration—both voluntary and forced—occasioned the problem of what would happen to European whites and African blacks relocated among the indigenous peoples of the Americas.

In "What is an American?" Farmer James suggests that European whites undergo a change that is racial in nature—making them markedly different from their European forebears but, importantly, still white. The American people, he writes, "are a mixture of English, Scotch, Irish, French, Dutch, Germans, and Swedes. From this promiscuous breed, that race now called Americans have arisen" (*L* 68). Certainly, this "new race" comes from "that strange mixture of blood" (*L* 69) of all these white Europeans, an early artic-ulation of America as the "melting pot."[28] However, the race "arise(s)" *also* because of its location on American soil. Given Crèvecoeur's knowledge of the language and theories of natural-historical racial formation, his use of plant imagery is not merely a rhetorical trope, but also a scientific observation that signifies literally. Natural historians used this type of language to describe the development of both vegetative and human life. Indeed, Kant writes that "in the course of wanderings and transplantations of animals and plants it seems to produce new sorts which, however, are nothing more than deviations and races of one and the same genus, whose germs and natural dispositions have merely developed appropriately at long periods in various ways;" he also uses "transplantations" to describe migratory movements of people.[29] In America, James attests, "Everything has tended to regenerate them: new laws, a new mode of living, a new social system; here they are become men: in Europe they were as so many useless plants, wanting vegetative mould and refreshing showers; they withered, and were mowed down by want, hunger, and war; but now, by the power of transplantation, like all other plants they have taken root and flourished!" (*L* 68–69).[30] James describes a two-part process: "Individuals of all nations are melted into a new race of men," but this race is also formed through "being received in the broad lap of our great Alma Mater" (*L* 70). Here, Mother Earth is the "nurturing Mother."[31]

Although *Letters* has been claimed by some literary critics as a national-istic text, the new "American" of whom James speaks is decidedly *not* a US citizen, as many might think of the term *American* today.[32] Rather, James de-scribes the "American" as a racialized condition that—still a British subject[33]—ironically would become a prerequisite for the national consciousness that was developing at the time Crèvecoeur was writing. As Benedict Anderson points out, Englishmen in the metropole considered American creoles—British nationals born in the Americas—"*irremediably*" inferior because of their births in "a savage hemisphere."[34] Because its "climate and 'ecology' had a constitutive impact on culture and character," this locale rendered American creoles "different from, and inferior to, the metropolitans."[35] James, in turn, reclaims the New World landscape as a beneficent environment in which to grow these new Americans who, for him, still remain British subjects.

Nevertheless, as Anderson makes clear, this "difference" between the creole and metropolitan—one, I contend, that James racializes here—serves as the basis of a "creole nationalism" that was developing in the colonies and would lead to a specific nation-state identity.[36] This racialized "American" identity plays a constitutive role in the way that a specifically "national" identity was coming to be, but in *Letters* it is not a fully formed nation-state identity, as scholarship once considered it to be. This "surprising metamorphosis" arises from being located in the new surroundings, encompassing both the natural habitat and the mode of living, which includes laws, government, and industry. "Americans," James writes, "were once scattered all over Europe; here they are incorporated into one of the finest systems of population which has ever appeared, and which will hereafter become distinct by the power of the different climates they inhabit" (*L* 70). James, as we shall see in the last letter, does not advocate a break from England. For him, Americanness is a racial identity that arises organically from the ground that makes possible a national identity that would eventually come into being—but not a national identity constituted by an unnatural rupture from the mother country.[37]

If *Letters'* European audience fears that white men decline in the New World, James describes the American environment as changing people racially, but making them into a distinctive, improved, and still light-skinned American race. The text does, however, consider the possibility that one *could* be darkened and degenerated in the colonies. James admits as much in this same letter. He writes that if "British America . . . does not afford that variety of tinges and gradations which may be observed in Europe, we have colours peculiar to ourselves. For instance, it is natural to conceive that those who live near the sea must be very different from those who live in the woods; the intermediate space will afford a separate and distinct class" (*L* 70–71). James follows this with an oft-quoted passage in which his environmentalist language reaches its apex: "Men are like plants; the goodness and flavour of the fruit proceeds from the peculiar soil and exposition in which they grow. We are nothing but what we derive from the air we breathe, the climate we inhabit, the government we obey, the system of religion we profess, and the nature of our employment" (*L* 71).[38]

When James tries to describe the "back settlers," he concedes that "the manners of the Indian natives are respectable compared with this European medley. . . . they grow up a mongrel breed, half civilized, half savage, except nature stamps on them some constitutitional propensities" (*L* 77). The settlers' "breed" seems to be both inherited and impacted by nature's "stamp": "Eating of wild meat, whatever you may think, tends to alter their temper, though all the proof I can adduce is that I have seen it . . ." (*L* 77). This diet, along with a lack of religious community, leads to the decline of the backwoods settlers. "Is it, then," James asks, "surprising to see men thus situated, immersed in great and heavy labours, degenerate a little?" (*L* 77). Although he starts out to show Raynal and all of Europe how America can support a white race—and, indeed, form its own version of whiteness through intermarriage and environmental influence—he ends up acknowledging that the surroundings can transform the white man into the Native.[39] James further notes that "our bad people are those who are half cultivators and half hunters; and the worst of them are those who have degenerated altogether into the hunting state. As old ploughmen and new men of the woods, as Europeans and new-made Indians, they contract the vices of both; they adopt the moroseness and ferocity of a native, without his mildness or even his industry at home" (*L* 77-78). James concludes that "as soon as men cease to remain at home and begin to lead an erratic life, let them be either tawny or white, they cease to be [religion's] disciples" (*L* 78). Some back settlers are affected more than others, depending on the "nation or province [to which] they belong," but they are always pictured in—and defined by—the process of moving from one racial state into another.

This idea of "contracting vices" and contagion—one that resonates with APS member Benjamin Rush's later "Account of the Vices peculiar to the Savages of North America" as I discussed in Chapter 2—returns in James's final letter. Here, he and his family are hemmed in by the violence of the Revolutionary War. Because James abstains from choosing sides in the revolution, he seeks to flee what he deems the madness of the conflict. When he decides to retreat into "the great forest of Nature" to join an unnamed, peaceful American Indian tribe, he relishes the fact that his family will reside among "inhabitants [who] live with more ease, decency, and peace" (*L* 211).[40] He hopes that his family's "mutual affection for each other will in this great transmutation become the strongest link of our new society, will afford us every joy we can receive on a foreign soil . . ." (*L* 211).[41] However, describing these Natives as "a people whom Nature has stamped with such different characteristics" (*L* 211), James also begins to wonder if Nature will impress him and his family with these very same traits.

The language of metamorphosis recurs in this letter, an epistle that is a litany of anxieties punctuated with reassurances about racial change. If James begins *Letters* by celebrating how America's Nature would impact European bodies, here he agonizes over the fact that those impressionable bodies could just as easily turn dark. For, as he begrudgingly admitted earlier, if the backwoods settlers might degenerate, what is to keep him and his family from doing the same? He recounts stories of white parents whose children were returned to them after enduring Indian captivity. These parents, James laments, often "found them so perfectly Indianized that many knew them no longer" (*L* 213). Even adult captives, he concedes, often choose to stay with Indian tribes once they are set free. "It cannot be, therefore, so bad as we generally conceive it to be;" he insists, "there must be in their social bond something singularly captivating and far superior to anything to be boasted of among us; for thousands of Europeans are Indians, and we have no examples of even one of those aborigines having from choice become Europeans!" (L 214).[42] James nevertheless worries that his children might become so "thoroughly naturalized to this wild course of life" (L 214) that they would never "[return] to the manners and customs of their parents" (L 219), and he plans ways to forestall what he considers his impending racial transformation. To keep his children from being "seize[d]" with the "imperceptible charm of Indian education," James plans "to employ them in the labour of the fields" (L 219). Because hunting and eating game produce "this strange effect" of "becoming wild," James says he will keep his family "busy in tilling the earth" (L 220). If Benjamin Franklin and Hendrick Aupaumut tend to dismiss the effect one's mode of living has on one's race, Crèvecoeur and, as we shall see, Marrant and Brown explore the ways in which one's practices help determine it.

Further, despite his "respect" for the "inoffensive society of these people," James confesses that "the strongest prejudices would make me abhor any alliance with them in blood, disagreeable no doubt to Nature's intentions, which have strongly divided us by so many indelible characters" (L 222). Thus, he endeavors to bring a suitor for his daughter along with them. Here, where James couples a flexible understanding of racial identity with a sense of it "in [the] blood" (L 222), twenty-first century readers find an uncannily familiar understanding of race as a biological state produced by and inherited from one's parents' conjugal union. Indeed, it is this sense of race that we find in later American literature, such as when Cooper's Natty Bumppo (self-described as a "man without a cross") denigrates interracial sex and the consequent mixed-raced progeny it produces. However, we should not let this more recognizable sense of race "in the blood" obscure how James—contradictorily and ambivalently—sometimes intertwines these two different ways of conceptualizing racial difference.[43] For James, racial identity is not influenced solely by intermarriage and the crossing of bloodlines. Otherwise, he would not keep obsessing over how his family's move might change them. Although he professes that Nature marks people with "indelible characteristics," he nevertheless suspects that the "divide" between whites and Natives may not be so strong after all.[44] He writes that "thus shall we metamorphose ourselves from neat, decent, opulent planters . . . into a still simpler people divested of everything beside hope, food, and the raiment of the woods: abandoning the large framed house to dwell under the wigwam, and the featherbed to lie on the mat or bear's skin" (L 222). In this passage, James seems to be content with this type of metamorphosis, but the racial reasoning he uses earlier—that men degenerate after eating "wild meat" and living in Nature (a concern also taken up by Brown)—returns.

Because James closes his letter before removing his family among this Native tribe, his readers never know what ultimately transpires. The Revolution exerts such pressure on James that he compulsively worries over becoming "lost in the anticipation of the various circumstances attending this proposed metamorphosis!" (*L* 225). The logic of transformable race that underwrites Europeans becoming American in the first half of *Letters* necessarily demands that—according to the same reasoning—backwoods settlers and James himself will probably *become* Natives when living *as* Natives. Both the possibilities and dangers inherent in this potential racial metamorphosis are linked to the violence of the Revolutionary War; James's dread of the underside of racial transformation (i.e., becoming savage) connects to his reluctance to embrace the patriots' break with the mother country—a linkage vividly highlighted here.

Since the European becomes American and backwoods settlers become Natives in part due to the influence of the American natural environment, it is also of particular importance that James suspiciously "naturalizes" the existence of slavery in the New World. In his ninth letter, he grapples with agrarian slave labor in the US south. As Dana Nelson points out, James blames the fact of slavery on "Nature" itself.[45] Here, his use of *nature* denotes both human disposition (with its "inclinations" and "propensities") and the physical landscape ("fruitful soil") [*L* 174]. In this letter, James encounters a slave caged above the ground outside of Charleston. Nature—which heretofore had supported the magnificence found in America—is unable to ward off the evil of slavery.[46] Lamenting the peculiar institution, James exclaims, "Strange order of things! Oh, Nature, where are thou? Are not these blacks thy children as well as we?" (*L* 169). As numerous scholars have noted, nature in this letter differs distinctively from the way in which James characterizes it in his other letters.[47] Indeed, it disappoints men, for "if Nature has given us a fruitful soil to inhabit, she has refused us such inclinations and propensities as would afford us the full enjoyment of it" (*L* 174). Here, James revises his earlier optimism, chastising his reader and himself by asking, "Where do you conceive, then, that nature intended we should be happy?" (*L* 177). As Nelson writes,

> James now orates on "the history of the earth" and in a fascinating twist of logic . . . is able actually to conclude that it is the very *cruelty of Nature* that creates slavery, allowing white Americans—barbarously or benignly—to enslave black Africans. . . . His "general review of human nature" thus confirms indeed that all men are slaves, that slavery is but relative; that human tyranny and the practice of slavery are ordained *by* Nature. And Nature here is something that can be objectively recorded by impartial observers but not challenged.[48]

James thus naturalizes what is a *social* institution in order to abnegate himself from agency and responsibility.

James does so in both his attribution of slavery to human nature and his incorporation of it into the landscape. Pointedly, the way in which he characterizes nature and slavery here is inextricably linked to the way he writes about nature and the New World transformation available for white Europeans in his third letter. Indeed, he metaphorically connects slavery to how the environment affects man. In James's imagery, slaves' bodies become part of the landscape and quite literally feed the earth. He writes that "no one thinks with compassion of those showers of sweat and of tears which from the bodies of Africans daily drop and moisten the ground they till" (L 168). The American environment is enabled by the essential fluids of black labor that saturate the earth. Thus, within James's logic, if the American natural landscape enables a New World transformation for white American men who are "like plants," its transformable qualities are made possible by black slave bodies.[49] In other words, if, in Letter III, the ground enables the European's racial transformation in the British colonies, then the practice of slavery makes this possible.

For James, the way that slave labor relates to New World transformation materializes when he travels through the woods outside Charleston. On his way to dine with friends, James encounters the "shocking spectacle" of a perishing black slave suspended in a cage, where "large birds of prey" have "picked out his eyes" (L 178). This scene presents a predicament that the text and that Farmer James cannot seem to resolve. If the New World landscape enables the transformation of Europeans to Americans, the tortured slave, curiously caged above the ground, is restricted from receiving the same kind of nourishment. While the land can help transmute different Old World nationalities, it cannot accommodate the black slave who must hang, fixed and racially immutable, above the soil. Metaphorically, he is incapable of becoming anything other than what he already is: simply a dying "Negro" (L 178).[50]

The image of the suspended cage is striking, not least because flesh-eating birds feeding on the slave's dying body obscure him from view. The cage, hanging in the air, literalizes the way that the black slave does not benefit from being "rooted" in the supporting American environment *even as* his very body fluid moistens it.[51] Just like the sweat and tears from numerous slaves that steeped the earth, here, the slave's "blood slowly dropped and tinged the ground beneath" (L 178). Far from a minor detail, this aspect of the slave's captivity reveals the gothic underpinnings of an American nature: slavery's human parasitism is literalized. The decomposing flesh and blood of the black slave feed the natural landscape which supports the plantlike white men who seek natural "American" transformations, but the sweat, tears, and blood of black slaves enter the ground and ironically also become part of the environment that can darken whites in the New World. In James's world, then, nature at once fails to eliminate the system of slavery while its own nurturing and transformative capabilities are enabled by James's naturalized version of that very same system. In James's depiction, the American metamorphosis available for European men is predicated on the suspension and fixity of the black "Negro."

John Marrant Becoming Cherokee

John Marrant paints a very different picture. In his *Narrative of the Lord's Wonderful Dealings with John Marrant, a Black* (1785), the wilderness outside of Charleston becomes the precise place where black men might experience a racial metamorphosis. Marrant's *Narrative* chronicles his childhood as a free black in British North America, his Christian conversion, his capture by the Cherokee tribe, and his acculturation to life within the Indian nation. When Marrant later returns to his family in full Cherokee attire, he remains virtually unrecognized. As I will show, Marrant bases his racial transformation on two rubrics: first, a natural-historical belief that adopting another people's "mode of life" would make a person into one of those peoples; and, second, the eighteenth-century Cherokee conception that living with, being incorporated into, and assuming the cultural accoutrements of the tribe turns one into a Native. Marrant's overlaying of these two epistemologies makes his act not one of passing as something he is not but, rather, transforming into something he becomes. If Crèvecoeur's *Letters* investigates the conflicted ways that racial transformation might play out in America, Marrant's *Narrative* raises questions about how this alteration occurs. Is it according to a natural-historical paradigm? Or could it happen according to a Native epistemology, or, perhaps, some combination of the two? In addition to engaging these questions, Marrant's depiction of his "becoming Indian" in Charleston just before the outbreak of the US Revolutionary War distances him from any nascent white or "American" identity and allows him to associate himself with the British.

Like *Letters from an American Farmer*, Marrant's *Narrative* was one of the most popular books of the 1780s. Becoming one of the top three captivity narratives in early America, it went into six editions in three years.[52] While their narrative structures are quite different, both texts imagine life among a Native tribe and envision Charleston's potential as a site of black transformation. However, while Crèvecoeur depicts the town as a literal place of fixity for black men, Marrant figures it as a space of transformation. In addition, the *Narrative* has a level of tribal specificity that *Letters* lacks in its last epistle. Readers do not know any details about the unspecified tribe to which Farmer James contemplates removing.[53] In contrast, Marrant illustrates particular aspects of the Cherokee worldview when recounting his return from their tribe to "civilization." Furthermore, while Farmer James fears "Indianization" and plots against it, Marrant portrays it as the natural, logical, and even desired result of a prolonged stay among the Indians. Indeed, the length of his time as a Cherokee is less about disguising himself for a certain duration than about becoming something different from his prior, and also temporary, state of blackness. Thus, the fact that Marrant transforms into the Native for a limited period of time accentuates the notion that any racial state was considered to be necessarily temporal in the late eighteenth century.

Narrative relates the story of young John Marrant, a free black born in New York who relocates to South Carolina with his mother. Both a conversion story and a captivity narrative, Marrant's text offers a seemingly simple account. Although he "intended [that he] should be put apprentice to some trade," he instead decides to train as a musician.[54] He makes a good living playing at local events, leading, however, to his "drinking in iniquity like water" and becoming "a slave to every vice suited to [his] nature and to [his] years" (*LWD* 50).[55] One night while en route to "play for some Gentlemen," Marrant comes upon a "large meeting house." His friend persuades him to interrupt the preaching (what Marrant calls "a crazy man . . . hallooing in there") by blowing his French-horn (*LWD* 51). Just as Marrant raises the horn to his mouth, the "crazy man"—the notable Rev. George Whitefield himself—calls out, "PREPARE TO MEET THY GOD, O ISRAEL" (*LWD* 51). Feeling that Whitefield looks "directly upon [him], and pointing with his finger," Marrant falls "both speechless and senseless near half an hour" (*LWD* 51). After being carried home, Marrant remains ill for three days until a minister sent by Whitefield converts Marrant to Christianity, thereby restoring his health.

While his conversion promises salvation, when Marrant returns to his mother's home outside of Charleston, his family mistreats him because of his new-found religiosity. In fact, their behavior toward him persuades Marrant "to go from home altogether" (*LWD* 56). Taking his Bible and an Isaac Watts' hymnbook along with him, Marrant heads off into the wilderness. Despite his troubles traveling in the back country, Marrant testifies that "the Lord Jesus Christ was very present, and that comforted me through the whole" (*LWD* 58). One day while he is walking through the woods, an "Indian hunter" stops him to ask if he knows how far he has wandered from home. Marrant informs him how he "was supported by the Lord" during his travel, even though the Indian can't see this god. The hunter then reveals that he knows Marrant and his relatives from his time spent trading "skins" in Charleston. Since Marrant does not want to return to his family, he is convinced to travel along with his new acquaintance. By the time they arrive at "a large Indian town, belonging to the Cherokee nation," Marrant has "acquired a fuller knowledge of the Indian tongue" (*LWD* 59).[56]

Once in the town, the tribe separates Marrant from his fellow traveler and demands that he account for his presence there or be put to death. Failing to provide a satisfactory answer, Marrant is jailed, and his execution is set for the next day. He is inspired to pray aloud in the Cherokee language, which, as he writes, "wonderfully affect[s] the people" (*LWD* 61). His invocation also converts the executioner, who immediately takes him to the king, where Marrant's presentation of his Bible and his testimony converts the king's daughter.[57] Just as Marrant did after hearing Whitefield's sermon, she suffers "bodily weakness," and the king threatens to kill Marrant if he cannot cure her. Marrant does so, and as a result of his subsequent prayer, a "great change [takes] place among the people; the king's house [becomes] God's house." The king and his fellow Natives convert to Christianity, and at this exact moment, Marrant becomes "treated like a prince." He "assume[s] the habit of the country, and [dresses] much like the king . . ." (*LWD* 64).

Experiencing such success converting the Cherokee, Marrant takes up itinerant preaching among the Creek, Choctaw, and Chickasaw tribes. He notes that "when they recollect, that the white people drove them from the American shores, they are full of resentment. These nations have often united, and murdered all the white people in the back settlements which they could lay hold of, men, women, and children" (*LWD* 64). As critics Joanna Brooks and Saillant point out, Marrant "link[s] Indian raids against white settlers to colonization and the usurpation of tribal lands,"[58] and, as we shall see, this linkage foreshadows the reception Marrant surprisingly receives as he makes his way toward Charleston. After a return to and prolonged stay with the Cherokee, he realizes he would like to go home to see his relatives. Initially frowning on this request, the king finally acquiesces. Marrant travels with Indian escorts much of the way, but he treks the final seventy miles to "the back settlements of the white people" (*LWD* 65) alone and unhindered.

A strange thing then happens. When Marrant comes upon a family eating dinner, they become frightened and run away. Undeterred and seemingly unsurprised by their fear, he proceeds to eat their meal *and only afterwards* endeavors to "see what was become of the family" (*LWD* 65). When a young girl sees him, she "faint[s] away" for "upwards of an hour" (*LWD* 65). Finally, Marrant coaxes them to come back to the house, and he finally reveals to the reader what triggers their terror: "My dress was purely in the Indian stile; the skins of wild beasts composed my garments; my head was set out in the savage manner, with a long pendant down my back[,] a sash round my middle, without breeches, and a tomahawk by my side" (*LWD* 65). Then, despite his savage appearance and odd behavior of feasting on the supper of people who had been scared away from their own table, Marrant gathers several families together for "prayer on the Sabbath days" (*LWD* 65). The black wanderer has become the Indian preacher.

As Marrant continues home, he runs into extended family members who do not recognize him. His uncle, refusing him lodging, relates how Marrant's mother was grieving the loss of her son. One of his "old school-fellows" tells how he thought his former friend had been "torn in pieces by the wild beasts" (*LWD* 66), since Marrant's relatives had found a mutilated carcass in the woods. When Marrant finally arrives at his mother's house, he recounts that the "singularity of my dress drew every body's eyes upon me, yet none knew me" (*LWD* 66). Unrecognized by his mother and older siblings, only Marrant's youngest sister "recollect[s]" him. After being chastised for claiming that the "wild man" is her brother, she asks him directly. When he answers yes, Marrant writes that "thus the dead was brought to life again; thus the lost was found" (*LWD* 67).

Numerous literary critics have noted how various scenes in Marrant's narrative are typologically patterned on several Biblical stories: those of Jesus, Daniel, Lazarus, Paul, John the Baptist, and, perhaps most significantly in the reunion scene, Joseph.[59] However, the typological relationship between Marrant's *Narrative* and the Biblical story of Joseph is not as straightforward as it first seems. While Marrant convincingly has been placed in religious contexts by a number of able scholars, I suggest that this focus obscures a deeper understanding of the interaction Marrant chronicles between himself and the Cherokee tribe,[60] including his Cherokee captivity, his time spent among the various Southeastern tribes, and his learning of Cherokee ways.[61] Marrant's repeated emphasis on the Cherokee dress he wears upon reentry into "civilized" society is not only a typological allusion to Joseph but also a reference to Cherokee understandings of how one might transform from being "black" to "Native."[62]

Eighteenth-century Cherokee culture did not think of race as being located solely on the body, as many of their non-Native contemporaries, influenced by natural-historical theories, did. The understanding of what makes one a member of a tribe is a matter of Native sovereignty, and it can differ radically from tribe to tribe *and* within the same tribe over time.[63] Clan membership—rather than bodily traits—constituted what it meant to "be Cherokee" for Native peoples at this time.[64] (Interestingly, this was the Cherokee understanding of the constitution of a particular identity that non-Native culture understood as racial.) Because the Cherokee had a matrilineal culture where clan determines one's place within the tribe, the children of white traders and Cherokee women stayed with the mother's family to be raised according to its customs, and mothers had complete authority over their children's schooling (*Racial* 35). These offspring usually grew up in their indigenous culture and remained with the Cherokee tribe, regardless of whether their fathers stayed (although many actually did). While white society termed these descendants "mixed-blood," the Cherokees just thought of them as "Indian" (*Racial* 25). Furthermore, as ethnohistorian Theda Perdue argues, the Cherokee willingly adopted many non-Natives into their tribes and "attempted to convert [captive African Americans and whites] who remained with them into Indians" (*Racial* 7). With the Cherokee, once one was adopted into a clan system, took on Native practices, and became initiated into the tribe, in their eyes, one *became* Cherokee.[65] As Perdue explains, "from the Native perspective . . . Europeans who were adopted, literally became Cherokee and Creek respectively because they became relatives . . ." (*Racial* 9). (The same could be said of African Americans who were lucky enough, as I will explore below, to be adopted into the tribe [*Racial* 4–11].)

As much ethnohistoriography shows, ritual plays a key role in how non-Natives could be brought into various tribes. The "rituals of adoption" could include stripping, bathing, and painting the non-Native-*cum*-Native (Dowd, *SR* 13). As Perdue puts it, "Native nations enjoyed both political and cultural sovereignty in the eighteenth century, and they incorporated foreigners into their societies on their own terms and for their own purposes" (*Racial* 2). As she contends, "through ritual, Indians transformed people . . . into harmonious members of the community" (*Racial* 11). Specifically for antebellum African Americans, acquiring the Cherokee language, ingesting traditional Cherokee food, and donning Cherokee dress were all ways that they became Indianized.[66] These customs were also practiced in other tribes, such as the Iroquois, where "transfers in clothing accomplished the transformation to a new identity."[67]

While white natural historians and Farmer James suspected that exposure to a Native "mode of living" could change one's racial characteristics, some Indians felt that becoming Native could occur by rituals of incorporation. Cherokee, unlike natural historians, did not credit environmentalism with causing changes to the body's appearance. Instead, for them, through adoption rituals, a sartorial change refashions one's identity.[68]

However, Marrant's *Narrative* brings these two ideas together when he describes his integration into Cherokee society: "A great change took place among the people . . . [I] had perfect liberty, and was treated like a prince. . . . I remained nine weeks in the king's palace, praising God day and night: I was never out but three days all the time. I had assumed the habit of the country, and was dressed much like the king. . . . Here I learnt to speak their tongue in the highest stile" (*LWD* 64). Marrant's ritualistic change in clothes is simultaneous with his integration into the family. He dresses "like the king" and is accepted into the family as a son ("like a prince"). Furthermore, in Marrant's description, *habit* serves as the conceptual nexus linking together ideas about dress, repeated practices, and the constitution of the body. The *OED* tells us that "habit" means "fashion or mode of apparel" or "dress," and here Marrant certainly describes his raiment. However, *habit* also denotes "custom" or "usage," even to the point of "a settled disposition or tendency to act in a certain way, esp. one acquired by frequent repetition of the same act until it becomes almost or quite involuntary; a settled practice." Containing this meaning as well, Marrant's use of *habit* links it to the "modes of living" or social practices that many natural historians thought could affect one's racial status (in addition to indicating one's "habitation"). Lastly, and most strikingly, *habit* also refers to one's "bodily condition or constitution" and "the outer part, surface, or external appearance of the body." Each of these three ideas is embedded and mutually imbricated in the etymology of the word *habit*. Thus, when Marrant says that he "assumed the habit of the country," he indicates that he dressed like the Cherokee, that he practiced their "mode of living" (such as learning their language), and that he took on the constitution or appearance of the Cherokee body.

The reference to Cherokee clothing differentiates Marrant's return from that of the Biblical Joseph in this key respect. Like Marrant, Joseph receives a new set of clothes from the Pharaoh as a sign of his acceptance into the Egyptian community. However, when Joseph's brothers unwittingly reunite with him in Egypt, the Genesis narrator does not mention Joseph's clothing. In contrast, Marrant's scene with the frightened family actually withholds the fact of his Cherokee garb, only to reveal it strikingly at the anecdote's conclusion. Marrant's *Narrative* also differs importantly from Joseph's story in that, unlike Joseph, Marrant is never sold into slavery. This fact would have struck eighteenth-century readers, as the Cherokee tribe was known to engage at times in aspects of and also to practice slavery themselves.[69] Since the 1730 Treaty of Dover between the Cherokee and England, the Cherokee pledged to return runaway slaves, but "they did disappoint British expectations at various times by aiding runaways, by keeping black slaves for themselves, and by adopting Africans into their own families."[70] In this case, Marrant was safe in part because the hunter he first meets recognizes him as a free black from Charleston and also because the grateful king welcomes Marrant into the tribe. Not in danger of being sold into slavery by the Cherokee, Marrant's incorporation is central to his narrative.[71]

This close affiliation between Marrant and the Cherokee and his sartorial alteration undergone in the wilderness frame the homecoming scenes toward the end of the *Narrative*. Because some Native Americans considered this change of clothes to be partly constitutive of identity, the garb does not disguise the "'real' me underneath," as Deloria might say. Rather, what we might call the "transformed me" is *produced through* the wearing of the new clothes.

Marrant also explores how this racial transformation could be temporary. He leads his readers to believe that he reverts to his former life, removes his Cherokee attire, and returns to being what the *Narrative*'s title page emphasizes: "JOHN MARRANT, A BLACK."[72] He begins preaching, including to slaves on the Jenkins plantation in Cumbee, and is impressed into service for the British forces at "the commencement of the American troubles" (*LWD* 68). He participates in the British siege of Charleston and remains unharmed.[73] Furthermore, when the British commander General Clinton rides into town, he is accompanied by Marrant's "old royal benefactor and convert, the king of the Cherokee Indians," who immediately knows Marrant and dismounts to greet him in the street (*LWD* 72).[74]

One must note that his association with Cherokees and transformation into an Indian does not ultimately produce a white American identity. Rather, the tableaux of Marrant's greeting the king of the Cherokee (who mostly sided with the British during the war) and the British commander in the midst of a city under the control of the English characterizes Marrant as a black man associated closely with the British empire.[75] Relatedly, the text presents a view of Charleston that contrasts with Crèvecoeur's. In *Letters*, although its slave-holding practices morally degrade Charleston, James' caged Negro scene metaphorically depicts slave resistance as contained above the South Carolinian ground in the figure of the caged black man.[76] In contrast, the *Narrative* alludes to black radicalism associated with Charleston, particularly the free and escaped blacks who joined the British forces during the Revolutionary War, assisted in the 1780 siege of Charleston, and later evacuated from the new US nation-state.[77]

But how do we make sense of the fact that while Marrant's black relatives do not recognize him in his Indian dress, his sister and the king know him regardless of his dress and racial status? Or that this repeatedly transformed Marrant can be, counterintuitively, both recognizable and completely unknowable? Much of the answer lies in the fact that it *doesn't* make sense, which seems to be the point. On one level, various aspects of both natural-historical thought and Cherokee conceptions of tribal inclusion would come to be seen, by the early nineteenth century, as nonsensical, giving way to biologized racial science in one case and more concretized membership requirements in the other, which seemed to make "more sense" to folks at the time. On another level, it has to do with the way Marrant draws on two separate racial epistemologies, even as he does so unevenly. Perhaps the Cherokee king recognizes Marrant because he first knew him as a black man. Or, perhaps, like Marrant's young sister, he has not yet been indoctrinated into thinking about race and the body as "civilized" society was. In other words, perhaps the young sister and the Cherokee king do not take notice of certain traits that natural-historical thinking had trained others to look for; to them, John Marrant is not all that different, whether he is a Cherokee or "a Black." My aim here is not necessarily to prove that Marrant's skin "really" became red or that he "really" became a member of the Cherokee tribe (although either very well could be the case) but, rather, to emphasize that within the contexts of natural-historical thought and Cherokee eighteenth-century worldviews, the *Narrative* does not show Marrant disguising himself as an Indian, but it explores instead the various means through which he might transform into one.

While the *Narrative* importantly defines race as always in motion, a potentially temporary state to be maintained, it also explores the particular points of intersection between these incongruent ways of thinking about race, racial constitution, and racial transformation. These two systems of thought, though different, both concern themselves with the external appearance that is transformed and thus makes a new me—rather than one identity laid over another. This quality of his "surprising metamorphosis"—like Crèvecoeur's example—illustrates his "becoming" Indian according to the Cherokee epis-temology, rather than pretending to be Native. In the end, Marrant depicts a world in which various ways of racial transformation can be considered equally valid.

Edgar Huntly's Unsettling Transformation

While Marrant undergoes a transformation process while wandering in the woods outside Charleston, Charles Brockden Brown's eponymous main char-acter in *Edgar Huntly; or, Memoirs of a Sleep-Walker* (1799) finds himself ram-bling through the wilderness surrounding Norwalk, an area imagined to be in rural Pennsylvania. Although self-consciously fictional, Edgar's story parallels Marrant's in the sense that once he relocates to the backcountry, he finds that his exposure to Indians' practices, the lands on which they live, and, indeed, their blood changes his racial status to the point that he is no longer recogniz-able by those both strange and familiar to him. And, as I will explore below, like Crèvecoeur's *Letters* and Marrant's *Narrative*, Brown's novel draws upon the discourses of transformable race to unsettle rather than to articulate an American national identity.

Edgar Huntly features a tortuous and entangled plot, a hallmark of Brown's fiction. The novel itself is an extended letter from Edgar to his fiancé, Mary Waldegrave, in which he chronicles his efforts to solve the mystery behind the murder of her brother and his beloved friend, Waldegrave. While Edgar perambulates through the countryside seeking clues to Waldegrave's murder under a specific elm tree, he encounters Clithero Edny, an Irish immigrant apparently sleepwalking over the same ground. Edgar initially surmises that Clithero must have been Waldegrave's murderer, but upon confronting him, he learns that Clithero's disturbed sleep results not from an attempted murder of Huntly's friend but, rather, of Clithero's benefactress in Ireland, Mrs. Lorimer. Telling his own meandering tale, Clithero relates to Huntly that after accidentally killing Mrs. Lorimer's estranged twin brother, he hastened to her chamber to kill her. He believed he must do so in order to save her from hearing the news of her brother's death, one she always maintained would cause her own. Clithero's attempted murder is forestalled when Mrs. Lorimer herself stops Clithero from mistakenly stabbing Clarice, his own fiancé and Mrs. Lorimer's stepdaughter. Although she stops him from killing herself and Clarice, when Clithero tells Mrs. Lorimer that he has killed her brother, she swoons to the ground, and Clithero assumes she is dead. Clithero then ab-sconds to America to punish himself for his attempt on Mrs. Lorimer's life. After relating his story to Edgar, he decides anew to remove himself from his current situation as a laborer on a neighboring farm and to lose himself in the caverns of the wilderness. Edgar suspends his search for Waldegrave's murderer and instead pursues Clithero in order to convince him that he should not seek out his own death to punish what was, to Edgar's mind, an act not born out of malice but "dictated by a motive allied to virtue."[78]

After resolving to correct what he sees as Clithero's faulty logic, Edgar awakens one night to find himself inexplicably located at the bottom of a cavern. In the meantime, a band of Lenni-Lenape (or Delaware) Indians begin an attack on the settlers to retaliate against white colonization of their lands. During his quest back to Solebury, Edgar kills and eats a panther to stave off hunger, encounters and murders several Lenni-Lenape warriors, mistakes his townspeople for Indians and is in turn mistaken for an Indian, and finally returns to find his uncle dead from fighting the Native tribesmen. He reunites with his long-absent friend and father-figure Sarsefield. (Since Edgar last saw him years ago, Sarsefield has married and impregnated Mrs. Lorimer, who fainted rather than died upon hearing the news of her brother's demise). Edgar learns that it was an Indian warrior, not Clithero, who murdered Waldegrave, and that he, like Clithero, has begun to sleepwalk, which is how he unconsciously relocated himself to the cave. He resumes his quest to find and rectify Clithero's reasoning behind blaming himself for killing Mrs. Lorimer. In so doing, he inadvertently renews Clithero's mad drive to murder her. When Edgar hastily sends Sarsefield a warning of Clithero's mission, Mrs. Lorimer first reads the letter, and the shock of the news terminates her pregnancy. The novel ends with the brief account from Sarsefield relating that Clithero did not reach Mrs. Lorimer but instead was intercepted by Sarsefield and put on a boat to a Pennsylvania hospital. En route, Clithero threw himself overboard where, according to Sarsefield, Clithero "forced himself beneath the surface, and was seen no more" (*EH* 285).

Charles Brockden Brown weaves a multidimensional tale in *Edgar Huntly*, and literary critics remain divided on several key points. Scholars have pointed to either Federalist or Republican aspects of Brown's novels, and, more recently, others have argued that the novels themselves (and perhaps Brown's own politics) are not quite that easily classified.[79] Critics have also debated the degree to which Brown's work typifies that of an "Indian-hater" or whether through an ironic distance from a narrator who does not serve as his own personal mouthpiece, it criticizes the viewpoint of such a person.[80] On a related issue, critics disagree on how to read Brown's entanglement in or critique of the imperialist acts that his novel depicts.[81] Here I seek not to resolve these debates but, rather, to show how our comprehending the way Brown engages with the possibility of racial transformation in light of these problematics in his fiction allows us to understand *Edgar Huntly* with more complexity. To wit, the Gothic horror of Brown's work does not come from the clear endorsement of a particular political position but arises instead from how important questions are left to linger, unresolved, continually haunting the narrative even at the close of the story.

Although many scholars have noted how Edgar becomes "like" an Indian, I read Edgar's metamorphosis into an Indian as another example of the exploration of the natural-historical understanding of how a white man's race might undergo transformation in the New World. Here, I first explore Brown's deep and surprisingly underappreciated engagement with natural-historical thought, including his 1804 translation of Constantin François Chassebœuf Volney's 446-page *A View of the Soil and Climate of the United States*. I then turn to the implications that Edgar's transformation into an Indian has in terms of the queries it raises about the nature of racial difference, the ability of the US landscape to support white civilization, and the ultimate viability of the colonial project. Like literary scholar Jared Gardner, I focus on Edgar's change into an Indian in the second half of the novel and see Brown using the possibility of racial change and this "fear of contamination" from close proximity with the Lenni-Lenape tribe as the "central nightmare of the novel."[82] However, in his understanding of the return from what he calls Edgar's "racial cross-dressing," Gardner argues that Edgar's "exorcizing the alien (be he Indian or, . . . Irish) from the land allows American identity to come into existence."[83] Here I diverge from Gardner's influential reading to emphasize how Brown depicts the Indians Edgar encounters (or, as I will detail below, those his family displaced from their ancestral lands and whom Edgar over years comes to know and to emulate in several key ways) not so much as the "Other" Edgar kills off in order to constitute the American "me" but, rather, as the "potential me" that Edgar is always already becoming.[84] Indeed, Edgar's transformation radically questions the articulation of a white, American national identity and, furthermore, the viability of the US nation-state that such identity ostensibly signifies.[85] Readers are left to grapple with the questions behind so much of environmentalist thinking: If the white man displaces the Native man from his land, and the land influences the human form, what will become of this white man? Or the land? And the nation-state he so recently founded? Brown probes these questions, and, as I will suggest below, offers his readers anything but a definitive and thus reassuring answer.

PUBLICATION, TRANSLATION, ANNOTATION, AND REVIEW:
CHARLES BROCKDEN BROWN'S TEXTUAL ENGAGEMENT
WITH NATURAL HISTORY

Although we are not used to thinking of him as a natural historian and while he did not himself write a natural-philosophical treatise, Charles Brockden Brown had a thoroughgoing engagement with the publication of natural-historical thought. One of the reasons we should seriously approach the way Brown depicts Edgar becoming Native American via natural-historical ideas is because of the seriousness with which Brown himself treated natural history. Growing up as a Quaker in Philadelphia around the time of the Revolution,

Brown was exposed to a wide variety of political, scientific, religious, and philosophical thinking. As scholars have shown, Brown read, learned, and thought about topics as heterogeneous as physiognomy, geography, Godwinian philosophy, and theories of sensibility, just to name a few.[86] Of particular importance here, Brown not only was cognizant of debates occurring over the origins of the varieties of humankind; he also published, translated, annotated, and reviewed numerous and important texts of natural history. A reader of Linnaeus, Buffon, Blumenbach, and Benjamin Rush, Brown was generally well-aware of the work of influential natural historians and their explanations of the differences among humankind.[87] As Bryan Waterman has so meticulously shown in *Republic of Intellect*, Brown was deeply influenced by his time spent as part of New York City's Friendly Club, a social circle comprised of members with varied intellectual outlooks, several of whom took up natural-historical thinking. For example, Brown was influenced by Rush through his involvement in the Friendly Club.[88] In addition, several Friendly Club members—including Elihu Hubbard Smith, central member of the Friendly Club, a former student of Rush's, and an intimate friend of Brown—challenged polygenesis in order to undermine scientific arguments used to support the slave trade.[89] Both Smith and Brown were also aware of natural historian Erasmus Darwin's *Zoonomia* and his translation of Linnaeus's work.[90] In the periodicals he himself edited, Brown often published news pieces concerning and articulating natural-historical arguments and printed materials from the American Philosophical Society; in addition, his serialized fiction sometimes appeared alongside natural philosophical pieces. While Brown himself may not have wholeheartedly endorsed a particular explanation for the cause of racial difference, his knowledge of and, in a material sense, his distribution of these different ideas help contextualize the transformation that Edgar undergoes in *Edgar Huntly*.

In the February 24, 1798, *Weekly Magazine*, an "Account of a singular Change of Colour in a Negro" reports on Henry Moss's incremental change in skin color from black to white, as I discussed in the introduction.[91] As Jay Fleigelman points out (specifically in relationship to Brown's novel *Wieland*), this report not only appeared in a magazine that published pieces of Brown's fiction prior to the publication of *Edgar Huntly*; it also undoubtedly influenced Brown's thinking on topics such as transformation.[92] As the article recounts, one of the first queries Moss's examiners have about the cause of his change in appearance was "whether the change had been effected by any alteration in his mode of life or diet," although they subsequently decide that it had not. The account itself concludes with a call for the abolition of slavery by suggesting that from "the history ... of the change of a negro to a white man" it logically follows that "the change from *white* to *black* must be admitted as equally possible," thus possibly leading to (presently) white peoples ultimately being enslaved. As I suggested in the introduction and will take up again in my analysis of the work of Hugh Henry Brackenridge, the Henry Moss case is fascinating in its own right, but what is pertinent here is how influential this case was on peoples' thinking about race *and*, given Edgar's own transformation, how it is first assumed that Moss's change occurred because of "mode of life" or "diet."

In 1799 in the *Monthly Magazine* that he edited, Brown republished an excerpt from Johann Friedrich Blumenbach's "Observations on the Conformation and Capacity of the Negroes."[93] The article itself argues that "the negroes, in their mental faculties, are not inferior to the rest of the human race" and does so in part by comparing various "negro skulls" and by mentioning the literary work of a "female negro, who was a poetess" (whom scholars generally identify as Phillis Wheatley), Francis Williams, and Ignatius Sancho. Although Blumenbach's earlier craniometry work leaned more toward polygenesis than monogenesis (and would influence later scientific racism), he also was well-known for attributing color to external circumstances, as for instance when he wrote in *On the Natural Variety of Mankind* in 1775 that "colour, whatever be its cause, be it bile, or the influence of the sun, the air, or the climate, is, at all events, an adventitious and easily changeable thing, and can never constitute a diversity of species."[94]

Later, in April 1800 in the *Monthly Magazine*, Brown ran a portion of physician Benjamin Rush's infamous "Observations Intended to Favour a Supposition That the Black Color (As It Is Called) of the Negroes Is Derived from the Leprosy," originally printed in the *Transactions of the America Philosophical Society*, which argued that Africans' blackness was a form of leprosy.[95] Although I discuss Rush's piece at length elsewhere in this study, suffice it to say here that the emphasis on "mode of life" and "diet" from the account of Moss's transformation recurs in Rush's reasoning: "Many facts recorded by historians and physicians show the influence of unwholesome diet in producing leprosy in the middle and northern parts of Europe, in the 13th and 14th centuries. The same cause, combined with greater heat, more savage manners, and bilious fevers, probably produced this disease among the natives of Africa." Rush also hypothesizes that due to the sometimes "infectious quality in the skin of a negro," close proximity—along with, he insinuates, sexual relations—can cause a white person to darken. "A white woman in North-Carolina acquired not only a dark colour, but several features of a negro, by marrying and living with a black man. A similar instance of change in colour and features of a woman in Buck's county, Pennsylvania, has been observed to arise from a similar cause. In both cases, the women bore children by their black husbands," Rush writes. While this piece focuses exclusively on white-black racial transformation, these themes recur throughout and frame Edgar's transformation.

But perhaps Brown's most thoroughgoing engagement with natural history occurred when, in 1804, he translated Volney's *A View of the Soil and Climate of the United States*. Volney was a well-known French natural philosopher who corresponded with and visited the plantation of Jefferson and would come to be a member of the APS.[96] Although published subsequent to *Edgar Huntly*, this text attests to Brown's ongoing interaction with natural-historical discourse around the topic of race. Brown quarrels with Volney over several points, and, as critics often point out, he defends many Native American tribes from Volney's denigrating assessments.[97] Volney's text outlines various arguments concerning racial difference and advances its own theory. Brown's translation of and occasional dissenting footnotes added to Volney's text exhibit several competing theories about racial transformation, even if the text as a whole does not make it clear if Brown endorses or dissents from each aspect of Volney's claims.

Volney offers a generally unflattering evaluation of the United States and its Native American inhabitants, and Brown's footnotes generally reprimand him for his unfavorable views.[98] Volney and Brown seem to disagree on whether one's natural environment or mode of life makes a bigger difference on one's constitution. When Volney claims that the high heat in Philadelphia causes its citizens to desert its streets from noon until five in the evening, Brown retorts that the afternoon nap "is taken only by the old, infirm, or indolent, and not by a larger proportion of the people than in the north of Europe."[99] Brown goes on to suggest that habits, rather than solely the natural environment, impacts a people:

> The truth is, that our manners do not accommodate themselves to the climate, either in winter or summer, but we follow, in most respects, the fashion of our ancestors, who came from the temperate atmosphere of Europe. Strangers, from the torrid zone, especially from the islands, complain exceedingly of the heats of Philadelphia, when the mercury reaches 85 degrees, though natives of that city read, write, or pursue their mechanical vocations, without sensible inconvenience, in a heat of from 86 to 89. (*View* 108)

Here using "natives" to mean Anglo-American creoles born in Philadelphia, Brown gives several examples of people who carry out their everyday tasks despite the heat: "These instances prove, at once, the great heats of the American climate, and the influence of constitution and bodily habit to enable the natives to support them. These principles operate beneficially, in spite of absurd modes in eating and dressing, and the almost general disuse of the bath" (*View* 108–9). Like natural historian Benjamin Smith Barton, with whom— as I shall discuss below—Brown generally agrees, Brown provides proof that the constitution and bodily habit of those descended from Europeans enable them to "support" (as in, "endure," *OED*) the American (and what the French considered "degenerate") environment.[100] In this instance, Anglos born in the New World are "native" to that environment but are only able to continue in the environment *as* Anglos because they practice the habits of their forebears (and not, one might suppose, of "Native Americans"), even if that includes wearing overly heavy clothing and eating "strong meats three times a day" (*View* 109).

Later, Volney muses on how each nation of men is best suited to its own climate:

> The Dane and the Englishman exclaim against the heat of the climate, which the Spaniard and Italian think temperate enough. The Pole and the Provencal complain of its moisture, while the Dutchman is rather inclined to think it too dry: each one, in these instances, being secretly governed by comparisons between what he sees with what he has been used to in his own country. . . .
>
> The Americans resent these censures of their climate almost as a personal offence. (*View* 261)

Brown responds that "Volney has given an air of mystery and singularity to a trite and universal fact, and makes no allowance *in this place* for the force of habit, which lessens the evils of a climate to the native, and aggravates them to the stranger" (*View* 262, emphasis in original). The underlying issue here, of course, is that the Americans are relatively new strangers-*cum*-"natives" in the New World climate, and it remains to be seen if their habits will actually "lessen the evils of a climate" that many claimed would degenerate white men into Natives. While they disagree on whether one's climate or one's habits within that climate affect the person to the greatest degree, it is of note that both writers assume that one's body is impacted by external circumstances (be it weather or practices) instead of solely dictated by one's "inside."

Volney's treatise most directly engages environmentalist ideas in his anecdote about Mishikinakwa (or Little Turtle), a Miami chief, and William Wells, a white man who lived among the Miami for many years and married Little Turtle's daughter.[101] Volney interviews them for information on the Miami language and tribe, and he "converse[s] with them on the climate and soil of the Miamis" (*View* 359). Then, even while speaking mainly with Wells, Volney inserts the following fascinating scene:

> While talking with Wells, I was not inattentive to the chief. Not understanding English, he took no part in the conversation, but walked about, plucking out the hairs from his chin, and even from his eye-brows. He dressed in the American style; in a blue suit, with round hat and pantaloons. I desired Mr. Wells to ask him how he liked his clothes. "At first," said he, "they confined my limbs unpleasantly; but I have got used to them; and as they defend me against *the heat* and the cold, I now like them well enough." Tucking up his sleeves, he showed me a skin, between the wrist and elbow, whose whiteness surprised me. It differed not at all from my own. My hands

were as much tanned as his, and we looked as we had a pair of gloves on. His skin was as soft and fair as a Parisian's.

We talked a good deal about the colour of the Indians. The copper or red hue is commonly supposed to be innate, and to discriminate this race, as black does the Africans; but I gathered from these interviews, that, though they distinguish themselves by the name of red men, and justly pride themselves on this distinction, yet they are born as white as we*, and continue so through infancy†, the copper hue being derived from exposure to the sun, and from the grease and juices with which they rub themselves. The women are always white about the middle, in those parts which are constantly covered. It is, therefore, far from true that the copper hue is innate to this people; nor indeed is it universal: on the contrary, many tribes of North America have different shades, and their diversity, in this respect, is one of their means of distinguishing each other.

Mr. Wells, who had lived, in their fashion, fifteen years among them, had their complexion. The real colour appeared to be that of soot, or of smoked ham, clear and shining, exactly similar to that of the peasants of Lower Poitou, who live like savages, in a hot, moist climate, or that of the Andalusians.

On mentioning this to Little Turtle, he replied: "That he had seen Spaniards in Louisiana, and saw no difference between their colour and his own. And why," said he, "should there be any? In them and us the sun, *the father of colours*, causes it by burning us. You yourselves see the difference between your faces and bodies." This reminded me that, when I quitted the turban, on leaving Turkey, half my forehead resembled bronze, while the other half, above it, was as white as paper. If, as philosophers believe, all colours flow from light, it is plain that the difference in human complexions is produced by the action of this fluid, in conjunction with some other, on the skin. It will one day be proved, that the sable hue of the negro arises from no other cause*.

_____ [Volney's footnotes:]
*So is the negro, but he grows black in a few hours.
†Oldmixon says the same.

_____

*New facts, corroborating this conclusion, daily occur. One of these is the remarkable case of Henry Moss, a negro of Virginia, descended in the third degree from natives of Congo, who, in the course of seven years, became white, with smooth brown hair, like any European. He is the same mentioned by Liancourt. (*View* 360–62)

This passage highlights several aspects of the debates occurring around the origin of racial difference. It at once claims that skin color is "commonly supposed to be innate" and also that it is something that develops over time because of external factors. It hypothesizes that differences in skin color occur incrementally due to "exposure to the sun," "grease and juices," or some mysterious process of producing (in the case of newborn babies) or losing (in the case of Henry Moss) blackness on the skin. It also does not resolve the question of whether Mishikinakwa, or Volney, for that matter, considers skin color to be the single determining trait of racial status or merely one sign among many. Mishikinakwa's *"father of colours"* indeed colors his creation differently; it is not entirely clear here whether Mishikinakwa also thinks he created one or several races.[102] The passage also insinuates that because the chief wears the clothes of the white man, he is in the process himself of becoming a white man. What Brown earlier called "the fashion of our ancestors" (*View* 108) thus seems to protect the white man from becoming savage and helps the savage man become white.

Volney goes on to attest that he and, once he asks him, Mishikinakwa believe that those who live in Asia probably descended from the Indians and not that, according to a more common theory, Native Americans issued from Asians. Brown disputes this hypothesis, footnoting that "if [Volney] really knew of no argument, no proof, in favour of the prior settlement of the eastern continent, he must indeed be as ignorant as his savage acquaintance" (*View* 363).[103] Indeed, in a May 1799 review of Benjamin Smith Barton's *New Views of the Origin of the Tribes and Nations of America*, Brown seems to endorse Barton's argument that Native Americans descended from those living on the Asian continent. Brown writes that

> The question is difficult and doubtful, in different degrees, to different persons. Those who credit the writings of Moses, are not only persuaded that mankind arose from a single pair, but can even point out the period of their origin, and the district which the primitive man inhabited. With these, there is no doubt but that the birth-place and cradle of the human species was Asia; and that the inhabitants of the rest of the world are descended from those who gradually dispersed themselves from this centre.
>
> Those who lay the authority of the Hebrew scriptures out of view, will still admit that all mankind are sprung from one pair; because this is consistent with that maxim in reasoning which requires us to assign effects to as few causes as possible, and to be contented with that cause which is sufficient to produce the effect. The time and place at which they began to exist, in the view of such, is more doubtful, as well as the progress of migration from one quarter to another.[104]

Brown then goes on to write that he agrees with Barton's theory that the Indian descended from those in Asia because of the similarities in their language. As humankind spread out across the globe, it underwent changes over time, but, for Brown, tracing these linkages shows how that development took place: "Mankind, in proportion as they approach to a common stock, are distinguished by various affinities and resemblances. That race of men in the old world, which bears the greatest and most numerous resemblances to the nations of America, must be supposed to approach nearest to the common stock. These resemblances consist either in the person, manners, or language; and if, in these respects, a stronger resemblance is discerned between the Siberians and Americans than between any other races of men, the conjecture which physical appearances produced, has received the utmost confirmation of which the nature of the thing is susceptible." Ultimately, Brown approves of Barton's work: "No pains seem to have been spared to make this catalogue accurate and extensive; and, as far as it goes, it seems a suitable foundation for the theory which the writer has erected on it." Volney (and Mishikinakwa) and Brown (and Barton) disagree on the direction of development from Asian to Native American (or vice versa), but they all seem to agree on the underlying premise: that human races develop, from one into another, over a period of time.[105]

This disagreement between Volney and Brown is quickly followed by debate on another related issue—namely, to what degree Native Americans could take up white cultural practices. Volney relates that "of late years, the quaker and moravian missionaries, who have succeeded the jesuits,* tell us, that their converts have become more strong and hardy, and less subject to sickness, than the untamed savages" (*View* 370). Brown, indirectly defending his own Quaker background, clarifies Volney's statement by footnoting that "*The quakers are missionaries on a new plan, since their object is not to influence the religious faith of the Indians, but merely to convert them into husbandmen, carpenters, smiths, and weavers" (*View* 370). Later, in 1805, Brown published "An Account of the Late Proceedings of the Society of Friends (or Quakers) for the Civilization of the Indian Tribes" in the *Literary Magazine*, wherein he recounted how Quaker missionaries were able to get Natives to take up white cultural practices.[106] The tribes with whom the Quakers worked included Hendrick Aupaumut's tribe, the Stockbridge who had moved to Oneida land, and, as I outlined in Chapter 2, this push to civilize the tribes helped lead to the further appropriation of Native land. In this piece, Brown discusses what he regards as the beneficence involved in "assisting" the Indians because the Quakers themselves have no "interested motive" to "lay claim to a part of their land."[107] In addition to Natives who take up white farming practices, some Indian children move into Philadelphia families where they learn to read and write.

In Brown's translation of Volney's *View*, Brown and Volney disagree about why an apposite practice proves true—that is, why young settler children taken into captivity so easily adopt the habits of their captors. Volney claims that these children take to a life in the wild because they dislike the rigors of formal education. Brown instead attributes it to the fact that since these children are removed at such a young age, the white cultural practices of their parents do not have enough time to become a consistent practice: "The true reason why the captive child soon becomes savage in his habits is the same that makes the savage himself persist in the course he has been accustomed to; because he was too young at the time of his captivity to have imbibed opposite habits and impressions, and young enough, therefore, to receive all those proper to the Indian mode of life" (*View* 372). (Indeed, this is exactly what Crèvecoeur's Farmer James fears in regards to his own children.) Here and in his "Account" of Quaker civilization efforts, Brown attests to the fact that Indians and whites can take up the practices of the other. When Volney asks Mishikinakwa why he would not accept the offer of "*the friends*" to live among the whites, he replies that while he is "pretty well accustomed to what [he] find[s] here," he cannot speak the language and thus is "deaf and dumb" (*View* 375). Nor can he perform a trade that whites do, and he feels in his old age, he would not be able to learn one quickly enough. While Brown disagrees with Mishikinakwa's reasoning, he concedes that it is the long time Mishikinakwa spent among his own tribe that causes him to feel he could not adapt. In an utterly bizarre footnote, Brown writes that

> These reasonings would have been easily confuted, but no reasonings could have changed his inclinations, already moulded and fixed irrecoverably by the force of habit. The Indian life is a thousand times preferable, as to ease, safety, and liberty, to that of a sailor, yet how many of civilized communities are sailors! and how impossible to change their inclinations by reasoning! Habit endears motion, hardship, and danger, and an Indian returns to his woods for the same reasons which influenced an old gentleman of easy fortune, in Rhode Island, after several years retirement, to equip a ship, and resume his early vocation of *transporting negroes from Africa to Jamaica.* Every body knows the terrors, dangers, discomforts, and privations that beset the master, and, above all, the mariner of a slave-ship. (*View* 376, emphasis in original)

On the one hand, Brown admits that while habits might be changed, this process becomes harder in old age. While Mishikinakwa's claims might be easily refuted by reason, reason also fails to convince mariners of the dangers of their employment. In an analogy as striking as it is unsettling, Brown claims that Indians return to their lives because they are used to it, despite all its shortcomings, just as masters and mariners on slave ships do. Inexplicably, the "*negroes*" brought on these ships, although marked by italics in the original text, do not receive comment as the individuals who surely know "the terrors, dangers, discomforts, and privations" on a slave ship "above," one might assume, even that of the sailor.

Volney goes on to outline the reasons why it is difficult for an Indian to incorporate himself into white civilization, including the "early habits and impressions of childhood," "the tie of friendship and kindred," and the "painful and laborious preparation, which our social state would demand from an Indian" (*View* 377). Brown, however, disagrees:

> The true problem is not why the Indian cannot be changed into a shop-keeper or mechanic, but why he cannot . . . add to the enjoyment of his native woods, to hunting and fishing, the keeping of a cow or a few sheep, and the occasional culture of a corn field or a potatoe patch. This is all that the welfare of the United States, and their own happiness and dignity require of them. Nobody would think of persuading Little Turtle or Corn Planter to idle away his life in the streets of a city, which any Canadian trader or Ohio planter would find as irksome and unnatural as he; but why he cannot, if in fact he cannot, be persuaded to use his influence and example to induce his tribe to provide against scarcity of game, or infirmity of age, by appropriating and cultivating a little ground, is the only mystery. (*View* 377)

Brown is not convinced that Indians cannot change, and as his "Account" shows, he certainly thinks that they can. When it is revealed that Mishikinakwa did indeed own a cow until one of his tribesmen killed it, Brown writes that "it appears, then, that Little Turtle was a man capable of seeing the benefits of turning farmer. His difficulties were unavoidable in his situation, but he is an example that an Indian can abjure his habits, and adopt all the modes of the whites which are worthy of adoption" (*View* 379). During Volney's interview, when Mr. Wells claims that the Miami have improved like the Creeks and Choctaws, Brown adds that "these hints would lead us to suppose that the Indian tribes have really derived some benefit from their vicinity to a civilized people. . . . They receive many useful, as well as some pernicious things, in the way of trade, and have already probably taken several steps towards a total assimilation to the customs of the whites, but they are hastening to extinction with a much quicker pace than to civilization" (*View* 381). In his translation of Volney's natural-historical treatise, Brown insists that the red man can indeed change.[108]

These pieces in the popular press, along with Brown's translation of Volney, do not necessarily show that Brown himself had a well-articulated and coherent natural-historical theory on the origin of the races, but they do illustrate, however, that Brown was very knowledgeable about these discussions and weighed in on certain disputable points of them. Indeed, his knowledge of these discourses allowed him to use them to explore Edgar's transformation into an Indian. Thus, when Edgar fights like an Indian, eats like an Indian, and is able to speak like an Indian, the text does not necessarily defend any particular natural-historical theory but, rather, explores some of the ways racial transformation might take place, in the exact natural-historical terms through which an eighteenth-century audience would have understood it.

FIGHTING, EATING, AND SPEAKING INDIAN

Critics such as Norman Grabo have pointed out how Brown's *Edgar Huntly* explores topics of crucial importance to the founders, who debated to what extent citizens could be trusted to be rational and, therefore, what type of governmental structure should be founded to ensure the liberty of—or, alternately, to control the irrational passions of—humanity.[109] By focusing on the discourse of transformable race in the novel, I want to emphasize how the novel raises additional underlying questions about whether the white man, now that he has relocated to this "New World," can stay there, unchanged. Given Edgar's transformation, can white civil practices be enough to keep one from degenerating into a savage when living on his land and emulating his habits? When Edgar transforms into an Indian in the Norwalk wilderness, he does so within the parameters that natural historians conjectured that the transformation of one's racial status could take place. Although in his narration, Edgar first writes about Indians when he encounters them in the cave, he reveals slowly and in a piecemeal fashion that for many years he had been immediately involved with them (in both violent and friendly ways) and had taken up certain practices of the Lenni-Lenape tribe. Although he may present himself as one, Edgar is no Indian-come-lately. On the contrary, he has been transforming into one for years.

Edgar relates, for example, that in his youth, he and his family resided "on the verge" of Norwalk, which was originally Lenni-Lenape territory. As Sydney Krause has pointed out, the elm tree under which Waldegrave was murdered holds special significance in Pennsylvania settler history since it alludes to the 1737 Walking Purchase Treaty wherein the colonial government defrauded the Lenni-Lenape of a great deal of their land.[110] This, Krause argues, is the land on which Edgar's family lived and, as a result, died. Edgar relates that "during former Indian wars, this rude surface was sometimes traversed by the Red-men, and they made, by means of it, frequent and destructive inroads into the heart of the English settlements. During the last war, notwithstanding the progress of population, and the multiplied perils of such an expedition, a band of them had once penetrated into Norwalk, and lingered long enough to pillage and murder some of the neighbouring inhabitants" (*EH* 165–66). Edgar's personal story thus intersects with the larger history of white-red warfare: "My parents and an infant child were murdered in their beds; the house was pillaged, and then burnt to the ground. Happily, myself and my two sisters were abroad upon a visit" (*EH* 166). During the novel, Edgar and his sisters live with his uncle also on former Native land. As Edgar makes known, he does not have to travel far into the woods to encroach upon indigenous territory; he has been living on it his entire life.

Edgar has conflicted feelings about how the Natives have responded to this historic dispossession. On the one hand, the massacre of his family has forever made him quake at the sight of a Native. "You will not be surprised," he tells

Mary Waldegrave, "that the fate of my parents, and the sight of the body of one of this savage band, who, in the pursuit that was made after them, was overtaken and killed, should produce lasting and terrific images in my fancy. I never looked upon, or called up the image of a savage without shuddering" (*EH* 166). But yet, perhaps unwittingly, Edgar—much like John Marrant— also presents a justification for the Natives, who had endured a "long course of injuries and encroachments" (*EH* 166).[111]

This ambivalence also plays out in his relationship to Old Deb, a Lenni-Lenape woman who refuses to relinquish her ancestral lands, even though her fellow tribespeople do. After they remove from the spreading settlements, she burns their "empty wigwams and retired into the fastnesses of Norwalk" (*EH* 198). Old Deb becomes almost a trickster figure in Edgar's retelling, one who exerts her sovereignty over her land while appearing laughable to Edgar and the townspeople.[112] Edgar mockingly nicknames her "Queen Mab," after one of the fairies in Shakespeare's *Romeo and Juliet* and at the conclusion of the novel calls her claims to the land "groundless and absurd."[113] He neverthe-less shows a Native woman whose declaration of governance over the settlers resembles that made by the founders initially in 1776. Edgar relates that Deb

> seldom left the hut but to visit the neighbouring inhabitants, and demand from them food and cloathing, or whatever her necessities required. These were exacted as her due: to have her wants supplied was her prerogative, and to withhold what she claimed was rebellion. She conceived that by re-maining behind her countrymen she succeeded to the government, and retained the possession of all this region. The English were aliens and so-journers, who occupied the land merely by her connivance and permission, and whom she allowed to remain on no terms but those of supplying her wants. (*EH* 199)

Old Deb's assumption of governmental power, though considered "a subject of mirth and good humour" (*EH* 199), becomes an uncanny doppelganger for the new US nation-state in this novel that abounds with doubles.[114] At the same time, the Huntly farm also mirrors the nation-state, since the "vil-lage inhabited by this clan was built upon ground which now *constitutes* my uncle's barn yard and orchard" (*EH* 198, emphasis added). The Delaware were removed to make room for Edgar's family; both Deb and his uncle claim sov-ereign right to the land. But while Deb seems well-suited to the land usurped from her tribe, nothing but catastrophes have befallen the Huntly family: Ed-gar's parents are killed, he comes to be more and more closely associated with the Indians, and, as readers later learn, this most recent Indian attack will claim his uncle's life.

When Edgar first meets Old Deb sometime after his parents are killed and the Lenape remove, she captures his attention, as he "delighted to ob-serve her habits" (*EH* 199). Indeed, Edgar relates that the two became casual acquaintances, exchanging visits to each other's homes, and "insensibly she seemed to contract an affection for [him], and regarded [him] with more complacency and condescension than any other received" (*EH* 200). Part of the reason they become so close is that Edgar learns to speak her language: "I had taken some pains to study her jargon, and could make out to discourse with her on the few ideas which she possessed. This circumstance, likewise, wonderfully prepossessed her in my favour" (*EH* 200).[115] Although the first encounter with Indians that Edgar recounts in the novel is the one in the cave, in actuality, Edgar has developed an intimate knowledge of their language and "habits" though his time with Old Deb, who appears to be closer to Edgar than she is to "any other" Norwalk resident (*EH* 200). Just as Marrant did, then, Edgar learns the language and emulates the "habits" of the main Indian characters in his story.

But while Edgar dismisses Deb's "pretensions to royalty" (*EH* 200), she actually proves to be more savvy than he realizes. She herself coordinates the attack on Norwalk, and although the novel never says specifically if her direct orchestration included Waldegrave's death, one of the warriors she dispatches into warfare does indeed murder Waldegrave under the elm. A fairly unreliable and unknowing narrator, Edgar suspects Clithero whereas his old acquaintance Deb is actually behind the murder that ostensibly frames the plot. Although Deb certainly loses in the end, in many ways, her machinations—not Edgar's—put the main action of the novel into play.

In addition to acquiring a knowledge of the Lenni-Lenape language from Old Deb, Edgar also has learned to use the "Tom-hawk" to "[severe] an oak branch and cut the sinews of a cat-o'mountain, at the distance of sixty feet" (*EH* 119). Although Edgar does not reveal to his reader exactly how he learned to use a weapon almost solely associated with Indian tribes, he does counterpoise it to the hunting done by white colonists. He himself is adverse to game hunting: "I found no pleasure in plunging into bogs, wading through rivulets, and penetrating thickets, for the sake of dispatching wood-cocks and squirrels" (*EH* 119). Thus, he "never loaded [him]self with fowling-piece or rifle" (*EH* 119).[116] However, with his tomahawk, he has killed many rattlesnakes and panthers, animals he considers to be "enemies of man" (*EH* 119). Although Edgar does indeed own a gun—one given to him by Sarsefield from his own colonialist exploits on the Indian subcontinent (*EH* 179)—here Edgar claims that, for him, a tomahawk works just fine.

Edgar first encounters a panther while searching for Clithero in the wilderness. The panther is both specified as an animal within a natural-historical taxonomy and linked metonymically to the Native Americans whom Edgar later kills. Edgar describes his "grey coat, extended claws, fiery eyes" and footnotes—in a way that echoes Brown's footnotes in Volney's natural-historical treatise—that "this animal has all the essential characteristics of a tyger. Though somewhat inferior in size and strength, these are such as to make him equally formidable to man" (*EH* 118). But the panther has "a cry which he at that moment uttered, and which, by its resemblance to the human voice, is peculiarly terrific, denoted him to be the most ferocious and untamable of that detested race" (*EH* 118). As critics have pointed out, the panther, here called a "detested race," is linked to the Native Americans Edgar will subsequently meet in a nearby cavern.[117] Indeed, Edgar dreads "being rent to pieces by the fangs of this savage" (*EH* 120). Inexplicably, the panther jumps into a pit, and Edgar, rushing over a tree downed across a cavern, is saved. He vows never again to wander the woods without his tomahawk.

Four chapters later, Edgar wakes up in a cave. As he regains consciousness, he finds that, even walking in his sleep, he upholds his resolution, finding an "Indian Tom-hawk" (*EH* 154) at his feet. He also finds himself ravenously hungry: "I tore the linen of my shirt between my teeth and swallowed the fragments. I felt a strong propensity to bite the flesh from my arm. My heart overflowed with cruelty, and I pondered on the delight I should experience in rending some living animal to pieces, and drinking its blood and grinding its quivering fibres between my teeth" (*EH* 156–57). He mirrors the first panther he had seen in the wilderness, who "was accustomed to assail whatever could provide him with a banquet of blood" (*EH* 119). However, when Edgar immediately meets a second panther, instead of the feline attacking and feasting on Edgar, the opposite occurs. Edgar hurls his tomahawk, which "penetrated the scull and the animal fell, struggling and shrieking, on the ground" (*EH* 159). Despite his protestations that he "review[ed] this scene with loathing and horror," Edgar "banquet[ed]" on the "yet warm blood and reeking fibres of a brute" (*EH* 160).

Edgar becomes the thing he eats. On one level, he becomes like the first bloodthirsty panther, who then cannibalizes its own. (Such an "appetite has sometimes subdued the sentiments of nature," Edgar attests, "and compelled the mother to feed upon the flesh of her offspring" [*EH* 160].) In addition, via the association between the "savage" Indian and the "savage" panther, Edgar becomes the Indian who feasts upon what he hunts. This symbolic linkage is concretized when considered in light of Volney's description of the diet of Indian warriors on the hunt:

> When, after a long fast, they light on prey, a deer, bear, or buffaloe, they fall on it like vultures, and leave it not till they are gorged to the throat. This custom makes them unmanageable guides on a regular journey. The quantity they will devour on such occasions, though the fact is supported by the strongest testimony, is scarcely credible. It is notorious that a couple of starving Indians will pick the bones of a deer clean at one meal, and be still unsatisfied. (*View* 369)

According to eighteenth-century natural-historical thought, what one ate was directly linked to what one would become. If Henry Moss's examiners first suspected that he had changed race because he had altered his "mode of life or diet" and Benjamin Rush also emphasizes "diet" and "savage manners" as determinates of racial identity, here readers would have understood Edgar becoming a "savage"/panther/Indian because he was eating and acting like a "savage"/panther/Indian.[118]

As he emerges from the cavern, Edgar encounters a band of Lenni-Lenape warriors and a captive white female sleeping at the mouth of the cave. Justifying his actions by claiming he must act to save his life, Edgar kills the Indians at the cavern. At Old Deb's home, Edgar continues this rampage that he claims he cannot understand, since, as he relates, "all my education and the habits of my life tended to unfit me for a contest and a scene like this" (*EH* 184). Indeed, he entreats Mary, "thus I have told thee a bloody and disastrous tale. When thou reflectest on the mildness of my habits, my antipathy to scenes of violence and bloodshed, my unacquaintance with the use of firearms, and the motives of a soldier, thou wilt scarcely allow credit to my story" (*EH* 185). But perhaps we should not entirely trust Edgar's self-assessment. He has already casually alluded to how his parents' deaths were vindicated when the Natives were "overtaken and killed" (although he does not make it clear if he himself were involved in this retributive violence) and how he could "cut the sinews of a cat-o'mountain, at the distance of sixty feet" (*EH* 119). Edgar's habits have not been as mild as he here claims, and habits—as Edgar knows—matter. Indeed, Edgar's habits have made a profound impression upon him. Beginning with his earlier acquisition of the Delaware language and his expertise in the use of the "Indian Tom-hawk" (*EH* 154), to his consumption of the panther and "savage" murder of the Native warriors, Edgar emerges from the wilderness an Indian. His "habits" have been in the process of changing, and with them, so is he. While Edgar claims that "the transition I had undergone was so wild and inexplicable" (*EH* 186), perhaps it is not that inexplicable after all.

Once all the nearby warriors are killed and the family of the captive rushes on the scene to retrieve her, Edgar faints to the ground, and the party, believing he is dead, departs. When Edgar awakes, he is reclined against the body of one of the slain Indians, their two bodies merging into one.[119] "My head had reposed upon the breast of him whom I had shot in this part of his body. The blood had ceased to ooze from the wound, but my dishevelled locks were matted and steeped in that gore which had overflowed and choked up the orifice" (*EH* 189), he writes. Edgar has "become red," reddened from the blood of the Indian that dyes his skin and perhaps mixes with his own and from taking up the cultural practices believed both to signify and to help produce Indian-ness.

Edgar has become what the white man considered savage not just in appearance but also in the fact that he has moved from being a rational to an irrational figure. When he is later walking through the woods, a search party led by his dear friend Sarsefield fires on Edgar because they mistake him for an Indian. As Sarsefield later reveals to Edgar when they meet, he had spotted someone lying on the ground and had conjectured that "there was something likewise in the appearance of the object that bespoke it to be man, but if it were man, it was, incontrovertibly, a savage and a foe" (*EH* 248). His suspicions are confirmed when Edgar jumps up, fires on the party, and leaps off a cliff into the river to avoid being killed. As Sarsefield says, "Your action seemed incontestably to confirm my prognostics" (*EH* 248). Interestingly, Edgar's actions that "confirm" Sarsefield's judgment that he was an Indian are both rational and completely irrational. On the one hand, it makes perfect sense that Edgar would try to preempt being fired upon by taking the first shot and then trying to escape enemy fire. At the same time, Edgar's—and Sarsefield's—discernments and the decisions they make based upon those discernments are terribly askew. Instead of rescuing one another, they are attacking each other in the wilderness. As Edgar stated earlier regarding his resolve to complete his hazardous journey, "I disdained to be out-done in perspicacity by the lynx, in his sure-footed instinct by the roe, or in patience under hardship, and contention with fatigue, by the Mohawk. I have ever aspired to transcend the rest of animals in all that is common to the rational and brute, as well as in all by which they are distinguished from each other" (*EH* 203). Even here, the distinctions are blurred: is the Mohawk grouped in "the rest of animals" or considered the "rational" that is contrasted to the "brute"? As Edgar exclaims about Clithero's thinking regarding his near-attack on Mrs. Lorimer, "How imperfect are the grounds of all our decisions!" (*EH* 88). If all men make irrational choices, what then is the difference between the Indian and the white man, besides just a gradation of degree? The distinctions between a rational being and an irrational one are provisional at best, and despite Edgar's intentions, the novel makes clear that Edgar does not always make the rational and wise choice.

Indeed, once Edgar does return successfully to the white settlements, his judgment is still called into question. Despite all that has transpired, he remains intent on convincing Clithero that he should not punish himself for his attempt on Mrs. Lorimer's life. Ignoring Sarsefield's warning that Clithero is not to be trusted, Edgar seeks him out again. He finds him residing in Old Deb's hut in an "unsocial and savage state" (*EH* 276). Clithero, linked through his own irrationality to the savage in addition to being the alien, displays no desire to return to civilization and its ways.[120] Indeed, when Edgar reveals to him that Mrs. Lorimer is alive and residing in New York, Clithero again takes up his mad quest to find her and end her life only to drown himself rather than be institutionalized.

That Clithero's continued savage irrationality stays with him to his end seems fairly obvious, but Edgar's "return" to rationality seems more vexed. He does indeed go back to the white settlements, but he continues to make poor decisions. He insists upon telling Clithero of Mrs. Lorimer's location and then hastily sends a letter to Sarsefield with the warning of Clithero's coming attack, a warning which then results in the death of Sarsefield's and Mrs. Lorimer's unborn child. In his final letter to Edgar, Sarsefield rebukes him for his rash and unwise decisions. If Edgar and Clithero have mirrored each other during the narrative and both continue to make nonsensical choices, how much can we assume that Edgar himself has returned to a non-savage state? The novel refuses to resolve this ambiguity.[121]

In his note "To the Public" that prefaces *Edgar Huntly*, Brown states that he proposes in the work "to exhibit a series of adventures, growing out of the condition of our country" (*EH* 3). In his reading of this statement in relationship to Brown's aesthetics, Ezra Tawil challenges us to understand "the condition of our country" to denote not an abstract nation-state but, rather, "to refer quite concretely to certain geographical and topographical features of 'America'" in order to appreciate Brown's understanding of the importance of the actual physical landscape in the United States.[122] I want to suggest that we should do so, too, in terms of thinking about how one's environment might affect one's race. Indeed, it is not so much that Edgar finds the savage within himself when he goes into the woods; by being on Indian land and practicing his habits, Edgar was already metamorphosing into one. The bloody scenes in the cavern and outside Deb's hut do not initiate Edgar's transformation process. Instead, they complete it. Indeed, *Edgar Huntly* asks its readers whether men are inherently irrational and need to be controlled by a strong central government. But it also asks the following questions: Does living like an irrational savage on his land make one into an irrational savage? Are white civil practices enough to keep one from "degenerating" into a savage when living in this new land? In *Edgar Huntly*, the racial status of US citizens being ostensibly solidified in Philadelphia during the setting of the novel is *not* called into stable being by the speech act of law or even "distinguished from the alien by his ability not to become an Indian."[123] One's racial status is a trait with an inherently temporal component; it is always-already in the process of possibly becoming the Other. Thus, the novel also raises this question: How *can* the nation-state, ostensibly established to govern white (potentially irrational) US citizens, do so when whites can always become red? And it is this question that this novel, questioning the colonial project and nation-state, does not answer.

***

The walks that the main characters take in Crèvecoeur's *Letters*, Marrant's *Narrative*, and Brown's *Edgar Huntly* explore not only Indian Country but also the conflicted way racial transformation might occur in the New World. Excavating the models underwriting the transformations these texts portray allows us to appreciate how they are concerned with racial change and how that concern relates to the attempted articulation of a new, American national identity. Crèvecoeur's *Letters* concludes with James fearing the looming break from England. Marrant's *Narrative* features Marrant, the Cherokee king, and General Clinton cheerfully gathering together in the middle of a British-controlled Charleston, and *Edgar Huntly* concludes with almost everything unresolved. If anything, these three texts illustrate the American Revolution and/or its aftermath from perspectives either particularly disidentified with the emerging American nation-state or not yet seamlessly congruent with it.

Each also meditates upon the option to and the outcome of adopting indigenous habits. If Farmer James studiously plans to avoid them, Marrant eagerly practices them and strategically deploys them to his own ends of halting his execution and evangelizing among the southeastern tribes. Poor Edgar seems to adopt them practically unknowingly, only to become aware of the result of this long practice toward the close of the novel, if ever. In this way, then, each text—much like a more formal natural-philosophical experiment—takes up the supposed mutability of racial identity and explores how racial transformation might work and what that process might look like. Thus, in their narrative action, these authors' texts stage a dialogue with the practice of natural history. However, Olaudah Equiano and Hugh Henry Brackenridge, as we shall see in the next chapter, will do so in a much more direct—sometimes challenging, sometimes satirizing—manner.

Doubting Transformable Race: Equiano, Brackenridge, and the Textuality of Natural History

It is probably most straightforward to state that Olaudah Equiano and Hugh Henry Brackenridge had lost hope. Or, perhaps not all hope, but it is safe to say that they were significantly skeptical about the idea of transformable race and the implications that might follow from that idea. In his work, Equiano, a former slave turned overseer turned abolitionist, professes explicit belief in a few prevalent natural-historical theories about the environmentally produced difference in chromatic appearance, but he nevertheless exhibits incredulity about various aspects of these same theories and, furthermore, their ability to bring about just treatment of slaves and free blacks. Brackenridge, a lawyer turned politician turned novelist, displays cynicism not only about environmentalist explanations of racial difference but also about all theories on the production of race. Indeed, both Equiano and Brackenridge question the limits of what others such as Phillis Wheatley and Samson Occom saw as the beneficial aspects of transformable race.

This chapter brings together two seemingly incongruent authors and texts. Olaudah Equiano composed *The Interesting Narrative of the Life of Olaudah Equiano, or Gustavus Vassa, the African. Written by Himself* initially in 1789, in part to contribute to the growing British anti–slave trade movement. Although, as we shall see, his identity has been questioned, Equiano claims to be a native-born African stolen from his homeland, transported through the Middle Passage, and forced into New World slavery. His narrative records his experiences as both a slave and a free black in the eighteenth-century Atlantic world. Differing a great deal from Equiano's slave narrative, Hugh Henry Brackenridge's *Modern Chivalry* is a sprawling, satirical novel that was published in seven volumes from 1792 to 1815. It strives to burlesque early American social, political, religious, and scientific culture by depicting the picaresque escapades of Captain John Farrago and his Irish servant, Teague O'Regan. But while Equiano's slave narrative largely has a serious tone that varies from Brackenridge's more mocking vein, both these texts explicitly engage late eighteenth-century natural-historical thinking and—though in contrasting ways—express remarkable reservations about the idea of transformable race. Demonstrating that not all writers accepted the hypotheses of transformable race whole cloth, this chapter contrasts other authors' strategic use of a notion of transformable race with Equiano's and Brackenridge's suspicion of it.

In this chapter, I argue that both Equiano's *Narrative* and Brackenridge's *Modern Chivalry* display an important distrust of natural-historical texts and, furthermore, textuality more generally. Equiano subscribes to specific natural histories and then questions them, both by troubling certain facets of their theories and by noting how they fail to influence white behavior. He indicates his investment in the notion of transformable race but remains cynical about the fulfillment of its promises. In addition, the *Narrative* demonstrates that written texts only have limited power to ensure the states of being that they supposedly constitute. Thus, as I will explain, in the sense that the *Narrative* tells an origin story like natural-historical texts, it is both as legitimate as other natural histories and also as open to critique. In the end, we can understand better Equiano's turn to economic arguments against the slave trade once natural-historical and religious arguments seem to fail. Brackenridge's *Modern Chivalry* similarly distrusts the reliability of prevalent natural histories. The novel takes primary aim at the American Philosophical Society (APS), the learned institution home to major debates over racial production. Importantly, Brackenridge satirizes both the conclusions *and* the methods of early American natural philosophers, revealing the gothic underside to the scientific Enlightenment. However, more widely, by emphasizing the textuality and narrativity of natural history, *Modern Chivalry* does not just parody *one* natural-philosopical theory but rather *all* theories. Underscoring how all these theorems are created through discourse, *Modern Chivalry* suggests the impossibility of ever articulating a definitive truth. As we will see, indeed, the book's own narrative cacophony destabilizes racial thinking itself.

In these ways, both *The Interesting Narrative* and *Modern Chivalry* highlight the interwoven relationship between literary writing, on the one hand, and scientific writing, on the other. Both works represent natural history as a textual and discursive practice. They evidence that we should not assume that "literary texts" simply or exclusively drew upon scientific facts but rather that literature and natural history existed as intertwined discourses. Equiano's and Brackenridge's works did not create the scientific facts per se, but by exploring, assessing, and altering these ideas, they contributed to the thinking around this topic of transformable race. *The Interesting Narrative* and *Modern Chivalry* do not just reflect or reflect upon but rather help form (both by coinciding with and by challenging) this constellation of ideas. In this way, because these texts render evident the way in which they—like natural histories—create, circulate, and constitute these ideas in discourse, they make us aware that literary pieces and scientific works were both efforts to narrate the world, and, thus, they demonstrate the interactive engagement between literature and natural history.

To Quote and to Question: Olaudah Equiano's Provocative Ends

A year before he published *The Interesting Narrative of the Life of Olaudah Equiano, or Gustavus Vassa, the African. Written by Himself* (1789), Olaudah Equiano published an open letter to Gordon Turnbull, author of "An Apology for Negro Slavery."[1] To counter Turnbull's "hypothesis" that "the Negro race is an inferior species of mankind," Equiano closes his letter by emphatically declaring, "Oh fool! See the 17th chapter of the Acts, verse 26, 'God hath made of one blood all nations of men, for to dwell on all the face of the earth &c.' Therefore, beware of that Scripture, which says, Fools perish for lack of knowledge."[2] Disputing Turnbull and similar thinkers like David Hume who thought not only that the "Negro" was a separate species from the white man but also that he was an "inferior" one, Equiano emphasized the Christian argument that all humans shared a single creation. Therefore, for Equiano, Africans were of the same species and stood on equal footing with white peoples because of that shared creation. The first chapter of his *Interesting Narrative* closes with a similar rhetorical gesture, alluding to natural-historical theories of monogenesis and to "God, 'who hath made of one blood all nations of men for to dwell on all the face of the earth; and whose wisdom is not our wisdom, neither are our ways his ways.'"[3] Equiano concludes both his letter to Turnbull and his first chapter of his *Narrative* by pointing to the Biblical account of humankind's origin and the equality that evidenced for the "Negro race." Furthermore, just as he directly calls Turnbull a "fool" for not taking God at his word on the Negro's origin and equality, Equiano uses the rest of his *Narrative* to point to the foolishness of those who do not agree. However, rather than envision that an understanding of a Biblical, monogenetic creation and its inherent equality might lead to outcomes that reflected that understanding—what one might call the promise implicit in the notion of transformable race—Equiano's text shows whites continually failing to live up to that potential result of this natural-historical theory.[4]

In this way, Equiano's *Interesting Narrative* registers a certain distrust of natural-historical texts and textuality more broadly. In what follows, I explore how Equiano displays skepticism about natural histories that follow the Biblical origin story despite the fact that he endorses them. The *Narrative* demonstrates that while the widely accepted scientific and religious understanding of humankind's creation, the subsequent development of racial difference, and the inherent equality of the black race should mean that just treatment of blacks would follow, this premise fails to make a substantial difference in the areas of economics and civil liberties for slaves and even free blacks. Thus, while he is invested in the idea of transformable race, he expresses doubt about the realization of its promises of equality. In addition, Roxann Wheeler has argued that Equiano's text shows some of the inconsistencies of aspects of eighteenth-century natural-historical thought (*CR* 236), and I would like to further this line of inquiry by emphasizing not so much where Equiano was unable to negotiate some of the difficulties in natural-historical thinking but more so where he himself registers skepticism about either their theorems or the ability of this body of thought to make much of a practical difference in his everyday life. Furthermore, as we shall see, Equiano troubles much natural-historical thought that claimed blacks could or should want to become physically white. In this sense, he revalues blackness and seems more interested in his own transformation from slave to free man to economic actor.

This skepticism, moreover, is not limited to just natural-historical texts. In the *Interesting Narrative*, just as a natural historian's text cannot ensure the equal position of the black man that it calls into being and for which it provides a scientific explanation, neither can a free black person's free papers ever fully ensure that he will not be impinged upon, enslaved, or reenslaved by white men. Indeed, in part because of the influence of Henry Louis Gates's notion of the Trope of the Talking Book, scholars tend to emphasize the importance of literacy and getting into print for early black writers, but in many ways, Equiano's *Interesting Narrative* displays an overlooked and important distrust of written texts.[5]

Reading Equiano's *Interesting Narrative* in this way means, in part, we should reconsider how we read the manners and customs section of the first chapter specifically and his chapters on Africa more generally. While the debate that has erupted around the veracity of this section of the *Narrative* is important, here I consider the truthfulness of that section less than the crucial way in which it is being used.[6] True or not, the account of Equiano's birth in Africa not only, as Vincent Carretta has argued, let Equiano add an "African" voice to the anti-slave trade movement (*B* 320). The inclusion of the African section also allows Equiano to link his text to natural-historical arguments and frame the entire book around the way whites fail to live up to the potential of them. Furthermore, although Equiano is not writing a natural-historical text per se, his *Narrative* constitutes a similar type of story of origins because it describes his own origin in Africa and also his race's origin in the Biblical creation. A similarity exists between natural-historical texts that try to write into being a simultaneously-created, equal black human; political texts that try to write into being free, economically enfranchised black humans; and his narrative text that tries to write himself into being as an African. In the sense, therefore, that it is a textual example of an origin story, the *Interesting Narrative* is just as legitimate as the other natural histories. Ironically, it also opens it up to a similar kind of scrutiny. That is, *The Interesting Narrative* demonstrates how, in relationship to natural-historical texts and political texts, just because a written document makes a statement, it does not necessarily make that statement true; ironically, the same type of questioning has been raised about his opening chapters on Africa themselves.

A second and related irony is that Equiano characterizes both Turnbull (in the letter) and whites (in his book) who fail to recognize and implement the equality implicit in a monogenetic origin as fools at the same time that he himself expresses doubt about certain aspects of natural history's tenets, and, more importantly, for their efficacy to make a significance difference in the social world. On the one hand, it is ironic that he at once points out that whites are foolish for not believing in the Biblical origin story while he himself displays doubts about certain aspects of natural-historical theories. And on the other hand, it is *precisely because* whites foolishly do not recognize and base their actions upon an equality implicit in the single origin story that Equiano himself is skeptical about the theories' ability to make a difference in the world. Understanding Equiano's vexed investment in natural historical theories and his skepticism about whether these theories and their implications can change white behavior also helps us comprehend his turn at the conclusion of his text to the economic argument he makes against the slave trade because, as we shall see, he advances it only after his narrative has shown how arguing the equality of Africans through natural-historical and/or religious means has not been effective.

***

When Mary Wollstonecraft reviewed Equiano's *Interesting Narrative* in the May 1789 pages of the *Analytical Review*, she opened her comments with an immediate reference to natural-historical thought:[7] "The life of an African, written by himself, is certainly a curiosity, as it has been a favourite philosophic whim to degrade the numerous nations, on whom the sun-beams more directly dart, below the common level of humanity, and hastily to conclude that nature, by making them inferior to the rest of the human race, designed to stamp them with a mark of slavery."[8] Wollstonecraft alludes to the prevalent belief that if Africans did indeed share a creation with white men, the heat of the sun's rays over time in locations close to the equator rendered them darker and, for some thinkers, inferior to lighter peoples. But although this belief makes Equiano's text a "curiosity," the theory's validity is not of direct concern to Wollstonecraft. She continues,

> How they are shaded down, from the fresh colour of northern rustics, to the sable hue seen on the African sands, is not our task to inquire, nor do we intend to draw a parallel between the abilities of a negro and European mechanic; we shall only observe, that if these volumes do not exhibit

extraordinary intellectual powers, sufficient to wipe off the stigma, yet the activity and ingenuity, which conspicuously appear in the character of Gustavus, place him on a par with the general mass of men, who fill the subordinate stations in a more civilized society than that which he was thrown into at his birth.[9]

Here, Wollstonecraft declines to evaluate whether or not this hypothesis about the Negro's color or his supposed inferiority is true. Rather, she focuses on Equiano's work itself. While she does not want to parallel Equiano's "abilities" with that of a "European mechanic," she nevertheless claims that even if his "volumes" do not adequately challenge the "stigma" of the claim, they do "place him on a par with the general mass of men."[10] Interestingly enough, less than six months prior to this, Wollstonecraft published a review of Samuel Stanhope Smith's *An Essay on the Causes of the Variety of Complexion and Figure in the Human Species*, a publication she describes as an "ingenious essay," one that "concludes that natural causes are sufficiently powerful to effect the changes observable in the human species, without recurring to vague conjectures, which shake our confidence in the validity of the Mosaical account."[11] There Wollstonecraft agrees with Smith's attribution of racial difference to both "climate" and the "state of society," thereby concurring with the idea that the sun's beams can cause blackness and that, while darker humans may have degenerated in an intellectual sense because of the sun as well, they began on an equal footing with lighter humans. It is striking, then, in her review of Equiano that she does not conclude that Equiano is "on a par" with the "general mass of men" because of any natural-historical theory—even one with which she agrees—but because of the quality of the *Narrative* itself.

But while Wollstonecraft's two *Analytical Review* pieces bring Smith's treatise and Equiano's autobiography into context with one another, both in the coverage she gives each of them in the same periodical and in the way her Equiano review begins with aspects of Smith's theorem, direct citation to Smith's work remains noticeably absent from Equiano's engagement with theories of natural history. While we do not know for certain whether Equiano knew of Smith's work, the fact that Smith's theory was prominent enough in order to garner a review from Wollstonecraft and to inform her later review of Equiano, its absence in *The Interesting Narrative* is striking. It is especially so considering that Equiano instead quotes both Thomas Clarkson's *Essay on the Slavery and Commerce of the Human Species, Particularly the African* (1786) and John Mitchell's "An Essay upon the Causes of the Different Colours of People in Different Climates" (1744). Although Equiano cites Mitchell because Clarkson himself first quotes him, Equiano's use of Mitchell's work is conspicuous because it was a text almost forty years old at the time Equiano used it, and, like Smith, Mitchell was a member of the APS.[12] That Equiano would opt for Mitchell's more dated text over Smith's recent and recently discussed text is notable. But, as we shall see, Mitchell's (and Clarkson's) natural-historical theories provided Equiano with a particular—and, in Equiano's *Narrative*, unspoken—natural-historical theorem that Smith's treatise noticeably lacked.

Before it alludes to the natural-historical texts specifically, *The Interesting Narrative* commences with "The Author's account of his country, and their manners and customs" (*IN* 31), and Equiano details what he views as particularly important aspects of Eboe culture. As others have noted, Equiano does so in part to demonstrate for his readers that despite what they might think, the eighteenth-century Eboes who live in Equiano's claimed home of Essaka were indeed quite civilized.[13] So much so, claims Equiano, that they remind him of what he would later come to learn were the practices of ancient Jews (*IN* 92). Vincent Carretta rightly points out that Equiano uses this comparison between eighteenth-century Africans and Old Testament Hebrews to counter very nascent polygenist beliefs and that he "uses his description of 'Eboe' to support the orthodox Christian monogenetic belief that all humans descended directly from Adam and Eve" (*B* 316). Indeed, Equiano emphasizes the ancient Jewish peoples "before they reached the Land of Promise, and particularly the patriarchs, while they were yet in that pastoral state which is described in Genesis" (*IN* 43). This, Equiano states, is "an analogy, which alone would induce me to think that the one people had sprung from the other" (*IN* 43–44). Not only does Genesis explicitly claim that all peoples shared in a single creation; Equiano's own observation that his people's "manners and customs" resemble those of the Jews described in Genesis lead him to argue for the Africans' and Jews' shared origin. Scholars have emphasized various implications that result from Equiano's Eboe-Jew comparison, but Carretta convincingly argues that Equiano uses the analogy and his subsequent turn in the next paragraph to natural histories to emphasize "the environmental causes of the difference in complexion" (*B* 317) and that the "inferiority [of Africans to Europeans] is apparent, not real, because complexion is superficial" (*B* 318).[14]

But in fact, much more is implied in Equiano's Eboe-Jew analogy. After citing several Biblical scholars whose work shows how the Africans descended from the Jews and providing a few more of his own observations of similarities (including governmental and familial structures; circumcision; and ritual sacrifices and cleansings), Equiano claims that "As to the difference of colour between the Eboan Africans and the modern Jews, I shall not presume to account for it" (*IN* 44). He does go on, however, to refer to Clarkson's *Essay*, which, for Equiano, "has ascertained the cause, in a manner that at once solves every objection on that account, and, on my mind at least, has produced the fullest conviction" (*IN* 44). Equiano then cites Clarkson's reference to Mitchell's *Essay*, "extracting a fact": that Spaniards who live in the New World become just as "dark coloured" as Native Americans in Virginia (*IN* 44).[15] Equiano also draws upon Clarkson's use of another example from *Treatise upon the Trade from Great Britain to Africa, by an African Merchant*: that the descendants of Portuguese colonizers and natives of Sierra Leona "are now become, in their complexion, and in the woolly quality of their hair, *perfect negroes*, retaining however a smattering of the Portuguese language" (*IN* 45). As Ralph Bauer points out, here Equiano's "draw[s] on the most authoritative texts in Enlightenment natural history"[16] and in these two examples, both America and Africa have the potential to turn people dark. For Equiano, despite his assertion that he will not "presume to account for" the African's color, Clarkson's examples lead to a very specific conclusion: "These instances, and a great many more which might be adduced, while they shew how the complexions of the same persons vary in different climates, it is hoped may tend also to remove the prejudice that some conceive against the natives of Africa on account of their colour. Surely the minds of the Spaniards did not change with their complexions!" (*IN* 45). As Roxann Wheeler points out, Equiano accepts climate as a cause of physical color, but he does not believe that the sun also makes Africans intellectually inferior (*CR* 263).[17] What Equiano calls the "apparent inferiority of an African" is not caused by climate but rather by his "situation," which includes being "ignorant" of European "language, religion, manners, and customs" and also "slavery," which "depress[es] the mind, and extinguish[es] all its fire, and every noble sentiment" (*IN* 45). The African appears to be "inferior" not as a result of the same cause of his color but rather because of different cultural situations and, importantly, slavery itself.

Equiano furthermore reminds his British readers that their own ancestors were "like the Africans, uncivilized, and even barbarous" (*IN* 45). Equiano questions his European readers: "Did Nature make *them* [the European ancestors] inferior to their sons? and should *they too* have been made slaves?" (*IN* 45). Equiano answers his own rhetorical question: "Every rational mind answers, No." Therefore, Equiano implies, just as those with "rational minds" would not argue that their own ancestors in their "uncivilized" state should be enslaved, neither should the Africans. "Let such reflections as these," Equiano continues, "melt the pride of their superiority into sympathy for the wants and miseries of their sable brethren, and compel them to acknowledge, that understanding is not confined to feature or colour. If, when they look round the world, they feel exultation, let it be tempered with benevolence to others, and gratitude to God, 'who hath made of one blood all nations of men for to dwell on all the face of the earth; and whose wisdom is not our wisdom, neither are our ways his ways'" (*IN* 45).

Werner Sollors has claimed that Equiano's statement here serves as a "theoretical starting point" for his examination of "the meaning of reciprocity implied by the golden rule," and Carretta points out that in Equiano's evocation of stadial theory, he "places Africans just one step below civilized Europeans," rendering them "closer to becoming equivalent to modern Englishmen than some Britons are" (*B* 318).[18] However, I want to suggest, Equiano's conclusion to his first chapter is even more radical than that in two ways. First, it serves as a much more far-reaching *challenge* to his readers. To wit, if God made all humankind of "one blood," where various climates gave rise to a myriad of colors and disparate situations resulted in different levels of "civilization," those who believe that Africans are destined to become slaves are not only fools like Turnbull but also irrational ones at that. Given the pressures placed on blacks to prove their rationality in the eighteenth century, Equiano's word choice could not be more apt.[19] Here, it is not blacks who are irrational but whites who believe that blacks' "apparent inferiority" is justification for their enslavement.

Second, Equiano's reference to Clarkson's and Mitchell's texts has an even more far-reaching implication. As I discussed in the introduction and Chapter 2, Mitchell, a Virginian physician and naturalist, was a correspondent of Peter Collinson, an important London Quaker and member of the Royal Society, and in 1743 Mitchell composed his essay and submitted it to Collinson. The paper was then discussed for four meetings of the Royal Society—no small achievement for a naturalist in the colonies—and subsequently published in the society's *Philosophical Transactions*. Mitchell's paper was widely read and, according to Whitfield Bell, greatly influenced Samuel Stanhope Smith's much later *Essay*.[20] Equiano draws upon Clarkson's later citation of Mitchell's earlier essay.[21] Like many naturalists, Mitchell advanced his theory in support of the Biblical account that both black and white peoples "descended from the same Stock" ("ECDC" 131). Instead of accounting for the Negro's blackness by claiming that the sun causes the skin to exhibit more blackness, Mitchell argued that the sun's intense rays cause the African's outer skin layers to become thicker which, then, "transmit no Colour thro' them" ("ECDC" 107). Claiming that the human's inner-most skin layer is white ("ECDC" 112), Mitchell argues that "both the internal Membranes and Humours of such swarthy People are of the same Colour in time of Health with those of the perfectest white Skins, as well as they are in Negroes" ("ECDC" 122). Indeed, "the thicker the Cuticle is . . . the more the Light will be intercepted in passing them, and the more the Colour of the Skin will degenerate from the pure White of the Membranes below it" ("ECDC" 121). Literally, for Mitchell, all humans are the same white color on the "inside." But, crucially, unlike many later eighteenth-century natural philosophers who explicitly claimed or just assumed that the complexion of the original humans was white, Mitchell argued that it was a "dark swarthy, a Medium betwixt Black and White: From which primitive Colour the *Europeans* degenerated as much on one hand, as the *Africans* did on the other; the *Asiatics* (unless, perhaps, where mixed with the whiter *Europeans*) with most of the *Americans*, retaining the primitive and original Complexion" ("ECDC" 146–47).

Clarkson extends this claim. He articulates that it would be vain for Englishmen to assume that the original color was white. Rather, he argues, it was "dark olive; a beautiful colour, and a just medium between white and black. That this was the primitive colour, is highly probable from the observations that have been made; and, if admitted, will afford a valuable lesson to the Europeans, to be cautious how they deride those of the opposite complexion, as there is great reason to presume, *that the purest white is as far removed from the primitive color as the deepest black*" (*ESC* 190, emphasis in original). For Clarkson, this not only means that whites have degenerated just as much as blacks have; it also gives him justification to poke fun at white slaveowners who base their actions on their supposed color superiority. He writes that

> It is evident, that if you travel from the equator to the northern pole, you will find a regular gradation of colour from black to white. Now if you can justly take him for your slave, who is of the deepest die, what hinders you from taking him also, who only differs from the former but by a shade. Thus you may proceed, taking each in a regular succession to the poles. But who are you, that thus take into slavery so many people? Where do you live yourself? Do you live in *Spain*, or in *France*, or in *Britain*? If in either of these countries, take care lest the *whiter natives of the north* should have a claim upon yourself. (*ESC* 185–86)

It is not only that *both* blacks and whites have degenerated but also that justifying slavery via color can lead to a slippery logical slope. "But the argument," he quips, "is too ridiculous to be farther noticed" (*ESC* 186). In addition, color has developed over years, but it also can continue to change in the future as people relocate around the globe. Clarkson is especially caustic addressing those who disagree with his formulations: "if any man were to point out any one of the colours which prevails in the human complexion, as likely to furnish an argument, that the people of such a complexion were of a different species from the rest, it is probable that his own descendants, if removed to the climate to which this complexion is peculiar, would, in the course of a few generations, degenerate into the same color" (*ESC* 213). This, of course, was the ultimate insult because it played upon the ultimate fear. Clarkson's treatise also would influence Samuel Stanhope Smith's *Essay*; indeed, Clarkson—not Smith—first articulated that the black complexion could be thought of as a "*universal freckle*" (*ESC* 210).[22] However, strikingly, Smith does not emphasize that whites have degenerated from an original norm but instead focuses on Native Americans and Africans degenerating *from* whiteness *into* darker shades.

Thus, the fact that Equiano endorses—but, "refer[ring] to that performance for the theory," (*IN* 44) does not directly quote—this much more radical theorem is key. In effect, Equiano's endorsement of Clarkson's theory implies that whiteness itself could be thought of as degenerative. Thus, first, it allows him to make his overall point about transformable race: that blacks and whites share a single origin from which *everyone* degenerated, but that this fact makes little impact on the treatment of blacks. Second, it helps him trouble the values associated with whiteness and blackness. Indeed, Equiano makes a point related to Clarkson's theory earlier in his chapter when he comments upon the "comeliness" of the Eboe, amongst whom "deformity is indeed unknown" (*IN* 38). Equiano claims that "Numbers of the natives of Eboe now in London might be brought in support of this assertion; for, in regard to complexion, ideas of beauty are wholly relative" (*IN* 38). If any of his readers should miss his subtle point that blackness can be considered attractive, he clarifies his stance in the next sentence: "I remember while in Africa to have seen three negro children, who were tawny, and another quite white, who were universally regarded by myself and the natives in general, as far as related to their complexions, as deformed" (*IN* 38). Equiano probably refers to children with what scientists now call albinism; more importantly, though, is the fact that here, Equiano characterizes lighter shades as deformity; blackness, as beauty.[23] Scholars have noted how Equiano separates whiteness from Britishness (*CR* 235), and here, we see that even as Equiano works throughout the book to take up British customs and manners (and indeed, in the final chapter, he advocates all Africans adopting them), he does not do so with the goal of making Africans physically "white." He revalues the retention of blackness. Taking into account the split historical perspective Equiano employs throughout the text—that of both a young boy experiencing his life and the adult man looking back and writing his life's story—we find in this scene that Equiano aesthetically valued blackness and denigrated whiteness both in Africa as a child *and* as an adult who comments on the blackness of the "natives of Eboe *now* in London" (*IN* 38, emphasis added).

Indeed, Equiano shows how he was taught about differences in complexion and learned that whiteness could be conceived as valuable. While serving in the British navy as a young man with his owner Michael Henry Pascal, Equiano famously records seeing the marvels of a clock, a portrait, and a book and naively reacting to each. In the same chapter, he meets one mate's young daughter, "with whome [he] used to be much delighted" (*IN* 69). As Equiano relates it, "I had often observed, that when her mother washed her face it looked very rosy; but when she washed mine it did not look so; I therefore tried oftentimes myself if I could not by washing make my face of the same colour as my little play-mate (Mary), but it was all in vain; and I now began to be mortified at the difference in our complexions" (*IN* 69). Thomas Jefferson cites blacks' inability to blush as proof of their inferior beauty,[24] but Mitchell's scientific theory claims that it is not that blacks do not have red-colored blood ever rise toward the epidermis, but rather that thinner white skin allows the color of one's blood to show through that skin more so than thicker black skin ("ECDC" 104–9). Here, it is not so much that the young Equiano wants to be white; he had just encountered another young European girl whose skin he does not envy but rather to whom Equiano "began to fear I should be betrothed" (*IN* 68).

Instead, he wants to be rosy, which—according to Mitchell—the difference in his complexion from that of the second little girl will not allow him to do. He does not value whiteness as a skin color, per se, but the rosy color that thin white skin allows one to display. It is not that he denigrates blackness as opposed to whiteness but that he wants his different skin to show the rosy blush that would evidence the physical and sentimental similarities between himself and lighter peoples. Thus, Equiano values the *functionality*, not necessarily the appearance, of white skin. Although some scholars have read this scene as a testament to Equiano's dislike of his own skin color, it is rather a dramatization of how a young Equiano learned to recognize what whiteness could do.[25] At this point he "*now began* to be mortified at the difference in our complexions" (*IN* 69, emphasis added). The young and innocent Equiano in this scene exhibits the same naiveté as the youth who earlier in the chapter thought that a clock and portrait were magic and that a book could talk. Not something that exists a priori, an awareness of the "difference in . . . complexions"—and the resulting functionality and social hierarchies that follow—is something that must be taught. The desire for the functionality of whiteness is instructed here and as an adult, Equiano also comes to desire the utility of whiteness in how it operates in an economic and social rights sense.

But even as Equiano draws up these two natural-historical texts in order to assert that blackness has aesthetic value and to frame the argument of his text overall, he also expresses doubt about some of the theories in both Mitchell's and Clarkson's works. Indeed, when Pascal sells Equiano and returns him to West Indian slavery, Equiano invokes climatic influence to signify his dejection at being returned to the Caribbean. Equiano asks God to strike him dead, "rather than permit me to become a slave, and to be sold from lord to lord" (*IN* 98). "In this state of my mind," he continues, "our ship came to an anchor, and soon after discharged her cargo. . . . And, to comfort me in my distress in that time, two of the sailors robbed me of all my money, and ran away from the ship. I had been so long used to an European climate that at first I felt the scorching West-India sun very painful, while the dashing surf would toss the boat and the people in it frequently above high-water mark" (*IN* 99). This attestation characterizes the pain the West Indies inflicts on Equiano, both metaphorically (in the sense that the milieu of slavery is worse in the West Indies than in England) and literally (in the sense that the sun "scorch[es]" his skin). In this second sense, Equiano's statement directly rebuts one of Mitchell's claims: "Negroes are never subject to be sun-burnt, or have their Skins blistered by any such Degree of Heat; as Whites are; but, if we consider, that a black Body retains more Heat than a white one, or any other Colour, it will be very plain, that their Skins must be thicker or denser, *i.e.* more cartilaginous or callous, to award off this Violence of the Sun's Beams" ("ECDC" 108). For Mitchell, black peoples withstand the sun more easily than whites, and their ability to do so makes their lives in hot climates easier:

For the different Colours of People have been demonstrated to be only the necessary Effects, and natural Consequences, of their respective Climes, and Ways of Life; as we may further learn from Experience, that they are the most suitable for the Preservation of Health, and the Ease and Convenience of Mankind in these Climes, and Ways of Living: So that the black Colour of the Negroes of *Africa*, instead of being a Curse denounced on them, on account of their Forefather *Ham*, as some have idly imagined, is rather a Blessing, rendering their Lives, in that intemperate Region, more tolerable, and less painful. ("ECDC" 146)

As Equiano is quick to point out, however, black slaves in the West Indies are indeed, in Mitchell's words, "subject to be sun-burnt" and, furthermore, unable to ward off the "Violence of the Sun's Beams," both in the sense of being singed by the sunlight and of enduring the physical violence perpetrated there in the hot sun. And, lest anyone assume that the color of "Negroes," as Mitchell says, "render[s] their Lives . . . more tolerable, and less painful" in the West Indies as Mitchell claims it supposedly does in Africa ("ECDC" 146), or that darker peoples are "most healthy" in "hot Countries" ("ECDC" 142), Equiano points out that this simply is not the case. Drawing upon both Anthony Benezet's *Some Historical Account of Guinea* and William and Edmund Burke's *An Account of the European Settlements in America*, Equiano points out that life in the West Indies is deadly for Africans because of slavery. Equiano contradicts Mitchell's claim that "the black Colour of the Negroes" is a "Blessing" because it enables them to be healthier in warmer climes, and here he emphasizes that black skin actually leads to lower life expectancy. This is because, secondary to the claim that black skin enables Africans to be healthier in warm climates, for some slave apologists, black skin justifies slavery (as Phillis Wheatley points out), which obviously leads to rampant and premature death. Claiming that a Negro's life expectancy is "but sixteen years! and yet the climate here is in every respect the same as that from which they are taken, except in being more wholesome" (*IN* 106), Equiano asserts that the African does *not* enjoy a more tolerable life in hot climates because of his skin.[26] Pointing out that it is said that the climate in the West Indies is similar to (indeed, "more wholesome" than) an African one, Equiano shows that the color of black skin does not make them more suitable for life in hot climates because the black skin that slave apologists argue is a justification for slavery results in blacks being enslaved, which causes their deaths in disproportionate numbers. Thus, black skin makes Negroes more susceptible to death in the West Indies, not because of its climate, but because of its practice of slavery. Equiano's paragraph's concluding lines drip with sarcasm: "Do the British colonies decrease in this manner? And yet what a prodigious difference is there between an English and West India climate" (*IN* 106). White people do not die at such a high rate in the West Indies despite the "torrid" heat; claims about whether hot climates are healthier for dark peoples ultimately are secondary to the brutality of slavery. Thus, Equiano registers skepticism about this natural-historical theory on two levels. One, contra the claim that Africans do not sunburn, he claims that he is susceptible to the "scorching West-India sun" (*IN* 99).[27] Secondly, and more importantly, even if it were true that blacks were necessarily more healthy in hot climates, they are *not* necessarily healthier in the West Indies because of slavery. Even if that natural-historical claim held true, it matters little in the social world.

Equiano also registers skepticism about the natural-historical claims that blacks could or would necessarily want to become white. Natural historians themselves disagreed about whether this change could happen in one lifetime, or if it would take generations; they also disagreed over the ways in which such a change might happen. Although Equiano cites Clarkson's two examples of European peoples becoming darker in America and Africa, he also includes examples in his narrative where he does not argue for black people trying to become white. As Carretta has pointed out, Equiano does work to adopt British manners and customs, and Roxann Wheeler maintains that Equiano attempts to split off Britishness from whiteness, precisely in order to claim "an authoritative public identity" (*CR* 235). I would like to extend this thinking and suggest that even in becoming like the British, Equiano does not envision becoming white, which is interesting given the context of the natural-historical thought on which he otherwise draws. While he talks freely about how whites can become darker, he does not approach talking about how blacks might become lighter. Equiano is quick to point out the British habits that he adopts, claiming, for instance, that becoming "inured" to the dangers of a sea life, he "soon grew a stranger to terror of every kind, and was, in that respect at least, almost an Englishman" (*IN* 77). Indeed, he attests, he "had the stronger desire to resemble them; to imbibe their spirit, and imitate their manners; I therefore embraced every occasion of improvement; and every new thing that I observed I treasured up in my memory" (*IN* 78). Equiano's main example is learning to "read and write" (*IN* 78). But here, even as he wants to "resemble" the British in terms of their ways of life, he does not necessarily want to change his complexion.

Indeed, in a bizarre scene where Equiano does ostensibly change complexions, he does so not to acquire whiteness per se, but rather to seize upon its functionality. Serving as a steward onboard a ship bound for Turkey, Equiano recommends John Annis, "a very clever black man" (*IN* 179), as a cook for the voyage. When Annis is removed from the ship under mysterious circumstances by William Kirkpatrick, a man with whom "he had formerly lived many years," and "from whom he parted by consent" (*IN* 179), Equiano attempts to orchestrate Annis's release. When approaching Kirkpatrick's residence, Equiano "whitened [his] face, that they might not know me" (*IN* 180). Trying to avoid the watch that Kirkpatrick had set out for him, Equiano temporarily lightens his face in order to fool the guards, which, he notes, "had the desired effect" (*IN* 180). Although Equiano successfully eludes the watchmen, he ultimately is unsuccessful at rescuing his friend, who was returned to the West Indies, endured torture, and later died. The inclusion of this scene testifies not to Equiano's desire to be white but rather to the usefulness Equiano sees whiteness having.

Equiano later alludes to another sense of whiteness, one that again emphasizes its utility. On a voyage from England to Jamaica, Equiano endeavors to convert a Musquito Indian prince onboard to Christianity. When the other, non-religious crew members dissuade the young prince from his religious studies by ridiculing him, he asks Equiano why he is so different from these other men. As Equiano records it, "At last he asked me, 'How comes it that all the white men on board, who can read and write, observe the sun, and know all things, yet swear, lie, and get drunk, only excepting yourself?' I answered him, the reason was, that they did not fear God" (*IN* 204). As Carretta points out, the Indian calls Equiano white not because of his skin color but because of the "culture, education, and religion" Equiano had acquired (*B* 183). The Indian considers Equiano "white" not because of his appearance but because of things Equiano does. Thus, although Equiano quotes natural-historical texts, he seems relatively uninterested in exploring how changes in climate and/or practices might render him physically more white, despite the fact that this was a concern of natural history. He is more interested in his transformation from slave to free man to economic actor but, like his engagements with natural history, this quest is also one that is quite vexed.

FREEDOM PAPERS

Just as Equiano endorses natural-historical texts that he then questions, he also notes the crucial importance and then the unreliability of written texts that ostensibly produce and document a black man's freedom. This conflictedness about the efficacy of written texts relates to the way *The Interesting Narrative* depicts the British North American colonies (in the narrative time frame) and the young US nation-state (when *The Interesting Narrative* was written and published). Equiano's *Narrative* uses the representation of Philadelphia, the city Equiano's readers would recognize as the setting for US freedom-making, on the one hand to emphasize themes of liberty and freedom due to its association with the American overthrow of the British monarchy and on the other hand to underscore Equiano's own British loyalties by exposing the contradictions in associating Philadelphia and the United States with "freedom."

In the book's sixth chapter, Equiano palimpsestically overlays his coming-to-freedom story with that of the US nation-state. First published in London in 1789 after the United States declared independence, won the Revolutionary War, and ratified the Constitution and after Equiano's release from slavery, the narrative depicts 1765 when the colonies were still a British impe-rial holding and Equiano was still a slave. (At the time the *Narrative* depicts, Equiano, his master, and the American creoles are British subjects; at the time that he writes and the *Narrative* is published, the Americans consider them-selves to have a different nationality from the British.) The chapter implies an uneasy homology between the status of a black slave and that of the colonies in an interesting and risky negotiation for a writer invested in underscoring his British loyalties. While it was common for blacks enslaved in the Brit-ish American colonies to (re)appropriate rhetorics of freedom and liberty in order to advocate for their own emancipation,[28] the British-affiliated Equiano surprisingly uses them to critique British slaveholding practices (which, ironi-cally, he himself participated in until he took up residence in England) along with the ways in which American colonists mistreated him as a black man.

Equiano's intertwined references to visiting Philadelphia and to gaining his freedom link his own desire for liberty with the recently acquired liberty (in terms of when the *Narrative* was written) of the US nation-state.[29] When talking about preparing for a voyage to "Philadelphia, in the year 1765," Equi-ano "worked with double alacrity, from the hope of getting money enough by these voyages to buy my freedom, if it should please God; and also to see the city of Philadelphia, which I had heard a great deal about for some years past" (*IN* 124). Equiano is shocked when his master, Robert King, al-leges that Equiano "meant to run away from him when [he] got to Philadel-phia" (*IN* 124) and announces his plans to sell Equiano to a "severe master" (*IN* 124). Equiano convinces his master that he did not plan to run away but that "if ever I were freed, whilst I was used well, it should be by honest means" (*IN* 125); his master thus decides to let Equiano work toward buying his own freedom.[30] His master and captain both associate Philadelphia with Equiano's alleged planned escape, and while he denies that he would run away, he also notes that his "mind was big with inventions, and full of schemes to escape" (*IN* 125). However he may gain it, Equiano narratively associates Philadelphia with his freedom.[31] Indeed, when Equiano finally does reach Philadelphia, he meets "a *wise* woman, a Mrs. Davis, who revealed secrets, foretold events, &c." who "told [him that he] should not be long a slave" (*IN* 127). As his read-ers knew, the prediction that this "wise woman" makes in Philadelphia that Equiano would gain his independence eventually came to pass, as it also did for the colonies.

But the freedom created for the United States in Philadelphia differs dra-matically from that of free black men. Equiano precedes his foretuneteller's assurances with a story of a free "mulatto-man, whose name was Joseph Clip-son" (*IN* 121), unrightfully seized from his maritime employment because a Bermuda captain simply declared that he was not free. Although the man produced "a certificate of his being born free in St. Kitt's" (*IN* 121), he was physically removed from the boat by "infernal invaders of human rights"

(*IN* 121) and forced into captivity. Equiano's anecdote illustrates the compli-
cated nature of liberty-bestowing speech acts. While the US Declaration of
Independence might have liberated the country and the people it at once created, for black or racially mixed men, even written documents stating one's
freedom did not necessarily ensure it.[32] Equiano comments that while he has
"often seen in Jamaica, and other islands, free men, whom I have known in
America, thus villainously trepanned and held in bondage" and that he has
"heard of two similar practices *even in Philadelphia*: and were it not for the benevolence of the quakers in that city, many of the sable race, who *now* breathe
the air of liberty, would, I believe, be groaning under some planter's chains"
(*IN* 122, emphasis added). He continues that "hitherto I had thought only
slavery dreadful; but the state of a free negro appeared to me now equally so at
least, and in some respects even worse, for they live in constant alarm for their
liberty. . . . In this situation, is it surprising that slaves, when mildly treated,
should prefer even the misery of slavery to such a mockery of freedom?"
(*IN* 122). If Equiano's white, US contemporaries such as Benjamin Franklin
could rest assured in their citizenship and free status, Equiano's narrative contrasts this sharply with the lives of nominally "free" black men.

Indeed, even as it might be becoming the "land of the free," the United
States specifically falls short of becoming an idealized place in which black
men might become fully enfranchised agents, and Equiano's further characterization of the American colonies in this chapter emphasizes his British loyalty. When he visits Charlestown, South Carolina, he witnesses the
"town illuminated" (*IN* 128) in local festivities over the repeal of the Stamp
Act. However, two white men who refuse to pay Equiano for his exchanged
goods mar this celebration of the loosening of British economic authority. As
David Kazanjian claims, "by juxtaposing the celebrations over the Stamp Act
repeal on the streets of Charleston with an account of being swindled by white
American colonials, Equiano tells us that he has been barred from the formal
and abstract equality of mercantile exchange that the repeal supposedly recognized."[33] While in Georgia, he encounters the "worse fate than ever attended
me" when two drunk white men beat him for unjust cause (*IN* 129). In these
situations, Equiano stresses the fact that as a black man, he has no legal recourse through which to register his complaints. As Equiano's simultaneous
and partially contradictory affiliations suggest, while the British American
colonies can revolutionize themselves into an independent nation, his own
evolution from black slave to free man to fully enfranchised economic agent
represents a more troubled and possibly incomplete transformation.

The presentation of Equiano's free papers is a case in point. When Robert
King decides to sell Equiano his freedom, Equiano immediately goes to the
Register Office to "get [his] manumission drawn up" (*IN* 135). When King
signs the manumission papers, Equiano rejoices that "I who had been a slave
in the morning, trembling at the will of another, now became my own master,

and compleatly free" (*IN* 137). Equiano even decides to include his manumission "before [his] readers at full length" (*IN* 137). Rather than include the manumission to show how free he has become, however, Equiano presents them to stress how *not free* he had been.[34] As he says, the manumission "expresses the absolute power and dominion one man claims over his fellow" (*IN* 137). This is underscored by the repetition of synonymous verbs in the document's most important clause:

> Know ye, that I the aforesaid Robert King, for, and in consideration of the sum of seventy pounds current money of the said island, to me in hand paid, and to the intent that a negro man slave, named Gustavus Vasa, shall and may become free, have manumitted, emancipated, enfranchised, and set free, and by these presents do manumit, emancipate, enfranchise, and set free, the aforesaid negro man-slave, named Gustavus Vasa, for ever; hereby giving, granting, and releasing unto him, the said Gustavus Vasa, all right, title, dominion, sovereignty, and property, which, as lord and master over the aforesaid Gustavus Vasa, I have had, or which I now have, or by any means whatsoever I may or can hereafter possibly have over him the aforesaid Negro, for ever. (*IN* 137)

King grants Equiano his freedom by saying so; he frees Equiano through the performative speech act of declaring that "by these presents [I] do manumit, emancipate, enfranchise, and set [him] free." Furthermore, by giving Equiano "all right, title, dominion, sovereignty, and property" over himself, the document—rather than demonstrate how free he became—alludes to how this ownership of himself that once was inherently his was taken from him in the slave trade. King does not give Equiano these things for the first time; he merely restores the "right, title, dominion, sovereignty, and property" *of* Equiano *to* Equiano, their rightful owner.

Nevertheless, as Equiano knew, the papers granting him these rights that he had already had—and had taken from him—were hugely important in the West Indies, as they enacted and provided proof of his freedom. Yet right after emphasizing their importance, Equiano stresses their unreliability. In a sense, the presentation of this document and what follows it repeats the Joseph Clipson episode; Equiano has his free papers and then nevertheless is imposed upon. Immediately following a paragraph describing his experience of becoming a "freeman" (*IN* 138), Equiano describes how a slave in Savannah "began to use [him] very ill" (*IN* 139). Equiano attempts to defuse the situation because "there was little or no law for a free negro here" (*IN* 139). Nevertheless, when Equiano loses his temper and "beat[s] him soundly" (*IN* 139), Mr. Read, the slave's owner, threatens to flog Equiano for attacking his slave. Realizing that even as a free black man he has no standing before the law, Equiano hides until his captain convinces Read to let the matter rest. As Kazanjian points out, this anecdote makes evident the cruel irony that in many senses one has more protection as a slave than he does as a free man because a slaveowner is invested in protecting his property.[35] Equiano acknowledges this directly in another scene recording similar misuse; when he later visits a friend named Mosa in Savannah, the night patrol insists that Equiano "go to the watch-house," where he will be either flogged or fined for having a light on after nine at night. When the patrol leaves Mosa alone, Equiano explains that "as the man of the house was not free, and had his master to protect him, they did not take the same liberty with him they did with me" (*IN* 158). While one member of the watch relents the next day, arguing, as Equiano attests, "that as I was a free man they could not justify stripping me by law," Equiano must enlist the help of a white man before the watch lets him go (*IN* 159). Much like with his depiction of the natural-historical texts, Equiano expresses faith in his man-umission papers but then shows how they are often ineffective. Furthermore, the promise of equality written into both the natural history texts and the free papers is not realized. Both the natural histories and his free papers show how he should not be mistreated, and yet he is.

Later, Equiano includes an additional example of misuse where the unreliability of a text figures prominently.[36] After working for Charles Irving as an overseer on his South American plantation, Equiano yearns to return to England. He finally requests his discharge from Irving, and the latter provides Equiano with a "certificate of [his] behaviour," which Equiano includes in full (*IN* 210). The document, one Carretta points out "he would need to prove that he was a free man and to find any other employment" (*B* 189), attests to Equiano's "honesty, sobriety, and fidelity," all which make him an "excellent servant" (*IN* 210). Irving accompanies Equiano to a sloop headed for Jamaica, where Equiano will go aboard a ship to England. However, soon after Irving departs, Hughes, the owner of the sloop, demands that Equiano work for him as a sailor on a schooner bound to Carthagena. When Equiano demurs, Hughes inveighs against Equiano's former master for freeing him and Doctor Irving for allowing him to leave, and he finally threatens to enslave Equiano if he does not follow his wishes. Hughes promptly orders for Equiano to be painfully suspended by a rope, where Equiano, as he says, "hung, without any crime committed, and without judge or jury, merely because I was a freeman, and could not by the law get any redress from a white person in those parts of the world" (*IN* 212). Despite the fact that Equiano possessed the certificate from Irving (who arranged Equiano's passage with Hughes), Hughes treats Equiano as he would a slave. Equiano is unfettered the next day and takes advantage of a disagreement between the captain and Hughes about his future to escape to the shore in a canoe and thus avoids being reenslaved (*IN* 213). Like the natural-historical texts, the import of the text on which Equiano often depends is counterbalanced with their uncertain nature.

BECOMING BRITISH, RETAINING BLACKNESS

Thus, when readers come to the end of Equiano's narrative, the text has endorsed both Mitchell's and Clarkson's natural-historical theories, indicated distrust of both these natural-historical texts and other texts ostensibly creating and documenting the black man's equal status with the white man, and then demonstrated how whites continually fail to live up to the promises inherent in both these kinds of documents. When these natural-historical and political arguments have seemed to fail, Equiano advances an economic argument for why the British empire should abolish the slave trade. If, as Equiano hopes, the slave trade were to be abolished by the British legislature and, as he proposes, a "system of commerce was established in Africa, [then] the demand for manufactures would most rapidly augment," (*IN* 233) making commerce more profitable than the slave trade.

As Geraldine Murphy points out, Equiano's proposition of expanded British trade *with* African peoples rather than *of* African peoples does not sit well with many contemporary readers who, with the privilege of historical hindsight, see the colonization and underdevelopment of parts of the African continent that have come into fruition.[37] In addition, one attentive to the way race was conceptualized in the eighteenth century also might pause. As Equiano writes, he believes that "the native inhabitants would insensibly adopt the British fashions, manners, customs &c." (*IN* 233). Furthermore, as they do so, "in proportion to the civilization so will be the consumption of British manufactures" (*IN* 233). As Carretta and Roxann Wheeler have pointed out, Equiano here proposes that the African will become move civilized, moving up several stages that are hypothesized by stadial theories (*B* 318; Wheeler, *CR*, 283–85). In addition, one should note, this idea of adopting a different country's "manners and customs" hews closely to what Samuel Stanhope Smith called "state of society" (*EC* 110) and what Mitchell called "ways of living" ("ECDC" 136). These ways of life were exactly what were considered by many to also influence color, complexion, and appearance. One could get the idea that, maybe, for Equiano, advocating these changes in manners relates to an effort to turn Africans white.

But maybe not. Perhaps, like him, they can become—just as his *Narrative* has documented—"civilized" while still remaining black. Indeed, Equiano stresses that just as the "Aborigines of Britain" became more civilized and thus consumed more manufactured goods, "It will be equally immense in Africa.—The same cause, viz. civilization, will ever have the same effect" (*IN* 233–34). However, here, the "same effect" is that the Africans will become consumers of British manufactured goods and, thus, contributors to the British economy, not that they will physically become white. Equiano proposes that the spread of civilization will change the Africans in terms of economic status, but he does not indicate, like Smith and Mitchell, that a change in custom and manners will necessarily result in a change in color. After all, these Africans, as Equiano proposes, will stay in their original African climate.

The fact that, in Equiano's proposal, these Africans would become more "civilized" but not necessarily more white—in some senses, an incomplete transformation in natural-historical thought—makes the "white negro" with which he begins his final chapter an important figure for him. When he opens chapter 12, Equiano signals he is nearing the close of his text, writing that "I therefore hasten to the conclusion of a narrative, which I fear the reader may think already sufficiently tedious" (*IN* 220). Yet after signaling his rush to the end, Equiano pauses to include a brief description of a "white negro woman": "Soon after my arrival in London, I saw a remarkable circumstance relative to African complexion, which I thought so extraordinary that I shall beg leave just to mention it: A white negro woman, that I had formerly seen in London and other parts, had married a white man, by whom she had three boys, and they were every one mulattoes, and yet they had fine light hair" (*IN* 220). Equiano clearly is interested in the racial status of the progeny of interracial marriage, a topic pertinent to him, perhaps, because of his own 1792 marriage to a white woman with whom he would later have two children. However, what fascinates Equiano about this particular example is the persistence of blackness, even in the progeny of a "white negro woman" (*IN* 220). Clarkson's treatise holds that when a people of one color are relocated to a new climate, those people will eventually become the "native colour" of the original inhabitants of that climate (*Essay* 206). He also emphasizes—repeatedly— that the children of those migrants will become lighter (in the case of darker peoples who move to colder climates) or become darker (in the case of lighter peoples who move to warmer climates) (*Essay* 202). However, Equiano is not so sure. This negro woman who now appears white raises questions: did she become lighter if and when she moved to London (as Clarkson claimed many blacks from the West Indies attested "they had found a sensible difference in themselves since they came to England" [*Essay* 203])? If she did undergo some sort of change, did she retain any blackness? Equiano's wedged-in example is quite subversive in a way. Given his earlier suggestion that Africans who are somehow lighter are considered "deformed" (*IN* 38), his inclusion of this woman suggests that he does not equate becoming white with becoming beautiful. Rather, he emphasizes how blackness—even when not on the woman's skin itself—is retained in her body and somehow passed on to her sons. Rather than be entirely "white," the young men are "mulattoes," with "fine light hair" (*IN* 220).

In this way, the *Interesting Narrative* has an interesting symmetry: the concern with how dark peoples acquired their darkness and might become lighter in the future bookends Equiano's text. He ends his first chapter with the natural-historical question of how Africans came to be dark and begins his last chapter with a white negro woman, a figure that raised the natural-historical question about how she came to be light. This is important because, first, Equiano's interest in this person contextualizes his ending argument about Africans adopting British "manners and customs." This particular woman, despite undergoing some sort of transformation and living out her days in London, still preserves a kind of blackness that she passes on to her children, and the fact that she does so frames Equiano's ending. While Equiano does propose making Africans more civilized, he does not necessarily advocate making them "white." She has moved to London's colder and ostensibly more civilized environment and yet her transformation remains incomplete, and her children are darker than she—not lighter, as Clarkson claimed they would be. Second, she is an ambiguous figure with which to frame the conclusion of the *Narrative*. That one could be "white" and "negro" simultaneously destabilizes racial boundaries. In addition, the "white negro" figure constitutes a conundrum for natural history because the figure could be used (and indeed, was used) both to prove and to disprove aspects of natural-historical thought. It could be said that this person's transformation into whiteness proved the fact of transformable race, that one could change if she moved to a new geographic location and undertook new social practices. However, it could also be said that this figure pointed to problems in natural-historical thinking, particularly in Equiano's example, because she does not change "fully." Her very ambiguity allows Equiano to suggest that even as some transformations take place, blackness persists. And this ambiguity that Equiano utilizes is exactly what scientists like Benjamin Smith Barton would consistently struggle to explain, an effort itself that a contemporaneous novelist, Hugh Henry Brackenridge, would mercilessly satirize.

Brackenridge and the Limits of Writing Natural History

On August 5, 1796, Benjamin Smith Barton, an APS member who was trained in medicine at the University of Pennsylvania and the University of Edinburgh, sat down to write out what he called "Notes for a paper on the colour, &c. of the Negroes."[38] On six-by-seven and a half inch scraps of paper, he jotted down notes on what various natural historians had conjectured about this topic. He wrote that "there is an analogical argument in favour of the idea that there is more than one species of *man*, considered as a *genus*. The more we have examined natural productions, the more reason we have to say that nature has not been fond of creating isolate species." He then, in various configurations, sketched out what others before him had argued and scrawled out phrases that included things such as "Pechlin had once seen a negro. . . . he asserted that the black colour resides in the cutaneous reticulum. . . . He asserts that the black colour is not derived from the sun, and that the Bile assists in tinging the skin.—" On another sheet, he jotted down that "Pallas thinks the albino negro is no more in a diseased state than the black negro. . . . Blumenbach is of a different opinion." On another paper, he noted that "Blumenbach is of opinion that all those mammalia which are destitute of the brown pigment of the internal eye, are mere *varieties* which have degenerated from the primitive *species*. . . ." Barton's musings were probably incited by his examination of Henry Moss, an African American man who, as I discussed in the introduction, appeared to be undergoing a whitening process and was examined by several Philadelphia naturalists in 1796. These notes show Barton struggling to understand and to articulate the causes of epidermal blackness.[39] Indeed, these initial formulations evince a natural philosopher working to comprehend where one's dark complexion might come from (and, hence, where it might go). But more fundamentally, part of the process of formulating his own hypothesis about the "colour . . . of the Negroes" and recording other scientists' differing opinions on it, his notes demonstrate that even in the articulation of one thesis about the production of color, it necessarily adds to and becomes one among many of the various and disparate hypotheses that have preceded it. Most importantly here, these material fragments themselves emphasize the *textuality* of natural history, the very fact that just like novelists, these natural historians engaged in the process of producing stories about what might cause color and participated in the very process of writing race into being.[40]

These papers most likely served as notes toward what would become, first, Barton's September 16 presentation to the APS ("Facts relative to Henry Moss, a white negroe, now in this city") and, second, Barton's paper ultimately published as "Account of Henry Moss, a White Negro: together with Reflections on the Affection called, by Physiologists, Leucaethiopia humana; Facts and Conjectures relative to the White Colour of the Human Species" in the *Philadelphia Medical and Physical Journal*.[41] Barton's talk mused on Henry Moss and what might cause the various colors of humankind. It narrates some of the basic facts of Moss's background, including his birthplace in Virginia and his mixed race genealogy. In his "Account," Barton details the circumstances of Moss's change from having black skin to having white skin, and he conjectures that Moss is not an albino. This chapter will return to Henry Moss and the various natural historians who examined him, but for the moment, I want to highlight the narrative structure of Barton's scientific treatise. Like the other natural historians who wrote about Moss, Benjamin Smith Barton narrativized Moss's situation. He outlined Moss's history, gave details about his condition, and reflected upon what might or might not have caused his appearance to change. And, like his fellow naturalists, Barton wrote just one version of the Henry Moss story that entered into public circulation, constructed a speculative storyline, and interpellated Moss as a particular kind of racial being.

It might be easy for readers with twenty-first century postmodern sensibilities to regard Barton's notes, presentation, and published essay in this light, perhaps in no small part because environmentalist, natural-historical explanations for the causes of racial difference have been replaced by later theories of what causes human variation and of how societies interpret those variations. However, in this eighteenth-century moment, Barton and his colleagues were considered serious scholars in weighty debates about the causes of human complexion. And while these and other thinkers certainly disagreed with one another, their interlocutors took them seriously and on the scientific terms that each offered.

Unless, that is, one's interlocutor was Hugh Henry Brackenridge. In 1792 this politician, lawyer, and eventual judge published the first volume of what would swell to become his seven-volume novel, *Modern Chivalry*. Derived from the structure of Cervantes's *Don Quixote*, *Modern Chivalry* follows the adventures of Captain John Farrago and his Irish servant, Teague O'Regan, and it satirizes multitudinous aspects of the US public. As numerous scholars have pointed out, *Modern Chivalry* parodies, among other things, the American Philosophical Society itself and the debates that took place there on the topic of race and racial difference. In what follows, however, I complicate our notion that Brackenridge's book simply parodies the APS. Indeed, Brackenridge does lampoon the Society, but as I will explore below, it uses burlesque to critique not only APS conclusions but also APS methods. Making apparent the negative characteristics of certain aspects of Enlightenment thinking, *Modern Chivalry* reveals the gothic underside that haunts the scientific "advancement" of the eighteenth century.[42] Those who examined Moss saw themselves investigating one of the world's most pressing questions, and certainly some of them were doing it to make arguments about the unity of humankind and the evils of slavery. Nevertheless, *Modern Chivalry* takes aim not only at their theories about the development of various skin colors but also at their means of getting to those ends—in one example, by subjecting Henry Moss to uncomfortable and at times degrading examination, all for the scientific acquisition of knowledge. It is not just that *Modern Chivalry* is a slapstick comedy but rather a much more highly complex burlesque whose content is not all a laughing matter. Much like a court jester's performance in front of a sovereign king, *Modern Chivalry* is so silly as not to be punishable by law and/or power but also daring enough in its caricatured depiction of the APS members' actions to draw attention to unsettling aspects of these scientific endeavors. As an unnamed character argues about another topic during a town meeting, "I take it, that scurrility may be useful to those that bear it, and are the subjects of it. It may bring to a man's knowledge and serve to correct foibles that he would not otherwise have been conscious of, or amended. Men will hear from the buffoon or the jester, things they would not take from a friend, and scarcely from a confessor. It was on this principle that in the middle ages of Europe, a profession of men was indulged, and rewarded, in the houses of the great, called the Joculators, or Jesters."[43] While, as we shall see, Brackenridge himself and his politics fell far short of advocating the rights of people of color, *Modern Chivalry* not only ridicules an idea that has since come to be dismissed—that people's bodies would respond to environmental factors in a way that could transform their appearance and social categorization—but also underscores troubling dimensions of this kind of scientific thinking and experimentation on real people.

This way of reading bridges the gap between two different bodies of scholarship on Brackenridge's novel. In "As Others Saw Us: Notes on the Reputation of the American Philosophical Society," published in a 1972 edition of the *Proceedings of the American Philosophical Society*, APS librarian Whitfield Bell attests to the Society's eighteenth-century esteemed reputation and also notes figures such as Brackenridge who attacked it.[44] Since then, scholars such as William Stanton, Winthrop Jordan, Charles Martin, and John Wood Sweet all describe certain aspects of environmentalist understandings of the development of skin color and the Henry Moss example and then, to varying degrees, briefly comment on how Brackenridge's *Modern Chivalry* parodies each.[45] In these accounts, these scholars view Brackenridge's text simply as a response to the APS and neglect the literary dimensions of the text itself. They also do not consider *Modern Chivalry* within the much broader context of the plethora of literary works that engaged with eighteenth-century natural-historical racial thinking. By contrast, my focus here renders more complex our understanding of the very specific method *Modern Chivalry* uses and puts it in context with the other approaches this book thus far has limned.

The other, more literary-focused body of Brackenridge scholarship analyzes various aspects of Brackenridge's text, but they neglect to consider *Modern Chivalry* in its full relationship to APS debates and eighteenth-century thinking on race. Cathy Davidson, Dana Nelson, and Christopher Looby, for instance, emphasize the discord of the novel, specifically the way that the text's different, although periodically overlapping, voices articulate various and sometimes irreconcilable points of view.[46] For my purposes here, it is not only that, as Paul Gilmore points out, *Modern Chivalry* advances different political stances.[47] As I will show, by advancing perspectives at odds with each other about raced characters and, furthermore, race theory, the book's cacophony, a hallmark of this text, problematizes racial thinking itself.

This reading of Brackenridge's book has important implications for demonstrating the complex relationship between literature and natural history in the eighteenth century. It is not only that *Modern Chivalry* pokes fun at what would quickly become the largely disregarded science of environmentalism. Instead, by adding its own tongue-in-cheek accounts of race, racial difference, and racial explanation to those coming out of the APS,

Modern Chivalry points up a crucial aspect about Barton's notes and published essay: that all of these accounts are, to a certain extent, written attempts at providing an explanation for any given human being's appearance and what society might take that appearance to mean. Reading *Modern Chivalry* not simply *as a response to* but rather as a document *written alongside* these other accounts shows the way the textuality of literature can bring to light the textuality of natural history. *Modern Chivalry* is not a piece of fiction that simply draws on scientific ideas. Literature, in this case, occupies a corresponding space in which racial stories are written, much like the ones APS members write; literature serves as an imbricated discourse with science. It is not just that the ludicrous nature of some of Brackenridge's stories call attention to the outlandish quality of some of the scientific treatises published at the same time; it is that the narrative qualities of Brackenridge's novel call attention to the narrative dimensions of the APS pieces. In other words, reading *Modern Chivalry* along with these other APS documents demonstrates how we should consider these scientific texts not so much as "truths" and more as written narratives that try to understand the world around them. Both the literature and the natural histories of the time period were efforts to narrate the world into existence. To wit, these natural historical texts do not describe the people that they ostensibly report upon; they—much like the literature of the moment—create them. *Modern Chivalry* forces its readers to ask, what, at the end of the day, is the precise difference between these two ways of "writing transformable race"?

THE MULTITUDES OF HUGH HENRY BRACKENRIDGE AND *MODERN CHIVALRY*

Over the course of his career, Brackenridge became known for advancing and then reversing—or, at least, appearing to backtrack or hedge on— various positions. After emigrating from Scotland with his family as a child, Brackenridge grew up in Pennsylvania. He attended the College of New Jersey, served as an army chaplain during the Revolutionary War, and was a practicing lawyer, judge, and politician.[48] In three key instances briefly outlined here, Brackenridge appeared to contradict himself. One of Brackenridge's most remembered conflicted stances includes his role in the 1794 Whiskey Insurrection. As Ed White delineates in his scholarly introduction to *Modern Chivalry*, this conflict arose between moneyed, metropolitan elites and rural, western, working-class farmers.[49] In 1791, Congress taxed the alcohol distilled from the grain that farmers raised for their primary income in an effort to pay down the national debt accrued during the Revolutionary War. As White explains, the farmers felt they had helped finance the war by buying bonds that afterwards lost their value and were then bought by wealthy elites. When the government imposed the tax in part to pay off the bonds at their original value, the farmers took the tax as "an attempt to re-distribute wealth from the poor and middling classes to the rich."[50] Western farmers began to resist the tax both by demonstrations and violence, and, as White attests, "by 1794, westerners had formed a large-scale congress, es-tablished a democratically-organized militia army, and talked more openly about resisting the elite interests of the national government."[51] As these events unfolded, Brackenridge became distrusted from both sides. Prior to this, he had supported the ratification of the Constitution, angering his rural constituents who subsequently voted him out of office for his seeming be-trayal to their interests, but he also disagreed with the new tax and worked against it, although not in the more confrontational approaches that some farmers used.[52] While Brackenridge sought a middle ground on the matter, in the end, he was regarded with suspicion by both rural farmers who did not see him as militant enough and federal officials who associated his resist-ance to the tax with the raucous citizens and, thus, with treason. When fed-eral armed forces moved to put down the rebellion, Brackenridge feared for his life. Ultimately, Brackenridge was able to convince Alexander Hamilton, Secretary of the Treasury, of his innocence, and he later published *Incidents of the Insurrection in Western Pennsylvania in the Year 1794*, an attempt to absolve further his actions and his name.[53]

The Whiskey Rebellion, however, was not the only place where Bracken-ridge advanced what would be seen as a somewhat inconsistent politics. In 1779, Brackenridge founded *The United States Magazine* to publish both po-litical and literary pieces.[54] In an essay published in December of that year entitled "Thoughts on the Enfranchisement of the Negroes," Brackenridge denigrates slavery, advocates its abolition, and admonishes those who "have been so grossly stupid as to assign the [black] color as a mark for servitude."[55] Nevertheless, after advocating for the freedom of African Americans, he proposes that freed slaves be relocated west of the Mississippi River in "that country forfeited by the native Indians in consequence of their hostilities against us."[56] Although he could imagine a world in which Africans would be free, Brackenridge fails to envision a world in which they would be incor-porated into the US body politic. This stance—which would not necessarily be viewed as "contradictory" in his day—nevertheless highlights the vexed nature of Brackenridge's racial politics and prohibits us from viewing his racial politics unilaterally.

Brackenridge's writings about Native Americans were also considered to be characterized by a similar, if perhaps more striking, confliction. Earlier the same year in *The United States Magazine*, Brackenridge published a two-part essay entitled "Establishment of These United States—An American Ac-count," in which he argues that Indians do not have a right to the land of North America just because they lived upon it before the white man. Indeed, Brackenridge argues, the right to the land goes to those who cultivate it, claiming that the "aborigines of this continent can therefore have but small pretense to a soil which they have never cultivated."[57] As Daniel Marder makes clear, Brackenridge had long been hostile to Native Americans.[58] In 1783, Brackenridge helped publish *Narratives of a Late Expedition against the Indians, with An Account of the Barbarous Execution of Col. Crawford; and The Wonderful Escape of Dr. Knight and John Slover from Captivity, in 1782.* The text responded to frontier violence, and Brackenridge hoped it would convince readers in the east of what he saw as the brutality of the Indians on the frontier (*Reader* 10). Brackenridge includes the narrative of Dr. Knight, and he serves as an amanuensis for that of John Slover. He also appends a note in which he "subjoin[s] some observations with regard to the animals, vulgarly called Indians."[59] He repeats several of his arguments from his "Establishment of These United States," and advances his opinions on negotiating with the Indians. "With regard to forming treaties or making peace with this race, these are my ideas:—They have the shapes of men and may be of the human species, but certainly in their present state they approach nearer the character of Devils: take an Indian; is there any faith in him?" (*LE* 36). Perhaps most vehemently, Brackenridge declares that "the tortures which they exercise on the bodies of their prisoners, justify extirmination" (*LE* 36) and that "These nations are so degenerate from the life of man, so devoid of every sentiment of generosity, so prone to every vicious excess of passion, so faithless, and so incapable of all civilization, that it is dangerous to the good order of the world that they should exist in it" (*LE* 37). However, just two years later, Brackenridge would soften his tone in his "Trial of Mamachtaga." As Marder succinctly describes, "having vindicated himself somewhat as a man who stood for the people, which meant against Indians and eastern subtleties, Brackenridge suddenly turned on them. He undertook the defense of an Indian who had ended a drunken spree by killing a carpenter working on the Brackenridge house" (*Reader* 11).[60] While "Trial of Mamachtaga"—written in 1785 but not published until 1806 (*Reader* 355)—certainly makes use of stereotypical ideas about Native Americans, it lacks the heated and aggressive tone of his notes in the captivity narratives. Instead, even while emphasizing the murder Mamachtaga committed, he underscores Mamachtaga's kindness, honesty, and honor, all the while painting a negative portrait of whites who wish to lynch the Indian instead of following the protocols of the law. "Trial of Mamachtaga" certainly does not reveal Brackenridge to be a friend to the Indians; however, he does appear to be an Indian-hater who finds admirable qualities in Indians. While, like his other two stances outlined above, this postition is one that is complex, Brackenridge's contemporaries and constituents were often puzzled and even angered by how he appeared to be of many minds on these issues.[61]

Modern Chivalry is characterized by the same contradictory nature. As White points out about its practically tortured publication history, *Modern*

Chivalry was published over a number of years from 1792 to 1815 and allows us to see Brackenridge writing at various points in his career.[62] It also voices a number of opinions of and views upon race and its raced characters. The text often gives its readers problematic, stereotypical depictions of its Irish, black, and Native characters; at the same time, it also lambasts white women and men. Additionally, at times the whites are the privileged characters, but at others, the book itself critiques improper treatment of raced characters. These competing perspectives in the novel are related to the debates scholars have had for years over the many voices in the novel, including whether one character "speaks" for Brackenridge or presents his perspective and which character serves as the book's protagonist. Vernon Parrington declared in 1930 that Farrago "is evidently Brackenridge himself,"[63] a stance later reworked both by Joseph Harkey who sees "Teague represent[ing] the unenlightened, impetuous majority, the Captain, the rational minority"[64] and by John Engell who views Farrago as the protagonist and Brackenridge as the narrator.[65] Subsequently, scholars have argued that the novel is host to a multitude of voices, including that of Teague, Farrago, the narrator, an "implied author"[66] and perhaps Brackenridge himself. Both White and Looby emphasize the difference between the narrator's voice and that of Brackenridge and also caution readers from seeing Farrago as the protagonist or overidentifying with him, since he himself is often the object of the text's critique.[67]

Given these scholarly debates, I want to suggest that in *Modern Chivalry*, the very conflictedness of the stances on race is not so much a narrative problem (i.e., what perspective is the one that Brackenridge or the text *really* takes?) but rather an important point in and of itself. First, Brackenridge's racial politics—inconsistent and problematic as they often are—cannot be considered exactly correspondent to either his intentions for or, more to the point, the cumulative effect of the book. Second, the discord in the text on issues of race theory does not just make fun of any one prevailing hypothesis of the time. Interestingly, the novel's own articulation of several, contradictory theories parallels Barton's notes in this way: by adding its own theories to the already-proliferating theories, it underscores the fact that they are all theories, or, in other words, ideas created through discourse. Indeed, with its many voices and contradictory stances, the form of the book itself unsettles assumptions not just about certain claims regarding the production of racial difference but also about the *nature* of those claims. In this way, the text ends up satirizing not only the outcomes and methods of this racial science but also the impossibility of trying to articulate the exhaustive truth about race in the first place. Like Barton's notes, *Modern Chivalry* shows that both the science and the literature were attempts to narrate race, to explain race, and to figure it through language and signification. But, unlike scientific treatises, the novel does this by spinning a yarn about the escapades of Farrago and Teague.

TEAGUE'S SKIN

Very early in Farrago and Teague's adventures, they come upon a large owl that had been shot and left to hang in a tree. Its size interests Farrago, so he has Teague tie the dead bird to his saddle. As they are "passing by the house of one who belonged to the society" (*MC* 15), the APS member comes out to ask the Captain about the bird, what the philosopher considers to be a scientific specimen fantastic enough to gain the Captain entry into the society. Farrago agrees to hand over the owl, but he declines admission into the organization since he considers himself "unqualified." When the Captain refuses the invitation, the philosopher offers a seat to Teague instead. A plot element that recurs throughout the novel, Teague over and again tries to obtain or is offered positions that Farrago thinks are beyond his capacities and qualifications. Farrago has already talked Teague out of becoming a public official, and he will soon prevent him from becoming a minister.[68] Here, Farrago must act quickly to prevent Teague from accepting what Teague sees as "a door open to his advancement" (*MC* 16).

To talk Teague out of accepting this invitation, Farrago describes what will happen to him as a member of the APS: the society will treat him either as a natural-historical specimen, a reconnoiterer of specimens, or a philosopher who is tortured until he can solve puzzling natural-historical problems. He asks Teague,

> Do you think it is to make a philosopher of you that they want you? Far from it. It is their great study to find curiosities; and because this man saw you coming after me, with a red head, trotting like an Esquimaux Indian, it has struck his mind to pick you up, and pass you for one. Nay, it is possible, they may intend worse; and when they have examined you awhile, take the skin off you, and pass you for an over-grown otter, or a musk-rat; or some outlandish animal, for which they will, themselves, invent a name. If you were at the museum of one of these societies, to observe the quantity of skins and skeletons they have, you might be well assured they did not come by them honestly. I know so much of these people, that I am well persuaded they would think no more of throwing you into a kettle of boiling water, than they would a tarapin; and having scraped you out to a shell, present you as the relics of an animal they had procured, at an immense price, from some Guinea merchant. (*MC* 16–17)

Here, Brackenridge satirizes the APS and the "invitation" it extends to Teague. But, as Christopher Looby has convincingly argued, even while Brackenridge parodies the APS as being too open to potential members, the text also criticizes Farrago, the ostensible voice of reason, as well. Indeed, Looby writes, "the Captain represents an outmoded pretense of rationality and a reactionary attachment to a deferential social protocol, while Teague represents emergent democracy. To say this isn't to deny that Brackenridge has misgivings about the emergent egalitarian social order; he obviously does. It is only to say that his irony cuts both ways, and that if the final effect of the satire of *Modern Chivalry* is to cut one way more vigorously than the other, it cuts against the Captain's nostalgia more violently than it does against Teague's optimistic, disorderly hopes for social change."[69] It is interesting to note how the narrator critiques the lack of objective, scientific evaluation in lieu of political favoritism (*MC* 18) and how Brackenridge's earlier "Memoir" jests at both the unnamed protagonist whose disingenuous scientific efforts fail to receive the society's attention and his servant whose ignorance makes him a better potential member, since he has so much to learn.[70] More to the point here, however, is how Farrago paints a gruesome scene of how the Society might treat Teague as a natural-historical sample himself. This scene commences a characterization of Teague that will continue throughout the text, namely, that of a person around whom many racial identifications condense.[71] First, Teague is an Irishman, and he therefore would have been discursively linked to African Americans.[72] This association is strengthened and made all the more explicit here with Farrago's reference to the "Guinea merchant." Farrago ostensibly uses the term here to mean a seaman who trades in exotic animals. However, "Guinea merchant" also means "one who trades with Guinea; hence, a slave-dealer" (*Oxford English Dictionary*). On the one hand, Farrago says that the APS members would present Teague as a type of exotic turtle they acquired from abroad; on the other, the text suggests that this "animal" is analogous to a black slave. Second, clearly, Teague is associated with Indians, as the APS members might try to "pass [him] for one" (*MC* 17). As Charles Martin points out, with the conjectured removal of Teague's outer membrane, his skin "becomes the body's sole signifier."[73] The reference to Teague's skin in this scene designates it as something that the natural historians might take off and as something that serves as a racial marker that associates him with these other racialized groups.

However, Farrago's outrageous warning likens the Irishman not only to African Americans and Native Americans but also to "curiosities" on which naturalists might perform experiments. And while part of the scene's humor arises from the incongruent juxtaposition of what might be done to humans versus to animals, it also eerily conjures up examples where Native and African peoples actually were subject to these types of natural-historical investigations.[74] For instance, five years after Brackenridge published this first volume of *Modern Chivalry*, Judge George Turner of the "Western Territory" presented to the philosophical society "a variety of very curious and interesting articles from different parts of the Western country . . . tending to throw some illustration on the Indian Antiquities of North America."[75] The articles included some quotidian items such as a stone pestle, arrows, and a hatchet in addition to sacred items such as a conjuror's mask, calumet, and Native remains taken from "an ancient Indian grave on the great Kenhawa."[76] However, the collection also contained items such as "Buffalo Dung," "petrified ordure, supposed to be human," the "skin of an Indian, taken from the side," and "Part of the Sea Otter skin from its blank, where the fur is shortest."[77] While Farrago's tirade is striking in part because it sounds preposterous, *Modern Chivalry* is oddly prescient in anticipating a moment when the APS would house both the "skin of an Indian" and that of a "Sea Otter."[78]

Another example, of which Brackenridge almost certainly knew, focused on the skin of African peoples. *Modern Chivalry* notes that the philosophers "published books, they called Transactions," and the second volume of *Transactions* (1786) included a paper by John Morgan entitled "Some Account of a Motley Coloured, or Pye Negro Girl and Mulatto Boy, Exhibited before the Society in the Month of May, 1784, for Their Examination, by Dr. John Morgan, from the History Given of Them by Their Owner Mons. Le Vallois, Dentist of the King of France at Guadaloupe in the West Indies."[79] Morgan was a founding member of both the College of Physicians of Philadelphia and the APS, and his paper describes a pair of two-year-old children of interest to the philosophers because of their striking appearances. Adelaide, much like Henry Moss, had splotches of white across her mostly black skin. The text reports that

> The eyes are black and lively, a little to the left and towards the middle of the chin a white spot begins, which is long in proportion to its breadth, but of less magnitude than that of the forehead: It stretches under the chin to the upper part of the throat. The neck, the upper and under part of the chest, the shoulders, the back, loins and buttocks to the junction with the thighs, and the pudendum, are of the colour of her face, but the loins and the thicker part of the buttocks are of a deeper black. ("SA" 392)

The account reports in excruciating detail the exact color of each of Adelaide's body parts, including her genitalia. Morgan compares her to Maria Sabina, "of whom Mons. Buffon gives an account" ("SA" 393) and describes her mother as "a negro of the Ibo nation" ("SA" 394) and father, "of the Mina Nation" ("SA" 394). The young boy, Jean Pierre, "is entirely of the colour of a mulatto, except that he has from nature a white aigrette in his forehead like that of Adelaide. The hair in that part is white mixed with black, which is not so in Adelaide. The stomach, and the legs from two inches above the ancles to the middle of the calf of the legs are entirely of a beautiful lively white; there is also a white spot in the upper part of the penis. Over the white parts of the legs there is a light white down, longer and thicker than children commonly have at this age" ("SA" 394–95). While Morgan records that Jean Pierre "was born at Grandterre, Guadaloupe, of a negro wench named Carolina and of a white man, an European, whose name I did not learn" ("SA" 394), he does not address the nature of the relationship between the parents, although the omission of the father's identity may hint that Jean Pierre very well could have been a product of the sexual exploitation of his slave mother. Although Morgan conjectures that the spots of lighter skin might be caused by maternal impression (a theory that claims that things a pregnant mother experiences or even sees become impressed upon her unborn child), Morgan writes that "Such is the natural history of those two extraordinary children; but what causes have produced those surprising phænomena and alteration of the natural colour of their skin, are left for others to investigate and explain" ("SA" 395). Both children, the essay tells us, "belong to Mons. Le Vallois" ("SA" 394).

Despite what some scholars have assumed, it is not at all certain whether Morgan exhibited the children at the meeting of the APS, examined them himself and then wrote up his observations, or presented his observations based upon "the History" given to him by Mons. Le Vallois.[80] The essay's title is full of ambiguous modifying phrases that do not give a clear sense of when, where, or how the physical inspection of the infants took place. The mysterious circumstances of the examination notwithstanding, the text itself is a result of it, and once published in *Transactions*, the essay circulated quite widely, as I mentioned in Chapter 2. In part because of some of the other natural-historical essays in this specific edition, the second volume of *Transactions* was sent to "Societies and particular persons in Europe, as they shall think entitled to this respect" (*Early Proceedings* 143) and was purchased by persons such as Benjamin Rush, Benjamin Franklin, William Bartram, and Charles Peale.[81] When read alongside this "Account," Farrago's tirade in *Modern Chivalry* appears remarkable not only in its outlandish description of scientific methods but also in its uncanny resemblance to the particularly unnerving aspects of this natural-historical document.

Once Farrago enumerates the ways Teague would be treated as a natural-historical curiosity himself, he then turns to the tasks the society might assign him in order to procure other curiosities, such as flies, mire-snipes, and pole-cats (*MC* 17). The most outrageous task would be to clean the stars themselves. However, if the society decides not to use Teague as a specimen and not to send him out to retrieve other specimens, they will treat him as a philosopher who they will "rack and torture . . . with hard questions" (*MC* 17). Farrago envisions that Teague will have to explain, among other things, "how the Indians got over to America. You will have to prove absolutely that the negroes were once white; and that their flat noses came by some cause in the compass of human means to produce" (*MC* 17). Here the text most likely gestures towards the general debates the society had on the issue of Indian origins and Samuel Stanhope Smith's *An Essay on the Causes of the Variety of Complexion and Figure in the Human Species*, given as the society's annual oration in 1787. Smith's talk articulated an environmentalist point of view, where Smith argued that external factors, over the course of time, produced bodily features that came to signify racial difference. While this topic arises briefly here before being explored much more thoroughly in subsequent sections of *Modern Chivalry*, Farrago uses it to summarize his argument to Teague. "These are puzzling questions," he says, "and yet you must solve them all. Take my advice, and stay where you are" (*MC* 17). Farrago's argument convinces Teague, and "without bidding the philosopher adieu, they [pursue] their route as usual" (*MC* 18). In the next chapter, as the narrator offers "observations" of the prior episode, he muses on the hyperbole of the previous scene. "It may be said," he advances, "that this is an exaggeration of the facts; and can be considered only as burlesque. I profess it is not intended as such, but as a fair picture of what has taken place. Should it be considered in the light of burlesque, it must be a very lame one; because where there is no excess there can be no caricatura" (*MC* 18–19). Here the narrator speaks specifically of the invitation issued to Teague to join the organization, but the same can be said for aspects of Farrago's argument themselves. The caricatural nature of Farrago's amplified descriptions of what might happen to Teague point to what the text works to characterize as excessive in and of itself.

ENDLESSLY PROLIFERATING RACIAL THEORIES

After Farrago convinces Teague to decline membership in the philosophical society, he has a more intimate encounter with the association once the travelers arrive in Philadelphia. Waking up one morning to find Teague missing from the inn, Farrago suspects that he may have gone to hear the "annual oration, delivered before the Philosophical Society, by a member" that some of their fellow lodgers plan to attend (*MC* 73). Farrago joins the meeting and is surprised to find a "black member" sitting before the society. Cuff, a slave of a Maryland man named Gorum, had found a large stone that the society ascertained to be "an Indian's petrified moccason" (*MC* 73). The APS extended an invitation to Gorum for membership, but he declined because he felt that since Cuff had found the stone, he was "more intitled to that honour than he was" (*MC* 73). As the narrator explains, since Gorum "made it a point to do his slaves justice in any perquisite of their own, he could not think of robbing one, on this occasion of any honour, to which he might be introduced by this discovery" (*MC* 73). Although, as Cuff's slavemaster, Gorum consistently "rob[s]" Cuff of his freedom and his labor, Gorum demurs to take away this honor from his slave. Farrago and Teague resemble Gorum and Cuff, except that Gorum allows his servant not only to become an APS member but also to deliver the annual oration. Here one should note that Brackenridge lampoons the society, its members, and its potential members by satirizing how the APS will stoop to extend membership "even" to a "bog-trott[ing]" Irishman and a black slave.

Cuff, hesitant to speak before the society, goes to his master for advice on what to say. Gorum, the narrator tells us, "attending a good deal to literary matters, had heard of an oration delivered before the society, the object of which was to prove that the Africans had been once white, had sharp noses, and long hair; but that by living in sun-burnt climates, the skin had changed colour, the hair become frizzled, and in the course of generation, the imagination of the mother, presenting obtuse objects, had produced an offspring with flat noses" (MC 73). Here, *Modern Chivalry* satirizes Samuel Stanhope Smith's 1787 APS oration and subsequent publication. As I explained in the introduction, Smith's text was the apogee of eighteenth-century environmentalism.[82] In his essay, published shortly after the oration, Smith passionately argues for the unity of humankind. He contends that the effects of both climate and states of society impact the human form in such a manner as to give rise to the various races of people. Although humans may have many different appearances, for Smith, they all descended from a single, Biblical origin. In the final paragraph of his treatise, he says that

> The unity of the human race I have confirmed by explaining the causes of its variety.—The first and chief of these I have shewn to be climate; by which is meant, not so much the latitude of a country from the equator, as the degree of heat or cold, that depends on many connected circumstances. The next, is the state of society, which greatly augments or corrects the influence of climate, and is itself the independent cause of many conspicuous distinctions among mankind. These causes may be infinitely varied in their degree, and in their combinations with other principles. And in the innumerable migrations of mankind, they are modified by their own previous effects in a prior climate, and a prior state of society. Even where all external circumstances seem to be the same, there may be secret causes of difference, as there are varieties in the children of the same family. The same country often exhibits differences among individuals similar to those which distinguish the most distant nations. Such differences prove, at least, that the human constitution is susceptible of all the changes that are seen among men. It is not more astonishing that nations, than that individuals should differ. In the one case, we know with certainty, that the varieties have arisen out of the same origin; and, in the other, we have reason to conclude, independently on the sacred authority of revelation, that from one pair have sprung all the families of the earth. (EC 110–11)

In many ways, Smith's explanation for the varieties of men came from an optimistic and egalitarian outlook on all of humankind. Indeed, it is this kind of thinking that Phillis Wheatley and Samson Occom draw upon in their articulations for equality. Differences among humans were not inherent, natural, or inevitable. For Smith, they were produced over time; originally, everyone was the same.

Smith's talk was a momentous event, and his argument was generally accepted. As a March 1787 article in the *Freeman's Journal* rhapsodizes about the address,

> The subject was managed with uncommon ingenuity, depth, and elegance. The Supreme Executive Council, the General Assembly of the State,— the trustees of the University, the magistrates, clergy, and a very great number of the principal people of this city, by particular invitation, were present on the occasion. The profound attention given by so venerable an audience, and the excellent order in which the whole business was conducted, did honor to the society, and placed in a very respectable point of view the general philosophic taste in Pennsylvania.[83]

On the day of the oration, the Society "met and proceeded to the Hall of the University" and afterward, it requested that at least one thousand copies of the speech be printed as pamphlets (*Early Proceedings* 148–49). As Winthrop Jordan attests, the "main argument of Smith's *Essay* carried far greater conviction [than Lord Kames *Sketches*], for it was in fact a well-sustained statement of long-standing and widely held views on the question of race. On the whole, it was well-received."[84] Jordan elaborates that "among American scientists of Smith's generation, the environmentalist cast of mind reigned virtually unchallenged. In natural history, it seemed axiomatic that forms of life changed only to the extent that they were affected by their surroundings—a very great extent."[85]

But however seemingly egalitarian and recognized Smith's talk originally appeared to be, *Modern Chivalry* reveals the racial hierarchy implicit in Smith's hypothesis by inverting it in the alternative explanation that Cuff offers.[86] Gorum initially suggests to Cuff that "it would be doing no more than justice to his countrymen, for he was a Guinea negro, if he should avail himself of this occasion, to prove that men were all once black, and that by living in snowy countries, and being bleached by the weather, the skin had gradually become white, and the hair moist and long, and the imagination presenting prominent objects to the mothers, or the fathers differing among themselves, and pulling one another by this part, had given the long and pointed nose" (*MC* 73–74). Cuff follows his master's advice to claim precedence for the black man and improves upon it in his "Oration," recorded in a caricature of black slave vernacular. Cuff, by claiming that blackness was the original appearance of humankind and inverting Smith's hierarchy, renders Smith's latent assumptions manifest. Cuff announces that "Now, shentima, I say, dat de first man was de black a man, and de first woman de black a woman; and get two tree children; de rain vasha dese, and de snow pleach, and de coula com brown, yella, coppa coula, and, at de last, quite fite; and de hair long;

an da fal out vid van anoda; and van cash by de nose, an pull; so de nose come lang, sharp nose" (*MC* 74). Just like with Smith's oration, the (here, fictional) APS moves immediately to put Cuff's speech into print circulation. As Looby brilliantly points out, "this leaves us to wonder if it is the published version of the oration that *Modern Chivalry* is here quoting, and whether the phonetic transcription of Cuff's black dialect is his own, or the philosophical society's, or the narrator's. . . ."[87] Earlier, the narrator explained that Gorum knew of Smith's oration because "attending a good deal to literary matters, [he] had heard of an oration delivered before the society" (*MC* 73). Like Cuff's speech, here it is unclear whether Gorum read Smith's printed essay (because he attends to "literary matters") or if he merely heard about the delivered oration or the published article through the grapevine. Either way, the manner in which *Modern Chivalry* depicts both orations emphasizes their textuality, their very existence in—and only as—discourse. It is not that Cuff's take on the origin of man refutes Smith's but rather that its existence highlights the discursive nature of both. The line between writing that makes claims to truth and that which presents itself in jest becomes blurred.

In addition, Cuff's speech shows the slave himself to be quite an interesting figure. On the one hand, he speaks in a problematic stereotypical black dialect that obviously emphasizes his use of nonstandard English. On the other hand, he seems to hold the belief that the stone is a stone—not a moccasin—but yet he is willing to go along with the his master's belief that it is a moccasin, perhaps because it results in him traveling to Philadelphia alone. While Cuff appears to be simpleminded, his manipulation of his discovery into a free pass to travel unimpeded leads one to believe otherwise. In addition, insomuch as Cuff is depicted as a dimwitted character, the text uses his ignorance to characterize both the society itself and Smith's original oration as seemingly just as unsophisticated.[88]

By highlighting the racial value judgment built into Smith's scientific theory, Cuff's oration calls attention to some of the less egalitarian aspects of it. As Jordan makes clear, Smith's theory "laid the foundations for an imposing case for human equality."[89] However, it is based upon an implicit belief that Africans and Native Americans are, in their present state, inferior to the original, white race, from which they degenerated. Furthermore, Smith claims that unlike field slaves, house slaves, who live under more similar conditions to their white masters, are slowly becoming more like their white masters (*EC* 57–58). He writes that "the field slaves are, in consequence, slow in changing the aspect and figure of Africa. The domestic servants have advanced far before them in acquiring the agreeable and regular features, and the expressive countenance of civilized society" (*EC* 58). He also adds that a Native American student brought to a white college was becoming more like his classmates, claiming that "the expression of the eye, and the softening of the features to civilized emotions and ideas, seems to have removed more than half the difference between him and us. His colour, though it is much lighter than the complexion of the native savage, as is evident from the stain of blushing, that, on a near inspection, is instantly discernible, still form the principal distinction. There is less difference between his features and those of his fellow-students, than we often see between persons in civilized society" (*EC* 61–62).[90] The implication of this line of thinking, as Jordan points out, is that "the Negro was going to be equal of the white man only when the Negro came to look like one" and that Smith held "the hope that Negroes would simply go away."[91] When put in conversation with Cuff's oration, Smith's oration—while egalitarian and utopian in conception—begins to show its dystopian aspects. And, in a further ironic twist, this wishful thinking that African Americans might somehow "go away" agrees with Brackenridge's public statement regarding the colonization of African Americans on Native American lands ("Thoughts on the Enfranchisement of the Negroes" 104).

After Cuff advances his theory of the causes of racial difference, the narrator takes his own try at explaining the origin of the races or, as he puts it, "how the descendants of Adam and Eve, both good looking people, should ever come to be a vile negro, or even a mulatto man or woman" (*MC* 74–75). The narrator articulates and then challenges several popular explanations before advancing his own. He first takes up the idea that the mark God placed on Cain for killing his brother Abel was one of "a black complexion, frizzled hair, a flat nose, and bandy legs" (*MC* 75). The narrator dismisses this theory, reasoning that if that were the case, all black peoples must have died in the great flood.[92] He then tackles the "curse pronounced upon Canaan, the son of Noah, for looking at his father's nakedness" (*MC* 75). Many early American proslavery apologists argued that the curse on Ham and his descendants was that they were black, and these apologists used that association to defend the practice of slavery.[93] However, the *Modern Chivalry* narrator argues, this cannot be the case because "by Moses' own account the Canaanites were the descendants of Canaan; and we do not hear of them being negroes" (*MC* 75). The narrator turns next to a well-known argument advanced by Lord Kames' *Sketches of the History of Man* (indeed, the very idea that Smith himself attacks in his *Essay*) that contends that at the Tower of Babel, God gave various complexions—in addition to languages—to the people there. But, the narrator contends, since historians did not record this part of the story, claiming it "introduc[es] a miracle, which we are not warranted in doing" (*MC* 75). When he turns his attention to Smith's theory, the narrator says simply, "This does not appear altogether satisfactory" (*MC* 75).

The narrator then gives his own explanation of the existence of a variety of people. "I have thought of one," he says, "which I would suggest with great diffidence; the authors of those before me being great men, and their hypothesis not lightly overblown" (*MC* 75). The narrator claims that Adam was a white man and Eve, a black woman. Some of their children resembled Adam and were "red haired, fair complexioned, blue eyed, proportionably featured boys and girls" (*MC* 75), while others resembled their mother. Indeed, all the descendents therefore were varied in the shades of their skin, a "diversifyed progeny, with a variety of features" (*MC* 75). On the one hand, the narrator advances a theory that celebrates differences when he questions why people think Adam and Eve would have looked the same, asking, "For what necessity to make them both of the same colour, feature, and form, when there is beauty in variety. Do not you see in a tulip, one leaf blue, and another white, and sometimes the same leaf white and red?" (*MC* 75). But on the other hand, he goes on to disparage black women. He acknowledges that some readers will challenge his theory the same way he challenged the curse of Cain—that many of these peoples would have met their end in the great flood. He flippantly answers by claiming that "it is but giving some of the sons negro wenches for their wives, and you have the matter all right" (*MC* 76). The fact that the narrator's tone is at once idealistic—"there is beauty in variety" (much like Phillis Wheatley)—and also denigrating to black peoples—give "some of the sons negro wenches for their wives"—is key. While here Brackenridge's text is off-putting, to say the very least, it is also true that this mixed tone points up the mixed tone that is characteristic of much of eighteenth-century natural-historical writing on race.

But even more important, the narrator's enumeration of theories to which he appends his hypothesis oddly mirrors Barton's notes; both men catalog other theories before adding their own. Specifically because the text offers the narrator's explanation of the existence of black peoples so obviously in jest, *Modern Chivalry* depicts the articulation of racial theories as something that will continue on into perpetuity. The narrator's hypothesis clearly does not resolve the debate; it is not advanced as the *correct* theory that should end discussion. Instead, it is just another supposition added to the pile. Certainly, Brackenridge satirizes Smith's monogenism in particular by putting a version of the 1787 oration into the mouth of an ostensibly uneducated slave. Nevertheless, rather than articulate a theory to disprove Smith's, *Modern Chivalry* simply contributes another to emphasize the endless proliferation of theories. Underscoring not the resolution of these discussions but rather the ongoing series of guesses, *Modern Chivalry* does not satirize the efforts to explain the existence of different races just because it believes they are wrong but also because scientists make the effort to articulate seemingly definitive theories at all.

Although the text satirizes the scientific theories produced in order to reconcile the existence of the various races with the belief in a single origin, it does not dismiss the single origin theory outright. Indeed, it goes on to emphasize how important it *could be* to arguments against the institution of slavery. For example, the Captain seems unconvinced by Cuff's hypothesis that black and white peoples come from the same origin, and this impacts what he believes about slavery and abolition. When he finally does locate Teague, he is in a playhouse, trying out his skills as an actor. Convinced that Teague will never return to him as his servant, Farrago decides "to purchase a negro" (*MC* 85). He mentions his idea at breakfast at the inn, and a Quaker inquires of Farrago whether he "canst reconcile it with thy principles, to keep a slave" (*MC* 85). Farrago argues that since the "great law is Force," one who holds power over other things, such as animals, also has a right to execute that power over them. When the Quaker protests that "a negro," unlike a horse or oxen, "is a human creature, and possesses all the natural rights of man," Farrago retorts that natural rights are "resolvable, as in the inanimate world, into power on the one hand, and weakness on the other" (*MC* 85). He thinks himself "justifiable in making any man a slave to answer my purposes, provided I treated him well while he was such. This I take to be the only condition which the law of reason annexes to the enjoyment of such property" (*MC* 85). Here, Farrago echoes arguments made by proponents of slavery who claimed the humanity of the system itself. He continues his paternalist argument by asserting that "as the slave has the master always to provide for him; so the master has the slave always to subserve him: and thus by a conjoint interest, the felicity of both is promoted, and the sum of human happiness increased" (*MC* 86). Furthermore, Farrago attests, one's race does not necessarily qualify one to be a slave. "It is difficult to determine," he claims, "*a priori*, who are intended for slavery or freedom. . . . It is in vain to be squeamish, and stick at colour. It is true, I would rather have a white person, if such could be got; as I prefer white to black, especially in the summer season, as being a more light and airy colour" (*MC* 87).

For all Farrago's fallacious reasoning to justify slavery, the Quaker calmly dismisses him. "Thy reasoning, said the Quaker, is more rhetorical than logical; and thy analogies of nature, and historical proofs, cannot so far oppress the light within, as to make me think, that it is given to thee, or me, to make slaves of our species" (*MC* 87). But this is the point upon which Farrago remains unconvinced. Although the Quaker—regardless of how he accounts for racial difference—believes that ultimately Africans are of the same species, Farrago disagrees. "As to that, said the Captain, I am not clear that a negro is of our species. You may claim kindred with him, if you please; but I shall not" (*MC* 87). Finally, the Quaker concedes that Farrago obviously does not "give credit to what the book says of the first man, and his descendants," but he challenges Farrago that even if he does not believe "the species of the white and the black [to] be the same," certainly he must admit that the African is a man. Farrago agrees, but then continues on to say that since the African is a man, this makes both the white man and the black man subject to the law of power with which he first began.

As Emory Elliott points out, the Quaker in this exchange wins a "quiet victory over Farrago," in part because Farrago's rhetoric seems so imbecilic in this caricature of the paternalistic slaveholder.[94] However, similar to Equiano's *Narrative*, it also illustrates a certain ambiguity around what the text sees as the usefulness of natural-historical proofs of single humanity in the fight against slavery. On the one hand, although Farrago has heard Cuff's oration, he remains unconvinced that white and black peoples are "of the same species," and thus, all arguments for a single origin (whether made by slaves, university presidents, or narrative voices) then put toward an abolitionist end will be ineffective. On the other hand, the text leaves open the possibility that a more reasonable and reasoned person besides Farrago might be open to the Quaker's line of argument: namely, that if the unity of mankind might be proved, then slavery itself, at one blow, would be shown to be inhumane and wrong.

The narrator, however, in commenting on this exchange, chooses to take a route different from Farrago to defend the institution. He, too, confesses that he believes "that there can be no moral wrong in catching a young African, and bringing him away from his own happiness to pursue ours" (*MC* 87). Some may believe that "the Captain was not serious in thus advocating the cause of slavery," but he nevertheless "omitted some serious arguments," which the narrator is happy to supply (*MC* 87).[95] He goes on to argue that if slavery were wrong, everyone who owns a slave would be as guilty as the first person who enslaved him; if that were true, "no man that pretends to humanity, much less to religion, would be safe in being the possessor of a slave. The only way therefore to get rid of the difficulty is to justify, *ab origine*, traffic in all such property" (*MC* 88). Since no religious group—save the Quakers—has declared it to be wrong, the narrator reasons, it must not be. In addition, some "weak minded powers, in Europe" argue that the trade is a moral wrong and advocate for gradual abolition. This, the narrator says, he can agree with, for if abolition wins the day, he is all for its gradual implementation, commenting that he has

> always thought a defect in the criminal codes of most nations, not giving licence to the perpetrators of offences, to proceed, for a limited time, in larcenies, burglaries, &c. until they get their hands out of use to these pursuits, and in use to others. For it must be greatly inconvenient to thieves and cutthroats, who have engaged in this way of life, and run great risks in acquiring skill in their employment, to be obliged all at once to withdraw their hands, and lay aside picking locks, and apply themselves to industry in other ways, for a livelihood. (*MC* 88)

Even in Pennylsvania, the government has turned to gradual abolition, "for those who have got them could not do without them, no more than a robber could do without the money that he takes, being pressed by some great necessity to make use of that expedient to recruit his purse" (*MC* 88). Like with Farrago, *Modern Chivalry*'s narrator's argument takes very common defenses of slavery and pushes them to their ad absurdum. And although the narrator calls abolition itself "absurd," it is clearly his extreme reiteration of these arguments that is so, both in the sense that it is laughably funny, and in the sense that it renders these arguments, when articulated in seriousness, completely flawed.

Toward the end of his "Remarks," the importance of the origin of man argument recurs. The narrator attests that it is crucial to prove that there is no "wickedness of enslaving men" because otherwise, the conscience of Pennsylvania Christians might never be put to rest. Because most of them "hold, that the African, though of a sable race, is of their own species; being descended from Adam," once they realize that this clearly implies that slavery is wrong due to the "favourite maxim of the gospel—'Do to others, as you would have others to do to you'" (*MC* 89), their consciences will be upset. The satire here is multilayered. First, clearly, in the text's ironic tone, it shows the degree to which proslavery Christians are hypocritical if they subscribe to these two Biblical dicta—that humankind shares one origin and that one should treat others well—and nevertheless engage in the practice of slavery. Second, however, the conscience of the narrator himself should be "unsettled," for as he has made clear, he believes in a version of the single origin and yet he still remains proslavery. *Modern Chivalry* depicts the narrator showing these Christians to be inconsistent in their origins of man and proslavery beliefs as it simultaneously shows the narrator himself being foolishly inconsistent in his origins of man and slavery beliefs. *Modern Chivalry* demonstrates how the single origin arguments can be put to different ends that fail to argue against slavery, and, at the same time, it shows how vacuous proslavery advocates can be when they refuse to acknowledge what the implications of that belief is, in terms of slavery. In different ways, both the Quaker at the inn and the narrator show that if one does believe in the unity of the species, it should follow that slavery is wrong. Although not convinced by racial theories that support a single origin, the text nevertheless shows that if one believes in a single origin, abolitionist sentiment should logically follow. The text does not work to dismiss the Adam and Eve story itself but rather both the natural-historical theories that make it compatible with the existence of different races and the proslavery arguments with which it is incompatible.

In an interesting way, much like with the racial theories, *Modern Chivalry* never seriously advances an argument to refute the various proslavery justifications lampooned here. The Quaker remains oddly, reasonably silent, and the narrator offers abolitionist reasoning only as examples of that with which he *doesn't* agree. He closes the chapter by confessing that he has "been under apprehensions, that some of our young lawyers in the courts, might plead the constitution of the state, by which it is established that 'all *men* are born equally free and independent'" (*MC* 89). After admitting that this would mean that if one accepts that "a negro is a man," then the negro "must be set at liberty" (*MC* 89), the narrator himself quickly grows silent. "I shall say no more on this head, lest I should furnish hints to pettifoggers, who may make an ill use of their information" (*MC* 90). Farrago is painted as a fool, and the narrator has been painted as a fool, but the text hopes the reader will be much the wiser.

PEALE'S CAVE

At least in the Captain's case, all of the discussion about slavery is for naught because when he reunites with Teague, the Irishman returns to being Farrago's servant. However, somewhat resigned to the fact that the early American public incessantly tries to elevate unqualified persons into positions of power and influence, Farrago decides to assist Teague in seeking an office. He takes Teague to a Presidential levee and introduces him to the President. Farrago trains him for engaging in public matters, and at last, his efforts are rewarded. The President, in spite of—and in light of—the Captain's "exact account of the education and history of the bog-trotter," appoints Teague as an excise officer (*MC* 178). As Teague departs Farrago to begin to collect taxes, Farrago employs Duncan Ferguson, a Scotchman, to take up Teague's former duties.

While they are traveling through the countryside, Farrago and Duncan spend two days exploring a "cave in the neighbourhood" of their inn, in a scene that attests to the vexed depiction of Native Americans, the philosophical society, and the relationship thereof. When the travelers arrive, they first notice "certain rude sculptures" in the "figure of the tarapin, the bear, the turkey, &c," and the captain wonders if these images were the result of these animals themselves making an impression on the rock before it hardened or whether Native Americans carved them into the stone. Moving further into the cave, they come into a "second apartment," where they find "a vast bed of human skeletons petrified, but distinguishable by their forms" (*MC* 194). The skeletons are "giant," and the narrator assumes it had been "a repository of savage chiefs, whose bodies, converted into stone" by virtue of the petrifying water that also formed stalactites in the cave. In the next apartment, they find "bows and arrows, all petrified, that these warriors had used in life" (*MC* 194). The next day, when Duncan and Farrago return, they enter the "petrified grove," an area of the cave "which appeared to have been once the surface of the earth" (*MC* 195). Here they are captivated by "an Indian man reduced to stone" (*MC* 195). Upon leaving this odd place where everything has been petrified, the Captain takes "the skin of a wild cat," and Duncan departs with "a petrified turtle" (*MC* 195).

As Christopher Looby points out, because Brackenridge endorsed the extermination of Native tribes, "it is not hard to see that this fantasy of instant Indian petrification—their immediate conversion into inert pseudoantiquities— expresses, at the very least, a genocidal wish."[96] But while this certainly is the case, the cave scene also contains moments where there is a certain kind of conflictedness around Native Americans.[97] When Farrago and Duncan come across the gigantic skeletons, they observe them in awe. Farrago is fascinated and wonders aloud, "What can have become of this breed?" When Duncan conjectures that "they have fought wi' ane another, 'til they are a' dead," the narrator simply comments, "this was the easiest way of accounting for the loss" (*MC* 194). The fact that the narrator attests that this is the "easiest way" to explain the passing of this "breed" signals that there is, indeed, a harder way to explain it, perhaps one that emphasizes the eradication of Native Americans as an effect of their colonial encounter with white settlers. On the one hand, it seems that the text enacts a certain kind of nostalgia for the loss of Native cultures that characterizes white advancement.[98] On the other, it is dismissive of Native cultures, but even in its dismissal, the text attests to the violence done to them.

The narrator himself, when commenting upon both Farrago and Duncan's exploration into the cave and some similar engravings that he has seen, also expresses divergent reactions. Hearing of engravings "on the Monongahela, about forty miles above Pittsburgh," the narrator traveled there to see them. Both because he observes that the human foot engraved in the wall had "the narrowness, and smallness of the heel" he attributes to the Indian and because the engravings do not bear any "alphabetic mark of any language," he attributes the artwork to the Indians.[99] He views these, he says,

> as the first rude essays of the fine art of engraving; and to have been the work of savages of taste, distinguished from the common mass, by a talent to imitate in wood or stone, the forms of things in nature, and a capacity of receiving pleasure from such an application of the mental powers. Whilst a chief of genius, was waiting for the assembling of other chiefs, to hold a council; or while the warrior was waiting at a certain points for others, that were to meet him, he may have amusd himself in this manner; or it may have been the means to cheat weariness, and solace the intellectual faculty, when there was no counseling in the nation, or wars to carry on. (*MC* 197)

The narrator comments that it is this ability to create art that allows the "happy savage" to "exercise his first preeminence over animals we call Beasts" (*MC* 197). The Native enjoys "these abstract pleasures, that feed the imagination" (*MC* 197). Here, the narrator characterizes the Native as more civilized and less animalistic.[100] However, he quickly comments that this likely holds true exclusively for older tribes. "It would seem," he conjectures, "that the sculptures of which I speak are the works of more ancient savages, than these which have lately occupied this country; these tribes not being in the habit of making any such themselves." These older groups of Native peoples "would seem to have been a more improved race, who had given way to barbarians of the north, who had over run the country" (*MC* 198). In an instant, the narrator both commends Native peoples (the ancient tribes) for their artistic accomplishments and derides them (the contemporaneous ones) for their lack thereof.

In addition to the ambiguity around the depiction of Native Americans, an unanswered question that permeates this section is whether what Farrago and Duncan find in the cave are pieces of art or frozen remains. The Captain wonders if the first images he sees were "impressions" made by "the tarapin, the bear, the turkey &c" or if it was the "work of the savages" (*MC* 194). Perhaps more crucially, when Farrago sees "an Indian man reduced to stone," the narrator juxtaposes it with European sculptures. He writes that "if the virtuosi of Italy, could have access to this vault, there would be danger of them robbing it of some of these figures, in order to compare with the statues that have been made by hands" (*MC* 195). The cave, thus, is an indeterminate space: it could be a museum, where Farrago and Duncan stare at the works wrought either by the Natives (in terms of the etchings) or by the petrifying water of nature (in terms of the frozen Native remains); or it could be a burial site, a resting place for those who have died. While contemplating the history of the first figures, Farrago "lament[s] that he had not a philosopher at hand, to determine this," and reflected on "how good a school this would have been for Teague, had he been admitted a member of the Philosophical Society, as had been proposed at any early period" (*MC* 194). The narrator also comments that when Farrago discovers arrow heads made not out of stone "by the dint of human labour" but rather by being "first formed in wood, and then put in this water to petrify" (*MC* 195), he would lose "no time in communicating to the Philosophical Society, as will in due time appear, from a publication of their transactions" *MC* (195).

When the question of whether or not these indeterminate figures are either dead animals and people or works of art is raised in proximity with explicit comments about the APS, the cave uncannily mirrors and comments upon Charles Willson Peale's museum. An APS member himself, Peale was well-known as both a naturalist and an artist, and he displayed both portraits that he himself had painted along with natural-historical specimens in his museum, what would become by the early nineteenth century the "most famous and prestigious proprietary museum in America and perhaps the world."[101] In 1794, Peale relocated his museum to Philosophical Hall, a space he rented from the APS, and it contained both preserved animals and numerous portraits.[102] Peale's museum was arranged according to Linnean classification, important because Linneaus thought that varieties developed over time within species. The museum included portraits of Revolutionary figures, wild animals, Indian arrows, and human (both Native and European) scalps.[103]

Both Peale's museum and the APS collections themselves, like the imagined cave, housed artworks and specimen that evince an interest in the bodies of people of color. In 1791, while on his honeymoon with his wife in Maryland, Peale learned of James, an African American man whose black skin was giving way to white spots. Peale painted his portrait, sent a letter detailing James to the APS, and published an "An account of a person born a Negro, or a very dark Mulatto, who afterwards become white" in the *National Gazette*, on October 31, 1791.[104] James was of interest to the APS because of his changing skin tone, and Peale's letter describing James was read aloud at the October 7, 1791, APS meeting (*Early Proceedings* 197). Most importantly here, Peale exhibited the portrait in his museum once he returned home. In addition to this visual representation of James, there were other bodily components on exhibit. In 1796, the *Scientific and Descriptive Catalogue of Peale's Museum* by Charles Willson Peale and A.M.F.J. Beauvois described part of a Native body there on display. One item was the "skin of the thigh, and part of the leg, of an Indian, dressed in the Indian manner." The catalogue claims that the "piece of skin belonged to a warrior, who was wounded in general Sullivan's expedition into the Genesee country, and who, not being able to defend himself, would not yield."[105] Peale already possessed a few bones of a "Mammoth,"[106] and although the publication of this section of *Modern Chivalry* predated it, in just a few years, Peale would display the bones of a large mastodon excavated in New York.[107] And while not in the Peale Museum, the APS Cabinet of Curiosities once held part of an Indian skeleton taken out of a grave in Cincinnati, sent to Benjamin Smith Barton by Colonel Jonathan D. Sergeant.[108] *Modern Chivalry*'s cave mirrors Peale's museum in that it is filled with objects of both art and human remains and raises questions about the difference between the two. Speaking of his speculation that artists might rob the cave of its "figures" to compare them with their "statues that have been made by hands," the narrator comments that "when this cave shall have gained due celebrity, there is no question, but that attempts of this nature will be made. I submit therefore, whether it would not be adviseable for the connoisseurs of America, to apply to the legislature of the state, where the cave is, to prevent such exportation" (*MC* 195). What is left undetermined about the narrator's suggestion is whether he means for the cave to be protected by the state as a sacred burial ground or as a repository of art.

By depicting the cave as a kind of museum, *Modern Chivalry* satirizes the pretentions of the philosophical society for what the text views as its tendency to view ordinary objects as extraordinary ones.[109] In his "Observations," the narrator relates that he had once heard the claim that "Ferdinando Soto, had been on the Ohio waters, and as high as the mouth of the great Kenaway," and that this was proven because an "imperial eagle was to be seen engraven on a rock" (*MC* 196). The "vestiges of fortifications" found in the area thus were assumed to be Spanish works, and even "the great Franklin had adopted this hypothesis with regard to these forts, from the sculpture of the eagle" (*MC* 196). However, the narrator remains skeptical of this theory and asks a surveyor who had seen the sculpture himself. When the surveyor replies that the sculpture is a turkey, "all the hypothesis of the holy Roman eagle, and Ferdinando Soto, fell to the ground" (*MC* 196). The narrator makes fun of Franklin for building his thesis on what he mistakenly takes to be an eagle and for turning attention to an object that the narrator views as quite mundane. "It is a turkey," he says, "which the fancy of the virtuoso and antiquarian, has converted into the king of birds" (*MC* 196).

But the cave scene also calls attention to the darker, more troubling aspects of Peale's museum and other collections of similar objects. The cave not only serves as an odd type of exhibit space where Farrago, Duncan, their guide, and previous and future sightseers visit; it is also the burial ground for these Native peoples. In the "second apartment," there was "a vast bed of human skeletons petrified," which the narrator comments without doubt "had been a repository of savage chiefs, whose bodies, converted into stone by the virtue of this water; were preserved more durably than the mummies of Egypt" (*MC* 194). This is no coincidental dumping ground for dead bodies; as a resting place for "chiefs," it is a sacred burial space. Farrago and Duncan are not only dimwitted tourists tromping about unseen lands but also intruders into a hallowed space who thoughtlessly take souvenirs with them. Farrago leaves with the "skin of a wild cat," which he breaks off "by giving it a sudden jerk as he turned around" while Duncan left with a "petrified turtle" (*MC* 195). Depicting what cannot be taken as mere buffoonery, this scene is tragicomic, being both silly and deeply upsetting. In this way, the text depicts not only the enlightened, natural-historical mind at work amongst scientific evidence but also the more troubling aspects of this sort of "research."

RESEARCHING TEAGUE

When Teague begins his duty as an excise officer, *Modern Chivalry* expands its depiction of the types of research carried out on subjects of color. By the time he published Volume 4 in 1797, Brackenridge had both lived through his experience in the Whiskey Rebellion and written about it in *Incidents of the Insurrection* (1795). *Modern Chivalry*'s depiction of Teague's short run as a tax collector draws upon Brackenridge's experience, and it muses on the types of research done on people of color. The scene humorously claims that the philosophers oftentimes do not know what they are talking about. In addition, it critiques the scientific methods the philosophers use when investigating cases such as Teague's, thus displaying the disconcerting facets to this scientific "advancement" and nuancing these philosophers' ostensibly egalitarian stances.

When Teague, Farrago, and Duncan enter into the district where Teague will collect the taxes, the townspeople quickly assemble to tar and feather him. While the Captain attempts to lecture the crowd on why the government might be justified in assessing taxes, the citizens grab Teague, strip him of his clothes, and "pouring the tar upon his naked body, empt[y] at the same time a bed of feathers on his head, which adhering to the viscous fluid, gave him the appearance of a wild fowl of the forest" (*MC* 214). Once Teague frees himself from the crowd, he makes his way to the wilderness, and the Captain and Duncan also leave town to avoid similar treatment.

Once he is tarred and feathered, Teague becomes metaphorically both a strange bird of unknown origins and an escaped slave. After spending a night in the forest, he is recaptured by two hunters. The hunters cannot determine whether Teague is a bear or a fowl and finally decide that he must be "at least a new species of animal, never before known in these woods" (*MC* 222). They tie Teague with ropes, put him into a cage, and take him to the capital, where his captors begin "to exhibit him as a curiosity" (*MC* 222). A reiteration of the earlier scene where Teague and Farrago find the owl, this episode depicts Teague as the intriguing bird. Members of the philosophical society show up in short order to examine this wild beast brought into town. They request "a leisurely examination of the animal" (*MC* 223). As the philosophers prepare for their examination, the hunters first describe how they found him. They "were disposed, as was natural, to assist with some particulars of fiction, the singular qualities of the animal they had in charge" (*MC* 223). They briefly describe finding the animal "flying from the mountain," attempting to feed it "boiled and roasted flesh," and determining that its voice was "of a mixed sound . . . but that it had come to have some imitation of the human voice, and even articulation, and might from that circumstance be probably a species of the parrot" (*MC* 223). These "particulars of *fiction*" (emphasis added) are striking here. Indeed, the scene highlights the production of the stories told about each of these natural-historical specimens. As soon as the philosophers get some time to examine Teague, they advance their own report on the animal, which the narrator includes in draft form. The hunters' conjectures and the report of the philosophers are flattened out and presented as comparable accounts, highlighting the discursive quality of each and their roles in creating this subject as a certain type of raced being.

In their report, the philosophers note that this strange fowl's features are "growing through a viscous substance resembling tar" (*MC* 223), that his face has "the appearance of a human face," and that his eye has the "look wild, but steady, like that of a person under an impression of amazement and wonder" (*MC* 224). If it were not for the birdlike features, the philosophers might take the animal for a "Negro" (*MC* 224). "If this animal is to be referred to the quadruped, or beast kind, it would most naturally be classed with the Ouran Outang, or Wild Man of Africa: If with the bird kind, we shall be totally at a loss to assign the genus," they decide (*MC* 224). They ultimately determine that Teague must be something between the two, "a link between the brutal and the human species" (*MC* 224).

The report is remarkable for what the philosophers see versus what they do not see and for some of their examination tactics. They notice, for instance, Teague's smirk: "It cannot be said to laugh, but rather grin," they note, "though once or twice in our presence, you would have thought that it exhibited a dilatation of the oscular muscles, as if attempting to laugh" (*MC* 224). Teague is amused at their wonder and, in addition, their misrecognition of his status as an excise officer who has escaped persecution because he is enacting the very animal-like qualities the tar and feathering citizens tried to bestow upon him. However, there's no doubt that the entire examination was not particularly amusing. The philosophers relate that Teague lacks a tail, which "was ascertained by one of us, who in the interval of his sleeping, felt his rump" (*MC* 225). They also decide that he is "prepared to preserve its species" because of "the circumstance of nature having furnished it with testicles" (*MC* 225). Teague is able to hide in plain sight but is subject to invasive examination in order to do so.

This scene most likely satirizes the popular and scientific attention raised by Henry Moss when he arrived in Philadelphia in 1796.[110] However, in addition to making fun of the philosophers for their explanations of Moss's surprising change, *Modern Chivalry* also critiques the naturalists for the disconcerting methods used to advance their scientific knowledge. When Moss came to Philadelphia, he captured the interest of the general public and Philadelphia naturalists. He first was exhibited at a tavern where people could come view him, and he was examined by some of the leading scientific and political figures of the time, including Barton, Rush, Thomas Jefferson, and George Washington. The examination of Teague performed by the two unnamed philosophers resonates with the assessment of Moss carried out by these men, and the scene renders both inspections less as objective, scientific inquires and more as self-interested exercises that prioritize their insatiable desire for information over the comfort of their specimen.

When Benjamin Smith Barton reports on Moss in his "Account of Henry Moss, a White Negro," he characterizes himself as an educated and disinterested scientist and Moss as an unschooled subject, but the account contains narrative moments that disrupt the text. He details Moss's history and tries to explain that Moss's thoughts "run much upon the future" because he does not understand the science that Barton thinks accounts for his change of appearance.[111] "If the philosopher contemplates with astonishment such a change as this, it must appear miraculous in the sight of this poor, ignorant man, who knows but little of the immense agency of physical causes, and in every thing that is wonderful, and to him inexplicable, thinks he perceives the *immediate* interference of a God. I do not wonder that his reflections are of a serious nature" ("AHM" 4). Although Moss's transformation was exceptional in its rapidity, Barton attributes this change in racial appearance to "physical causes," and he thinks of Moss as a "poor, ignorant man" because he attributes his change less to a scientific than to a religious rationale. In addition, when enumerating aspects of Moss's life, Barton notes that "Perhaps, it is not important to observe, that *he* says, that his ability for the enjoyment of veneral pleasures is not impaired" ("AHM" 6). Given the intimacy of this remark about Moss's sexual practices, it is striking that Barton laments that his assessment of his subject has not yielded all the information that he desires. "With respect to the alterations which have taken place in the sensations and in the functions of the body of Moss," Barton notes, "I have not obtained all the information which I sought for" ("AHM" 14). Barton's readers are left to wonder exactly what type of information this might have been.

Benjamin Rush, Barton's APS colleague, also examined Moss. As I discussed in the introduction, Rush pasted a copy of the broadside advertising Moss's arrival in Philadelphia into his commonplace book.[112] It entices people to come see Moss's changing skin, claiming that the "sight is really worth the attention of the curious, and opens a wide field of amusement for the philosophic genius." Rush conducted his own examination of Moss on July 27, 1796,[113] and he used what he surmised of Moss's condition in his July 14, 1797, presentation to a special meeting of the APS entitled "On the black colour of the Negroes" (*Early Proceedings* 260). This talk would eventually inform Rush's published essay, "Observations Intended to Favour a Supposition that the Black Color (As It Is Called) of the Negroes is Derived from the Leprosy."[114] In the published version of the essay, Rush agrees with Samuel Stanhope Smith's assertion that the four factors of climate, diet, state of society, and diseases cause the varieties in the appearance of humankind. Rush then goes on to elaborate that he believes that blackness specifically is caused by leprosy. As scholars have noted, Rush's piece is marked by its simultaneous egalitarian and biased remarks.[115] For instance, Rush adamantly insists that understanding blackness as a result of leprosy means that "all the claims of superiority of the whites over the blacks, on account of their color, are founded alike in ignorance and inhumanity" ("Leprosy" 295). For Rush, helping to prove that "the whole human race . . . descended from one pair" demands what he calls "universal benevolence" to all peoples ("Leprosy" 297). Nevertheless, Rush thinks of blackness as a disease, one whites could possibly acquire, and Rush claims that two white women who slept with their black husbands did just that ("Leprosy" 294). Rush conjectures that "science and humanity" might "endeavour to discover a remedy for it" ("Leprosy" 295). The "cure [of] this disease of the skin in negroes," Rush reasons, will "destroy one of the arguments in favor of enslaving the negroes, for their color has been supposed by the ignorant to mark them as objects of divine judgments, and by the learned to qualify them for labor in hot, and unwholesome climates" ("Leprosy" 297). During the late eighteenth century, Rush was a leading advocate for abolition, publishing his "An Address to the Inhabitants of the British Settlements in America, upon Slave-keeping" in 1773, and he worked with African American ministers in order to build black churches in Philadelphia.[116] He was an early member of the Pennsylvania Society for the Abolition for Slavery, and in many ways, was noted for his work with and for black communities.[117] However, he himself once owned a slave, and, as his writings show, he thought of blackness as a disease that should be cured in blacks and rigorously avoided by whites.[118] *Modern Chivalry*, in caricaturing scientists like Rush who examined Moss, not only points to this troubling undercurrent in Rush's thought but also highlights the disturbing methods they employed to come to some of their conclusions about human equality.

It seems that several of the men who examined Moss did use invasive methods to explore Moss's condition. As John Wood Sweet points out, Moss later related to Moses Brown, an antislavery activist in Rhode Island, that Rush used the procedure of blistering to determine where the color might reside in his skin. Charles Caldwell, a student of Barton's, also used this method, what Sweet calls a "painful procedure that involved either applying a caustic chemical on the skin or creating a vacuum over part of the skin with a heated glass, which then cooled and sucked up the skin, thus separating the skin layers."[119] Extraordinarily interested in Moss's case, Caldwell, as he himself describes it, "took him in some measure under my care, procured for him suitable lodging and accommodation, induced many persons to visit him, kept him under my own strict and constant observation, and, by his permission, and for a slight reward, made on him such experiments as suited my purpose"[120] In one that he recounts, Caldwell "induced [Moss] frequently to excite, by exercise, a copious perspiration, that I might ascertain, by suitable tests, whether the fluid perspired, by the colored portions of the skin, was *itself* colored."[121] When it is not, Caldwell conjectures that Moss's rete mucosum, what Caldwell considers "the seat of the human complexion," was removed by absorption.[122] James Pemberton, an abolitionist in Philadelphia, used a magnifying glass to examine Moss's skin and combed his fingers through Moss's hair to inspect its texture.[123] Although Moses Brown's interview and examination of Moss occurred later in 1803, Moss also related to Brown that he had been examined and viewed by luminaries such as George Washington and Thomas Jefferson.[124]

It is no wonder, then, when the *Modern Chivalry* philosophers "proposed to make a purchase of this animal, for the purpose of examining it more fully, in their own hall," that Teague vocally protests. Recalling what Farrago had previously told him about the "use to which they would apply him," Teague implores his owners, "do not sell me to dese filosophers, that will cut me up as you would a dead cat, and put my skin upon a pitchfork, just to plase deir own fancies" (*MC* 225). He begs to stay in the cage, where people can "gape and stare" but will not try to bite him. Teague objects not so much to observation but rather to the experimentation he fears at the hands of the philosophers. And, while played for humor, it is significant that here the specimen is given a voice that allows him to talk back to the philosophers who talk so much *about* him.

The philosophers answer Teague's protest in a way that not only addresses his claims but also notes the shift beginning to take place—and will be explored in the next chapter—at the end of the eighteenth century from a natural-historical focus on the body's exterior traits to a comparative anatomical concern with its interior. They assure that they will not dissect him, "at least until he died a natural death" (*MC* 226). While they might want to examine the "internal structure of his body" to determine "to what genus or class of animals he might belong," for the time being, they can concentrate on "the observations drawn from external structure" (*MC* 226). The proposed transaction and Teague's protests of it are both interrupted when an officer of the court delivers a writ of habeas corpus to Teague's captors.

Because the townspeople cannot come to a consensus on whether Teague is either a "monster, or new animal in the creation" or a "real man," a chief justice of the state—concerned that if Teague were man whether "confining him in that manner was a restraint upon the liberty of the subject" (*MC* 226)—demands a trial. The argument between the two sides over whether or not Teague is a man raises the specters both of slavery and of the famous three-fifths clause in the Constitution. The dispute centers around "whether this creature is of the brutal or the human kind" and thus reflects the point upon which the discussion of the three-fifths clause turned, namely, whether black slaves in Southern states should be considered property (animals that can be owned) or persons. It also speaks to the institution of slavery more broadly, of course, because if it can be established that Teague is a "man," the text raises the question of whether he should have his liberty taken from him.[125] Despite the fact that the philosophers are interested parties in the case, the court allows them to provide testimony "to establish [Teague's] brutality" (*MC* 227). Once the officers declare that although they don't know exactly what kind of animal Teague is, they can say for certain he is "not of the human race," the court rules in favor of the keepers and sends Teague back into their custody.

The "keepers" quickly sell Teague to the APS members who study Teague for a year before deciding to circulate him among other international learned societies, particularly those in France. Once they have an opportunity to "[ascertain] its structure and properties" (*MC* 227), they ship Teague off, and in so doing, he comes to resemble many of the natural-historical items exchanged across the Atlantic and specifically the panther, mammoth, and moose that Jefferson sent over a number of years to Buffon in a desperate attempt to get him to recant his degeneration theory.[126] Going from being considered as a fowl, then a raced person, then an animal once again, when Teague resembles these other natural-historical specimens sent abroad, he is always a figure that speaks to early American culture and its interest in race and how it forms. In the end, the trip over wears off "the tar and feathers from his back-side," so that when Teague lands in France, he is "mistaken for a sans culotte" and is freed by the mob (*MC* 227).[127] Although Teague eventually returns to continue his adventures with Farrago for three more volumes, when the fourth volume closes, Teague's fate is left uncertain. Likewise, similar to the ambiguous white negro woman in Equiano's *Narrative*'s final chapter, at the end, readers know less—not more—about these changing racial figures. Despite all the scientific efforts to explain them, these figures typify the skepticism both *The Interesting Narrative* and *Modern Chivalry* express about eighteenth-century natural-historical thought that would, by the end of the century, come under even more intense scrutiny.

Interiorizing Racial Metamorphosis:
The Algerine Captive's Language of Sympathy

What happened to transformable race? As the eighteenth century drew to a close, exactly what happened when beliefs about how the environment might impact the physical body changed over to newer hypotheses about how racial truth was located within the body? Scholars have approached various aspects of this shift. Michel Foucault depicts a larger epistemological change at the turn of the nineteenth century in which thinkers altered the way they thought about science, language, and economics from comparing external similarities to creating and analyzing interior structures—most pertinent for our purposes here, the difference between the earlier practice of natural history and the later ones of biology and comparative anatomy. Robyn Wiegman, extending Foucault's line of thinking into race science specifically, describes how changes in the conceptualization of the human body located "racial truth" inside that body.[1] Winthrop Jordan conjectures that perhaps environmentalist thinking collapsed under its own weight, and Joanne Pope Melish examines how the switch to inherent racial differences helped mitigate the instability caused by gradual emancipation.[2] Dana Nelson helps us understand how nineteenth-century race science helped negotiate power relations among white men and stabilized white manhood; Ezra Tawil explores how the frontier romance of the 1820s helped redefine race as both a biological and sentimental difference in the nineteenth century; and George Boulukos demonstrates the role that the trope of the grateful slave plays at the end of the eighteenth century in initially suggesting human similarity between whites and blacks only to come to be seen ultimately as signifying meaningful difference between racialized groups.[3] And Bruce Dain shows us how the ideas of environmentalism do not simply disappear at the end of the eighteenth century but rather get picked up, reworked, and used by African American writers, intellectuals, and political actors well into the nineteenth century.[4]

This book has argued that the significantly different ways of looking at race in the eighteenth century impacted the way that literature imagined the formation of racial categories; therefore, it has advanced a model of reading early American literature that takes eighteenth-century thought into account. Thus, tarrying a bit longer at the close of the eighteenth century before the moment in the nineteenth century when transformable race would not be the dominant way of conceptualizing racial difference, I'd like to conclude this study by pondering how literature itself moved into a different understanding of the racial body. To consider this question, I take up Royall Tyler's *The Algerine Captive or, The Life and Adventures of Doctor Updike Underhill* (1797) to suggest that it demonstrates one way that we can understand the piecemeal way the thinking of the eighteenth century began to give way to that of the nineteenth and what that means for our understanding of this literary text. In the last fifteen years of the eighteenth century, the interactions between the new United States and what were then known as the Barbary States—Tripoli, Algiers, and Tunis—captivated the American reading public. The white citizens of the American slave-holding republic were outraged that North African pirates commandeered US ships in the Mediterranean Ocean, captured US sailors, and enslaved them in Africa. In addition, because of still-lingering environmentalist understandings of the racialization of the body, white Americans at home wondered what might happen to their fellow countrymen if they remained in North Africa for too long. As Melish asks,

> Under radically different conditions, enslaved in a tropical climate by a "savage" people of color, could free white Americans become . . . something else? Slaves? And how profound and permanent would such a change be? Was whiteness part of some stable, essential nature, or did the conditions of their existence have the power to transform the "nature" of Americans and Europeans too, as Buffon and [Samuel Stanhope] Smith suggested?[5]

This book thus far has analyzed early American texts that explore what might happen to Europeans and Africans when they relocate to the New World. This epilogue now examines a novel that imagines what could transpire when a white American is forced to live in Africa.

Royall Tyler's *The Algerine Captive*, a fictional Barbary captivity story claiming to be an authentic narrative, depicts what may occur if a white, US male citizen were to undergo an unwilling racial alteration. Part farce and part historical fiction, the narrative chronicles the story of Dr. Updike Underhill. The travels of this buffoonish New Englander take him through the recently formed United States, to England and West Africa as a surgeon on a slave ship, to Algiers as a slave himself, and back to the United States as a free man. In this epilogue, I argue that *The Algerine Captive* registers a shift in the understanding of race from a malleable feature of a person's exterior to a trait lodged within one's corporeal interior. I first examine how several competing racial epistemologies inform the text. Secondly, I show how *The Algerine Captive* uses eighteenth-century theories of sentiment to illustrate racial difference moving "inside" the body. Drawing upon Adam Smith's eighteenth-century model of (unraced) sympathetic identification and building upon Christopher Castiglia's reworking of that model to account for cross-racial sympathy as an exchange of racialized interior states, I demonstrate how in the novel, Dr. Underhill's profound sympathetic identification with African slaves "blackens" his soul in a metaphorical, interior racial metamorphosis. It is not that Underhill "really" becomes black on the inside but rather that the novel's use of the language of sympathy to posit a racialized interior parallels in exact historical synchronicity the way that scientific thinking was beginning to relocate race to the body's interior.

Because his cross-racial sympathy rhetorically alters his racial interior and is linked to his capture by the Algerines, Underhill, upon his return to freedom, disavows that identification and his prior abolitionist tendencies in order to reclaim his white US citizenship. Or to be more specific, in the re-telling of his story, Underhill-as-narrator either forgets his earlier abolitionist feelings or, more problematically, as he narrates his "Life and Adventures," the recording and reperforming of his sentiment toward black slaves that might lead to abolitionist action serves as the abolitionist action itself; the recording is the doing. While the text envisions that the white citizen can transform into the metaphorically internally raced slave through cross-racial compassion, the narrative guarantees firmly grounded white US citizenship only inasmuch as it can deny white-black affective identification and the abolitionist sentiment it causes. This helps explain the "amnesia" Underhill seemingly undergoes in terms of his abolitionist promises and aspects of the confusing split narration—wherein an older, more experienced Underhill, upon his return to the US, depicts the younger, naive Underhill he once was, all brought into being by Tyler's writing—two formal characteristics of Tyler's novel that have continually puzzled scholars.[6] In this sense, *The Algerine Captive* helps us understand how we eventually get not only to the nineteenth century thought that race resides "inside" the body but also to Harriet Beecher Stowe's admonishment to "feel right." Some critics have understood this novel as one that shows the hypocrisy of the United States because its satire ultimately is aimed at showing the absurdity of American slavery.[7] However, this critique of hypocrisy is not as trenchant as we might want it to be because the initial comparison between the white slave in Algiers and the black slave in the United States is displaced by that between the white captive in Algiers and the white citizen in the United States. Indeed, as the book's title makes clear, thinking about Underhill's character as a slave (and thus comparable to black slaves) is subordinated to thinking about him as a (temporary) *captive* who eventually becomes free.[8]

Tyler's *Algerine Captive* fantastically demonstrates the messiness at the end of the eighteenth century. We see the ad hoc work the novel must do to tack together those things always threatening to break apart: Underhill's body, the novelistic text (itself one that conjoins the somewhat dissonant genres of personal narrative, picaresque, travelogue, burlesque, ethnography, captivity narrative, and political tract), and the US nation-state (which, according to the logic of the novel, must be consolidated according to Federalist principles in order to persist). But these are Frankensteinian stitches—crude sutures that call attention less to the coherent entity they make possible and more to the building pressures only partially concealed that could burst forth to disintegrate the whole. In addition, *The Algerine Captive* in this way also helps us understand the way that literature dealt with these changing discordant racial epistemologies. Moving from Phillis Wheatley's use of environmentalist thinking to talk about how the sun might "die" the exterior of the skin to Tyler's use of sympathetic language to metaphorically blacken the soul in order to imagine a raced interior may not necessarily explain—but certainly gives us a better way to think about—the subsequent shift to how racial identity was thought to be in "the blood," something we see wrestled with by later authors from Stowe to Twain to Larsen. Indeed, the blood is no more literally black than the soul; each can only be thought to be black metaphorically. Thus, this helps us understand over and again—but this time with a new, longer, and more nuanced history—how race is read and how it is read metaphorically from the body.

The Algerine Captive and the Sciences of Race

Tyler's 1797 novel is informed by both the Barbary captivity crisis and multiple theories of racial difference. As much scholarship on Barbary captivity narratives is quick to point out, the twenty-first century engagement of the United States with various Muslim states has a long history with its origins in the post-Revolutionary era. In *The Cultural Roots of American Islamicism*, Timothy Marr demonstrates how early and antebellum Americans used orientalist depictions of Islam to help forge their own national identity and moral legitimacy within a global framework, and he gives specific attention to a "series of conflicts with the Islamic world" that were crucial to this era.[9] Indeed, beginning in the seventeenth century, Algiers, Tunis, and Tripoli interfered with European trade in the Mediterranean Sea, capturing sailors and demanding ransom for their return. Toward the latter part of the eighteenth century, the British government's practice of paying tributes to the leaders of North Africa protected imperial ships from pirating. However, when the United States officially won its independence from Britain in 1783, the mother country's protection evaporated, leaving American ships vulnerable to attack. To make matters worse, many Americans felt that Great Britain publicized the news of America's self-rule to the Barbary States to encourage them to assault

US vessels. As Marr points out, because of the young nation's inexperience, this entire episode highlighted the relative weakness of the United States in international affairs.[10]

For the next decade, Barbary pirates captured US sailors and pressed them into slavery. Stateside, Americans held events to raise money, increased awareness, and petitioned the government to force an end to this North African practice, and as Robert Allison argues, the Algerian situation and American responses shed light on the vexed position in which US citizens found themselves: protesting slavery abroad while practicing it at home.[11] After much negotiation, the United States signed a treaty on July 12, 1796, that freed the Algerian captives, but this resolution, Marr explains, caused Americans deep humiliation, as the United States ended up paying ransom and giving lavish gifts to North African officials. While the ongoing spectacle engrossed American readers, captivity narratives both true and fictionalized flooded the popular press. And although this particular set of captives regained their freedom, US-North African interaction and the public interest it engendered showed no signs of attenuation. Published just a year after the 1796 treaty, *The Algerine Captive* found a reading public primed for its tale of travel, capture, and eventual liberation.

Although important, however, the publicity of the Barbary captivity crisis was not the only historical discourse within which *The Algerine Captive* is situated. Although often overlooked by literary critics, Tyler's novel also indexes several competing theories of American racial thought, including Biblical, natural-historical, and polygenetic explanations for racial difference, and these various strands of racial thought demonstrate the novel's placement within multiple epistemological regimes. Indeed, the novel illustrates not an abrupt shift from an eighteenth-century conceptualization of race to a nineteenth-century one but rather the slow and disjointed manner in which one way of thinking was coming to replace another. Furthermore, the novel does so through a particular type of narration. The events of the novel are narrated by an Underhill who lived through and ostensibly learned from his various experiences. However, especially at the beginning of the novel, the older Underhill depicts the naiveté of the younger Underhill, and while the distance between the narrative voice and the naive protagonist is almost imperceptible, there are moments in the text that evidence the perspective of a more senior Underhill looking back upon his juvenile self. In a way, as the novel progresses, the (voice of) Underhill-as-character becomes closer to the (voice of) Underhill-as-narrator, in large part merely because at the end of the narrative, the Underhill-as-character becomes the Underhill-as-narrator who will then narrate his tale from the beginning.[12]

Using Biblical imagery that had taken on a racialized connotation in early American culture, Tyler's narrator twice depicts scenes that illustrate a monogenetic explanation of the differences among races. While detailing his

New England ancestral background, Underhill describes an absurd charge
of "adultery" leveled at his forbear, John Underhill, for staring too long at
a married woman in church. Tyler lampoons Puritan zealousness, but more
important here is Underhill's justification of the anecdote's inclusion in his
narrative. "I would rather," he claims, "like the sons of Noah, go backwards
and cast a garment over our fathers' nakedness; but the impartiality of a historian . . . will excuse me to the candid [sic]."[13] Underhill alludes to the Biblical
scene in which Noah's son Ham witnesses Noah's "nakedness" when he lay
in a drunken stupor in his tent, while brothers Shem and Japheth avert their
eyes and cover their father with a blanket. When Noah awakens, he curses
Ham and his descendants for not turning away from the scene (Genesis 9).
As intellectual historian Thomas Gossett explains, American slave apologists
claimed that Africans were descendants of Ham to justify the system of racial
slavery.[14] Though absent from the original Biblical account, this association
emerged later and was a commonly understood aspect of the "curse of Ham"
by the eighteenth century.[15]

While this example ostensibly characterizes Underhill as an "impartial"
historian, it also places him in the position of Ham. In doing so, Underhill
hints at his own link to blackness, foreshadowing the pivotal blackening scene
to come later in the text,[16] and he also draws upon a Biblical explanation for
the existence of different races. Although the story of Ham is not frequently
discussed in terms of its implications for theories of monogenism, the structure of the anecdote supports it. If, as Christian slave apologists claimed, Africans are descendents of Ham, then all races could trace their familial lineage
through Ham and Noah back to Adam and Eve.

Later, when contemplating his service as physician aboard a slave ship,
Underhill again invokes monogenism to condemn (his own) inhumane treatment of Africans:

> I cannot reflect on this transaction yet without shuddering. I have deplored
> my conduct with tears of anguish; and, I pray a merciful God, the common
> parent of the great family of the universe, who hath made of one flesh and
> one blood all nations of the earth, that the miseries, the insults, and cruel
> woundings, I afterwards received, when a slave myself, may expiate for the
> inhumanity, I was necessitated to exercise, towards these MY BRETHREN
> OF THE HUMAN RACE. (AC 96)

In the same manner as Occom and Wheatley, Underhill points to humankind's common origin. Like Occom, Underhill uses the "one flesh and one
blood" language from the Biblical account of creation in Genesis, and, like
Wheatley, he envisions God as a "common parent" of humankind who "made"
each individual "nation" from one, original flesh. It necessarily follows from
this thinking that the various "races" within the one human race developed
after their shared creation. Underhill even plays upon the multiple meanings

of the term *race*, using it here to denote the whole of humanity and preferring the term *nation* to denote the differences among humankind.[17] This echoes an earlier scene wherein a friend comments to Underhill on how Underhill had described his own beliefs to him; Underhill's friend related that he

> saw the master hand of the great Creator, in the obvious difference that was between man and man: not only the grosser difference between the Indian, the African, the Esquimeaux, and the white man; but that which distinguishes and defines accurately, men of the same nation, and even children of the same parents. You observed, that as all the children of the great family of the earth, were compounded of similar members, features, and lineaments, how wonderfully it displayed the skill of the Almighty Artist, to model such an infinite variety of beings, and distinctly diversify them, from the same materials. (*AC* 38)

This explanation echoes environmentalist thinking, where the different "varieties" of humankind were nevertheless believed to be part and parcel of the same species, partaking of the same "materials."

Natural history, a "scientific" way of thinking that was itself underwritten by theories of monogenism, appears in Tyler's text as well, when Underhill stops to inspect the museum at Harvard College and is surprised to find "curiosities of all countries," except the United States. When he inquires about American "specimens," he finds a hodge-podge of underwhelming pieces, including a gourd shell, a stuffed duck, and a "miniature birch canoe, containing two or three rag aboriginals with paddles, cut from a shingle" (*AC* 60). Upon seeing this cliched Native American diorama, Underhill nurses his wounded national pride. He laments that "I felt then for the reputation of the first seminary of our land. Suppose a Raynal or Buffon should visit us; repair to the museum of the university, eagerly inquiring after the natural productions and original antiquities of our country, what must be the sensations of the respectable rulers of the college, to be obliged to produce, to them, these wretched, bauble specimens" (*AC* 60–61).

As I have mentioned often in this book, the mere mention of Raynal and Buffon alludes to, and, in this instance, pokes fun at the heated debate between them and American natural philosophers like Thomas Jefferson over the effect the New World environment would have on both its Native and newly arrived European populations. Gesturing toward this well-known scientific dispute, Underhill alludes to the underpinnings of this racial debate: if humankind descended from one ancestor and the effects of the environment produced differences among humans, what kind of effect would the American environment have on its inhabitants? Sandwiched between several of Underhill's foolhardy encounters, this scene gently mocks Underhill's mildly histrionic mortification, and it illustrates how the novel is informed by these multiple theories of racialization.[18] Indeed, Tyler had demonstrated his awareness of various accounts of racial difference a year earlier in a 1796 entry in the "Colon & Spondee" series, a satirical newspaper column he coauthored with fellow Federalist, Joseph Dennie.[19] Posing as an "Indian editor," Tyler composes an essay on the topic of race. "'The creatures,' Tyler's Indian editorializes, 'are whitened by disease, like the decaying leaves of the woods.'"[20] As Jared Gardner points out, Tyler probably satirizes Benjamin Rush's theory (discussed herein in Chapters 3 and 4) that blackness was a form of leprosy.[21] One of the most influential and well-known early environmentalist thinkers, Rush argued that since blackness was a disease, it could be cured by freeing Africans from slavery and moving them to comfortable and humane surroundings.[22]

However, even with its multiple references to natural-historical and Biblical monogenetic thought, *The Algerine Captive* also alludes to nascent theories of polygenism that were beginning to gain credence in scientific circles. When he begins training in medicine, Underhill studies the works of John Hunter, among others. As Gardner attests, this British physician and anthropologist, "whose carefully hierarchized 'gradation of skulls' provided a foundation for several theorists on race," laid the groundwork for later race theorists who would expand upon this "evidence" to argue for separate creations.[23] Scientists such as Georges Cuvier, Samuel George Morton, Dr. Josiah Nott, and George R. Gliddon would draw upon such scientific research to show what they saw as the utter alterity and distinction of the races, an argument that would develop into full-blown scientific racism in the nineteenth century.[24] The work of Hunter and like-minded scientists would provide one of the first steps to conceiving of race as something not merely residing on the surface of the body, but as a trait emanating outward from the body's interior.

Thus, in the waning years of the eighteenth century, scientific models began to conceptualize racial "truth" as something located within the body. This shift in thinking provoked new cultural anxieties: If racial truth was an interior phenomenon, where was it located inside the body and what did it look like? Furthermore, what did one's outside look like? And perhaps most importantly, if racial truth resided inside where it could not be seen (and might not be indicated by one's skin), how would people know who was "really" black or "really" white? *The Algerine Captive* brings together the discourses of race science and sympathy to explore the problems that arise when race begins to be conceptualized as located on the "inside."

Turning Black on the Inside

Considering the role of sentiment in *The Algerine Captive*, twentieth-century literary critic James R. Lewis praises the novel for steering clear of maudlin, emotional scenes in its efforts to condemn slavery.

The only worthwhile piece of literature to emerge out of the Barbary conflict, Royall Tyler's *The Algerine Captive*, was untainted by the cult of sentimentality. The author's refusal either to engage in sensationalism or to employ the conventions of romantic heroism makes it difficult to classify. Tyler does, however, have an axe to grind against slavery, although the principal target of his critique is Anglo-American rather than North African slavery.[25]

In marked contrast to Lewis and in agreement with Ed White's related emphasis on sentiment,[26] I argue that Tyler *does* engage eighteenth-century theories of sentiment and that his use of sympathetic exchange serves key purposes in the novel. First, Tyler's use of the language of sympathy illustrates the late eighteenth-century shift in thinking about race from an exterior feature to an interior trait of the body. When Underhill extends sympathy to the black slaves, they state that God has placed "a *black* soul" inside a "*white* body" (*AC* 101, emphasis in original). Thus, the novel imagines that this cross-racial sympathetic identification can potentially cause a metaphorical racial transformation—but that this rhetorical blackening takes place not on the surface of the skin, but rather "within the body." As I shall explain, the novel closely associates Underhill's racial sympathy with his enslavement, thus characterizing such sympathetic identification as a dangerous threat to one's own freedom. Furthermore, while Underhill's enslavement initially gives rise to his impassioned profession of abolitionism, in the end, he forgets or represses his promises of antislavery activism and instead focuses on reclaiming his citizenship in the slave-holding United States.

Underhill first encounters slaves on his trip to a "Southern State," where he accompanies a friend to church.[27] As the congregation waits for the service to begin, they observe the parson make his belated arrival. "The absence of his negro boy, who was to ferry him over" causes the parson's tardiness. Switch in hand, the minister strikes "the back and head of the faulty slave, all the way from the water to the church door; accompanying every stroke with suitable language" (*AC* 79–80). Making his way to the pulpit, the parson preaches "an animated discourse, of eleven minutes, upon the practical duties of religion, from these words, remember the Sabbath day, to keep it holy" (*AC* 80). After such a display, the whole congregation makes their way to the horse track, where the parson serves as both bookie and finish-line judge for the races.

Appalled, Underhill remarks that "the whole of this extraordinary scene was novel to me. Besides, a certain staple of New England I had with me, called conscience, made my situation, in even the passive part I bore in it, so awkward and uneasy, that I could not refrain from observing to my friend my surprise at the parson's conduct, in chastising his servant immediately before divine service" (*AC* 80). After his friend defends the parson, swearing that he himself would have just "killed the black rascal" for causing his tardiness,

Underhill closes the scene by emphasizing the profane language used by both the parson and his friend. As Underhill notes, this encounter with the violence of slavery is indeed "novel;" the word both characterizes Underhill's first experience with slavery and comments upon the text's own status as a literary artifact that explores these very issues. Here, Underhill is duly shocked but focuses more on the perpetrator's language and less on his action or even the experience of the slave himself.

A later scene in which Underhill witnesses the horrors of slavery stands in stark contrast. His inability to find stable work as a physician forces him to seek employment as a surgeon on a ship. Although it is unclear whether Underhill understands that the vessel is a slave ship, he finds happiness in securing a job. Once aboard the significantly named *Sympathy*, Underhill realizes the extent of the slave trade's dehumanization. The traders' conversations about "the purchase of human beings, with the same indifference, and nearly in the same language, as if they were contracting for so many head of cattle or swine, shocked [Underhill] exceedingly" (94). In striking sentimental language, Underhill laments various tableaux of slavery.

> But, when I suffered my imagination to rove to the habitation of these victims to this infamous, cruel commerce, and fancied that I saw the peaceful husbandman dragged from his native farm; the fond husband torn from the embraces of his beloved wife; the mother, from her babes; the tender child, from the arms of its parents and all the tender, endearing ties of natural and social affection rended by the hand of avaricious violence, my heart sunk within me. (*AC* 94–95)

Underhill suggests that he unknowingly enlisted and now certainly regrets boarding the slaver: "When the captain kindly inquired of me how many slaves I thought my privilege in the ship entitled me to transport, for my adventure, I rejected my privilege, with horrour; and declared I would sooner suffer servitude than purchase a slave" (*AC* 95). Underhill's feelings toward the slaves single him out from all the other white men on the ship. As we shall see, his statement—that he would rather be a slave than buy one—ultimately proves to be prophetic.

Underhill records his moral revelation about the degradation of slavery and his efforts to assuage the suffering of the captives, and his specific description of the slave ship have led scholars to conjecture that Tyler drew extensively on black slave narratives published during this time period.[28] Recoiling at the conditions in the ship's hold, Underhill informs the captain "that it was impracticable to stow fifty more persons between decks, without endangering health and life" (*AC* 99). However, Underhill attests, "it was in vain I remonstrated to the captain. In vain I enforced the necessity of more commodious births [sic], and a more free influx of air for the slaves. In vain I represented, that these miserable people had been used to the vegetable diet, and pure air of a country life" (*AC* 99). The captain suspects Underhill's compassion is a reaction to the slaves' plight. "He observed that he did not doubt my skill, and would be bound by my advice, as to the health of those on board his ship, when he found I was actuated by the interest of the owners; but, he feared, that I was now moved by some *yankee nonsense about humanity*" (*AC* 99, emphasis in original). However, when above sixty percent of the slaves becomes ill, Underhill convinces the captain to land the ship on the African coast so that the sick may be taken ashore and restored to health.[29]

The slaves recover quickly. Underhill relates that they "looked on me as the source of this sudden transition from the filth and rigour of the ship, to the cleanliness and kindness of the shore. Their gratitude was excessive" (*AC* 100). The captives gather berries for Underhill in appreciation. Underhill writes that "our linguist has told me, he has often heard them, behind the bushes, praying to their God for my prosperity, and asking him with earnestness, why he put my good *black* soul into a *white* body" (*AC* 100–101, emphasis in original).[30] As scholars have noted, here the novel ironically inverts the traditional moral association between blackness as evil and whiteness as virtuous.[31] For these slaves, whiteness—not blackness—represents wickedness. However, in addition, the slaves perceive Underhill's soul as black because of his intense sympathetic identification with them.

The black slaves can perceive Underhill's soul as black in part because sympathy at this time was understood to be a phenomenon of one's interior. In his monumental *The Theory of Moral Sentiments*, leading eighteenth-century theorist of sympathy Adam Smith writes that sympathetic identification (for Smith, imagined as unraced) occurs when a spectator tries to comprehend the pain of the sufferer by imagining himself into the position of that sufferer. Smith describes that "It is the impressions of our own senses only, not those of his, which our imaginations copy. By the imagination we place ourselves in his situation, we conceive ourselves enduring all the same torments, we enter as it were into his body, and become in some measure the same person with him, and thence form some idea of his sensations, and even feel something which, though weaker in degree, is not altogether unlike them."[32] Here, Smith imagines that a spectator would imaginatively enter into the body of the sufferer in order to get some sense of his feelings. This becomes even more pronounced when he speaks of how living persons might try to understand what it would be like to be a dead person, and, in the case of Underhill, we can productively extend Smith's analysis to think not only of the physically dead but also of the socially dead. "We sympathize even with the dead. . . . The idea of that dreary and endless melancholy, which the fancy naturally ascribes to their condition, arises altogether from our joining to the change which has been produced upon them, our own consciousness of that change, from our putting ourselves in their situation, and from our lodging, if I may be allowed to say so, our own living souls in their inanimated bodies, and thence conceiving what would be our emotions in this case" (*TMS* 12–13). Here, one places his "living soul" into that of the dead in order to imagine what the dead Other feels. Furthermore, sympathy works according to a logic of imagined trading of places. In a later example, Smith explains how feeling flows between both spectator and sufferer, who tries to render his experience in such a way that the non-suffering onlooker will be able to understand.

> In order to produce this concord, as nature teaches the spectators to assume the circumstances of the person principally concerned, so she teaches this last in some measure to assume those of the spectators. As they are continually placing themselves in his situation, and thence conceiving emotions similar to what he feels; so he is as constantly placing himself in theirs, and thence conceiving some degree of that coolness about his own fortune, with which he is sensible that they will view it. As they are constantly considering what they themselves would feel, if they actually were the sufferers, so he is as constantly led to imagine in what manner he would be affected if he was only one of the spectators of his own situation. As their sympathy makes them look at it, in some measure, with his eyes, so his sympathy makes him look at it, in some measure, with theirs, especially when in their presence and acting under their observation: and as the reflected passion, which he thus conceives, is much weaker than the original one, it necessarily abates the violence of what he felt before he came into their presence, before he began to recollect in what manner they would be affected by it, and to view his situation in this candid and impartial light. (*TMS* 22)

As scholar of eighteenth-century sentiment Julia Stern explicates, here "the object of compassion and the viewing subject *exchange interiorities*."[33] Stern further describes Smith's "mirror of sympathy": "By attempting to imagine the predicament of the other, the compassionate subject circulates fellow feeling back to the suffering object, who then reflects it back to the subject again."[34] Furthermore, as Christopher Castiglia points out, Adam Smith's originally unraced notion of sympathy also provided a language for whites to visualize themselves as internally black. According to this logic of sentiment, Castiglia explains, "racial difference persists . . . as differentiated *interior states* requiring different relationships to nationalism and social agency. . . . White reformers took on blackness, not on the surface of the skin, but as a suffering interior."[35] Although Castiglia specifically describes radical abolitionists, this logic also applies to Underhill's experience with the black slaves. Drawing on this understanding and using the language of sympathy, the novel stages Underhill's empathetic encounter as an imagined exchange of interiorities with the black slaves. Thus, as Castiglia's extension of Smith's theory helps us understand, the slaves themselves see Underhill's interior as black because Underhill, through his sympathetic exchange, reflects their "black souls" back to themselves. To be clear, I am not arguing that souls are raced or have a color;

nor am I arguing that eighteenth-century thought always conceptualized the soul being inside the body. Nevertheless, while "fellow feeling" does not have a color per se, the black slaves use language of racialization, language of the soul, and language of the interior to characterize Underhill's consideration for them. By asking why God "put [Underhill's] *black* soul *into* a *white* body" (*AC* 101, middle emphasis added), the slaves crucially conceptualize Underhill's empathy toward them as something raced and *inside* the body. The black slaves' description of Underhill's kindness towards them finds perfect expression in this envisioned exchange of a metaphorically black interior.[36]

But, one may ask, what does Underhill's metaphorical black soul have to do with his actual racial status? And furthermore, what does this internal blackness have to do with his enslavement by the "Mahometans"? This scene depicts a sympathetic identification that is symbolized by a metaphorical blackening "on the inside." This location of blackness is crucial because it is in this precise historical moment that the discourse of race science—in addition to the discourse of sympathy—begins to posit a bodily interior that can be raced. As Robyn Wiegman attests, at this time, "the theoretical assumptions on which race is apprehended undergo a profound rearticulation."[37] Wiegman explains that "comparative anatomy begins to break with the assurance of the visible to craft interior space, to open the body to the possibilities of subterranean and invisible truths and meanings. . . . Natural history, in other words, was replaced by biology and in this, race was situated as potentially more than skin deep."[38] Drawing on Foucault, Wiegman attests that the shift from natural philosophy to biology "assigned to 'man' a new sphere of specificity, the racial determinations wrought through this sphere produced not simply the constancy of race as an unchanging, biological feature, but an inherent and incontrovertible difference of which skin was only the most visible indication."[39] The incident in which Underhill becomes represented as inwardly black is certainly about his emotional exchange with enslaved Africans. However, because the language of sympathy perfectly intersects here with evolving theories of racialization, the scene also speaks to the changing "location" of racial difference.

As leading scholars of sympathy such as Julie Ellison, Nichole Eustace, and Sarah Knott have shown us about this particular period, the language of sympathy was never "just about" feelings but had everything to do with politics, social community, status, and even the basis of affiliation among citizens in the new nation-state.[40] Extending their insights, we can see the language of sympathy working in conjunction with that of racialization.[41] Indeed, Underhill's soul is metaphorically blackened because of his sympathetic identification with the black slaves. However, because theories of both sympathy and race science imagine a racialized interior, the novel raises the uneasy question of whether Underhill's internal, metaphorical blackness should also be considered his racial "truth" because it is located "inside" his body, despite the fact that this may not be indicated by his skin. In this way, the novel explores the possibility that the racialization of one's interior could change and, furthermore, that there might be a problematic slippage between one's internal racial "essence" and one's external bodily appearance.

It is important, then, to consider how the novel associates Underhill's sympathetic identification and internal blackness with his subsequent enslavement. The novel distinguishes Underhill as the only white man aboard the *Sympathy* who actually extends sympathy to the black slaves. The day after the slaves note his black soul, Barbary pirates chase off the *Sympathy* and capture Underhill and one black slave still on shore.[42] The solitary white man left to treat the slaves, Underhill is the only white man forced to become one. This radical change occurs, furthermore, at the break between the two volumes of the novel, a split underscored all the more in the book's first edition wherein the two volumes were published as two separate physical entities. The novel singles Underhill out for enslavement because he extends compassion to the slaves. Since many of the "white slave narratives" based on Barbary captivity had already established the narrative of whites being taken captive by racial "Others," *The Algerine Captive*, with Underhill's rhetorical blackening scene, is not only ironizing US white-black slavery by illustrating its inverse in North Africa. The novel specifically links Underhill's empathy and his internal blackness with his enslavement in order to illustrate not just the dangers of whites enduring enslavement but also the hazards of whites experiencing intense compassion for black slaves in their own country.[43] If Underhill's sentiment toward the black slaves results in his internal, metaphorical blackness, the novel literalizes that blackness insomuch that the consequence of that blackening is enslavement. (And, interestingly, in this manner, Underhill anticipates many nineteenth-century characters such as William Wells Brown's Clotel, Hannah Crafts's mistress, and Dion Boucicault's Zoe who are in or are forced into slavery not because they are black on the outside—their skin color is white—but because they are considered to be black within.) Thus, this punishment teaches Underhill a lesson about sympathetically identifying with slaves. The scene depicts the disciplining of Underhill's sympathies and, as we shall see, his political allegiances, and it dramatizes the cultural anxiety arising around trying to determine what race one "really" is.

Underhill experiences racial metamorphosis, not on his external body as his contemporary environmentalists might have anticipated, but within his body's interior. If J. Hector St. John de Crèvecoeur, John Marrant, and Charles Brockden Brown portray racial transmutation happening externally, for Tyler the racial change takes place internally, while externally Underhill remains visibly the "same." Furthermore, the novel shows Underhill's soul being metaphorically blackened in the same historical moment that race science was beginning to literalize blackness "on the inside." On the one hand, this incident illustrates the shift Wiegman describes where the "truth" of race moves inside; on the other, it still makes use of eighteenth-century theories of racialization that assumed one's racial status to be a reaction to circumstances. Thus, Underhill's narrative straddles—rather than rests on either side of—what Foucault characterizes as an epistemological chasm that opens up between classical and modern "epistemes of knowledge."[44]

My repositioning of Tyler in this gradual transition between racial epistemologies troubles the way critics have tended to assume a fixed sense of whiteness in the novel. Joanne Pope Melish claims that in the fictional encounters that Barbary captivity narratives stage between environmental theory and the constancy of race, racial fixity wins out. These narratives, Melish attests,

> proclaimed the whiteness and virtue of true republicans—northern, free, white citizens—to be innate and inherited, as was the slavishness and dependency of people of color. . . . In every case the answers challenged environmental theory, proposing a radically different conception of human difference: that whiteness and citizenship, savagery and servility were innate characteristics; that there was indeed an immutable human nature that was not subject to substantial change by external experience—a fixed nature to which the somatic or physiognomic could after all provide reliable cues.[45]

Melish is correct in that Tyler does ostensibly remain white, and racial truth is imagined to be inside the body. However, the stability of this whiteness is not quite as assured as she claims. Underhill's sympathetic identification with the black slaves metaphorically racializes him internally; the racial metamorphosis occurs, but this time, it takes place subcutaneously.

Furthermore, if cross-racial compassionate interchange works imperfectly (because the white spectator can never understand *exactly* and thus empathize with the black sufferer's situation), Underhill's sympathetic identification is imperfect because it works all too well. Within the logic of the novel, Underhill so intensely sympathizes with Africans that he literally takes the enslaved position of an African who is a slave on board the *Sympathy*. When they are both taken captive by the Algerines, the African enjoys freedom while Underhill is enslaved. Underhill's profusion of compassion complicates the racial logic of his former Western world: dark Africans of various backgrounds experience personal autonomy while Underhill, whose US citizenship and external whiteness is rendered useless, finds himself in chains. Before, this "affectionate Negro" had slept "at [Underhill's] feet" (*AC* 104). Later, when Underhill is "thrust into a dirty hole" on the Algerine vessel, a mysterious hand reaches through the hatchway to present him "a cloth, dripping with cold water, in which a small quantity of boiled rice was wrapped" (*AC* 105, 106). When Underhill receives the same nourishment the next day, he begs to see his "benefactor" and discovers the tearful "face of the grateful African, who was taken with [him]" (*AC* 106). These characters not only imaginatively exchange interiors; they completely trade subject positions.

Underhill's prior sympathetic identification with Africans, coupled with his gratitude toward this particular slave, causes abolitionist sentiment to well up in him:

> Is this, exclaimed I, one of these men, whom we are taught to vilify as be-
> neath the human species, who brings me sustenance, perhaps at the risk of
> his life, who shares his morsel with one of those barbarous men, who had re-
> cently torn him from all he held dear, and whose base companions are now
> transporting his darling son to a grievous slavery? Grant me, I ejaculated,
> once more to taste the freedom of my native country, and every moment of
> my life shall be dedicated to preaching against this detestable commerce. I
> will fly to our fellow citizens in the southern states; I will, on my knees, con-
> jure them, in the name of humanity, to abolish a trafic [sic], which causes
> it to bleed in every pore. If they are deaf to the pleadings of nature, I will
> conjure them, for the sake of consistency, to cease to deprive their fellow
> creatures of freedom, which their writers, their orators, representatives,
> senators, and even their constitutions of government, have declared to be
> the unalienable birth right of man. (AC 106)

Underhill's dangerous sympathy leads to his internal, metaphorical racial metamorphosis and change of subject positions. This man's compassion toward
Underhill results in this kind treatment. Both these outcomes furthermore
cause Underhill to vow to fight for the end of slavery.[46] This illustrates, one
might be led to believe, a perfect example of sympathetic exchange resulting
in social action. However, as we shall see, upon his eventual return to freedom
in the United States, Underhill's easily made promises evaporate in the face
of his desire to preserve the very nation-state that engages in this "detestable
commerce."

Bathing with the Balm of Mecca

The way that Underhill's racial metamorphosis scene registers two roughly
historically successive conceptions of race is restaged during his captivity
in North Africa. Exhausted from forced manual labor, Underhill decides
to take advantage of a policy particular to North African slavery: Muslim
captors frequently would evangelize their bondsmen and even free them if
they converted to Islam. Enticed at "the prospect of some alleviation from
labour, and perhaps a curiosity to hear what could be said in favour of so
detestably ridiculous a system" (AC 127), Underhill agrees to meet with
the Mollah. Before the meeting, however, Underhill undergoes a ritual
cleansing process, the description of which speaks volumes about his racial
status:

Immediately upon my entering these sacred walls, I was carried to a warm bath, into which I was immediately plunged; while my attendants, as if emulous to cleanse me from all the filth of errour, rubbed me so hard with their hands and flesh brushes, that I verily thought they would have flayed me. While I was relaxed with the tepid, I was suddenly plunged into a contiguous cold bath. I confess I apprehended dangerous consequences, from so sudden a check of such violent perspiration; but I arose from the cold bath highly invigorated.* I was then anointed in all parts, which had been exposed to the sun with a preparation of a gum, called the balm of Mecca. This application excited a very uneasy sensation, similar to the stroke of the water pepper, to which "the liberal shepherds give a grosser name." In twenty four hours, the sun browned cuticle peeled off, and left my face, hands, legs, and neck as fair as a child's of six months old. This balm the Algerine ladies procure at a great expense, and use it as a cosmetic to heighten their beauty. (*AC* 128–29)

Underhill notes that after his bath, he is "clothed in the drawers, slippers, loose coat, and shirt of the country" and "my hands and feet were tinged yellow: which colour, they said, denoted purity of intention" (129). After this bizarre whitening-then-yellowing process, Underhill emerges ready to meet the Mollah.

It first appears that Underhill's bath simply remedies the effects of the sun. But in the eighteenth century, a sunburn is never just a sunburn. When describing the movement from the hot to the cold bath, Underhill footnotes that this strange process is also practiced by "*The Indian of North America." With a "process founded on similar principles," the Indian "patient . . . was confined in a low hut . . . which had been previously heated by fire" before being carried to "the next stream, and plunged frequently through the ice into the coldest water" (*AC* 129). "This process," Underhill documents, "ever produced pristine health and vigour" (*AC* 129). Underhill compares North African and Native American practices, and he does so in the context of the bathing scene that ostensibly impacts racial identity by erasing a sunburn. Thus, this juxtaposition of these two rituals gestures toward a belief in the eighteenth century that Native Americans, upon acquiring a darkened skin tone from exposure to the sun, retained that color long-term and even passed it down to their children.[47]

James Adair, in his widely read *History of the American Indians* (1775), articulates the specifics of this theory:

The parching winds, and hot sun-beams, beating upon their naked bodies, in their various gradations of life, necessarily tarnish their skins with the tawny red colour. Add to this, their constant anointing themselves with bear's oil, or grease, mixt with a certain red root, which, by a peculiar property, is able alone, in a few years time, to produce the Indian colour in those who are white born, and who have even advanced to maturity. These metamorphoses I have often seen. . . .

We may easily conclude then, what a fixt change of colour, such a constant method of life would produce: for the colour being once thoroughly established, nature would, as it were, forget herself, not to beget her own likeness.[48]

Writing to "overturn" developing theories of the "separate races of man," Adair labors to show how the Indian's "colour" results entirely from environmental factors.[49] The sun does not just tint the skin temporarily; here, it permanently alters it. And, as Adair claims, once it is "thoroughly established," it "beget(s)" itself. For many eighteenth-century readers of Tyler's scene, then, Underhill's "sun browned cuticle" would have carried racialized connotations, especially when linked to American Indians. Furthermore, according to the *Oxford English Dictionary*, "cuticle" denotes the "epidermis" or "scarf-skin." *Scarf-skin* is the exact term natural historians like Thomas Jefferson and Samuel Stanhope Smith used to attempt to identify the "layer of skin" in which one's color resided.[50]

It is unclear exactly how Underhill becomes white again, and readers are not told for certain if his skin was brown temporarily or not. Underhill first suggests that the scrubbing of the attendants, nearly "flay(ing)" him, exfoliates the top layer of his skin. This is just another instance where Underhill's body is threatened with disintegration. While pregnant with Underhill, his mother experienced a nightmare wherein once Underhill was born, Indians broke into their home, grabbed Underhill from his cradle, and played "foot ball with [his] head" in front of their home (*AC* 22). Underhill's mother dreams his head will be removed, slaves envision that his soul is somehow differentiated from the rest of his body, and here his bath attendants work to strip off his outer layer of skin. However, he additionally mentions the "balm of Mecca," which itself seems to help slough off Underhill's outer layer *and also* to whiten it. The balm, a "cosmetic" used by "the Algerine ladies . . . to heighten their beauty" makes Underhill's "face, hands, legs, and neck as fair as a child's" (*AC* 129).[51] The difference between scrubbing off the outer skin to reveal the white skin beneath or dying the brown skin white may seem like a negligible one. However, its very ambiguity illustrates—like the metaphorical blackening of Underhill's interior—how the novel draws upon two epistemic understandings of racial difference as an outer or an inner phenomenon. Perhaps Underhill's manual labor in the sun has caused only surface changes to his body; his outer brown cuticle is removed to reveal the white skin beneath it. Or perchance his exposure to drastically different circumstances (from a moderate to a sweltering climate, from a civilized to a "savage" society) has begun to inflect his racial identity, a process that can only be reversed by dying his skin white (and then yellow). Literary critics such as Philip Gould rightly note the "uncannily and significantly protean" nature of Underhill's racial identity in this scene, but they generally overlook the undecidability regarding the different epistemologies through which that identity takes form.[52] Like the earlier sympathetic racial metamorphosis scene, Underhill manages to retain his whiteness, but the fixity of his race—or even the epistemological frameworks readers might use to understand it—is anything but definitive.

Unfinished Business

Although the analogies between black slaves in the United States and white slaves in North Africa pepper the text, Underhill's narrative ultimately does not end with a condemnation of the practice of slavery but rather with a celebration of restored white citizenship. Increasingly throughout the novel, Underhill positions the enlightened US citizen as opposite not to the black chattel slave but rather to the white slave held by the Orientalized, Islamic "Other." He asks the reader, "Let those of our fellow citizens, who set at nought the rich blessings of our federal union, go like me to a land of slavery, and they will then learn how to appreciate the value of our free government" (AC 124). In a sense, he himself becomes the contrast by which US citizens realize their own freedom.[53] Describing an altercation with his master, Underhill directly addresses his citizen-readers: "Judge you, my gallant, freeborn fellow citizens, you, who rejoice daily in our federal strength and independence, what were my sensations. I threw down my spade with disdain, and retired from my work, lowering indignation upon my insulting oppressor" (AC 123). Underhill reacts negatively to his treatment as a slave because he had once lived as a free citizen. As he later states explicitly, his enslavement makes him appreciate and understand American liberty. "A slave myself," he writes, "I have learned to appreciate the blessings of freedom. May my countrymen ever preserve and transmit to their posterity that liberty, which they have bled to obtain" (AC 144).

After lengthy discussions with the Mollah, Underhill refuses religious conversion and emancipation, but a Portuguese rescue mission eventually restores him to freedom. Upon release from Algerian slavery, Underhill realizes his love for his US citizenship and the importance of national union, as the status of his whiteness destabilized in international travel is reinstated once he is safely relocated within US boundaries. Despite what critics such as Benilde Montgomery have claimed, his enslavement does *not* motivate him to challenge the unjust system of institutional slavery.[54] Indeed, what had become a main concern for Underhill while performing his duties as a slave ship physician drops out of the conclusion of the novel. Describing his return, Underhill writes that "I had been degraded to a slave, and was now advanced to a citizen of the freest country in the universe. I had been lost to my parents, friends, and country; and now found, in the embraces and congratulations of the former, and the rights and protection of the latter, a rich compensation for all past miseries" (*AC* 225). Underhill has come full circle, from citizen to slave and back again. However, he forgets or represses his promise that if he were "to taste the freedom of my native country," he would dedicate "every moment of [his] life . . . to preaching against this detestable commerce" and to press citizens "to cease to deprive their fellow creatures of freedom, which their writers, their orators, representatives, senators, and even their constitutions of government, have declared to be the unalienable birth right of man" (*AC* 106).

Instead, when Underhill lays out his future plans, abolitionist activity is noticeably absent. Underhill decides "to contribute cheerfully to the support of our excellent government, which I have learnt to adore, in schools of despotism; and thus secure to myself the enviable character of an useful physician, a good father and worthy FEDERAL citizen" (*AC* 225). In the closing sentence of his narrative, Underhill beseeches his fellow Americans, not to abolish slavery, but to consolidate the nation-state. "Our first object is union among ourselves. For to no nation besides the United States can that antient (sic) saying be more emphatically applied; BY UNITING WE STAND, BY DIVIDING WE FALL" (*AC* 226). Like his own body and like the book itself (in both a material and a generic sense), the nation-state threatens to fall apart.[55]

By becoming a federalist, Underhill works through the paradox of American history, as stated years ago by historian Edmund Morgan: in a country founded on liberty and freedom, the citizens continually enslave others.[56] Because of this contradiction, for instance, Thomas Jefferson somehow had to reconcile his dual role as slavemaster and leader of a "free" country. But because Underhill was not a slave owner but a slave himself, this paradox manifests itself and is resolved quite differently. The sympathetic identification between Underhill and the black slaves depicts his internal metaphorical blackening, which the novel closely associates with his enslavement. This experience initially provokes abolitionist sentiment, but ultimately Underhill's time as a slave disciplines him instead to cherish his citizenship and nation-state unity that provides it. In the end, Underhill chooses to advocate for a federalism free of abolitionism to foreclose the possibility of a return to slavery because, for him, a strong nation can provide the "rights and protection" that will ensure he remains "a citizen of the freest country in the universe" (*AC* 225). Thus, Underhill's experience of slavery—what enables him to learn this "lesson" about valuing citizenship—is *exactly* what he must repress because it also gives rise to abolitionism and the possibility of sectional conflict. Underhill does *not* "fly to [his] fellow citizens in the southern states" to beg them "for the sake of consistency" to end slavery (*AC* 106). On the contrary, he does nothing. Or, to be more specific, he does nothing at the conclusion of the narrative, and once he returns home, he writes his story wherein he professes feelings of abolitionism; the profession of abolitionist feeling in a sense becomes the abolitionist action itself.[57] Underhill's (as character) feeling of abolitionist sentiment and Underhill's (as narrator) recording of that feeling—not the promised action based upon that feeling—secures his position as a US citizen. Both for Underhill in the novel and, as we know, for the US citizenry in this post-Revolutionary moment, the contradiction of black slavery and its ongoing horrors in the free country were denied, repressed, and forgotten in order to keep the fragile unity of the nation-state—and the citizenship that it ensured—secure. At the novel's conclusion, Underhill focuses on how American citizenship continues to be endangered because, for him, it is threatened not only from outside the nation-state (from North African white slavery) but also from within it (by the potential split between North and South over slavery and by the disagreement between Federalist and Anti-Federalists). Within the logic of the novel, this is one reason why a former slave such as Underhill becomes a federalist instead of an abolitionist.

Because his cross-racial sympathetic identification metaphorically transformed his racial interior and coincided with his enslavement and disenfranchisement at the hands of the Algerines, Underhill disallows that identification and those abolitionist tendencies in order to guarantee his reclaimed white US citizenship. David Blight has helped us understand how the postbellum efforts for sectional reunion after the Civil War worked at the cost of racial reconciliation, and here, the key imperative becomes not freeing the black slave but rather denying the slave's problematic status within the nation.[58] Indeed, the novel's emphasis on the contrast between the free white and the enslaved white helps enable that amnesia. Michael Rogin usefully analyzes the way that spectacle and collective amnesia function to allow the American republic to forget certain examples of how race and gender underpin imperial politics. He writes that "political amnesia works . . . not simply through burying history but also through representing the return of the repressed."[59] His insight applies here; perhaps it is through Underhill's hyper-representation of racialized slavery that allows him simply to forget black African Americans still enslaved in the "united" country he celebrates at the conclusion of the novel.[60] If, as Underhill claims, "our first object is union among ourselves," *The Algerine Captive* suggests that sympathetic identification must be reserved for Underhill and his fellow white citizens only.[61] Indeed, *object* not only signifies Underhill's goal. It also denotes, as in Adam Smith's theory, the correct object with which a subject should sympathetically identify: white citizens, not black slaves.

It seems fitting that this book closes, then, with the unfinished business at the conclusion of Tyler's novel. *The Algerine Captive* charts the move between eighteenth-century and later beliefs about internal versus external and flexible versus fixed racial differences. It supplies a vantage point from which to reflect on the racial epistemologies at the close of one century and to consider how they were altering at the beginning of the next. However, at the same time, the narrative shows how even as conceptualizations about what constitutes race were beginning to change, as citizens increasingly worried over how they could correctly identify a racial status if its "truth" moved "inside," the centrality of race itself as a national issue and concern remained constant. At the conclusion of this novel, the national blight of American racial slavery is left to fester. The black slave's status in both the narrative and the nation remains unresolved.

{ NOTES }

Introduction

1. John Mitchell, "Essay upon the Causes of the Different Colours of People in Different Climates, M.D. Communicated to the Royal Society by Mr. Peter Collinson, F. R. S." *Philosophical Transactions* 43 (1744–45), 147. Further references to this edition will be cited parenthetically as "ECDC."

2. Phillis Wheatley, *Poems on Various Subjects, Religious and Moral. Complete Writings*, ed. Vincent Carretta (New York: Penguin, 2001), 3–65. Further references to this edition will be cited as *P*.

3. Thomas Clarkson, *Essay on the Slavery and Commerce of the Human Species, Particularly the African* (London: J. Phillips, George-Yard, Lombard-Street, and sold by T. Cadell, In The Strand, and J. Phillips, 1786). Indeed, Clarkson includes excerpts from Wheatley's "An Hymn to the Evening," "An Hymn to the Morning," and "On Imagination" in *Essay* to argue that "where they [slaves] have received an education, and have known and pronounced the language with propriety, these defects [incoherence and nonsense] have vanished, and their productions have been less objectionable" (171). Further references to this edition will be cited parenthetically as *ESC*.

4. Benjamin Banneker, "Copy of a Letter from Benjamin Banneker to the Secretary of State, with his Answer," in *Unchained Voices: An Anthology of Black Authors in the English-Speaking World of the Eighteenth-Century*, ed. Vincent Carretta (Lexington: The University Press of Kentucky, 1996), 320.

5. Winthrop Jordan, *White over Black: American Attitudes Toward the Negro, 1550–1812* (Baltimore: Penguin Books, 1968). Further references to this edition will be cited parenthetically as *WOB*. John Wood Sweet, *Bodies Politic: Negotiating Race in the American North, 1730–1830* (Philadelphia: University of Pennsylvania Press, 2006). Further references to this edition will be cited parenthetically as *BP*. See also Bruce Dain, *A Hideous Monster of the Mind: American Race Theory in the Early Republic* (Cambridge: Harvard University Press, 2002), and Joanne Pope Melish, *Disowning Slavery: Gradual Emancipation and "Race" in New England, 1780–1860* (Ithaca: Cornell University Press, 1998). Ian Finseth also notes this kind of racial thinking in *Shades of Green: Visions of Nature in the Literature of American Slavery, 1770–1860* (Athens: University of Georgia Press, 2009), particularly its relationship to the debate over slavery, as does Ezra Tawil, *The Making of Racial Sentiment: Slavery and the Birth of the Frontier Romance* (Cambridge: Cambridge University Press, 2006), 1–68.

6. For more on the role of Biblical interpretation and racial ideology, see Colin Kidd, *The Forging of Races: Race and Scripture in the Protestant Atlantic World, 1600–2000* (Cambridge: Cambridge University Press, 2006), esp. 1–120.

7. I follow W. Jordan's use of the term *environmentalism*, in the sense that one's surroundings help dictate one's racial characteristics. See W. Jordan, *WOB*, 286–90, 513–25, and passim.

8. For more on Henry Moss, see Sweet, *BP*, 271–86. See also Melish, *Gradual Emancipation*, 137–50; W. Jordan, *WOB*, 521–25; William Stanton, *The Leopard's Spots: Scientific Attitudes toward Race in America, 1815–59* (Chicago: University of Chicago Press, 1960), 5–7; and Dain, *Hideous Monster*, 1–39.

9. Kariann Yokota, *Unbecoming British: How Revolutionary America Became a Postcolonial Nation* (New York: Oxford University Press, 2011), 213–25.

10. See note 5.

11. Ralph Bauer, *The Cultural Geography of Colonial American Literatures: Empire, Travel, Modernity* (Cambridge: Cambridge University Press, 2003); Susan Scott Parrish, *American Curiosity: Cultures of Natural History in the Colonial British Atlantic World* (Chapel Hill: University of North Carolina Press for the Omohundro Institute of Early American History and Culture, 2006); Finseth, *Shades of Green*; and Cristobal Silva, *Miraculous Plagues: An Epidemiology of Early New England Narrative* (New York: Oxford University Press, 2011).

12. George Levine, "Why Science Isn't Literature: The Importance of Differences," in *Realism, Ethics and Secularism: Essays on Victorian Literature and Science* (Cambridge: Cambridge University Press, 2008), 167. As Levine makes clear, most studies of science and literature used to be preoccupied "with the way scientific ideas shaped literary ones" (167) before reading both science and literature as texts. As he writes, "the critical question for students of science and literature is how to mediate between the total obliteration of distinction between the two and the old positivist assertion of absolute difference" (174). See also Finseth on this distinction, *Shades of Green*, 21–22.

13. This is part of what gives rise to the contentious tenor of the exchange between Eric Lott and Henry Louis Gates, Jr., about racial formation, literary studies, and science in the pages of *PMLA*. See Lott, "Criticism in the Vineyard: Twenty Years after 'Race,' Writing, and Difference" *PMLA* 123.5 (2008), 1522–27; and Gates, "Rereading 'Race,' Writing and Difference" *PMLA* 123.5 (2008), 1534–39. Priscilla Wald and others take up the dialogue between scientific and literary studies in a Forum on "Biocultures: An Emerging Paradigm" in *PMLA* 124.3 (2009), 947–56. More recently, *Genetics and the Unsettled Past: The Collision of DNA, Race, and History* approach the topic of racial formation and developments in science in a decidedly interdisciplinary way. See *Genetics and the Unsettled Past: The Collision of DNA, Race, and History*, eds. Keith Wailoo, Alondra Nelson, and Catherine Lee (New Brunswick: Rutgers University Press, 2012).

14. For more on various aspects of eighteenth-century racial thought, see W. Jordan, *WOB*, 216–565; Dain, *A Hideous Monster of the Mind*, 1–39; Sweet, *BP*; Roxann Wheeler, *The Complexion of Race: Categories of Difference in Eighteenth-Century British Culture* (Philadelphia: University of Pennsylvania Press, 2000). Further references to this edition will be cited parenthetically as *CR*. Andrew Curran, *The Anatomy of Blackness: Science and Slavery in the Age of Enlightenment* (Baltimore: Johns Hopkins University Press, 2011); Bernard W. Sheehan, *Seeds of Extinction: Jeffersonian Philanthropy and the American Indian* (Chapel Hill: University of North Carolina Press for the Institute of Early American History and Culture, 1973), 1–116; Reginald Horsman, *Race and Manifest Destiny: The Origins of American Racial Anglo-Saxonism* (Cambridge: Harvard University Press, 1981), 98–115; Robert F. Berkhofer, Jr., *The White Man's Indian: Images of the American Indian from Columbus to the Present* (New York: Alfred A. Knopf, 1978), 38–44; Roy Harvey Pearce, *Savagism and Civilization: A Study of the Indian and the American Mind* (Berkeley: University of California Press, 1988), 91–100; Nancy Shoemaker, *A Strange Likeness:*

Becoming Red and White in Eighteenth-Century North America (New York: Oxford University Press, 2004), 125–40; Yokota, *Unbecoming British*, 192–225; Gregory Dowd, *A Spirited Resistance: The North American Indian Struggle for Unity, 1745–1815* (Baltimore: Johns Hopkins University Press, 1992). Further references to this edition will be cited parenthetically as *SR*. Daniel Richter, *Facing East from Indian Country: A Native History of Early America* (Cambridge: Harvard University Press, 2001), 179–201; George Boulukos, *The Grateful Slave: The Emergence of Race in Eighteenth-Century British and American Culture* (Cambridge: Cambridge University Press, 2008); William Stanton, *Leopard's Spots*, 1–23; Thomas Gossett, *Race: The History of an Idea in America* (New York: Oxford University Press, 1997), 3–53; James Drake, *The Nation's Nature: How Continental Presumptions Gave Rise to the United States of America* (Charlottesville: University of Virginia Press, 2011), 56–62; and Dror Wahrman, *The Making of the Modern Self: Identity and Culture in Eighteenth-Century England* (New Haven: Yale University Press, 2004). A spectacular overview of the "study of human races" (16) can be found in Urmila Seshagiri, *Race and the Modernist Imagination* (Ithaca: Cornell University Press, 2010). See also Tawil, *Racial Sentiment*, 26–68.

15. See Sweet, *BP*, 275–86; and Curran, *Anatomy*, 74–166, esp. 102–4. For more instances of this phenomenon, see also Melish, *Gradual Emancipation*, 137–50; and W. Jordan, *WOB*, 521–23.

16. Melish, *Gradual Emancipation*, 142.

17. This book will examine many throughout the following chapters. Even more examples that this text will not discuss in detail include: Lycurgus, "The History of White Negroes" (*The New Haven Gazette, and the Connecticut Magazine*), April 1786; William Byrd, "An Account of a Negro-Boy That is Dappel'd in Several Places of His Body with White Spots" (*Philosophical Transactions 19*), 1697, 781–782; Richard Clayton, "Observations on the Cretins, or Idiots, of the Pais de Vallais, in Switzerland" (*The Universal Asylum and Columbian Magazine*), July 1791, 23; and Thompson Westcott, *A History of Philadelphia, From the Time of the First Settlements on the Delaware to the Consolidation of the City and Districts in 1854* (Philadelphia: Pawson & Nicolson, 1886), 1107: "'A white negro boy, born in South Carolina,' was exhibited in the year 1800 at Mrs. Beatty's, No. 127 Water Street, first door below the drawbridge, at the sign of the Liberty Tree."

18. Charles Caldwell, *Autobiography of Charles Caldwell* (New York: Da Capo Press, 1968), 268.

19. See also Curran's excellent examination of Buffon's thinking, *Anatomy*, esp. 74–166.

20. For more on creole identity, see Ralph Bauer and José Antonio Mazzotti, "Creole Subjects in the Colonial Americas," in *Creole Subjects in the Colonial Americas: Empires, Texts, Identities*, eds. Ralph Bauer and José Antonio Mazzotti (Chapel Hill: University of North Carolina Press for the Omohundro Institute of Early American History and Culture, 2009), 1–57. See also Bauer, "The 'Rebellious Muse': Time, Space, and Race in the Revolutionary Epic," in *Creole Subjects in the Colonial Americas: Empires, Texts, Identities*, eds. Ralph Bauer and José Antonio Mazzotti (Chapel Hill: University of North Carolina Press for the Omohundro Institute of Early American History and Culture, 2009), 442–64.

21. Parrish, *American Curiosity*, 102; Drake, *Nation's Nature*, 56–62; and Yokota, *Unbecoming British*, 192–225.

22. I focus here on this terminological distinction rather than the "origins debate," so ably discussed by others, about whether race or slavery preceded the other. See Boulukos, *Grateful Slave*, esp. 10–20; and Tawil, *Racial Sentiment*, 34–41.

23. Colete Guillaumin, *Racism, Sexism, Power and Ideology* (London: Routledge, 1995), 70; Ivan Hannaford, *Race: The History of an Idea in the West* (Baltimore: Johns Hopkins University Press, 1996).

24. Tawil, *Racial Sentiment*, 40. As Tawil rightly notes: "As scholars have begun to put a finer point on the shifts in the conceptualization of human variety during the seventeenth and eighteenth centuries, and more carefully to guard against the retrojection of nineteenth-century categories of thought onto them, the question of terminology has become invested with greater importance. Some scholars prefer not to use the term 'race' to refer both to the earlier and later conceptions; to do so, it can be argued, is to proceed as if the object toward which both terms gestured was identical—race itself—and thus to falter at the very opening of the inquiry. In any case, it has become quite common to find scholars defining and defending their terminological choices, typically in their introductions or in long footnotes" (40–41).

25. Roxann Wheeler also writes that "During the late eighteenth century, the word *race* was used by some writers in a recognizably incipient form of its modern sense—denoting a fairly rigid separation among groups. At this time, skin color was the most typical way to differentiate 'races'" (*CR* 31).

26. On Kant, see "Of the Different Human Races," in *The Idea of Race*, eds. Robert Bernasconi and Tommy L. Lott (Indianapolis: Harckett Publishing Company, Inc., 2000), 8–22. See also Robert Bernasconi, "Who Invented the Concept of Race? Kant's Role in the Enlightenment Construction of Race," *Race*, ed. Robert Bernasconi (Malden, MA: Blackwell Publishers, 2001), 11–36.

27. Nicholas Hudson, "From 'Nation' to 'Race': The Origin of Racial Classification in Eighteenth-Century Thought," *Eighteenth-Century Studies* 29.3 (1996), 258.

28. Ibid., 253, 255.

29. Andrew Curran notes that these are "troublesome categories (variety, race, species) within the specific eighteenth-century contexts in which they appeared" and that "some (but not all) biblically minded thinkers initially referred to the *nègre* as a 'people'; that many Buffon-influenced naturalists tended to use the botanical term 'variety'; that a number of thinkers employed the zoological term 'race' in order to emphasize the anatomical or conceptual separation of human categories; and that the most extreme polygenists often claimed that the African was *a different species*" (*Anatomy* x–xi). Audrey Smedley and Brian Smedley also note the difficult terminology: "From the sixteenth to the eighteenth centuries, *race* developed as a classificatory term in English similar to, and interchangeable with, *people, nation, kind, type, variety, stock*, and so forth. By the latter half of the eighteenth century, when scholars became more actively engaged in investigations, classifications, and definitions of human populations, *race* was elevated as the one major symbol and mode of human group differentiation applied extensively to non-European groups and even to those groups in Europe who varied from the subjective norm. Of all the terms commonly employed to categorize human beings, *race* became, as we shall see, the most useful one for conveying the qualities and degrees of human differences that had become increasingly consonant with the English view of the world's peoples." See Audrey Smedley and Brian Smedley, *Race in North America: Origin and Evolution of a Worldview* (Boulder: Westview Press, 2012), 37–38.

30. On the role of natural history in racializing human difference in the eighteenth century, see Emmanuel Chukwudi Eze, Introduction, in *Race and the Enlightenment:*

A Reader, ed. Emmanuel Chukwudi Eze (Malden, MA: Blackwell Publishers, 1997), 1–9; Roxann Wheeler, *CR*, 1–48; Dain, *Hideous Monster*, 1–39; Smedley and Smedley, *Race in North America*, 159–212; Henry Louis Gates, Jr., *Figures in Black: Words, Signs, and the "Racial" Self* (New York: Oxford University Press, 1989), 61–79; Parrish, *American Curiosity*, 77–102; W. Jordan, *WOB*, 216–565; Boulukos, *Grateful Slave*, 1–37; Tawil, *Racial Sentiment*, 26–68; Wahrman, *Making of the Modern Self*, 83–126; and Curran, *Anatomy*.

31. Linnaeus published thirteen editions of his work during 1735–1770. In his 1758 edition, Linnaeus divided the category of *Homo sapien* into *ferus, americanus, europaeus, asiaticus*, to hierarchize his divisions according to the Great Chain of Being. However, Linnaeus did feel that all mankind developed from an original whiteness into the different "varieties," establishing whiteness as the original standard. Furthermore, according to historians Audrey Smedley and Brian Smedley, Linnaeus believed that "species [were] distinct primordial forms dating from creation that remained essentially the same throughout all time, whereas varieties were clusters within a species that had acquired superficial differences in appearance" (218). Smedley and Smedley write that varieties "reflected changes caused by such external factors as climate, temperature, and geographic features" (218). See also W. Jordan, *WOB*, 216–22; Dain, *Hideous Monster*, 9–13.

32. For more on Buffon, see Curran, *Anatomy*. See also Buffon, *Barr's Buffon. Buffon's Natural History* (London: printed for proprietor, and sold by Symonds, 1797).

33. Smedley and Smedley, *Race in North America*, 220.

34. For more on the shift from natural history (and its emphasis on the visible surface of the body) to comparative anatomy (and its opening up of the body's interior space) toward the end of the eighteenth century, see Michel Foucault, *The Order of Things: An Archaeology of the Human Sciences. Les Mots et les choses*, by Editions Gallimard, Paris, 1966 (New York: Vintage Books, 1994); and Robyn Wiegman, *American Anatomies: Theorizing Race and Gender* (Durham: Duke University Press, 1995), 21–42.

35. Curran, *Anatomy*, 124.

36. *CR* 7. As Roxann Wheeler explains, four-stages theory came out of Scottish common sense philosophy. Four-stages theorists looked not at skin color per se but at "socioeconomic factors" in order to establish a hierarchy that privileged white Europeans. These four stages included primitive societies, shepherd-based societies, agriculturally based societies, and commercial civilization (35). But, as Wheeler points out, while natural history increasingly emphasized the body, four-stages theory was "keeping alive" an emphasis on cultural conceptions. Also, an idea of polygenesis was beginning to emerge, though still a "minority theory" among European intellectuals. Ultimately, these different paradigms could be "mutually reinforcing or at odds" (37). For more on the flexibility of eighteenth-century British identity in general, see Wahrman, *Making of the Modern Self*.

37. For more on how "geohumoralism" influences ideas about racial and ethnic distinctions during the British Renaissance, see Mary Floyd-Wilson, *English Ethnicity and Race in Early Modern Drama* (Cambridge: Cambridge University Press, 2003).

38. For more on this nativist movement and the war it helped inspire, see Dowd, *Spirited Resistance* and *War Under Heaven: Pontiac, the Indian Nations, and the British Empire* (Baltimore: Johns Hopkins University Press, 2002); Richter, *Facing East*, 179–201; Alfred A. Cave, *Prophets of the Great Spirit: Native American Revitalization Movements in Eastern North America* (Lincoln: University of Nebraska Press, 2006), 11–44; and Gary Nash, *Red, White, and Black: The Peoples of Early America* (Englewood Cliffs, NJ: Prentice-Hall, 1974), 258–64.

39. Dowd, *SR*, 30; and Richter, *Facing East*, 193–98.

40. Richter, *Facing East*, 181.

41. David Silverman, *Red Brethren: The Brothertown and Stockbridge Indians and the Problem of Race in Early America* (Ithaca: Cornell University Press, 2010). See also Linford Fisher, *The Indian Great Awakening: Religion and the Sharping of Native Cultures in Early America* (New York: Oxford University Press, 2012).

42. Samson Occom, "To all the Indians in this Boundless Continent," in *The Collected Writings of Samson Occom, Mohegan: Leadership and Literature in Eighteenth-Century Native America*, ed. Joanna Brooks (New York: Oxford University Press, 2006), 196–97. All references to this edition will follow Brooks's editorial decision in transcribing Occom's manuscripts to use carets to denote Occom's interlineations.

43. Hendrick Aupaumut, Letter to James Monroe (1819). Stockbridge Indian Papers. Cornell University Library Archives, Rare and Manuscript Collections, Carl A. Kroch Library. #9185, Folder 5, Box 1.

44. For more on how Aupaumut queers familial rhetorics, see Mark Rifkin, *When Did Indians Become Straight? Kinship, the History of Sexuality, and Native Sovereignty* (New York: Oxford University Press, 2011), 99–142.

45. Kidd brilliantly points this out about nineteenth-century Pequot writer William Apess who wrote that "I humbly conceive that the natives of this country are the only people under heaven who have a just title to the name, inasmuch as we are the only people who retain the original complexion of our father Adam" (qtd. in Kidd, *Forging*, 31).

46. For more on this, see Joanna Brooks, "Hard Feelings: Samson Occom Contemplates His Christian Mentors," in *Native Americans, Christianity, and the Reshaping of the American Religious Landscape*, eds. Joel W. Martin and Mark A. Nichols (Chapel Hill: University of North Carolina Press, 2010), 23–37; and Rachel Wheeler, "Hendrick Aupaumut: Christian-Mahican Prophet," in *Native Americans, Christianity, and the Reshaping of the American Religious Landscape*, eds. Joel W. Martin and Mark A. Nichols (Chapel Hill: University of North Carolina Press, 2010), 225–49.

47. Benedict Anderson, *Imagined Communities: Reflections on the Origin and Spread of Nationalism*, 1983, rev. ed. (London: Verso, 1991), 60.

48. See also John Wood Sweet on this issue, *BP* 272–75.

49. For two recent, competing takes on this question, see Yokota, *Unbecoming British*, and Leonard Tennenhouse, *The Importance of Feeling English: American Literature and the British Diaspora, 1750–1850* (Princeton: Princeton University Press, 2007).

50. W. Jordan, *WOB*, 335–36. The dialogue about the environment's ability to produce change in physical and cultural characteristics took on an increased import due to both a scientific curiosity and an investment in the republican project. As Sweet puts it, "at this time, human nature became central to theories of republican citizenship, the significance of emerging national boundaries, and more subtle ways in which physical appearances might manifest invisible qualities of mind" (*BP* 274). W. Jordan elaborates that "republican scholarship was anxious to advance the study of natural philosophy and especially to explain to hostile or uncomprehending Europeans the nature of men and of nature in America. In an era of nation-building, the character—perhaps even the complexion—of the American population was bound to come under consideration" (*WOB* 264). W. Jordan also links this with the "quest for a national identity": "the prevailing view that Americans were Englishmen remodeled by New World conditions tended to throw the whole question of the Negro's Americanness into the lap of the American environment, where natural

philosophers pondered it cautiously and arrived at strange conclusions" (*WOB* 341). Joanne Pope Melish also argues that later, "post-Revolutionary instability" (*Gradual Emancipation* 137) helped lead to the fading of environmentalism, as thinkers turned from ideas of environmentalism to those of innate difference; indeed, she claims, "the whites' need to resolve post-Revolutionary uncertainty over susceptibility to enslavement and eligibility for citizenship provided a political justification for emerging [nineteenth-century] scientific notions of 'race'" (6). As W. Jordan writes, "The mood for the Revolution itself, the prevailing sense of incompleteness and of embarking upon a new era in the course of human events, was itself bound to dissipate as Americans came quite rapidly in the early years of the nineteenth century to take the existence and the viability of an American nation more for what it had never been before—granted. In these circumstances it is perhaps no wonder that views about the relationship of men to their surroundings should have changed" (*WOB* 537–38).

51. Thomas Jefferson, *Notes on the State of Virginia. The Portable Thomas Jefferson*, ed. Merrill D. Peterson (New York: Penguin Books, 1977), 23–232. Further references to this edition will be cited parenthetically as *Notes*. For more on the Jefferson–Buffon debate, see Lee Alan Dugatkin, *Mr. Jefferson and the Giant Moose: Natural History in Early America* (Chicago: University of Chicago Press, 2009); Ralph Bauer, "The Hemispheric Genealogies of 'Race': Creolization and the Geography of Colonial Differences across the Eighteenth-Century Americas" in *Hemispheric American Studies*, eds. Caroline Levander and Robert Levine (New Brunswick, NJ: Rutgers University Press, 2007), 36–56; Tawil, *Racial Sentiment*, 26–68; W. Jordan, *WOB*, 475–82; Betsy Erkkilä, *Mixed Bloods and Other Crosses: Rethinking American Literature from the Revolution to the Culture Wars* (Philadelphia: University of Pennsylvania Press, 2005), 37–61; Peter Coviello, *Intimacy in America: Dreams of Affiliation in Antebellum Literature* (Minneapolis: University of Minnesota Press, 2005), 25–57; Sheehan, *Seeds*, 66–88; Pearce, *Savagism*, 91–100; Dain, *Hideous Monster* 14–19, 26–39; Jared Gardner, *Master Plots: Race and the Founding of an American Literature 1787–1845* (Baltimore: Johns Hopkins University Press, 1998), 17–21; Berkhofer, *White Man's*, 42–44; Drake, *Nation's Nature*, 231–37; and Sean X. Goudie, *Creole America: The West Indies and the Formation of Literature and Culture in the New Republic* (Philadelphia: University of Pennsylvania Press, 2006), 179–82.

52. As Douglas Egerton puts it, "Although typically regarded as a disciple of the Enlightenment, not only was Jefferson out of step with prevailing scientific trends of the late eighteenth century, he also foreshadowed what would become the scientific racism of the late nineteenth century." See Egerton, "Race and Slavery in the Era of Jefferson," in *The Cambridge Companion to Thomas Jefferson*, ed. Frank Shuffelton (Cambridge: Cambridge University Press, 2009), 79. The scholarship on Jefferson and race is vast. Key texts include Peter S. Onuf, *The Mind of Thomas Jefferson* (Charlottesville: University of Virginia Press, 2007); Gordon M. Sayre, "Jefferson and Native Americans: Policy and Archive," in *The Cambridge Companion to Thomas Jefferson*, ed. Frank Shuffelton (Cambridge: Cambridge University Press, 2009), 61–72; Lucia Stanton, "Jefferson's People: Slavery at Monticello," in *The Cambridge Companion to Thomas Jefferson*, ed. Frank Shuffelton (Cambridge: Cambridge University Press, 2009), 83–100; Timothy Sweet, "Jefferson, Science, and the Enlightenment," in *The Cambridge Companion to Thomas Jefferson*, ed. Frank Shuffelton (Cambridge: Cambridge University Press, 2009), 101–13; Bauer, "Hemispheric Genealogies;" Coviello, *Intimacy*, 25–57; and Dugatkin, *Giant Moose*. See Annette Gordon-Reed's amazing work on Thomas Jefferson's relationship with his slave Sally Hemings in *Thomas*

Jefferson and Sally Hemings: An American Controversy (Charlottesville: University of Virginia Press, 1998) and *The Hemingses of Monticello: An American Family* (New York: Norton, 2008). See also "'Hidden in Plain Sight': Colloquy with Annette Gordon-Reed on *The Hemingses of Monticello*," in *Early American Literature* 47.2 (2012), 443–59. See also the much discussed "Slavery at Jefferson's Monticello: Paradox of Liberty" exhibit at the Smithsonian National Museum of African American History and Culture. (An online version may be viewed at: www.slaveryatmonticello.org.) In addition, other important thinkers who disputed the monogenetic account of humankind include Henry Home, Lord Kames.

53. Onuf, *Mind*, 207. Onuf continues that "Jefferson did not simply discover racial boundaries already inscribed and fixed in nature: he helped construct them, contributing significantly to the racial 'science' that would in subsequent decades naturalize racial hierarchy" (211).

54. Bauer, "Hemispheric," 51.

55. Banneker, letter, 319, emphasis added.

56. Samuel Stanhope Smith, *An Essay on the Causes of the Variety of Complexion and Figure in the Human Species. To Which are added Strictures on Lord Kaims's "Discourse, on the Original Diversity of Mankind"* (Philadelphia: Aitken, 1787). Further references to this edition will be cited parenthetically as *EC*. W. Jordan, *WOB*, 486. For more on Smith, see W. Jordan, *WOB*, 442–44, 486–88; and Dain, *Hideous Monster*, 40–80.

57. See Sheehan, *Seeds*, 1–116; Horsman, *Manifest*, 98–115; Pearce, *Savagism*, 76–104; Berkhofer, *White Man's*, 38–44; and James H. Merrell, "Declarations of Independence: Indian-White Relations in the New Nation," in *The American Revolution: Its Character and Limits*, ed. Jack P. Green (New York: New York University Press, 1987), 197–223. Berkhofer notes how environmentalism became a more common explanation for Indian difference during the Enlightenment: "A minor line of reasoning [prior to the Enlightenment] focused upon the effects of climate and physical environment to explain the varieties of lifestyles, but this hypothesis was not generally accepted until the eighteenth century, when new assumptions about social process provided a revitalized context for applying this old theme in Western thought to Native Americans" (37).

58. Sheehan, *Seeds*, 41.

59. Timothy Dwight, *Travels in New England and New York*, ed. Barbara Miller Solomon (Cambridge, MA: The Belknap Press of Harvard University Press, 1969), vol. III, 127. Further references to this edition will be cited as *T*.

60. Parrish, *American Curiosity*, 77–102.

61. Natural historians who used the term "degeneration" in a racialized way include John Mitchell, Thomas Clarkson, and Samuel Stanhope Smith, for instance. In current scholarship, Dugatkin (*Giant Moose*) pursues the concept of degeneration mainly in terms of size; Curran (*Anatomy*) brilliantly explores the racial dimension of eighteenth-century degeneration theories.

62. Yokota, *Unbecoming British*, 218.

63. Ibid., 221.

64. Sheehan, *Seeds*, 1–44.

65. While Roxann Wheeler does point out that "civil society could also enhance color's mutability" (*CR* 4), she emphasizes how skin color and civil society operated for the majority of the eighteenth century as two axes (which she notes could be "mutually informing"). In the New World context, society was thought not only to inform rubrics of skin color but also to influence skin color itself.

66. This might be, in part, because of the influence of both four-stages theory and degeneration theories on Smith and of Scottish common sense philosophy on other American environmentalist thinkers. See Roxann Wheeler, *CR*, 251–52; Pearce, *Seeds*, 82–100; and Dain, *Hideous Monster*, 23–24, 42–43.

67. Dana Nelson, *The Word in Black and White: Reading "Race" in American Literature, 1638–1867* (New York: Oxford University Press, 1992) and *National Manhood: Capitalist Citizenship and the Imagined Fraternity of White Men* (Durham: Duke University Press, 1998); Philip Gould, *Barbaric Traffic: Commerce and Antislavery in the Eighteenth-Century Atlantic World* (Cambridge, MA: Harvard University Press, 2003); Gardner, *Master Plots*; and Joanna Brooks, *American Lazarus: Religion and the Rise of African-American and Native American Literatures* (New York: Oxford University Press, 2003).

68. Julia Stern, *The Plight of Feeling: Sympathy and Dissent in the Early American Novel* (Chicago: University of Chicago Press, 1997); David Kazanjian, *The Colonizing Trick: National Culture and Imperial Citizenship in Early America* (Minneapolis: University of Minnesota Press, 2003); and Andy Doolen, *Fugitive Empire: Locating Early American Imperialism* (Minneapolis: University of Minnesota Press, 2005).

69. Robert Levine, "Introduction: New Essays on 'Race,' Writing, and Representation in Early American Literature," *Early American Literature* 46.2 (2011), 199. One can see this especially in an earlier, provocative roundtable, "Historicizing Race in Early American Studies," where J. Brooks, Gould, and Kazanjian confront the issue, and the vehement tone of this exchange speaks volumes about the topic of race in early American literary study. Joanna Brooks, "Working Definitions: Race, Ethnic Studies, and Early American Literature," *Early American Literature*, 41.2 (2006), 313–320; Philip Gould, "What We Mean When We Say 'Race,'" *Early American Literature*, 41.2 (2006), 321–27; and David Kazanjian, "'When They Come Here They Feal So Free': Race and Early American Studies," *Early American Literature*, 41.2 (2006), 329–37.

70. In addition, historians have documented various aspects of these eighteenth-century ideas about race, and the British literary scholarship of Roxann Wheeler, Dror Wahrman, and George Boulukos have begun excavating how eighteenth-century Britons conceptualized human difference. But while this book shares with these scholars an attention to eighteenth-century, natural-historical theories of race, it considers the details of North American natural history (often related to the particular problem raised by migration and contact of various peoples in the "New World" and the establishment of the United States) and the idea of the changing racialized body, in addition to the changing of various rubrics that delineate racial difference.

71. Nelson, *Reading Race* and *National Manhood*; Tawil, *The Making of Racial Sentiment*; and Wiegman, *American Anatomies*. This book also shares with Parrish and Finseth an attention to natural history in early America but focuses less on the transatlantic exchange of scientific knowledge and the depictions of the natural environment in writings on slavery. See Parrish, *American Curiosity*; and Finseth, *Shades of Green*.

72. See, for instance, Lisa Brooks (Abenaki), *The Common Pot: The Recovery of Native Space in the Northeast* (Minneapolis: University of Minnesota Press, 2008); J. Brooks, *American Lazarus*; Phillip Round, *Removable Type: Histories of the Book in Indian Country, 1663–1880* (Chapel Hill: University of North Carolina Press, 2010); Hilary Wyss, *English Letters and Indian Literacies: Reading, Writing, and New England Missionary Schools, 1750–1830* (Philadelphia: University of Pennsylvania Press, 2012); Kelly Wisecup, *Medical Encounters: Knowledge and Identity in Early American Literatures* (Amherst: University of

Massachusetts Press, 2013); Birgit Brander Rasmussen, *Queequeg's Coffin: Indigenous Literacies and Early American Literature* (Durham: Duke University Press, 2012); and Matt Cohen, *The Networked Wilderness: Communicating in Early New England* (Minneapolis: University of Minnesota Press, 2009). Native-centered and tribal-centered approaches have been influenced greatly by the developments in thinking about indigenous sovereignty, particularly the concept of intellectual sovereignty explored by Robert Allen Warrior (Osage) in *Tribal Secrets: Recovering American Indian Intellectual Traditions* (Minneapolis: University of Minnesota Press, 1995), 97–8. Intellectual sovereignty is related to, but not necessarily coterminous with, ideas of Native American literary separatism and/or American Indian literary nationalism, two methodological approaches that emphasize analyzing Native American literatures on their own terms, according to their own aesthetics, and in relationship to their individual tribal contexts, both of which have been hugely influential. For more, see Craig Womack (Oklahoma Creek-Cherokee), *Red on Red: Native American Literary Separatism* (Minneapolis: Minnesota University Press, 1999); and *American Indian Literary Nationalism*, eds. Jace Weaver (Cherokee), Craig S. Womack, and Robert Warrior (Albuquerque: University of New Mexico Press, 2006).

73. Toni Morrison, *Playing in the Dark: Whiteness and the Literary Imagination* (New York: Vintage Books, 1993); Eric Lott, *Love and Theft: Blackface Minstrelsy and the American Working Class* (New York: Oxford University Press, 1993); and David Roediger, *The Wages of Whiteness: Race and the Making of the American Working Class*, Revised ed. (London: Verso, 1991). For how racialized identities form in opposition to each other in later periods, see also Philip J. Deloria, *Playing Indian* (New Haven: Yale University Press, 1998); Shari Huhndorf, *Going Native: Indians in the American Cultural Imagination* (Ithaca: Cornell University Press, 2001); Claire Jean Kim, "The Racial Triangulation of Asian Americans," in *Asian Americans and Politics: Perspectives, Experiences, Prospects*, ed. Gordon H. Chang (Stanford: Stanford University Press, 2001), 39–78; Abdul R. JanMohamed, "The Economy of Manichean Allegory: The Function of Racial Difference in Colonialist Literature," *Critical Inquiry*, 12.1 (1985), 59–87; and Richard Dyer, *White* (London: Routledge, 1997).

74. Morrison, *Playing in the Dark*, 8.

75. Ibid, 38.

76. Sandra Gustafson, "Historicizing Race in Early American Studies: A Roundtable with Joanna Brooks, Philip Gould, and David Kazanjian," *Early American Literature*, 41.2 (2006), 310.

Chapter 1

1. John Wheatley, letter, in *Poems on Various Subjects, Religious and Moral. Complete Writings* by Phillis Wheatley, ed. Vincent Carretta (New York: Penguin, 2001), 7. On Wheatley's life, see Vincent Carretta, *Phillis Wheatley: Biography of a Genius in Bondage* (Athens: University of Georgia Press, 2011).

2. David Grimstead, "Anglo-American Racism and Phillis Wheatley's 'Sable Veil,' 'Length'ned Chain,' and 'Knitted Heart,'" in *Women in the Age of the American Revolution*, eds. Ronald Hoffman and Peter J. Albert (Charlottesville: University Press of Virginia, 1989), 388.

3. Phillis Wheatley, Letter to Samson Occom, *Connecticut Gazette; and the Universal Intelligencer* (March 11, 1774), 3. The *Connecticut Gazette* published the letter as "a Specimen of her Ingenuity," placing the Wheatley-Occom relationship in a debate about "authenticity."

The letter appeared in over ten New England newspapers in March and April of that year. See William Robinson, "On Phillis Wheatley and Her Boston," in *Phillis Wheatley and Her Writings*, ed. William H. Robinson (New York: Garland Publishing, 1984), 44.

4. David Silverman explores Occom's position within what he calls "The Christian Indian movement," which is contrasted with the "nativist" thinking outlined by Dowd and Richter. See Silverman, *Red Brethren*, passim. On Native engagement with Christianity, see also Fisher, *The Indian Great Awakening*, esp. 65–76, 122–26, and 164–87. See also Dowd, *SR*; and Richter, *Facing East from Indian Country*, 179–201.

5. For details on how Wheatley might have done this, see Joanna Brooks, "Our Phillis, Ourselves," *American Literature* 82.1 (2010), 1–28; Henry Louis Gates, Jr., *The Trials of Phillis Wheatley: America's First Black Poet and Her Encounters with the Founding Fathers* (New York: Basic Civitas Books, 2003); and David Waldstreicher, "The Wheatleyan Moment," *Early American Studies* 9.3 (2011), 522–51.

6. L. Brooks, *The Common Pot*, 51–105, on Occom's history and his role in the Mohegan land case.

7. Joanna Brooks, "'This Indian World': An Introduction to the Writings of Samson Occom," in *The Collected Writings of Samson Occom, Mohegan: Leadership and Literature in Eighteenth-Century Native America*, ed. Joanna Brooks (New York: Oxford University Press, 2006), 33.

8. Situating Occom's work in this way has its drawbacks; certainly, an execution sermon, natural-historical studies, and nativist visions transcribed on animal skin are not the same "kinds" of texts comprised of identical types of ideas. However, partly because of this very disjuncture and the problem of never translating these ideas into the *exact* same idiom, I suggest we must bring these things into conversation. Necessary to destabilize any one type of "gaze," comparison of these different thought systems results in inevitable incommensurability. My thinking here is informed by Jacques Rancière's notion of "dis-agreement" and Ronald Judy's "unfungible local value." Ed White also approaches this "familiar problem of conceptual translation, whereby Native American concepts are distorted by European parallels," which is "exacerbated by the connotations of each side of the (false) equation" (759). See Jacques Rancière, *Dis-agreement: Politics and Philosophy* (Minneapolis: University of Minnesota Press, 1999); Judy, *(Dis)Forming the American Canon: African-Arabic Slave Narratives and the Vernacular* (Minneapolis: University of Minnesota Press, 1993); Ed White, "Invisible Tagkanysough," *PMLA* 120.3 (2005): 751–67.

9. On how Occom was a crucial historical figure in the Mohegan articulation of tribal sovereignty and acquisition of federally-recognized status, see Caroline Wigginton, "Extending Root and Branch: Community Regeneration in the Petitions of Samson Occom," *Studies in American Indian Literatures* 20.4 (2008), 24–55.

10. LaVonne Brown Ruoff, "Introduction: Samson Occom's *Sermon Preached by Samson Occom . . . At the Execution of Moses Paul, an Indian*," *Studies in American Indian Literatures* 4.2–3 (1992), 75.

11. On black and Indian participation in the Great Awakening and its effect on the tensions between Old Lights and New Lights, the evangelical movement at large, and the inability of eighteenth-century evangelists to craft a theological approach to race, see J. Brooks, *American Lazarus*, 21–49. For more on the specific contours of indigenous interaction with Christianity, see Fisher, *The Indian Great Awakening*, esp. 65–76, 122–26, and 164–87.

12. The full-length studies by William DeLoss Love and Harold Blodgett are generally considered to be the most definitive—and at times problematically antiquated—Occom

biographies. Love, *Samson Occom and the Christian Indians of New England*, 1899 (Syracuse: Syracuse University Press, 2000); and Blodgett, *Samson Occom* (Hanover, NH: Dartmouth College Publications, 1935). For more on Occom's life, see L. Brooks, *Common Pot*, 51–105; Eve Tavor Bannet, *Transatlantic Stories and the History of Reading, 1720–1810: Migrant Fictions*, (Cambridge: Cambridge University Press, 2011), 158–85; Silverman, *Red Brethren*, passim; Round, *Removable Type*, 52–72; Drew Lopenzina, *Red Ink: Native Americans Picking up the Pen in the Colonial Period* (Albany: SUNY University Press, 2012), 195–322; Bernd Peyer, *The Tutor'd Mind: Indian Missionary-Writers in Antebellum America* (Amherst: University of Massachusetts Press, 1997), 54–116; J. Brooks, "Indian World" and *American Lazarus*, 51–63; Hilary E. Wyss, *Writing Indians: Literacy, Christianity, and Native Community in Early America*, (Amherst: University of Massachusetts Press, 2000), 123–53, and *English Letters and Indian Literacies*, 64–73; Sandra Gustafson, *Eloquence is Power: Oratory and Performance in Early America* (Chapel Hill: University of North Carolina Press for the Omohundro Institute of Early American History and Culture, 2000), 90–101; Jace Weaver, *That the People Might Live: Native American Literatures and Native American Community* (New York: Oxford University Press, 1997), 50–53; Fisher, *Indian Great Awakening*, esp. 65–76, 122–26, and 164–87; Brad E. Jarvis, *The Brothertown Nation of Indians: Land Ownership and Nationalism in Early America, 1740–1840* (Lincoln: University of Nebraska Press, 2010), passim; and Ruoff, "Introduction." On Occom in relationship to Scottish society, see Margaret Szasz, *Scottish Highlanders and Native Americans: Indigenous Education in the Eighteenth-Century Atlantic World* (Norman: University of Oklahoma Press, 2007), 162–96. For a detailed history of Occom's involvement in what would become Dartmouth College, see Colin Calloway, *The Indian History of an American Institution: Native Americans and Dartmouth* (Hanover, NH: Dartmouth College Press, 2010), 15–37. For more on the Mohegan Tribe, see the work of Mohegan tribal historian Melissa (Fawcett) Tantaquidgeon Zobel and Mohegan tribal archivist David Freeburg at www.mohegan.nsn.us.

13. Richter, *Facing East*, 181.

14. Ibid., 193. Religion was one of many factors that led to Pontiac's War. For more on the various influences of the rebellion, see Dowd, *War Under Heaven*.

15. The Iroquois Confederacy, or Six Nations, consisted of the Mohawk, Oneida, Onondaga, Cayuga, Seneca, and Tuscarora tribes. Different tribes had various levels and kinds of active involvement in the conflict. For instance, an Onondaga "received revelations critical of the Anglo-Americans and laced with separation theology on the eve of Pontiac's War," and Senecas actually took part in the violent uprising in 1763 (*SR* 35). Eventually the rest of the generally accommodationist Iroquois tribes subdued the more militant and nativist-leaning Seneca (*SR* 37). Dowd elsewhere notes that "by the spring of 1763 Neolin had achieved intertribal influence, even among the Six Nations. Genesee Senecas attended to his message, only to be chided by league authorities for admiring 'Wizards'" (*War Under Heaven* 101). While the more eastwardly-located Oneidas didn't actively engage in the conflict, they were well-aware of its existence. See Silverman, 61–69, 89–105, passim.

16. Dowd writes that the "chill of terror went beyond the backcountry" to far east areas like Philadelphia and Orange County, New York, where the sound of gunfire from colonial hunters inadvertently caused almost five hundred families to flea the area in fear of Indian attack. Also, rumors of an Iroquois Confederacy uprising pervaded New York. See Dowd,

War Under Heaven, 142–47. Eventually, while the majority of the violence was quelled by the British military response, Pontiac continued to struggle against the British for two more years. See Nash, *Red, White, and Black*, 262–63.

17. Love, *Occom*, 38. A November 25, 1761, letter to Rev. George Whitefield from Occom's teacher, Eleazar Wheelock, details that "Numbers from distant Nations came to hear [Occom], and some seemed really desirous to understand and know the truths which most nearly concerned them" (qtd. in Love, *Occom*, 92). In a September 16, 1762, letter to Whitefield, Wheelock writes that "the Boys and Girls which I expected from Onoyada were detained by their Parents on accot of a Rumour, & Suspicion of a War just comencing between them and the Nations back of them and in such a case they said they did not chuse to have their Children at such a distance from them, but perhaps they were Suspicious yt they should be obliged to Joyn those Nations against the English." Wheelock additionally related that Occom had also recently written him that "he was apprehensive he must return before the Time appointed—that he lived in fear of being killd, tho' the Indians had promised him in case a war should break out, they would send him under a Sufficient Guard, down as far as the English Settlements" (qtd. in Love, *Occom*, 96). Although it is unclear whether Occom's fears were fueled by the Six Nations' involvement in the Seven Years' War or outbreaks of the nativist movement, his concerns demonstrate his knowledge about Oneida intertribal affairs.

18. L. Brooks, *Common Pot*, 90; J. Brooks, *Collected Writings*, 70.

19. Melissa Jayne (Fawcett) Tantaquidgeon Zobel, *The Lasting of the Mohegans, Part I: The Story of the Wolf People* (Uncasville, CT: Mohegan Tribe, 1995), 17.

20. See L. Brooks, *Common Pot*, 51–105; Wigginton, "Extending;" and Silverman, *Red Brethren*, 64–68.

21. While we lack an extant document where Occom records an encounter with nativism, his writings demonstrate familiarity with indigenous tribal religions and customs. See "Account of the Montauk Indians, on Long Island" (50), "When He Drowned His Reason" (227), and Journal 5 (263). He is also aware of intertribal political affairs in New York and the Ohio Valley. See Journal 4 (261–62) and letter to Wheelock (67). These writings are all included in *The Collected Writings of Samson Occom, Mohegan: Leadership and Literature in Eighteenth-Century Native America*, ed. Joanna Brooks (New York: Oxford University Press, 2006). See also L. Brooks, *Common Pot*, 51–105, on Occom's travels among the Six Nations. Interestingly, Occom's beliefs on land rights converged somewhat with that of the nativists. When he returned to Mohegan, he got involved in the struggle to secure their tribal land from the British government. For more on what is sometimes known as the "Mason Controversy," see L. Brooks, *Common Pot*, 51–105; Love, *Occom*, 119–29; Peyer, *Tutor'd*, 72–74; Linford, *Indian Great Awakening*, 59–64; and Blodgett, *Occom*, 74–77.

22. When Occom visited England, Europeans were fascinated with "Red Indians." See Margaret Szasz, Introduction, in *Samson Occom and the Christian Indians of New England*, by William DeLoss Love, 1899 (Syracuse: Syracuse University Press, 2000), xxi. Occom preached sermons to packed churches, was introduced to the Earl of Dartmouth and the Countess of Huntingdon by George Whitefield, and was shown about Court. Occom even had a limited engagement with the King. His visit was so well known, in fact, that Occom records in his diary that "—this Evening I heard, the Stage Players, had been Mimicking of me in their Plays" (Journal 6, *Collected Writings*, 272). By the time he and fellow traveler

Nathaniel Whitaker returned home, Occom had raised over £12,000 for Wheelock and had become a transatlantic religious figure. For more on Occom's trip to England, see Leon Burr Richardson, *An Indian Preacher in England* (Hanover, NH: Dartmouth College Publications, 1933). See also Love, *Occom*, 130–51; Silverman, *Red Brethren*, 80–82; and Bannet, *Transatlantic*, 158–85.

23. James Axtell, "Dr. Wheelock's Little Red School," in *Natives and Newcomers: The Cultural Origins of North America*, 1974 (New York: Oxford University Press, 2001), 176.

24. Sweet, *BP*, 142. If this transformation did not happen in one's lifetime, it was imagined to occur in the afterlife. As Sweet has shown, eighteenth-century New England whites had contradictory views about whether religious conversion would cause racial transformation, holding a deep ambivalence about how Native Americans and Africans might or might not "become" white—culturally, religiously, and physically. As more people of color became members of the church, they were increasingly and paradoxically marked as different because white colonists "learned to draw new lines of difference," erasing "ethnic" differences, but inventing "racial" identities (106). Sweet details how the conversion of Indians and blacks ironically caused settlers to draw "new lines of exclusion," supplanting a "potentially *mutable* form of difference—culture—with the more stubborn, essentialist identities of race" (110; 108). While his important point about how Christian conversion reinforced racial difference is well-taken, Sweet overemphasizes the supposed "essentialism" of race—a highly disputable notion in this time period. Nevertheless, he crucially articulates that Christianity did not necessarily establish equality within New England culture, arguing that the more Occom and Wheatley became acculturated to British culture, the more they were scripted as exceptions to the Indian and African American rule.

25. Love, *Occom*, 152.

26. Peyer, *Tutor'd*, 74. The commissioners also had opposed Occom's trip to England partly because they had supported Occom's education and wanted more credit for it (Love, *Occom*, 134).

27. Peyer claims that "Occom undoubtedly had every intention of reaching the general public with his autobiographical sketch" because it is written in a twenty-six page notebook separate from his other journals, contains genre traits of salvationist literature, is subdivided into sections, and has been edited. Peyer suspects that Occom's angry diatribe kept Wheelock and the missionary societies from circulating it (*Tutor'd Mind* 89–90). The sketch was first published as "A Short Narrative of My Life" in Peyer's 1982 anthology, *The Elders Wrote*. For more on the print history of his autobiography, see Bannet, *Transatlantic*, 158–85; and Round, *Removable Type*, 52–58.

28. Joanna Brooks, however, convincingly argues that the majority of white eighteenth-century ministers actually "failed to develop a clear theological outlook on race or to enlarge on the potentially progressive energies of revivalism" (*American Lazarus* 24).

29. In detailing his early life and conversion, Occom dwells very little on his emotional or intellectual response to missionaries' messages. His record of conversion avers that "it pleased the Ld, as I humbly hope, to Bless and Acompany . . . ^with^ Divine Influences, to the Conviction and Saving Conversion of a Number of us; Amongst which, I was one that was Imprest with the things, Which we had heard" (53). By noting his reaction with the word "Imprest," Occom renders the effect that the sermons had on him as a physical change stamped or imprinted upon him *and* foreshadows how his body would be put into service for the Lord. See also Eileen Razzari Elrod on how Occom's narrative differs from

other Great Awakening spiritual autobiographies by focusing "on the material circum-stances resulting from the racist treatment he experienced" rather than "the interior self in its spiritual progression" by comparing it to Jonathan Edwards' "Personal Narrative" (22). Elrod, *Piety and Dissent: Race, Gender, and Biblical Rhetoric in Early American Autobiog-raphy* (Amherst: University of Massachusetts Press, 2008).

30. Samson Occom, "Autobiographical Narrative, Second Draft (A Short Narrative of My Life)," in *The Collected Writings of Samson Occom, Mohegan: Leadership and Literature in Eighteenth-Century Native America*, ed. Joanna Brooks (New York: Oxford University Press, 2006), 57–58. Further references to this edition will be cited parenthetically as "SN." All references to this edition will follow Brooks's editorial decision in transcribing Occom's manuscripts to use carets to denote Occom's interlineations. For more on Brooks's edito-rial markings, see "A Note on the Texts," in *The Collected Writings of Samson Occom*, xvii–xx.

31. Kimberly Roppolo, "Samson Occom as Writing Instructor: The Search for an Inter-tribal Rhetoric," in *Reasoning Together: The Native Critics Collective*, eds. Craig S. Womack, Daniel Heath Justice, and Christopher B. Teuton. (Norman: University of Oklahoma Press, 2008), 317–18.

32. Elrod and Keely McCarthy read Occom's insertion "(I speak like a fool, but I am Constrained)" as an allusion to Paul's similar comment in his second letter to the Corinthi-ans that "I speak as a fool" (II Corinthians 11:23). Dana Nelson links it to the "structural hegemony of colonialism" that will always render Occom "foolish" precisely because he is "constrained" within that system. See Elrod, *Piety*, 30; McCarthy, "Conversion, Identity, and the Indian Missionary," *Early American Literature* 36.3 (2001), 364; and Nelson, "'(I Speak Like a Fool but I Am Constrained)': Samson Occom's *Short Narrative* and Econ-omies of the Racial Self," in *Early Native American Writing: New Critical Essays*, ed. Helen Jaskoski (Cambridge: Cambridge University Press, 1996), 58–59.

33. Almost all critical interpretations of Occom's piece read this final paragraph by pointing out the tension created by what Occom writes he "*must* Say" as opposed to what he is "*ready* to Say." See Elrod, *Piety*, 32; McCarthy, "Conversion," 265; Gustafson, *Elo-quence*, 96–97; and David Murray, *Forked Tongues: Speech, Writing and Representation in North American Indian Texts* (Bloomington: Indiana University Press, 1991), 54. On the "communitism" of this paragraph, see Weaver, *That the People*, 52.

34. The *Oxford English Dictionary* gives one meaning of "so": "Representing a word or phrase already employed: Of that nature or description; of or in that condition, etc." Crit-ical accounts that credit Occom's use of "poor" here to a critique of colonial missions over-look Occom's emphasis on God's involvement in the making of the "poor Indian." Nelson sees Occom "asking his readers to see the 'poor Indian' as the *result* of the colonial mis-sionary project," showing how the project and the economic structure needs these Indians "for their own furtherance" ("Racial Self" 61). Laura Stevens claims that colonial missionary texts used the word "poor" to denote a "figure worthy of pity" in describing Indians to elicit a sympathetic response from British readers that they could then exploit; thus, the idea of the "poor Indian" became a representation peddled by these colonial societies in order to underwrite their own missions. See Laura M. Stevens, *The Poor Indians: British Missionar-ies, Native Americans, and Colonial Sensibility* (Philadelphia: University of Pennsylvania Press, 2004). Stevens contends that Occom uses the term ironically, showing not his own lack of religion and culture to be solved by missionary efforts but rather "revealing the

abysmal treatment that such pity rationalized." She states that "as he revised the trope of the 'poor Indian' to expose the hypocrisy of his would-be benefactors, Occom revealed the processes by which pity, under the auspices of the word *poor*, can be linked to the very sorts of treatment that would seem to inspire it in the first place" (*Poor Indians* 21). Both these readings neglect how Occom here focuses not on the commissioners, but rather on God and how he "makes" the Indian. I do agree with Stevens that Occom ironizes the phrase "poor Indian" as one who deserves pity from the missionaries themselves because it begs the question of what he means when he claims that God has made him that way. The emphasis returns to how the missionaries define the condition of the "poor Indian" as God's creation. If the "poor Indian" is one who has not yet and therefore needs to receive the missionary society's benevolence for conversion, then that Indian must have shared a creation with the white man. The opposite view—that he was created separately and necessitated his own religion—would clearly undermine the very missionary project and religious belief system on which it is based. For Occom's use of the "poor Indian type" in letters to Wheelock, see Wigginton, "Extending." See also Lopenzina's reading of "poor," *Red Ink*, 238.

35. McCarthy makes a somewhat similar argument about "make" by claiming that "'I did not make my self so' is not a confession bemoaning his state. He shows that his Indianness is a problem only because whites make it so." However, McCarthy emphasizes Occom as an "object of [white] prejudice" and his "position as 'despised'" rather than his creation ("Conversion" 366). Michael Elliott argues a similar point: "In his final sentence, Occom declares, 'I did not make my self so.' Yet his liminal position required him to make and remake himself continually in order to fashion his multiplicity into a permanent presence." Michael Elliott, "'This Indian Bait': Samson Occom and the Voice of Liminality," *Early American Literature* 29.3 (1994), 249. Both Elliott and McCarthy read "make my self so" in a Franklinian, self-made sense, pointing out how the narrative testifies to the way Occom actually did "make" himself in a certain way. In contrast, I read "make my self so" in a creationism sense. For another reading that considers God's role in this "making," see Elrod, *Piety*, 35.

36. According to the *Oxford English Dictionary*, *difference* contains both senses. First, it can mean a "discrimination or distinction viewed as conceived by the subject rather than as existing in the objects. Now only in phr. *to make a difference*: to distinguish, discriminate, act or treat differently." It also can mean "the condition, quality, or fact of being different, or not the same in quality or in essence; dissimilarity, distinction, diversity; the relation of non-agreement or non-identity *between* two or more things, disagreement." My reading here is influenced by Foucault's claim that power "produces reality[,] . . . domains of objects[,] and rituals of truth. The individual and the knowledge that may be gained of him belong to this production" (194). As the body is subjected to regimes of power, signs are produced, read, and interpreted. Foucault writes that "the examination is the technique by which power, instead of emitting the signs of its potency, instead of imposing its mark on its subjects, holds them in a mechanism of objectification. In this space of domination, disciplinary power manifests its potency, essentially, by arranging objects. The examination is, as it were, the ceremony of this objectification" (187). See Michel Foucault, *Discipline and Punish*. I am grateful to Jay Grossman for his insight into how Foucauldian notions of power operate within Puritan cultures, especially during the infamous witch trial examinations. Later in his life, ironically Occom himself would note distinctions between

blacks and Natives and work against black integration into Native tribes. See Silverman, *Red Brethren*, 101–6; and Daniel R. Mandell, *Tribe, Race, History: Native Americans in Southern New England, 1780–1880* (Baltimore: Johns Hopkins University Press, 2008), 53–59.

37. Occom's narrative implies that the "difference" between whites and Indians could be accounted for by two mutually exclusive theses. On the one hand, following the monogenetic story recently undergirded by natural philosophy, the Indian has transformed over time from his shared Adamic creation with whites to his current state. In this view, environmental factors produce the "difference" between Indians and whites, which is then made to signify in a certain way. In other words, this distinction is that which the Boston Commissioners themselves "make," not an inherent one placed there by God. On the other hand, if the Indian body is unable to metamorphose, then this "difference" is God-made; more closely aligned with radical nativist beliefs, this stance contradicts the Edenic creation story. By linking missionary officials' beliefs about the status of the Indian body to Christian epistemology, Occom makes it an expressly *spiritual* issue: if the commissioners discount the Edenic creation story (and how it accounts for difference between the varieties of men), then they accept as true a racial epistemology utterly irreconcilable to Biblical authority.

38. Possibly because it chastised Indian drinking, the printed version was wildly popular with both Native and white readers and appeared in nineteen different editions in thirty-five years (Love, *Occom*, 174–75), making Occom one of the most published authors in 1771–80. See *The Colonial Book in the Atlantic World, Vol. 1 of A History of the Book in America*, eds. Hugh Amory and David D. Hall (Cambridge: Cambridge University Press, 2000), 518. See Round, *Removable Type*, 67–72; and Bannet, *Transatlantic*, 174–80, on the sermon's print history. As it turns out, Occom delivered what is considered to be a fairly standard execution sermon. Ronald Bosco outlines the typical traits of the execution sermon in colonial New England and describes them as a "primary vehicle for social comment even more than for doctrinal investigation" (162). Most scholars who examine the sermon's text comment upon either the degree to which Occom reworks traditional notions of Protestant religion to produce a distinctive Indian Christianity or how he criticizes various colonial practices of white society. A notable exception is Sandra Gustafson, who argues that Occom's particular use of the "performance semiotic of speech and text" revises notions about the "'savage' speaker." See Bosco, "Lectures at the Pillory: The Early American Execution Sermon," *American Quarterly* 30.2 (1978), 156–76; and Gustafson, *Eloquence*, 90–101. For how eighteenth-century narratives of Indian crime, including Occom's sermon, challenged emerging notions of race, see Katherine Grandjean, "'Our *Fellow-Creatures* & our *Fellow-Christians*': Race and Religion in Eighteenth-Century Narratives of Indian Crime," *American Quarterly* 62.4 (2010), 925–50. For thinking about Occom within the genre and print history of execution sermons, see Karen Weyler, *Empowering Words: Outsiders and Authorship in Early America* (Athens: University of Georgia Press, 2013), 114–44.

39. According to Ava Chamberlain, the manuscript originally read: "And considering that we are of the same nation and tribe," with "and tribe" marked through. Chamberlain reads this as proof that Moses Paul was not Mohegan, despite some evidence to the contrary. Furthermore, it indicates a pan-Indian identity to which Paul refers, even if he and Occom are of different tribes. See Chamberlain, "The Execution of Moses Paul: A Story of

Crime and Contact in Eighteenth-Century Connecticut," *New England Quarterly* 77.3 (2004), 445. Lopenzina notes that Moses Paul's "grandchildren would be amongst the first baptized by Occom when the Brothertown settlement was established in Upstate New York. In fact, Occom's daughter would marry Moses Paul's son, making Paul's grandchildren Occom's grandchildren as well" (*Red Ink* 298).

40. Chamberlain, "Execution," 437.

41. Ibid., 438.

42. Ibid., 438.

43. The August 21, 1772, *Connecticut Journal and the New-Haven Post-Boy* had advertised that "the Rev. *Samson Occom*, (one of the Mohegan Tribe of Indians) has engaged to deliver a Discourse previous to the Execution of Moses Paul" (3). Paul might have been encouraged by William Samuel Johnson, Paul's appeal lawyer, who probably knew of Occom from his involvement in Mohegan land claims. Furthermore, a letter from Occom's associate, Mohegan Joseph Johnson, might have influenced him. The letter, published April 1772, is considered the first publication by a North American Indian; Occom's sermon was second. Preaching an execution sermon was a prestigious honor; further, Chamberlain claims, the minister chosen for this particularly notorious occasion "could expect a congregation of several thousand in attendance and . . . an immediate and popular publication" (444). See Chamberlain, "Execution," 442–45.

44. Nelson, "Racial Self," 48.

45. For more on the events of this day, see Chamberlain, "Execution;" Peyer, *Tutor'd*, 91–95; Blodgett, *Occom*, 139–44; Love, *Occom*, 169–74; and Gustafson, *Eloquence*, 97–101.

46. Samson Occom, *A Sermon, Preached at the Execution of Moses Paul, an Indian* (New Haven: T. & S. Green, 1772), 6. Further references to this edition will be cited parenthetically as *S*.

47. For how the term *race* changed during the eighteenth century, see Hudson, "From Nation;" and Roxann Wheeler, *CR*, 31.

48. Occom notes in his preface that "it was a stormy and very uncomfortable day, when the following discourse was delivered, and about one half of it was not delivered, as it was written, and now it is a little altered and enlarged in some places." As imperfect a "true record" of the "original" sermon the printed edition may be, I nevertheless want to consider it within the context of its actual delivery, given that the transcript of the first performance is unrecoverable. For more on the sermon's print history, see Round, *Removable Type*, 67–72; and Bannet, *Transatlantic*, 174–80.

49. Several scholars note Occom's stress on the universality of sin. See Stevens, *Poor Indians*, 174; Elliott, "This Indian," 234; Gustafson, *Eloquence*, 97–98; Chamberlain, "Execution," 448; Bannet, *Transatlantic*, 174–75; and Ruoff, "Introduction," 78–79.

50. See also Silverman for another reading of the language of being "cursed," *Red Brethren*, 125–148.

51. Here I purposefully use the masculine pronoun. Occom seems to consider the abstracted Native American as inherently male. In one of the few times that he mentions women in the sermon, he chastises specifically female drinking practices.

52. Elliott, "Indian Bait," 234. Elliott makes a similar point about how Occom uses these terms to describe "the lowly state of 'man'" (233).

53. Like Occom, Paul was what historian Margaret Szasz would term a "cultural intermediary" ("Samson Occom: Mohegan as Spiritual Intermediary" in *Between Indian and*

White Worlds: The Cultural Broker, ed. Margaret Szasz [Norman: University of Oklahoma Press], 61). The Jewish Paul grew up a Roman citizen in Greek culture. Known as Saul and a member of the strict Pharisee sect, he brutally persecuted Jews who converted to Christianity until his own Christian conversion. He then went by the Greek name Paul and was charged to preach specifically to the gentiles. Jews often considered the non-Jewish gentiles to be inferior, and other proselytizing apostles like Peter had previously ignored them. Both Paul and Occom are located in a conflicted position among contentious groups. Given tensions between gentiles and Jews, Paul's ministry required delicate negotiation. For other ways that Occom employs Pauline theology in his writing, see McCarthy, "Execution," 364; Elrod, *Piety,* 30; J. Brooks, *American Lazarus,* 72; and Gustafson, *Eloquence,* 99–100. On his use of the flesh metaphor, see also Silverman, *Red Brethren,* 53–54, 87–88.

54. Paul uses "according to the flesh" to differentiate Abraham ("our father, as pertaining to the flesh" Romans 4:1) from, one assumes, God, the spiritual father. Paul's expression connotes the kinship among those with Jewish heritage, which was still not to be superseded by the relationship with the spiritual Father and brethren.

55. Much of Paul's letter deals with the sensitive issue of how the message of God's redemption is directed "to every one that believeth; to the Jew first, and also to the Greek" (Romans 1:16). In his letter, Paul walks a delicate line: God's message, intended first for God's chosen people, also is meant to invite everyone to join the metaphysical body of Christ. Paul continually emphasizes the openness of God's message: "Glory, honour, and peace, to every man that worketh good, to the Jew first, and also to the Gentile: For there is no respect of persons with God" (Romans 2:10–11). Paul and Occom both stress the universal availability of God's kingdom but speak to different constituencies within that group. As Occom does with his Indian auditors, Paul regrets some of his fellow Jews' specific resistance to Christian conversion. In addition, Paul's consideration of physicality and spirituality inflects how he uses the flesh metaphor to talk about nationality and race. In Romans 8, Paul contrasts living life according to the spirit and not by way of the flesh; he focuses on spiritual concerns rather than those of the flesh, which is primarily linked to sinful nature. However, this sense of a sinful flesh contrasts sharply with Paul's later use of the body to highlight his Jewish heritage and to lament the way Jews were not converting to Christianity. Here, a tension exists in the way fleshy materiality works in religion. On the one hand, Paul aligns it with a sinful nature, but on the other, he uses it to identify specifically with Jews. The flesh is something that should be denied and also something that constitutes the relations among people. Although "St. Paul" himself shows up in Occom's sermon as an example of living "the life of the soul," Occom draws on Paul's corporeal metaphors to denote his kinship to other Natives.

56. Occom's bodily metaphorics resonate in multiple racialized discourses even at this date. Although Pontiac's rebellion had not realized the goals he had set for it, nativist thinking still circulated in Indian Country. In fact, the execution took place at the height of Shawnee nativism. See Dowd, *SR,* 41. Furthermore, because Moses Paul served the Connecticut Regiment that fought against Pontiac's forces, he himself probably would have been familiar with nativist beliefs. See Chamberlain, "Execution," 419.

57. Occom often uses the Christian creation story to talk about race. He challenges Christian slaveholders that "if you can prove it from the Bible that Negroes are not the Race of Adam, then you may keep them as Slaves, Otherwise you have no more right to keep them as slaves as they have to keep you as Slaves" (206). See "Thou Shalt Love Thy

Neighbor." As I shall explain below, in the sermon "To all the Indians in this Boundless Continent," Occom details the Adam and Eve creation story. This sermon also signals simultaneously the special relation Natives have among themselves and the universality shared among all humans. See *Collected Writings*. Occom also writes against slavery in "The Most Remarkable and Strange State Situation and Appearance of Indian Tribes in this Great Continent," 58–59, and "Cry Aloud, Spare Not" (II), 217–18.

58. Chamberlain, "Execution," 447.

59. Other scholars also note Occom's emphasis on alcohol's role in influencing Indian behavior. See Elliott, "Indian Bait," 235; Gustafson, *Eloquence*, 97; and Stevens, *Poor Indians*, 175. Bannet, *Transatlantic*, 175–78, furthermore, sees Occom's call for Indians to forsake alcohol akin to similar instructions given by nativist Indians.

60. Occom refigures humankind's "degeneration" as an effect of sin through his sermonic oeurve. See "Saying What Ye Think of Christ" (175); "Cry Aloud, Spare Not" (I) (211); and "Cry Aloud, Spare Not" (II) (215). See *Collected Writings*.

61. Pearce, *Savagism*, 86.

62. See Peyer, *Tutor'd*, 95; Stevens, *Poor Indians*, 176; D. Murray, *Forked*, 47; Weaver *That The People*, 53; and Elliott, "This Indian," 235.

63. "To all the Indians in this Boundless Continent," *The Collected Writings of Samson Occom, Mohegan: Leadership and Literature in Eighteenth-Century Native America*, ed. Joanna Brooks (New York: Oxford University Press, 2006), 197. Further references to this edition of this essay will be cited parenthetically as "BC."

64. Robert Warrior's notion of "intellectual sovereignty" has in many ways inaugurated a "sovereignty turn" in Native American literary studies, one that emphasizes Native intellectual concepts, indigenous practices and knowledges, and tribal land claims. See Robert Allen Warrior, *Tribal Secrets*, 97–98. For studies that have continued to develop Warrior's concept of "intellectual sovereignty," see, for instance, Lisa King (Lenape [Munsee]), "Speaking Sovereignty and Communicating Change: Rhetorical Sovereignty and the Inaugural Exhibits at the NMAI," *American Indian Quarterly* 35.1 (2011), 75–103; Qwo-Li Driskill (Cherokee), "Stolen from Our Bodies: First Nations Two-Spirits/Queers and the Journey to a Sovereign Erotic," *Studies in American Indian Literatures* 16.2 (2004), 50–64; *Queer Indigenous Studies: Critical Interventions in Theory, Politics, and Literature*, eds. Qwo-Li Driskill, Chris Finley, Brian Joseph Gilley, and Scott Lauria Morgensen (Tucson: University of Arizona Press, 2011); Mark Rivkin, *The Erotics of Sovereignty: Queer Native Writing in the Era of Self-Determination* (Minneapolis: University of Minnesota Press, 2012), 2; and Round, *Removable Type*.

65. At least two other creation stories exist in Mohegan literature. One, recorded in Melissa Tantaquidgeon Zobel's *The Lasting of the Mohegans*, was recited by Witapanoxwe/ Walks With Daylight (also known as James Weber), a Lenni Lenape Medicine Man, to Mohegan Medicine Woman Gladys Tantaquidgeon:

> In that place, there was nothing at all times above the earth. At first, forever lost in space the Great Manitou [or Gunche Mundu] was . . . He made the sun, the moon and the stars . . . Then the wind blew violently and it cleared and the water flowed off far and strong. And groups of islands grew newly [atop the domed back of a giant turtle whom we call "Grandfather"][1] and there remained. . . .

> [1]: Bracketed inserts are Mohegan additions to the Lenni Lenape Creation Story. (7)

Another exists in the Mohegan Sun Casino, where a mural depicts a man growing from a tree. *The Secret Guide*, a tourist-directed history of the Mohegan nation produced by the Mohegan Tribe and edited by Tantaquidgeon Zobel, addresses this mural in a section entitled the "Mohegan Creation Story": "To the left of the Tree of Life, is a large mural depicting the Mohegan Creation Story. The story is told as such; after the Earth was created long ago, a tree grew in the middle of the Earth. The root of the tree sent forth a sprout beside it, and there grew the first man. Then the tree bent over its top and touched the Earth, and there shot another root, from which came forth another sprout, and there grew the first woman" (29). Instead of asking which story is *the* Mohegan origin story, it might suit us better to inquire what *is* a Mohegan origin story. Most likely Occom would claim a Mohegan origin story is one told by a Mohegan, for a Mohegan purpose, and to a Mohegan end. In addition, all these stories have much in common: the emphasis on the natural world, the presence of a single Creator, and (in at least two of them) the importance of the relationship of the tree to that of human life. As Caroline Wigginton has pointed out about the many petitions Occom penned during the 1760s-80s, Occom often used the imagery of the "Sacred Tree" from Mohegan oral history in his writings, something Wigginton claims "spread[s] an Indigenous Christianity" ("Extending" 36). Furthermore, Silverman emphasizes how the elm bark story box sent from the Mohegan Indians who had removed to Oneida back to Occom's sister, Lucy, features "multiple roots feeding into a single strong trunk, hearkening to the Indian metaphor (ubiquitous among the Iroquois, including the Brothertowns' Oneida hosts) of the community as a great tree, with branches providing shelter to the people and reaching up to future generations and the roots plunging down into the earth where the ancestors are buried" (*Red Brethren* 30). Anthony Appiah theorizes a type of cosmopolitanism we might find useful in thinking about Occom's creation story. In Appiah's view, where one is from is crucially important to one's identity, but one's local place and one's local practices are never "pure;" rather, they are productively, always already "contaminated" (101–13). Here, we might consider this less a "replacement" of traditional Mohegan origin stories with a Christian one and more a certain kind of "contamination" that flows both ways among these cultural products. See Melissa Tantaquidgeon Zobel, *The Secret Guide* (Uncasville, CT: Little People Publications, 1998), and Appiah, *Cosmopolitanism: Ethics in a World of Strangers* (New York: Norton, 2007).

66. On nativism, see Dowd, *Spirited Resistance* and *War Under Heaven*; Ritcher 179–201; Cave, *Prophets of the Great Spirit*, 11–44; and Nash, *Red, White, and Black*, 258–64. See also Silverman, *Red Brethen*, passim.

67. See also Silverman and Fisher on how Occom and other New England Natives articulated a specific kind of "*Indian* Christianity, something related to but also distinct from the faith practiced by whites" (*Red Brethren* 56). Both scholars call attention to a story recounted by someone who heard Occom share a telling anecdote, where he talked "somewhat at length of what he called a traditionary religion; and he told an anecdote by way of illustration. An old Indian, he said, had a knife which he kept till he wore the blade out; and then his son took it and put a new blade to the handle, and kept it till he had worn the handle out; and this process went on till the knife had had half a dozen blades, and as many handles, but still it was all the time the same knife" (William B. Sprague, *Annals of the American Pulpit, or, Commemorative Notices of Distinguished American Clergymen of Various Denominations*, 4 vols. [New York: 1857–59], 3:195). See Silverman, 56; Fisher, 88.

In addition, Occom's general antislavery stance serves as an interesting counterpoint to the way he and other Mohegan leaders stood against interracial marriage between blacks and Natives and envisioned Brothertown, the removal town Occom and others founded on Oneida lands, as one exclusionary of blacks. See Silverman, *Red Brethren*, 101–6; and Mandell, *Tribe*, 53–59. On how Occom's interaction with Wheelock and white society led up to this separatist movement, see Bannet, *Transatlantic*, 158–85. For more generally on Brothertown, see J. Brooks, *American Lazarus*, 51–86; Wyss, *Writing Indians*, 123–53; Jarvis, *Brothertown*; and Drew Lopenzina, *Red Ink*, 253–313.

68. Weaver, *That The People*, xiii.

69. Silverman, *Red Brethren*, 97.

70. Samson Occom, "Brotherton Tribe to United States Congress," *The Collected Writings of Samson Occom, Mohegan: Leadership and Literature in Eighteenth-Century Native America*, ed. Joanna Brooks (New York: Oxford University Press, 2006), 148–49. Further references to this edition will be cited parenthetically as "BT."

71. Occom repeats this kind of language in "Montaukett Tribe to the State of New York," *The Collected Writings of Samson Occom, Mohegan: Leadership and Literature in Eighteenth-Century Native America*, ed. Joanna Brooks (New York: Oxford University Press, 2006), 150–52. For more on these fascinating documents, see Wigginton, "Extending."

72. This was "the first portrait of a black with a name to be painted in America." Sidney Kaplan, *The Black Presence in the Era of the American Revolution, 1770–1800* (Greenwich: New York Graphic Society, 1973), 178. Most Wheatley scholars conjecture that Scipio Moorhead (probable subject of Wheatley's poem "To S.M. a young African Painter, on seeing his Works"), artist and black servant to Rev. John Moorhead (the subject of "An Elegy, To Miss. Mary Moorhead, on the Death of her Father, *The Rev. Mr. John Moorhead*"), drew Wheatley's likeness in Boston. Wheatley then transported it with her when she traveled to England in May, 1773 (Robinson, "Wheatley and Her Boston," 31–33).

73. Astrid Franke, "Phillis Wheatley, Melancholy Muse," *New England Quarterly* 77.2 (2004), 227. For more on Wheatley's engagement with sentiment, see J. Brooks, "Our Phillis, Ourselves;" and Julie Ellison, *Cato's Tears and the Making of Anglo-American Emotion* (Chicago: University of Chicago Press, 1999), 114–22; and Peter Coviello, "Agonizing Affection: Affect and Nation in Early America," *Early American Literature* 37.3 (2002), 439–68. On mourning and Wheatley's elegies, see Max Cavitch, *American Elegy: The Poetry of Mourning from the Puritans to Whitman* (Minneapolis: University of Minnesota Press, 2007), 186–93; Weyler, *Empowering Words*, 23–75; Eric Wertheimer, *Underwriting: The Poetics of Insurance in America, 1722–1872* (Stanford: Stanford University Press, 2006), 62–78; Joseph Fichtelberg, *Risk Culture: Performance and Danger in Early America* (Ann Arbor: University of Michigan Press, 2010), 95–122; Christine Levecq, *Slavery and Sentiment: The Politics of Feeling in Black Atlantic Antislavery Writing, 1770–1850* (Durham, NH: University of New Hampshire Press, 2008), 52–69; and Katherine Clay Bassard, *Spiritual Interrogations: Culture, Gender, and Community in Early African American Women's Writing* (Princeton: Princeton University Press, 1999), 58–70.

74. Franke, "Melancholy Muse," 229.

75. Ibid.

76. Franke attributes the selection of the pose to the Countess; the similarity between the Wheatley portrait and one of Selina herself "suggests that the Countess wanted to

present Wheatley as her black double" ("Melancholy" 227). However, since we lack conclusive evidence, one could just as likely hypothesize that perhaps Wheatley herself suggested the pose to Scipio Moorhead or that it resulted as a collaboration between them. For more on natural-historical theories, including that about exposure to the sun, see Roxann Wheeler, *CR*, 1–48; Dain, *Hideous Monster*, 1–39; Smedley and Smedley, *Race*, 159–212; Gates, *Figures*, 61–79; Parrish, *American Curisotiy*, 77–102; and W. Jordan, *WOB*, 216–565.

77. Eric Slauter attributes the review to Dr. John Langhore. See Slauter, *The State as a Work of Art: The Cultural Origins of the Constitution* (Chicago: University of Chicago Press, 2009), 183.

78. Qtd. in *Critical Essays on Phillis Wheatley*, ed. William H. Robinson (New York: G.K. Hall & Co., 1982), 30.

79. Gates, *Figures*, 63–68.

80. *State* 183. Julian Mason points out that "this was a major review that month (not in the 'Monthly Catalogue'), approximately one and one-half pages long," in a crucially important review magazine of the day. See Mason, "On the Reputation of Phillis Wheatley, Poet," in *The Poems of Phillis Wheatley*, 1966, ed. Julian D. Mason (Chapel Hill: University of North Carolina Press, 1989), 25.

81. While the notion about the sun's influence on blackness dates back to the Hebrew Bible, in eighteenth-century natural philosophy, it accrued a "scientific" validity (Dain, *Hideous Monster*, 6–7), used by some natural historians to account for the development of human difference since the Edenic creation.

82. Roxann Wheeler explains that humoral/climate theory underwent a shift between ancient writers in the Mediterranean region and seventeenth- and eighteenth-century British writers. Ancient thought believed that southern zones like Africa produced "intellectual and creative people. Their black complexions signified this array of qualities" (*CR* 23). In this schema, white Britons were considered "dull-witted" laborers who excelled in the mechanical and manual arts. Peoples in the Mediterranean region enjoyed the perfect mix of the two. In later British writing, either the northern regions no longer had these negative connotations *or* Britain itself was conceived as part of the temperate zone. Additionally, Africans—still blackened by the sun—were considered to be lazy and enfeebled. See Roxann Wheeler, *CR*, 21–28.

83. On the critical history of discussing Wheatley's alleged imitation versus ironic appropriation, see Slauter, "Neoclassical Culture in a Society with Slaves: Race and Rights in the Age of Wheatley," *Early American Studies* 2.1 (2004), 104–5. Furthermore, this analysis moves away from the seemingly pervasive "assimilative versus subversive" critical dichotomy characterizing much Wheatley scholarship. On the debate over Wheatley's accommodation versus subversion, see Russell Reising, *Loose Ends: Closure and Crisis in the American Social Text* (Durham: Duke University Press, 1996), 76–84; Robert Kendrick, "Re-membering America: Phillis Wheatley's Intertextual Epic," *African American Review* 30.1 (1996), 71–88; and Gates, *Trials*. Also, for another view on Phillis Wheatley and aesthetics, see Edward Cahill, *Liberty of the Imagination: Aesthetic Theory, Literary Form, and Politics in the Early United States* (Philadelphia: University of Pennsylvania Press, 2012), 58–63.

84. Scholars have attributed Wheatley's sun metaphorics to Christian imagery, African sun worship, classical mythology, or Enlightenment philosophy. Grimstead notes that

"Africa was also the sun's chosen residence . . . and eighteenth-century science interpreted dark skins as direct reflection of people's closeness to the sun" (364), although he does not use this connection to read her poetry. See Grimstead, "Anglo-American Racism," 338–444. For views on Wheatley's sun imagery, see Shields, "Phillis Wheatley's Use of Classicism," *American Literature* 52.1 (1980), 97–111; Betsy Erkkilä, *Mixed Bloods*, 77–88; Reising, *Loose Ends*, 73–115; Robinson, "Wheatley and Her Boston;" and Regina Jennings, "African Sun Imagery in the Poetry of Phillis Wheatley," *Pennsylvania English* 22.1–2 (2000), 68–76.

85. Jefferson, well-versed in these theories, utterly misses Wheatley's implication that the sun makes her black *and* poetic. Gates chronicles how scientists debated the "Negro's" intelligence and pointed to Wheatley's poetry as evidence. See Jefferson, *Notes*, 189; and Gates, *Figures*, 61–79.

86. Reading Wheatley's poetry in this way provides new insight into how she transvalues light/dark metaphorics. Where her readers in the past have either attributed her some-times negative connotations attached to "dark" metaphors to a Christian and/or Enlighten-ment tradition, I argue that it gives us insight into her particular conception of life as a black poet. Important exceptions are Robert Kendrick and Russell Reising. Reising argues that Wheatley's "trafficking in whiteness" periodically reverses traditional values of black and white. See Reising, *Loose Ends*, 73–115. Kendrick sees this reversal in terms of signifyin(g) and the sublime. See also Kendrick, "Re-membering America," and "Sntaching a Laurel, Wearing a Mask: Phillis Wheatley's Literary Nationalism and the Problem of Style," *Style* 27.2 (1993), 222–51.

87. On the relation between slavery and the gothic, see Teresa A. Goddu, *Gothic Amer-ica: Narrative, History, and Nation* (New York: Columbia University Press, 1997).

88. Also leader of the nine muses, Apollo has often been associated with poetic inspira-tion. This is particularly so in Ovid's *Metamorphosis*, where his pursuit of Daphne leads to her transformation into the laurel tree, which holds symbolic meaning of poetic genius.

89. "Classicism" 100. Shields calls Wheatley's sun imagery "the central image pattern of her entire body of work" ("Classicism" 102–3). In "Phillis Wheatley's Struggle for Freedom in Her Poetry and Prose," Shields quantifies his earlier claim: "The Latin name for the dawn, 'Aurora,' appears nine times in Wheatley's poetry; she repeats the Greek names for the sun, 'Apollo' and 'Phoebus,' seven and twelve times, respectively, and uses the Latin 'Sol' twice. The word 'sun,' a classical name for it, or such a phrase as 'light of day' occurs in almost all of her fifty-five extant poems. Such regularity is certainly unusual if not unique in the work of poets from any age" (241). See Phillis Wheatley's "Struggle for Freedom in Her Poetry and Prose," in *The Collected Works of Phillis Wheatley*, ed. John C. Shields (New York: Oxford University Press, 1988), 229–70.

90. For more on the significance of Terence, see Paula Bennett, "Phillis Wheatley's Vo-cation and the Paradox of the 'Afric Muse,'" *PMLA* 113.1 (1998), 64–76.

91. See for instance Erkkilä, *Mixed Bloods*, 82; Frances Smith Foster, *Written by Herself: Literary Production by African American Woman, 1746–1892* (Bloomington: Indiana Uni-versity Press, 1993), 40; Franke, "Melancholy," 245–46; Bennett, "Vocation," 68; Marsha Watson, "A Classic Case: Phillis Wheatley and Her Poetry," *Early American Literature* 31.2 (1996), 103–32; and Shields, "Phills Wheatley's Subversion of Classical Stylistics," *Style* 27.2 (1993), 252–70.

92. Shields also notes the presence of Apollo and Aurora here. See Shields, "Classicism," 100.

93. This very question has prompted a number of different scholarly explanations. Reising claims it is the overpowering of imagination by the impact of slavery, figured in

Wheatley's poem as the winter. Erkkilä calls it "the chill of Northern white oppression" (86). For a related reading, see Shields, *The American Aeneas: Classical Origins of the American Self* (Knoxville: University of Tennessee Press, 2001), 245; Cahill, *Liberty of the Imagination*, 61; and Fichtelberg, *Risk Culture*, 115–16. Like me, Franke has a more literal reading; she attributes the sudden "return to a somber mood" to melancholy, perhaps caused by the cold weather ("Melancholy" 244). Ellison locates it in Atlantic slavery. See Reising, *Loose Ends*, 73–115; Erkkilä, *Mixed Bloods*; and Ellison, *Cato's Tears*, 114–22. For more on Wheatley's general knowledge of theories of imagination, see Shields, *Phillis Wheatley and the Romantics* (Knoxville: University of Tennessee Press, 2010).

94. Somewhat relatedly, Shields notes that "Memnon, a prince of Ethiopia," is produced by Tithonus and Aurora's coupling (*Romantics* 54). See also Fichtelberg, *Risk Culture*, 117, on this scene.

95. For instance, in "To the Rev. Dr. Thomas Amory," Wheatley accounts for God's existence by citing his influence on shaping the human form and setting the planets in their courses: "As if the clay without the potter's aid / Should rise in various forms, and shapes self-made, / Or worlds above with orb o'er orb profound / Self-mov'd could run the everlasting round" (17–20). Although it is unclear whether Wheatley studied the works of her contemporaneous scientists, many of them most certainly read hers, and she engaged them in oblique ways. Most famously, Thomas Jefferson cited her in his scientific "assertion only" that whites may have enjoyed a separate creation from blacks (*Notes* 189), and Gilbert Imlay responds to Jefferson via recourse to Wheatley in his scientific rebuttal (Mason, "Reputation," 30). Benjamin Franklin read Wheatley's works and visited her while she was in London (Robinson, "Phillis Wheatley and Her Boston," 36), and Wheatley's 1779 proposals for her second collection of poems shows that she planned to dedicate the volume to him (Robinson, "Phillis Wheatley and Her Boston," 56). Benjamin Rush cited her in his 1773 *Address to the Inhabitants of British Settlements in America, upon Slave Keeping,* and Robinson suggests that Wheatley's husband, John Peters, sold her manuscripts to Rush's son James Rush, who had an avid interest in Africa-Americana (Robinson, "Phillis Wheatley and Her Boston," 66). In the concluding pieces of *Poems,* "A Rebus, by *I.B.*" and "An Answer to the *Rebus,* by the Author of these Poems," Wheatley most likely engages with James Bowdoin, a scientist and politician, and one of the signatories of *Poems'* infamous prefatory "Attestation" (Gates, *Trials,* 11–12). Voltaire cited Wheatley in 1774 to counter Baron Constant de Rebecq's claim that there was so such thing as a black poet (Carretta, Introduction, *Wheatley,* xv), and Johann Friedrich Blumenbach also "wrote favorably of her poems" (Robinson, Introduction, 1). Lastly, in one of her most famous poems addressed "To the University of Cambridge, in New-England," Wheatley admonishes the students, who she calls "ye sons of science" (10) and "Ye blooming plants of human race divine" (27), which Dain links to "natural classification" (*Hideous Monster* 8). For more on contemporaneous reactions to Wheatley's poetry, see Shields, *Phillis Wheatley's Poetics of Liberation* (Knoxville: University of Tennessee Press, 2008), 43–69; and *Romantics,* 65–113; Jeffrey Bilbro, "Who Are Lost and How They're Found: Redemption and Theodicy in Wheatley, Newton, and Cowper," *Early American Literature* 47.3 (2012), 561–589; and Waldstreicher, "Wheatleyan Moment."

96. See Gates, *Figures,* 61–79; Dwight McBride, *Impossible Witnesses: Truth, Abolitionism, and Slave Testimony* (New York: New York University Press, 2001), 103–119; Erkkilä, *Mixed Bloods,* 77–88; William J. Scheick, "Phillis Wheatley's Appropriation of Isaiah," *Early American Literature* 27.2 (1992), 135–40; Bennett, "Vocation;" Kendrick, "Re-membering America;"

Sondra O'Neale, "A Slave's Subtle War: Phillis Wheatley's Use of Biblical Myth and Symbol," *Early American Literature* 21.2 (1986), 144–65; Marsha Watson, "A Classic Case;" James A. Levernier, "Style as Protest in the Poetry of Phillis Wheatley," *Style* 27.2 (Summer 1993), 172–93; Mary McAleer Balkun, "Phillis Wheatley's Construction of Otherness and the Rhetoric of Performed Ideology," *African American Review* 36.1 (2002), 121–35; Shields, *Liberation,* 78; Colleen Glenney Boggs, *Transnationalism and American Literature: Literary Translation 1773–1892* (New York: Routledge Press, 2007), 39; and Reising, *Loose Ends,* 73–115. See also Bassard, who argues that Wheatley's ventriloquism of a white-centered viewpoint about Africans in the poem's sixth line shows her understanding of white viewpoints of blackness (*Spiritual* 39).

97. Erkkilä, *Mixed Bloods,* 233–34.

98. Kendrick makes a similar observation, calling Wheatley's use of "die" in "Works of Providence" a "reply of sorts to the voice in 'On Being Brought from Africa to America, . . .'" ("Re-membering America" 85).

99. Wheatley's religious theorization of blackness challenges other theological explanations, such as the story of Ham. Citing how God cursed Ham when he looked upon his father Noah's nakedness, some slave apologists interpreted the curse of Ham to be a justification for slavery. Abolitionists argued that this curse had no link to blackness. For more on Ham, see Curran, *Anatomy,* 76–79; Kidd, *Forging,* 35; Smedley and Smedley, *Race,* 200, 216, 244; Thomas F. Gossett, *Race: The History of an Idea in America* (Dallas: Southern Methodist University Press, 1963), 5; and Dain, *Hideous Monster,* 126–27.

100. Shields sees Wheatley's use of sun imagery here as a synthesis of classical allusions, Christian elements, and aspects of African sun worship. Jennings contends that Wheatley's sun imagery "reach(es) far back into ancient Africa" ("African" 74). See Shields, "Classicism." On how Wheatley combines knowledge of Newtonian physics and Christian theology, see Cedrick May, *Evangelism and Resistance in the Black Atlantic, 1760–1835* (Athens: University of Georgia Press, 2008), 51–4; and Shields, *Liberation,* 102–3, 140–42.

101. For a related point, see Kendrick, "Re-membering America," 85. Grimstead notes the "ideal . . . Newtonian balance, specifically tied to enough but not too much sun" ("Anglo-American" 367).

102. W. Jordan, *WOB,* 525. Rev. George Whitefield himself partially justified slavery by his belief that Africans were more able "to support the hot sun" (Willard 247; 255). For more on Wheatley and Whitefield's ownership of slaves, see Carla Willard, "Wheatley's Turns of Praise: Heroic Entrapment and the Paradox of Revolution," *American Literature* 67.2 (1995), 233–56.

103. Similarly, in a cluster of four poems ostensibly on "health" ("Ode to Neptune. On Mrs. W—'s Voyage to England," "To a Lady on her coming to North-America with her Son, for the Recovery of her Health," "To a Gentleman on his Voyage to *Great-Britain* for the Recovery of his Health," and "A Farewel to America. To Mrs. S.W."), Wheatley uses the topic of slavery to rework the strand of environmentalist thought that argued that certain climates were better for one's health. In this hierarchy, the North American climate was better than tropical regions, while Europe's climate was considered best. For how these poems enable Wheatley to reinscribe the slave trade, see Bassard, *Spiritual Interrogations,* 47–57. For how the 1772 *Somerset* decision (understood by many to undermine slavery by denying slaveowners the right to remove their slaves to the colonies with them) resulted in Wheatley's association of London with restorative health and Jamaica with the disease of

slavery, see Carretta, Introduction, *Wheatley*, xxix–xxxi. See also Shields, "Subversion of Classical Stylistics;" and Kristen Wilcox, "The Body into Print: Marketing Phillis Wheatley," *American Literature* 71.1 (1999), 1–29.

104. See also Shields, *Imagination*, 143 on a related point regarding Genesis.

105. Reising reads this Aurora figure as a reference to Susanna Wheatley, who paraded Wheatley throughout polite Boston, requesting that her slave poet perform for her circle of female friends and public authority figures. See Reising, *Loose Ends*, 103. He associates the sun with whiteness, which "obliterates the . . . African American poet who would aspire to linguistic and cultural competence in an environment where she is quite clearly marginalized" (104). See also Grimstead on the poem's "mutuality of light and dark" ("Anglo-American" 368).

106. For a reading that links this to the sublime, see Kendrick, "Snatching a Laurel." Also on the sublime, see Fichtelberg, *Risk Culture*, 95–122; and Levecq, *Sentiment*, 52–69. Shields links the poem to Africa (*American Aeneas* 238–39).

107. Scholars contend that Wheatley most likely saw William Woollett's engraving of Richard Wilson's *Niobe* (Slauter, *State*, 199–200).

108. For more on Wheatley's use of classical sources, see Shields, *Classicism*; William W. Cook and James Tatum, *African American Writers and Classical Tradition* (Chicago: University of Chicago Press, 2010), 7–47; Tracey L. Walters, *African American Literature and the Classicist Tradition: Black Women Writers from Wheatley to Morrison* (New York: Palgrave Macmillan, 2007), 39–50; and (especially on translation) Boggs, *Transnationalism*, 37–60. Jennifer Thorn reads the poem in the context of American and British responses to Latin poetry; see "'All Beautiful in Woe': Gender, Nation, and Phillis Wheatley's 'Niobe,'" *Studies in Eighteenth-Century Culture* 37.1 (2008), 233–58. See also Christopher Phillips who claims that "Wheatley is unusually attentive to Apollo's place in the story, placing the blame for Niobe's 'woes' solely on his shoulders in the invocation (she bids the muse to sing 'Apollo's wrath' in the first line), and this is in part because of her interest in the Wilson picture" (*Epic in American Culture: Settlement to Reconstruction* [Baltimore: Johns Hopkins University Press, 2012], 57).

109. Shields, *American Aeneas*, 266.

110. Wheatley interpolates this epic simile (Shields, "Classicism," 109); Ovid did not relate the daughters' beauty to the productions of the sun.

111. Langley links the grief a sympathetic Niobe feels over the loss of her children to African and slave mothers whose families are destroyed by the slave trade; see April C. E. Langley, *The Black Aesthetic Unbound: Theorizing the Dilemma of Eighteenth-Century African American Literature* (Columbus: Ohio State University Press, 2008), 57–95. Walters (*Classicist* 39–50) has a similar reading. Slauter links it to both the situation of slave mothers and the petitions slaves made to the Massachusetts colony (*State* 198–203).

112. "Classicism" 110.

113. Scholars conjecture that the final stanza could be by Mary Wheatley or perhaps that Nathaniel Wheatley, Joseph Sewall, Samuel Cooper, or Mather Byles influenced it (Shields, *American Aeneas*, 294). Whoever might have written this final stanza, it leads one to believe that part of the anxiety around Wheatley's writing was not whether she had the ability to write it but that she composed it *alone*. In other words, in addition to "judging" Wheatley to be "qualified to write them," the prefatory Attestation also mediates worries over miscegenetic authorial collaboration and, perhaps, fears over the female collaboration of

Susanna and Phillis. For another reading of Niobe's transformation into stone, see Tim Armstrong, *The Logic of Slavery: Debt, Technology, and Pain in American Literature* (Cambridge: Cambridge University Press, 2012), 116–20.

Chapter 2

1. For more on the publication history of Franklin's *Autobiography*, see Stephen Carl Arch, "Benjamin Franklin's *Autobiography*, then and now," in *The Cambridge Companion to Benjamin Franklin*, ed. Carla Mulford (Cambridge: Cambridge University Press, 2008), 159–171; Joyce Chaplin, "Introduction," in *Benjamin Franklin's* Autobiography, ed. Joyce Chaplin (New York: Norton, 2012), xii-xxvi; and Douglas Anderson, *The Unfinished Life of Benjamin Franklin* (Baltimore: Johns Hopkins University Press, 2012), 1–2, passim. Sandra Gustafson's new, abridged edition of Aupaumut's "Narration," along with her historical and cultural contextualization of it, is perfect for teaching to students, particularly if one wants to teach Franklin and Aupaumut in relation to one another. See Gustafson, "Historical Introduction to Hendrick Aupaumut's *Short Narration*," in *Early Native Literacies in New England: A Documentary and Critical Anthology*, eds. Kristina Bross and Hilary E. Wyss (Amherst: University of Massachusetts Press, 2008), 237–42; and "Hendrick Aupaumut and the Cultural Middle Ground," in *Early Native Literacies in New England: A Documentary and Critical Anthology*, eds. Kristina Bross and Hilary E. Wyss (Amherst: University of Massachusetts Press, 2008), 242–50. This edition also includes an excerpt from Aupaumut's work. Aupaumut, "A Short narration of my last Journey to the Western Contry," in *Early Native Literacies in New England: A Documentary and Critical Anthology*, eds. Kristina Bross and Hilary E. Wyss (Amherst: University of Massachusetts Press, 2008), 223–37.

2. Even a sense of "red" identity resulted in various ways from colonial contact. See Dowd, *SR*, 23–46; Richter, *Facing East*, 179–87; and Shoemaker, *Strange Likeness*, 126–40. For more on Christianized Indians during the eighteenth century, see Silverman, *Red Brethren*; and Fisher, *Indian Great Awakening*.

3. This specific form of nativist thought among the Ohio Valley Indians, of course, does not begin to account for the distinctive origin stories of numbers of Native American tribes.

4. See note 51 from Introduction. For more on Jefferson sending the moose, see Dugatkin, *Mr. Jefferson*; and I. Bernard Cohen, *Science and the Founding Fathers: Science in the Political Thought of Thomas Jefferson, Benjamin Franklin, John Adams, and James Madison* (New York: Norton, 1995), 86.

5. I. Cohen, *Science*, 73–88. For more on Jefferson's and Franklin's respective responses to the degeneration controversy, see Gilbert Chinard, "Eighteenth Century Theories on America as a Human Habitat," *Proceedings of the American Philosophical Society* 91.1 (1947), 27–57; I. Cohen, *Science*, 72–88; Dugatkin, *Giant Moose*, 49–50; and David Waldstreicher, *Runaway America: Benjamin Franklin, Slavery, and the American Revolution* (New York: Hill and Wang, 2004), 214–16. Jim Egan argues that Franklin's preface to Alexander Dalrymple's 1771 *A Plan for Benefiting the New Zealanders* responds to "America's supposed degeneracy as an attempt to fashion a *theory of identity* rather than a theory of *American* identity" (207). Egan claims that Franklin "substitutes 'exchange' for 'climate' as the determining factor in collective identity" (207). See Jim Egan, "Turning Identity Upside

Down: Benjamin Franklin's Antipodean Cosmopolitanism," in *Messy Beginnings: Postcoloniality and Early American Studies*, eds. Malini Johar Schueller and Edward Watts (New Brunswick: Rutgers University Press, 2003), 203–22. For how Franklin portrays Native Americans in terms of four-stages theory in "Remarks Concerning the Savages of North America," see Carla J. Mulford, "Benjamin Franklin, Native Americans, and the Commerce of Civility," in *Revolutionary Histories: Transatlantic Cultural Nationalism, 1775–1815*, ed. W. M. Verhoeven (New York: Palgrave, 2002), 48–61. See also Sean Goudie on how Franklin characterizes a "regenerative North America" in contradistinction to a "degenerative West Indies," in *Creole America: The West Indies and the Formation of Literature and Culture in the New Republic* (Philadelphia: University of Pennsylvania Press, 2006), 25–63.

6. Jefferson, "Anecdotes of Benjamin Franklin," included in a letter to Robert Walsh, December 4, 1818. Rpt. in *The Complete Jefferson: Containing His Major Writings, Published and Unpublished, Except His Letters*, ed. Saul K. Padover (New York: Duell, Sloan & Pearce, Inc.), 894.

7. Benjamin Franklin, *The Autobiography*, in *Autobiography, Poor Richard, and Later Writings*, ed. J. A. Leo Lemay (New York: The Library of America, 1997), 567. Further references to this edition will be cited parenthetically as *A*.

8. Waldstreicher has interestingly argued that Franklin was more involved in race-based slavery that we have previously acknowledged, and he has expanded the understanding of how Franklin wrote about African Americans (*Runaway America*). See also Alan Houston, *Benjamin Franklin and the Politics of Improvement* (New Haven: Yale University Press, 2008), 200–16. However, scholars seem less interested in Franklin's thoughts on natural historical claims about race. Joyce E. Chaplin touches on them locally in *The First Scientific American: Benjamin Franklin and the Pursuit of Genius* (New York: Basic Books, 2006).

9. Franklin describes this kind of light-touched rhetorical approach as much himself:

I . . . retain[ed] only the Habit of expressing my self in Terms of modest Diffidence, never using when I advance any thing that may possibly be disputed, the Words, *Certainly, undoubtedly*, or any others that give the Air of Positiveness to an Opinion; but rather say, *I conceive*, or *I apprehend* a Thing to be so or so, *It appears to me*, or *I should think it so or so for such & such Reasons*, or *I imagine* it to be so, or *it is so* if *I am not mistaken*.—This Habit I believe has been of great Advantage to me, when I have had occasion to inculcate my Opinions & persuade Men into Measures that I have been from time to time engag'd in promoting.—And as the chief Ends of Conversation are to *inform*, or to be *informed*, to *please* or to *persuade*, I wish well meaning sensible Men would not lessen their Power of doing Good by a Positive assuming manner that seldom fails to disgust, tends to create Opposition, and to defeat every one of those Purposes for which Speech was give us, to wit, giving to receiving Information, or Pleasure: For If you would *inform*, a positive dogmatical Manner in advancing your Sentiments, may provoke Contradiction & prevent a candid Attention. If you wish Information & Improvement from the Knowledge of others and yet at the same time express your self as firmly fix'd in your present Opinions, modest sensible Men, who do not love Disputation, will probably leave you undisturb'd in the Possession of your Error; and by such a Manner you can seldom hope to recommend your self in *pleasing* your Hearers, or to persuade those whose Concurrence you desire. (*A* 581–82)

Indeed, the text not only describes how Franklin takes this rhetorical posture—the *Autobiography* itself performs it. See also Michael Warner, *The Letters of the Republic: Publication and the Public Sphere in Eighteenth-Century America* (Cambridge, MA: Harvard University Press, 1990), 73–96. See also Joseph Fichtelberg, "The Complex Image: Text and Reader in the *Autobiography* of Benjamin Franklin," *Early American Literature* 23.2 (1988), 202–16.

10. For a brilliant analysis of Franklin and the concept of imitation, see William Hunting Howell, *Against Self Reliance*, forthcoming from University of Pennsylvania Press.

11. Chaplin offers an account of Franklin as primarily a scientist who was continually pulled away, with much reluctance, from his scientific scholarship to his political and diplomatic endeavors. See Chaplin, *Scientific American*.

12. Ibid., 125.

13. Chaplin claims that over the course of his life, Franklin "never made up his mind about human difference" (83). Chaplin charts Franklin's developing thought on these issues, claiming that he at times asserted that all humans were inherently the same, while at others he conjectured that Indians' bodies were fundamentally different from the white man's. However, later in life he began to think that difference was not inherent or reflected a natural inferiority. See *Scientific American* 82–83; 180–82. Waldstreicher emphasizes the strategic nature of shifts in Franklin's views on slavery and black capacity for achievement in *Runaway America*, 192–209.

14. Christopher Looby, *Voicing America: Language, Literary Form, and the Origins of the United States* (Chicago: University of Chicago Press, 1996), 102.

15. J. A. Leo Lemay, *The Life of Benjamin Franklin, Volume 1: Journalist 1706–1730* (Philadelphia: University of Pennsylvania Press, 2006), 296. For more on how the climate might cause one to lose one's Englishness, see Parrish, *American Curiosity*, 1–17, 77–102; and Karen Kupperman, "Fear of Hot Climates in the Anglo-American Colonial Experience," *William and Mary Quarterly* 41.2 (1984), 215.

16. Lemay, *Life*, 297.

17. Thomas Tryon, *The Way to Health, Long Life and Happiness: or, A Discourse of Temperance*, 2nd ed. (London: Printed by H.C. for R. Baldwin, 1691). Further references to this edition will be cited parenthetically as *Way*.

18. Because of his aversion to violence inflicted on living things, Tryon was also anti-slavery when few people were, although, as Chaplin points out, "it took time for Tryon's larger moral program to surface in any of Franklin's thinking" (*Scientific American* 75). See also Waldstreicher, *Runaway America*, 66–7.

19. See Kim Hall for how Tryon bases his views "on a vision of national bodies with discrete boundaries that are linked to their geographic origin" (96). As Hall states, Tryon's "positing of the absolute incompatibility of foods produced in tropical regions with those produced in Northern Europe slides into an affirmation of absolute difference in color: racial difference itself and the mixture of foreign and domestic produce monstrosity that sickens the English body" (98). "The wonderful and wise Creator," Tryon writes, "hath endued every Country and Climate with such a permanent Nature, even in the beginning, as bring forth *Herbs, Fruits* and *Grains*, which are proper and most agreeable to the Natures and Constitutions of the People born in that place" (*Way* 161). See Kim Hall, "'Extravagant Viciousness': Slavery and Gluttony in the Works of Thomas Tryon" in *Writing Race Across the Atlantic World Medieval to Modern*, eds. Philip D. Beidler and Gary Taylor (New York: Palgrave Macmillan, 2005), 93–112.

20. Benjamin Franklin, "Observations Concerning the Increase of Mankind" 1751, in *Silence Dogood, The Busy-Body, and Early Writings*, ed. J. A. Leo Lemay (New York: The Library of America, 2002), 374, last emphasis added. This document itself eventually influenced Buffon to alter his assumptions about "the climate and soil of America." See Stephen Fender, "Franklin and Emigration: The Trajectory of Use," in *Reappraising Benjamin Franklin: A Bicentennial Perspective*, ed. J. A. Leo Lemay (Newark: University of Delaware Press, 1993), 340; and Chinard, "Theories," 36. On "Observations," see also Goudie, *Creole*, 36–54. Houston considers "Observations" in terms of its racialized rhetoric in *Politics of Improvement*, 131–39.

21. Franklin, "Observations," 374.

22. Ibid, 374. Here, "Blacks and Tawneys" are Africans, and "Red" means Native American. For more on the racial logics of this Franklin essay, see Waldstreicher, *Runaway America*, 136–39; Fender, "Emigration;" and Edmund Morgan, *Benjamin Franklin* (New Haven: Yale University Press, 2002), 72–80.

23. Stephen Jay Gould, "The Geometer of Race," *Discover* 15 (1994), 67. Rpt. in *The Concept of "Race" in Natural and Social Science*, ed. E. Nathaniel Gates, (New York: Garland Publishing, 1997).

24. Erkkilä has written convincingly about Franklin's "revolutionary body," emphasizing that "for all of Franklin's efforts to subject the body to regimes of discipline and control, his *Autobiography* is grounded in a reconceptualization of the self as fleshly, worldly, fluid, and ungodly" (718). See "Franklin and the Revolutionary Body," *ELH* 67.3 (2000), 717–41.

25. Lemay, *Life*, 216.

26. Erkkilä, "Revolutionary Body," 722.

27. *Transactions of the American Philosophical Society*. Vol 1 (Philadelphia: American Philosophical Society, 1771), ii; iii. Further references to this edition will be cited parenthetically as *Transactions I*.

28. Hugh Williamson, "An Attempt to account for the Change of Climate, which has been observed in the Middle Colonies in North-America," in *Transactions of the American Philosophical Society*, vol 1 (Philadelphia: American Philosophical Society, 1771), 276.

29. *Runaway America*, 6–7.

30. "A Conversation on Slavery," in *The Public Advertiser*, January 30, 1770, in *Silence Dogood, The Busy-Body, and Early Writings*, ed. J. A. Leo Lemay (New York: The Library of America, 2002), 646. David Roediger reads Franklin's description of slavery as an example of eighteenth-century rhetoric that characteristically depicts slavery without direct references to race. Roediger argues that the notion of whiteness and the privileges thereof became fused with the working class only *after* the Revolution established economic and political independence for white males but not black slaves. Because Franklin articulated this explication during what Roediger terms the "prehistory of the white worker" and included all persons toiling under brutal labor conditions, it illustrates Roediger's point that at this juncture in US history, whiteness and independence were not fully united, nor were blackness and servitude. Roediger writes that "Franklin's definition, a rare direct connection by an (albeit prosperous) white artisan of economic dependency and slavery, covered not only Black slavery but also indentured servitude and even the apprenticeship Franklin himself had served." See Roediger, *Wages of Whiteness*, 19–31.

31. Franklin, "Conversation," 645.

32. Roediger, *Wages of Whiteness*, 25. On the labor alliances between blacks and whites in seventeenth-century Virginia, see Edmund Morgan, *American Slavery, American Freedom: The Ordeal of Colonial Virginia* (New York: Norton, 1975). Rhetorically speaking, Franklin's narrative resonates with slave narratives by Britton Hammon and Frederick Douglass. Franklin escapes the brutal beatings of his master, passes for a young man avoiding the ramifications of getting "a naughty Girl with Child" (*A*, 585–86), and travels by commercial vessel to his freedom in New York and then to Philadelphia. He begins a new life after relocating to a distant location, analogous to the ways in which Hammon forges his life in both Jamaica and then England. Franklin's narrative utilizes similar tropes of enslavement, abuse, escape, and passing that call to mind not only the condition of indentured servants and apprentices but also that of black slaves. See Briton Hammon, *A Narrative of the Uncommon Sufferings, and Surprizing Deliverance Of Briton Hammon, a Negro Man,–Servant to General Winslow, of Marshfield, in New-England* (Boston: Green & Russell, 1760); and Frederick Douglass, *Narrative of the Life of Frederick Douglass*, 1845 (New York: Dover Publications, 1995). See also Rafia Zafar, "Franklinian Douglass: The Afro-American as Representative Man," in *Frederick Douglass: New Literary and Historical Essays*ed. Eric J. Sundquist (Cambridge: Cambridge University Press, 1990), 99–117.

33. Gary Nash notes that at the outbreak of the Revolution, numerous antislavery opinions were based upon the same natural rights and religious morality arguments that buttressed the colonists' struggle to separate from Great Britain, and many African Americans in the colonies appropriated these arguments in agitating for their own rights and freedoms. By conflating the two revolutionary tropes of the child separating from the parent and the slave breaking away from the master into one story, Franklin's short tale inextricably links the paradox of slavery and liberty in the colonies with the proposed separation of the colonies and the formation of a new nation. See Nash, *Race and Revolution*, 3–23.

34. Erkkilä, "Revolutionary Body," 719.

35. For a related reading on the undecidability of this scene, see Waldstreicher, *Runaway America*, 46–7. Waldstreicher footnotes that "*saucy*, of course, was a term often used for children, slaves, and servants in the eighteenth and early nineteenth century, and by employing it Franklin reveals the ambiguity of what in fact constituted tyranny or arbitrary power in such cases" (255).

36. See *The Autobiography of Benjamin Franklin: A Genetic Text*, eds. J. A. Leo Lemay and P. M. Zall (Knoxville, TN: University of Tennessee Press, 1981), 18–20.

37. Other literary scholars have read this early portion of Franklin's *Autobiography* in terms of his familial and colonial situation. Erkkilä calls attention to the historical perspective with which Franklin composes his narrative and views the story as representing "a transformation in the relations of father and son, master and apprentice, minister and parishioner, government and subject that anticipates even as it is shaped by the revolutionary impulses that would lead to the break with England in 1776" (720). Mitchell Breitwieser deemphasizes the role of Franklin's father, concentrating rather on his brother James's "excessive usurped authority" (245), likening Franklin's relationship with James to that of the colonies to the English Parliament and its improper appropriation of the power of the English king. Breitwieser believes that framed as a struggle between two brothers, Franklin's less-than-revolutionary story "allows him to represent himself as correcting an unnatural abuse of power rather than as rebelling against natural authority" (246). Looby contends that Franklin's *Autobiography* is organized around his allegorical relationship to his

father and reads it as an "Oedipal drama," wherein Franklin, like the new nation, struggles both to rebel against patriarchal power and to reinscribe that same power in order to structure a post-Revolutionary society. See Erkkilä, "Revolutionary Body," 720–1; Breitwieser, *Cotton Mather and Benjamin Franklin: The Price of Representative Personality* (Cambridge: Cambridge University Press, 1984), 245–8; and Looby, *Voicing America*, 99–144.

38. For more on the role of Franklin's cockpit hearing, see Sheila Skemp, *The Making of a Patriot: Benjamin Franklin at the Cockpit* (New York: Oxford University Press, 2013).

39. Ed White, *The Backcountry and the City: Colonization and Conflict in Early America* (Minneapolis: University of Minnesota Press, 2005), 181.

40. For more on the *Somerset* decision, see Carretta, "Introduction," *Wheatley*.

41. See *The First Scientific American*, Chapter 8, "The Science of War."

42. Whitfield J. Bell, Jr., *Patriot-Improvers: Biographical Sketches of Members of the American Philosophical Society, Volume 1: 1743–1768* (Philadelphia: American Philosophical Society, 1997), 25.

43. Qtd. in Bell, *Patriot-Improvers*, 25.

44. Ibid., 26. This solicitation of information about the New World mirrors, of course, François Barbé-Marbois's request for answers to his questions about the New World posed to Jefferson, which resulted in *Notes on the State of Virginia*.

45. This happened to be the same year that Jefferson brought his *Notes* manuscript with him to Paris for private circulation (Cohen, *Science*, 73).

46. Chinard, "Theories," 40. One of these "positive affirmations" could include Franklin's "Information to Those Who Would Remove to America," a document (written in 1782 and published the same year Franklin wrote the second section of his *Autobiography*) that strives to correct "mistaken Ideas & Expectations of what is to be obtained [in America]" (235). The essay claims that "from the Salubrity of the Air, the Healthiness of the Climate, the Plenty of good Provisions, and the Encouragement to early Marriages, by the certainty of Subsistance in cultivating the Earth, the Increase of Inhabitants by natural Generation is very rapid in America, and becomes still more so by the Accession of Strangers" (238). While not a direct reply to degenerationists' claims like Jefferson's contemporaneous *Notes*, Franklin's essay and his famous dinner at Passy indicate the subtlety of his involvement with these debates. See Franklin, "Information to Those Who Would Remove to America," 1784, *Autobiography, Poor Richard, and Later Writings*, ed. J. A. Leo Lemay (New York: The Library of America, 1997), 235–43.

47. Jean Feerick, "A 'Nation . . . Now Degenerate': Shakespeare's *Cymbeline*, Nova Britania, and the Role of Diet and Climate in Reproducing Races," *Early American Studies* 1.2 (2003), 48. As Feerick points out, Hector Boetius' "Description of Scotland" "charts a genealogical break stemming from bad diet and bad daily practice: the Scots through proximity to their English ancestors came to 'learne also their maners,' and so to lose themselves" (49–50). For Boetius, both dietary and sexual abstinence "produced bodies that are 'more hard of constitution . . . to beare off the cold blasts, to watch better, and absteine long,' and making them 'bold, nimble, and thereto more skilfull in the warres'" (49). Several of these histories also displayed a high suspicion of "leisured activities" instead of work (54).

48. Benjamin Rush, "An Account of the Vices peculiar to the Savages of N. America." *The Columbian Magazine*, September 1786, 1. Andrew Curran writes that according to *Réflexions critiques sur la poésie et sur la peinture* (1719) by Abbé Jean-Baptiste Dubos, "climatic variables were ultimately responsible—via the blood—for orienting whole nations

toward 'certain vices' or 'certain virtues'" (*Anatomy* 80). On Rush's list of vices, see also Ronald Takaki, *Iron Cages: Race and Culture in Nineteenth-Century America* (New York: Knopf, 1979), 28–35.

49. For more on Franklin's table of virtues, see Alan Houston, *Benjamin Franklin and the Politics of Improvement* (New Haven: Yale University Press, 2008), 33–40; and Anderson, 55–71.

50. As Erkkilä notes, this version of Franklin-as-model-American was a far cry from "the cosmopolitan and elite body of Franklin who drank, flirted, and flourished in France in the 1780s" ("Revolutionary Body" 728). Furthermore, she links the difference between the Franklin who credits his success to his program and the Franklin who abandons it for a "speckled Axe" to a narrative split "between the moral idealism of the [nation's] founding and an uneasiness with the lofty ideals and abstractions of the Revolution" ("Revolutionary Body" 729).

51. Franklin, "I-Doll-Ized in This Country," letter to Sarah Bache, in *Autobiography, Poor Richard, and Later Writings*, ed. J. A. Leo Lemay (New York: The Library of America, 1997), 268.

52. To confound matters even further, Joyce Chaplain claims that the hat not only signaled a "plain style" but also "resembled fur-capped French philosophes" (*Scientific American* 253–54).

53. Chaplin, *Scientific American*, 316.

54. John Morgan, "Some Account of a Motley Coloured, or Pye Negro Girl and Mulatto Boy, Exhibited before the Society in the Month of May, 1784, for Their Examination, by Dr. John Morgan, from the History Given of Them by Their Owner Monf. Le Vallois, Dentist of the King of France at Guadaloupe in the West Indies," *Transactions of the American Philosophical Society* 2 (1786), 392–95.

55. Ibid., 395.

56. APS Archives, 1791 January 31.

57. Anon, *Early Proceedings of the American Philosophical Society for the Promotion of Useful Knowledge, Compiled by One of the Secretaries, from the Manuscript Minutes of its Meetings, from 1744–1838* (Philadelphia: Press of McCalla & Staverly, 1884), 143. Further references to this edition will be cited parenthetically as *Early Proceedings*.

58. Ibid., 148.

59. W. Jordan, "Introduction," in Samuel Stanhop Smith, *An Essay on the Causes of the Variety of Complexion and Figure in the Human Species*, 1810, ed. Winthrop Jordan (Cambridge, MA: Belknap Press of Harvard University Press, 1965), xv.

60. Anon, *Early Proceedings*, 149.

61. See Sean Goudie on how Franklin "creolizes" his Britishness (*Creole America* 25–63).

62. This brief exchange appears in the third section of Franklin's narrative, which Franklin began composing in 1788 after he had helped pen the Declaration (1776), witnessed the Revolutionary War, become President of the Pennsylvania Society for the Abolition of Slavery (1787), and attended the Constitutional Convention (1787). For an extensive treatment of Franklin's changing views on slavery and black capacity for achievement, his begrudging acquiescence to an antislavery stance, his involvement in the Declaration and Constitution, and his late-in-life abolitionist activities, see Waldstreicher, *Runaway America*.

63. For a related point about how Franklin turns the humor of this joke against the governor and how "blackness" signifies in various registers, see Waldstreicher, *Runaway America*, 145–49.

64. Taken in context, this short scene wherein the rhetorical blackness of a sullied reputation interconnects with racial blackness partakes of 1780s debates over race, embodiment, and political representation because whiteness becomes the metaphor for and unstable prerequisite for citizenship. If, as Roediger argues, post-Revolutionary freedom extended to many white men connected whiteness with independence, Franklin's story exemplifies how one's ownership of himself by virtue of whiteness helps legitimate one as a republican citizen, relying on a rhetoric that equates blackness with disruptive behavior. It is of historical significance to note how Franklin was disgraced in front of the Privy Council in London in 1774, himself unwillingly "blackened" by Alexander Wedderburn who compared him to "the bloody African" (235) and later in writing by Peter Oliver who associated Franklin with the "black" Art of "forcing the Press often to speak the Thing that was not" and who said Franklin possessed a character "which a Savage would blush at" (240). See "Benjamin Vaughan's Account" and Peter Oliver's *Origins & Progress of the American Revolution*, reprinted in *Benjamin Franklin's Autobiography*, eds. J. A. Leo Lemay and P. M. Zall (New York: Norton, 1986).

65. See also Anderson, *Unfinished Life*, 158–61.

66. Surprisingly few literary scholars have commented upon Franklin's portrayals of Native Americans. In writing about Franklin's *Narrative of the Late Massacres*, Carla Mulford argues that Franklin does not, in fact, exhibit sympathy for the attacked Native Americans depicted in his brief 1764 pamphlet but, rather, links Christian with capitalist values that allow humane treatment of the Indians to be aligned with protecting the white man's commercial interests. Offering a more sympathetic reading of Franklin, Michael Warner contends that Franklin's "Remarks Concerning the Savages of North-America" actually addresses the manner of politeness rather than any innate nature of the Indians themselves. Warner views Franklin as cognizant of the "cultural relativism" between the white man and the Native American, "dissolv[ing] the distinction between savagism and civilization" (79). Mulford reads "Remarks" as Franklin's portrayal of Native Americans in terms of four-stages theory. These readings of Franklin, while not addressing the *Autobiography* specifically, gesture toward the complex ways that Franklin writes about Native Americans. See Mulford, "*Caritas* and Capital: Franklin's *Narrative of the Late Massacres*" in *Reappraising Benjamin Franklin: A Bicentennial Perspective*, ed. J. A. Leo Lemay (Newark: University of Delaware Press, 1993), 347–58; "Benjamin Franklin, Native Americans, and the Commerce of Civility," in *Revolutionary Histories: Transatlantic Cultural Nationalism, 1775–1815*, ed. W. M. Verhoeven (New York: Palgrave, 2002), 48–61; and Warner, "Savage Franklin," in *Benjamin Franklin: An American Genius*, eds. Gianfranca Balestra and Luigi Sampietro (Rome: Bulzoni, 1993), 75–87.

67. During this time, the French and British empires fought for control over the land of the Ohio Valley, which historian Richard White points out was considered the "key to the continent." Both sides felt that the domination of this territory would carry international implications for the land in Canada, Louisiana, the French Caribbean, and Spanish Mexico. See Richard White, *The Middle Ground: Indians, Empires, and Republics in the Great Lakes Region, 1650–1815* (Cambridge: Cambridge University Press, 1991), 223.

68. On how Franklin "played the role of the savage" in his diplomatic visit to France in the 1770s and 1780s, see Warner, "Savage Franklin," 83–84.

69. Erkkilä, "Revolutionary Body," 734.

70. This triangulation of American, British, and Native American over combat strategies stands in contrast to Franklin's earlier bifurcation of these strategies as Indian and

European. "Every Indian is a Hunter;" he writes "and as their Manner of making War, *viz.* by Skulking, Surprizing and Killing particular Persons and Families, is just the same as their Manner of Hunting, only changing the Object, Every Indian is a disciplin'd Soldier. Soldiers of this Kind are always wanted in the Colonies in an Indian War; for the *European* Military Discipline is of little Use in these Woods" (445). See Franklin, "To James Parker," March 20, 1950/I, *Silence Dogood, The Busy-Body, and Early Writings*, ed. J. A. Leo Lemay (New York: The Library of America, 2002), 442–46.

71. R. White, *Middle Ground*, 232–36.

72. Franklin's passage also infantilizes the Indians just as it considers them worthy of government negotiations. Assuming the role of a foreboding father figure, Franklin "strictly forbad the selling any Liquor to them" and notes how they "misbehav'd" (*A* 682). Carla Mulford observes a similar tendency in the *A Narrative of the Late Massacres*. She writes that "the conception of Anglo-American paternalism is invoked as a model for the protection the state can provide the individual. The rhetoric plays upon the conceptual commonplace . . . that figured Indians as children and the English king and his proprietary or royal representatives in America as 'great' or 'good' fathers" ("*Caritas* and Capital" 350). Mulford claims that this paternalism and tendency to equate and then denigrate Indians does not portray them as identical to the white man: "*Narrative of the Late Massacres* is, I find, premised upon a rhetoric that at once seems to locate Native Americans in a moral sphere equal to whites while ultimately placing them in a social position subordinate to white colonists" ("*Caritas* and Capital" 355). This reinscription of the Native Americans in a paternalistic system speaks to a post-Revolutionary urge to stifle any sort of rebellion against the nation lately articulated by the founding fathers. Looby sees this as a central tenet of the *Autobiography*, specifically in terms of Franklin's relationship with his father: "Franklin's initial rebellion against his father's authority, and then his eventual imitation of his father's role, figure in the *Autobiography* as a model that he proposed not only to other individuals, but also to the nation that had recently founded itself in a revolution against the authority of British institutions and now needed to establish institutions of its own" (*Voicing America* 100). On this scene with native Americans, see also Anderson, *Unfinished Life*, 169–72.

73. Chaplin claims that Franklin viewed Indian bodies "as significantly weaker than those of rum-resistant whites" (*Scientific American* 332).

74. *Middle Ground*, 235.

75. Franklin composed this portion of his text just a month after the final ratification of the Constitution, and in its historical context, the scene signals Franklin's apprehension of internal dissensions within the newly-formed nation that must be controlled. In the speech that Franklin delivered at the conclusion of the Constitutional Convention in September, 1787, he repetitively suggests that although an individual may see "errors" in the document, he should surrender that critique in order that the assembly may act "unanimously in recommending this Constitution" (401). See Franklin, "Speech in the Convention at the Conclusion of its Deliberations," September 17, 1787, in *Autobiography, Poor Richard, and Later Writings*, ed. J. A. Leo Lemay (New York: The Library of America, 1997), 399–401. Franklin even decides to "sacrifice" his own criticisms for the "public good." Because he believes that a form of government can only be as good as the people it governs, he worries over what Erkkilä calls the "excess of corruption in the people" ("Revolutionary Body" 731) and about the control of displeased citizens who might revolt against the US government. In fact, such a riot as Franklin anticipated occurred on December 26, 1787, in Carlisle, located in strong

Anti-Federalist territory. Immediately after Pennsylvania ratified the Constitution, a small group of victorious Federalists attempted to stage a demonstration there. Although the Federalists brought with them a cannon and barrels for a bonfire, the Anti-Federalists overtook the town square and burned a copy of the Constitution in the fire, shouting protests against Pennsylvania legislators who voted for its ratification. The following day, the Federalists were able to proceed with their celebration. See Robert L. Brunhouse, *The Counter-Revolution in Pennsylvania, 1776–1790* (Harrisburg: Pennsylvania Historical Commission, 1942), 210. Resonating eerily with Franklin's description of the Ohio Indian treaty negotiations, this account locates Carlisle as a place of dissension that threatens the nation's founding on the basis of unanimous consent. Written a year after this riot occurred, Franklin's scene can be read as replacement of so-called savage Indians, for the savage behavior of the Anti-Federalists during the Constitutional debates occurring nationally. Indeed, as Chaplin points out, "Franklin had forgotten what he had actually written about the incident in 1753: that the fault lay with the traders who plied Indians with liquor, threatening all the careful diplomacy" (*Scientific American* 331). Franklin's mis-remembering of the encounter and his original recording of it is a particularly striking one. Just as protestors of the 1773 Boston Tea Party seized upon the notion of Indian-ness to register their malcontent toward British imperial policy, in this scene, the savage Indians double for the behavior of the Anti-Federalists who protested the newly established federal government. This "savageness" of the Anti-Federalists, then, is exactly the type of oppositional behavior that Franklin condemns as a threat to the nation in speaking to the Constitutional Convention. For more on how Indian disguise helps produce (white) American national identity, specifically in the Boston Tea Party, see Deloria, *Playing Indian*, 10–37.

76. E. White, *Backcountry*, 208.

77. Hendrick Aupaumut, "A Short Narration of My last Journey to the Western Contry," in *Memoirs of the Historical Society of Pennsylvania* (Philadelphia: Carey, Lea & Carey, 1827), 104. Further references to this edition will be cited parenthetically as "N." R. White's monumental *Middle Ground* details the "rebel" group with which Franklin and his associates treated (130–35). See also Gustafson on the ritual and communicative techniques in "Cultural Middle Ground."

78. As I shall explore in more detail below, ethnohistorian Alan Taylor argues that Aupaumut's people should be called "Stockbridge" or "Mohican" (rather than "Mahican") Indians. On the removal of the Mohegan Indians to Brothertown and the Mohican/Stockbridge Indians to New Stockbridge, see Jarvis, *Brothertown Nation*; Silverman, *Red Brethren*, passim; Laura Murray, Introduction, in *"To Do Good to My Indian Brethren": The Writings of Joseph Johnson, 1751–1776*, ed. Laura Murray (Amherst: University of Massachusetts Press, 1998), 168–77; Wyss, *Writing Indians*, 123–153; Love, *Occom*, 207–30; Alan Taylor, "Captain Hendrick Aupaumut: The Dilemmas of an Intercultural Broker," *Ethnohistory* 43.3 (1996), 431–57; Blodgett, *Occom*, 169–99; J. Brooks, *American Lazarus*, 51–86; Wyss, *Writing Indians*, 123–53; Lopenzina, *Red Ink*, 315–22; and Mandell, *Tribe*, passim.

79. Rpt. in Blodgett, *Occom*, 196.

80. Ibid., 197.

81. R. White, *Middle Ground*, 442.

82. For accounts of Hendrick Aupaumut's personal and tribal history, see Dorothy Davids, *A Brief History of the Mohican Nation, Stockbridge-Munsee Band* (Bowler, WI: Stockbridge-Munsee Historical Committee, Arvid E. Miller Memorial Library Museum,

2001); L. Brooks, *Common Pot*, 106–62; Wyss, *Writing Indians*, 105–22; Rachel Wheeler, *To Live Upon Hope: Mohicans and Missionaries in the Eighteenth-Century Northeast*, (Ithaca: Cornell University Press, 2008), 233–44; and "Christian-Mahican Prophet;" Silverman, *Red Brethren*, 157–60; Taylor, "Intercultural Broker;" Gustafson, *Eloquence*, 257–65; Gustafson, "Historical Introduction;" Gustafson, "Cultural Middle Ground;" Dorothy Mayer, Elaine Doxtator Raddatz, and William Leach, *The Stockbridge Story* (Stockbridge, WI: Stockbridge Community Historical Society, 1978); Lopenzina, *Red Ink*, 258–84; and Jeanne Ronda and James P. Ronda, "'As They Were Faithful': Chief Hendrick Aupaumut and the Struggle for Stockbridge Survival, 1757–1830," *American Indian Culture and Research Journal* 3.3 (1979), 43–55. For more on Mohican tribal history, see Ted J. Brasser, *Riding on the Frontier's Crest: Mahican Indian Culture and Culture Change* (Ottowa: National Museums of Canada, 1974); Patrick Frazier, *The Mohicans of Stockbridge* (Lincoln: University of Nebraska Press, 1994); and Shirley Dunn, *The Mohican World, 1680–1750*, Fleischmanns (New York: Purple Mountain Press, 2000). On Stockbridge Indian service in the war, see Colin G. Calloway, *The American Revolution in Indian Country: Crisis and Diversity in Native American Communities* (Cambridge: Cambridge University Press, 1995), 85–107; and Helen Hornbeck Tanner, "The Glaize in 1792: A Composite Indian Community," *Ethnohistory* 25.1 (1978), 15–39. For more on the relationship between Occom, Aupaumut, and their respective tribes, see Love, *Occom*, 231–46; and Blodgett, *Occom*, 169–214. At this historical moment, in addition to Occom's tribe removing from Mohegan to Brothertown (1774–1776/7) and the Stockbridges relocating to New Stockbridge in Oneida territory in 1783–1785, the American Revolutionary War had been fought and won by the patriot-rebels. In the same year when the Mohicans penned their letter to Occom (1787), the Constitutional Convention was meeting in Philadelphia to write the Constitution (May–Sept. 1787) while "discussion [was breaking] out" on the origin and division of the races of mankind due to the English publication of Jefferson's *Notes* (1787) and Smith's *An Essay on the Causes of the Variety of Complexion and Figure in the Human Species* (1787). For more on the Stockbridge-Munsee Band of the Mohican Nation, see the work of Librarians Nathalee Kristiansen, Leah Miller, and Betty Groh; Elder Dorothy Davids, and Historic Preservation Officer Sherry White at www.mohican-nsn.gov.

83. For more on the separate messages the United States sent via Aupaumut and Brant, see L. Brooks, *Common Pot*, 143.

84. This happened to many Revolutionary War soldiers. See Catherine Kaplan, "Theft and Counter-Theft: Joseph Plumb Martin's Revolutionary War," *Early American Literature* 41.3 (2006): 515–34.

85. For more on Washington and early national federal Indian policy, see Francis Paul Prucha, *American Indian Policy in the Formative Years: The Indian Trade and Intercourse Acts, 1790–1834* (Lincoln: University of Nebraska Press, 1970); Merrell, "Declarations;" R. White, *Middle Ground*, 413–68; and Wiley Sword, *President Washington's Indian War: The Struggle for the Old Northwest, 1790–1795* (Norman: University of Oklahoma Press, 1985). The US government wrote and ratified its new Constitution (1787–1788), established Philadelphia as the country's first national capital (1790), and passed the Naturalization Law (1790) during this time period. See also David Andrew Nichols, who emphasizes class differences between white settlers and governmental elites and the "federationism" among Native Americans, "the belief that Indians had common racial interests that transcended intertribal rivalries and differences, and should unite to protect their land from encroaching

whites" (14) in *Red Gentlemen and White Savages: Indians, Federalists, and the Search for Order on the American Frontier* (Charlottesville: University of Virginia Press, 2008).

86. When the 1783 Peace of Paris that Franklin negotiated had officially ended the Revolutionary War and established the Mississippi River as the western boundary line between the new nation and Indian Country, the US government had begun to claim Native lands "by right of conquest," viewing the tribes as conquered peoples since they had allied themselves with the British. See Colin G. Calloway, *Crown and Calumet: British-Indian Relations, 1783–1815* (Norman: University of Oklahoma Press, 1987), 5. (The 1783 Peace of Paris boundary line replaced the Royal Proclamation of 1763 boundary line of the Appalachian Mountains and the 1768 Treaty of Fort Stanwix line of the Ohio River, to which the western tribes had agreed [Prucha, *Policy*, 13–20].) In the Peace of Paris, the British government had made no mention of the Indian tribes that had fought with them and ceded much of Indian Country to the United States; accordingly, the US government treated the Native tribes that had fought on the side of the British as "vanquished people(s)" (Calloway, *Crown*, 8). By contrast, viewing themselves as sovereign entities strategically engaged in a war not of their own making, Native American tribes hotly disputed this designation. In their view, they had simply defended their own ancestral homelands, fully expecting "that their sacrifices and achievements would earn them lasting gratitude and protection from George III" (Calloway, *Crown*, 7). No Indian tribes participated in the negotiation of the Peace of Paris; although they had fought alongside the British, many western tribes in the Ohio Valley did *not* view themselves as subjugated. For more on the history of the establishment of this boundary line and its implications for white-red relations, see Prucha, *Policy*, 26–50; Merrell, "Declarations;" Taylor, "Intercultural Broker;" Richter, *Facing East*, 223–35; Nichols, *Red Gentlemen*; R. White, *Middle Ground*, 413–68; and Calloway, *Crown*, 3–23.

87. Merrell, "Declarations," 204. Merrell demonstrates how early environmentalist beliefs about Indians' shared humanity with whites and potential convertibility undergirded the US shift to a policy of assimilation. Even if these government officials did not believe Indians would physically "become white" through the adoption of these practices, the influence of this belief on federal Indian policy signals the way that environmentalist thinking, broadly conceived, became imbricated in transnational politics during this period.

88. On the historical context of the frontier wars and the 1792 negotiations, see Tanner, "Glaize;" Taylor, "Intercultural Broker;" and R. White, *Middle Ground*, 413–468. See also Sword, *Washington*; Nichols, *Red Gentlemen*; Randolph C. Downes, *Council Fires on the Upper Ohio: A Narrative of Indian Affairs in the Upper Ohio Valley until 1795* (Pittsburgh: University of Pittsburgh Press, 1940); Alfred Cave, *Prophets of the Great Spirit*, 45–63; and Isabel Thompson Kelsay, *Joseph Brant, 1743–1807: Man of Two Worlds* (Syracuse: Syracuse University Press, 1984), 458–82.

89. The term "accommodationist"—coined by historians trying to understand this time period rather than the Native Americans themselves—should not be taken to mean that these tribes always acquiesced to white demands. For instance, the "accommodationist" Natives affiliated with the confederacy were adamantly opposed to the new government.

90. *Crown*, 45–6.

91. Taylor, "Intercultural Broker," 437.

92. On Aupaumut's trip to Philadelphia, see Gustafson, *Eloquence*, 260. On the competing visions and approaches to dealing with the United States between Aupaumut and Brant, see L. Brooks, *Common Pot*, 106–62; and Taylor, "Intercultural Broker." See also

R. White, *Middle Ground*; and Tanner, "The Glaize," on the broad implications of this historical moment.

93. For more on "the Glaize," see Tanner.

94. See Maureen Konkle, *Writing Indian Nations: Native Intellectuals and the Politics of Historiography, 1827–1863* (Chapel Hill: University of North Carolina Press, 2004), 1–41. I take up the issue of sovereignty and Hendrick Aupaumut in much more detail in "Tribal Sovereignty, Native American Literature, and the Complex Legacy of Hendrick Aupaumut," *Tennessee Studies in Literature*, forthcoming.

95. On the text's publication history, see Round, *Removable Type*, 103–9; Gustafson, *Eloquence*, 260; and Taylor, "Intercultural Broker," 431–32. Gustafson identifies Aupaumut's text as a "performance semiotic of speech and text."

96. Richter, *Facing East*, 181.

97. Cultural practices played an interesting role in the debate over how race was produced in the New World. As I discussed in the introduction, at the close of the eighteenth century, American natural historians tended to consider "society" and cultural practices as not only a delineation of difference but also as an agent in producing racial difference. Perhaps surprisingly, nativists—such as the Delaware prophet Neolin—held much in common with this line of thinking. Although stopping short of professing that adopting white ways might physically make them white, they invested social practices with a racialized tenor and, furthermore, felt "that proper [Indian] behavior could restore Indian power" (*SR* 36). Refusing whites' alcohol, European gender-mixed dancing, and European trade goods (Richter, *Facing East*, 180), some strict nativists also adhered to "a ritual diet that included the frequent consumption of an herbal emetic, after which they would be purified of the 'White people's ways and Nature'" (*SR* 33). Ritual drinking and vomiting was "a regular feature of Ohio Valley nativism in the 1760s" (*SR* 33). The importance of "modes of living" is not to be overlooked. Much of the energy animating red–white hostility arose from white governmental efforts to make Natives adopt white cultural practices (Merrell, "Declarations," 204) and from Natives' resistance to such efforts (*SR* 105–6).

98. See Dowd, *Spirited Resistance*; Richter, *Facing East*; and Prucha, *Policy*, 35–40.

99. Tanner, "Glaize," 31.

100. Shoemaker, *Strange Likeness*, 12.

101. Ibid., 130. Furthermore, according to Shoemaker, tribes could be known to alter the origin stories that they presented to white settlers.

102. Rachel Wheeler, "Christian-Mahican Prophet," 240.

103. Hendrick Aupaumut, Letter to James Monroe (1819). Stockbridge Indian Papers. Cornell University Library Archives, Rare and Manuscript Collections, Carl A. Kroch Library. #9185, Folder 5, Box 1.

104. For more similarities and contrasts between Aupaumut and nativist leaders and how Auapaumut's "Christian republicanism . . . stands in marked contrast to the increasingly racialized and nativisitc philosophies embraced by many of his contemporaries, both Euro-American and Indian" (226), see Rachel Wheeler, "Christian-Mahican Prophet." David Silverman, *Red Brethren*, emphasizes the connections between race and religion in Aupaumut's thinking.

105. Wyss, *Writing Indians*, 111–12.

106. Taylor, "Intercultural Broker," 432. Taylor is adamant that these "Mohicans" not be confused with seventeenth-century Mohegans (Samson Occom's tribe) or Cooper's fictive

Mohicans in his nineteenth-century romance, *The Last of the Mohicans*. See also Lopenzina, *Red Ink*, 253–313.

107. For more on Aupaumut's use of the "rhetoric of kinship," see Rifkin, *Straight*, 127–37.

108. For more on Aupaumut's use of the Condolence Ritual, see Gustafson, "Cultural Middle Ground," 246; Wyss, *Writing Indians*, 109–12; and L. Brooks, *Common Pot*, 158.

109. L. Brooks, *Common Pot*, 106–62.

110. In "A Narrative of the Late Massacres, in Lancaster County," Franklin displays a similar understanding of the fractured nature of racial groupings. "If an *Indian* injures me," he writes, "does it follow that I may revenge that Injury on all *Indians*? It is well known that *Indians* are of different Tribes, Nations and Languages, as well as the White People. In *Europe*, if the *French*, who are White People, should injure the *Dutch*, are they to revenge it on the *English*, because they too are White People? The only Crime of these poor Wretches seems to have been, that they had a reddish brown Skin, and black Hair; and some People of that Sort, it seems, had murdered some of our Relations" (540 in *Silence Dogood, The Busy-Body, and Early Writings*, ed. J. A. Leo Lemay [New York: The Library of America, 2002]).

111. R. White, *Middle Ground*, 456–59.

112. Taylor, "Intercultural Broker," 128.

113. Wyss, *Writing Indians*, 122.

114. On Aupaumut's challenging the basis of the confederacy because of his very diplomacy, see Wyss, *Writing Indians*, 113–14.

115. Merrell, "Declarations," 204. As Merrell writes, "from the Revolution to the Jacksonian era, thoughtful Americans agreed that societies progressed along the same path (a path which reached its 'present state of perfection' with Euro-American culture), that differences among peoples could be attributed to environmental influences, and that therefore native Americans could be guided along the path toward 'civilization'" (206).

116. Wyss, *Writing Indians*, 105–6.

117. Aupaumut's "History" exists only as "copied" in three nineteenth-century texts. The most complete version appears as Hendrick Aupaumut, "History," in *Stockbridge, Past and Present; or, Records of an Old Mission Station* by Electa Jones (Springfield, MA: Samuel Bowles, 1854), 15–23. Further references to this edition will be cited parenthetically as "H." For more on the text's print history, see Wyss, *Writing Indians*, 184.

118. Wyss, *Writing Indians*, 117.

119. Taylor, "Intercultural Broker, 441.

120. Gustafson, *Eloquence*, 258. Rachel Wheeler emphasizes how Aupaumut used both Christianity and the Mohican's role as cultural intermediaries to ensure community survival (*Live Upon Hope* 225–44).

121. Ronda and Ronda, "Faithful," 44.

122. Merrell, "Declarations," 204.

123. Rachel Wheeler notes that part of the reason Aupaumut advocated European-style agriculture was because he believed that if Natives worked the land themselves—instead of leasing it to whites—they would be more likely to retain ownership. See Wheeler, "Christian-Mahican Prophet," 236.

124. Importantly, this contrasts with the "report" sent to Timothy Dwight from Mr. Hart on how Elijah Wampey, Jr., Andrew Carrycomb, Ephraim Pharaoh, and Samuel Adams, all members of Native groups that had removed to Brothertown, NY, had indeed started to "becoming white." See Dwight, *Travels*, 124–29.

125. Jeremy Belknap and Jedidiah Morse, *Report on The Oneida Stockbridge and Broth-erton Indians*, 1796, reprinted in *Indian Notes and Monographs* Number 54 (New York: Museum of the American Indian Heye Foundation, 1955), 22. On Belknap, Morse, and Aupaumut, see also James W. Oberly, *A Nation of Statesmen: The Political Culture of the Stockbridge-Munsee Mohicans, 1815–1972* (Norman: University of Oklahoma Press, 2005), 21–29.

126. On Franklin and appearance, see Christopher J. Lukasik, *Discerning Characters: The Culture of Appearance in Early America* (Philadelphia: University of Pennsylvania Press, 2010), 1–10.

Chapter 3

1. J. Hector St. John de Crèvecoeur, *Letters from an American Farmer and Sketches of Eighteenth-Century America*, ed. Albert E. Stone (New York: Penguin, 1986), 213. Further references to this edition will be cited parenthetically as *L*.

2. For more on this shift from the exteriority to the interiority of the body in human classification, see Foucault, *The Order of Things*. For an extension of Foucault's thought in the context of US racialization, see Wiegman, *American Anatomies*, esp. 21–42.

3. Amy Robinson, "It Takes One to Know One: Passing and Communities of Common Interest," *Critical Inquiry* 20.4 (1994), 719. Critical scholarship on the logics of passing abounds. As Elaine Ginsberg writes, "as the term [passing] metaphorically implies, such an individual crossed or passed through a racial line or boundary—indeed *trespassed*—to assume a new identity, escaping the subordination and oppression accompanying one identity and accessing the privileges and status of the other" (3). See Elaine K. Ginsberg, "The Politics of Passing," in *Passing and the Fictions of Identity*, ed. Elaine K. Ginsberg (Durham: Duke University Press, 1996), 1–18. See also Kathleen Pfeiffer, *Race Passing and American Individualism* (Amherst: University of Massachusetts Press, 2003); Gayle Wald, *Crossing the Line: Racial Passing in Twentieth-Century U.S. Literature and Culture* (Durham: Duke University Press, 2000); and Teresa Zackodnik, *The Mulatta and the Poli-tics of Race* (Jackson: University Press of Mississippi, 2004). For an insightful analysis of disguise and passing that works within a nineteenth-century concept of racial identity, see Julia Stern, "Spanish Masquerade and the Drama of Racial Identity in *Uncle Tom's Cabin*," in *Passing and the Fictions of Identity*, ed. Elaine K. Ginsberg (Durham: Duke University Press, 1996), 103–30. On the rhetorical structure of passing, see Marcia Alesan Dawkins, *Clearly Invisible: Racial Passing and the Color of Cultural Identity* (Waco, TX: Baylor University Press, 2012). On "white-to-black passing," see Baz Dreisinger, *Near Black: White-to-Black Passing in American Culture* (Amherst: University of Massachusetts Press, 2008). For an analysis of "racechanges," in terms of blackface minstrels and racial imita-tion, see Susan Gubar, *Racechanges: White Skin, Black Face in American Culture* (New York: Oxford University Press, 2000).

4. Robinson, "Know," 716.

5. Certainly I do not mean to claim that racial truth resides in the body, an idea that much racial identity and performance theory have shown to be false. Rather, I am drawing a contrast between quotidian understandings of race in the eighteenth century from those in later centuries. Indeed, it is this everyday understanding of one's "racial interior" that passing both buttresses and questions. (As Ginsberg writes, "For the possibility of passing

challenges a number of problematic and even antithetical assumptions about identities, the first of which is that some identity categories are inherent and unalterable essences: presumably one cannot pass for something one *is not* unless there is some other, prepassing, identity that one *is*" ["Politics" 4].) Furthermore, my aim here is not to argue for a re-essentialism of racial identity by emphasizing the body. Rather, I want to understand better these historical discourses of race. This eighteenth-century notion of transformable race—while in conversation with and understood in relationship to natural history—is also *constituted* in particular ways across these literatures. This framework wherein one does not have an interior that can be raced is more about circumstance and habit, which is its own type of performative model.

6. In her extension of Judith Butler's theoretical work, Elin Diamond highlights Butler's emphasis on the repetition of recognizable acts that constitute identity. As Diamond puts it, "when being is de-essentialized, when gender and even race are understood as fictional ontologies, modes of expression without true substance, the idea of performance comes to the fore" (5). Exploring how Butler further develops her early notion of performativity along the lines of Derrida's citationality, Diamond notes how Butler "deconstructively elaborates a temporality of reiteration as that which instantiates gender, sex, and even the body's material presence" (5). See Judith Butler, *Bodies that Matter: On the Discursive Limits of "Sex"* (New York: Routledge Press, 1993); and Elin Diamond, Introduction, *Performance and Cultural Politics*, ed. Elin Diamond (New York: Routledge Press, 1996), 1–12.

7. Eve Sedgwick and Paul Gilroy both posit subtle and distinctive models of performative identity. In Axiom 4 in her introduction to *Epistemology of the Closet*, Sedgwick offers up "minoritizing/universalizing" understandings of homosexuality as "an *alternative* (though not an equivalent) to essentialist/constructivist" understandings because of the "essentially gay-genocidal nexuses of thought through which [the latter terms] have developed" (40–41). As she explains, if homosexuality is considered "constructed," it can be assumed to be easily "changed." If it is considered "essential," it can be assumed to be treatable. In his discussion of "blackness" in *The Black Atlantic*, Paul Gilroy offers "anti-anti-essentialism," an understanding that "sees racialised subjectivity as the product of the social practices that supposedly derive from it" as part of a "model whereby identity can be understood neither as a fixed essence nor as a vague and utterly contingent construction to be reinvented by the will and whim of aesthetes, symbolists, and language gamers" (102). Gilroy's position further develops, of course, in *Against Race*. See Eve Sedgwick, *Epistemology of the Closet* (Berkeley: University of California Press, 2008); Paul Gilroy, *The Black Atlantic: Modernity and Double-Consciousness* (Cambridge, MA: Harvard University Press, 1993); and *Against Race: Imagining Political Culture Beyond the Color Line* (Cambridge, MA: The Belknap Press of Harvard University Press, 2000).

8. Butler, *Bodies*, 14. Butler has warned us that "Performativity is thus not a singular 'act,' for it is always a reiteration of a norm or set of norms, and to the extent that it acquires an act-like status in the present, it conceals or dissimulates the conventions of which it is a repetition" (*Bodies* 12), what Diamond calls "a doing and a thing done" ("Introduction" 1). This chapter seeks, as Butler's work does, to "constitute partial and overlapping genealogical efforts to establish the normative conditions under which the materiality of the body is framed and formed" (*Bodies* 17).

9. What today we might think of as "ethnicity" (and its relationship to living in a certain place, speaking in a particular manner, or practicing the culture of a specific group) was not

differentiated from the idea of race in the eighteenth century. In terms of Cherokee episte-mology, see Circe Sturm, *Blood Politics: Race, Culture, and Identity in the Cherokee Nation of Oklahoma* (Berkeley: University of California Press, 2002), 50–51. On Cherokee literary culture, see Daniel Heath Justice (Cherokee), *Our Fire Survives the Storm: A Cherokee Literary History* (Minneapolis: University of Minnesota Press, 2006); Jace Weaver, *That the People*; Weaver, *Other Words: American Indian Literature, Law, and Culture* (Norman: University of Oklahoma Press, 2001); and Christopher B. Teuton (Cherokee), *Cherokee Stories of the Turtle Island Liars' Club* (Chapel Hill: University of North Carolina Press, 2012). On the protocols of engaging with native literatures from a nationalist perspective, see *American Indian Literary Nationalism*, eds. Jace Weaver, Craig S. Womack, and Robert Warrior. On earlier forms of race as they intersected with European ideas of "Indians," see Jonathan Gil Harris, "Forms of Indography," in *Indography: Writing the Indian in Early Modern England* (New York: Palgrave Macmillan, 2012), 1–21.

10. Philip Deloria has convincingly shown how white Anglos from the Revolution to the Cold War have engaged in "playing Indian" in order to form white American national identities, and Shari Huhndorf demonstrates how whites' "going native" helps "maintain European-American racial and national identities." See Deloria, *Playing Indian*; and Shari Huhndorf, *Going Native*, 8. As Deloria writes, "disguise readily calls the notion of fixed identity into question. At the same time, however, wearing a mask also makes one self-conscious of a *real* 'me' underneath. This simultaneous experience is both precarious and creative, and it can play a critical role in the way people construct new identities" (*Playing Indian* 7). See also Carroll Smith-Rosenberg's extension of Deloria's formation in *This Violent Empire: The Birth of an American National Identity* (Chapel Hill: University of North Carolina Press for the Omohundro Institute of Early American History and Culture, 2010), 191–206.

11. The way *Letters* partakes of several generic forms supports this reading. It falls within the eighteenth-century tradition of epistolary writing. See Elizabeth Heckendorn Cook, *Epistolary Bodies: Gender and Genre in the Eighteenth-Century Republic of Letters* (Stanford: Stanford University Press, 1996), 140–72; and Eve Bannet, *Empire of Letters: Letter Manuals and Transatlantic Correspondence, 1680–1820* (Cambridge: Cambridge University Press, 2009), 275–87. While also a natural history, it differs from Jefferson's *Notes on the State of Virginia* in that it uses a fictional persona. Crèvecoeur's use of James places the text in the eighteenth-century convention of presenting information through a character ostensibly in order to engage disinterestedly in rational-critic debate (Warner, *Letters of the Republic*, 34–72). For how Crèvecoeur stages "democratic personality" through James's persona, see Nancy Ruttenburg, *Democratic Personality: Popular Voice and the Trial of American Authorship* (Stanford: Stanford University Press, 1998), 274–89. See also Grantland S. Rice, *The Transformation of Authorship in America*, (Chicago: Unversity of Chicago Press, 1997), 99–124. Ed White's detailed attention to Dennis Moore's collection of Crèvecoeur's unpublished essays provocatively "trouble[s] our sense of Crèvecoeur's writing, signaling different levels of irony, different narrative personas, and different degrees of historical reference" (385). See Ed White, "Crèvecoeur in Wyoming," *Early American Literature* 43.2 (2008), 379–407; Crèvecoeur, *More Letters from the American Farmer: An Edition of the Essays in English Left Unpublished by Crèvecoeur*, ed. Dennis D. Moore (Athens: University of Georgia Press, 1995).

12. On a related point, see Finseth, *Shades*, 86–87.

13. Many scholars retroactively project a sense of nationalism onto Crèvecoeur's "American," thus closing down its meaning around the nation-state. On this point, see Ali Behdad, *A Forgetful Nation: On Immigration and Cultural Identity in the United States* (Durham: Duke University Press, 2005), 34–35; and Bryce Traister, "Criminal Correspondence: Loyalism, Espionage and Crèvecoeur," *Early American Literature* 37.3 (2002), 469–96. Ed White writes against this tendency in *The Backcountry and the City*, 35–39, and Edward Larkin argues for seeing Crèvecoeur as a loyalist in his "The Cosmopolitan Revolution: Loyalism and the Fiction of an American Nation," *Novel: A Forum on Fiction* 40.1–2 (2006), 52–76.

14. Larkin, "Cosmopolitan," 68.

15. See Harold Kulungian, "The Aestheticism of Crèvecoeur's American Farmer," *Early American Literature* 12.2 (1977), 197–201; and Ned Landsman, "Pluralism, Protestantism, and Prosperity: Crèvecoeur's American Farmer and the Foundations of American Pluralism," in *Beyond Pluralism: The Conception of Groups and Group Identities in America*, eds. Wendy F. Katkin, Ned Landsman, and Andrea Tyree (Urbana: University of Illinois Press, 1998), 105–24. On immigration and the idea of the melting pot, see Dorren Alvarez Saar, "The Heritage of American Ethnicity in Crèvecoeur's *Letters from an American Farmer*," in *A Mixed Race: Ethnicity in Early America*, ed. Frank Shuffelton (New York: Oxford University Press, 1993), 241–56.

16. For how the term "race" was used increasingly over the course of the eighteenth century in ethnographic scholarship to denote groups with common physical and mental characteristics, see Hudson, "From 'Nation.'" On how *race* replaced *variety* in the eighteenth-century lexicon, see Roxann Wheeler, *CR*, 31.

17. See also Larkin, "Cosmopolitan," 68, on a related point.

18. While others have considered the relationship between *Letters* and general tenets of eighteenth-century Enlightenment thought articulated by Raynal, my argument is most concerned with his specifically racial theories. For how "Crèvecoeur's book lays out an abbreviated fictional history of America loosely based on Raynal's nascent theory of civilizational decline," see Grantland Rice, "Crèvecoeur and the Politics of Authorship in Republican America," *Early American Literature* 28.2 (1993), 92. For views on Raynal's general influence on Crèvecoeur's thought, see Finseth, *Shades of Green*, 79–80; Christopher Iannini, *Fatal Revolutions: Natural History, West Indian Slavery, and the Routes of American Literature* (Chapel Hill: University of North Carolina Press for the Omohundro Institute of Early American History and Culture, 2012), 131–176; Ralph Bauer, *The Cultural Geography of Colonial American Literature: Empire, Travel, Modernity* (Cambridge: Cambridge University Press, 2003), 200–40; Christine Holbo, "Imagination, Commerce, and the Politics of Associationism in Crèvecoeur's *Letters from an American Farmer*," *Early American Literature* 32.1 (1997), 20–65; and Yael Ben-Zvi, "Mazes of Empire: Space and Humanity in Crèvecoeur's *Letters*," *Early American Literature* 42.1 (2007), 73–105. On how Crèvecoeur uses *Letters* as a "testing ground" for aspects of eighteenth-century Enlightenment thought, see Elayne Antler Rapping, "Theory and Experience in Crèvecoeur's America," *American Quarterly* 19.4 (1967), 707–18; Mary E. Rucker, "Crèvecoeur's *Letters* and Enlightenment Doctrine," *Early American Literature* 13.2 (1978), 193–212; and Stephen Carl Arch, "The 'Progressive Steps' of the Narrator in Crèvecoeur's *Letters from an American Farmer*," *Studies in American Fiction* 18.2 (1990), 145–58.

19. Indeed, Samuel Ayscough was so worried that Crèvecoeur's depiction of America might cause many Britons to emigrate there that he dedicates his entire "Remarks on the _Letters from an American Farmer_" to disputing Crèvecoeur's "contradictions." See Samuel Ayscough, _Remarks on the Letters from an American Farmer; or, a Detection of the Errors of Mr. J. Hector St. John; Pointing out the Pernicious Tendency of These Letters to Great Britain_ (London: J. Fielding, 1783).

20. For more on _Letters'_ early readers, see Russel Nye, "Michel-Guillaume St. Jean De Crèvecoeur: _Letters From an American Farmer_," in _Landmarks of American Writing_, ed. Hennig Cohen (New York: Basic Books, Inc., 1969), 34; and Stone, "Introduction," 8. On European assumptions about New World degeneration, see Parrish, _American Curiosity_, 77–109; J. A. Leo Lemay, "The Frontiersman from Lout to Hero: Notes on the Significance of the Comparative Method and the Stage Theory in Early American Literature and Culture," _Proceedings of the American Antiquarian Society_ 88 (1978), 191–92; and Ralph N. Miller, "American Nationalism as a Theory of Nature," _The William and Mary Quarterly_ 12.1 (1955), 74–78.

21. Bauer emphasizes how _Letters_ critiques natural history's imperialist geographic division of labor and then shows James's moving from "eyewitness observer" to "historian-philosopher" (_Geography_ 216). I stress _Letters'_ overall investment in the discipline of natural history. Its environmentalist perspective informs the text and serves as the basis for a variety of James's claims. (On Crèvecoeur's use of climate theory, see Pamela Regis, _Describing Early America: Bartram, Jefferson, Crèvecoeur, and the Influence of Natural History_ [DeKalb: Northern Illinois University Press, 1992], 127–31; and Parrish, _American Curiosity_, 20, 95, and 292–93.) Also Crèvecoeur was involved in the science of his day and endeavored to become a credible player in transatlantic natural-historical circles. While in Paris in 1782–1783, he "dined twice a week with Buffon, frequented the salon of Mme d'Houdetôt, and attended meetings of the Royal Agricultural Society and the Academy of Sciences" (Cook, _Epistolary Bodies_, 147). Accepting membership to the American Philosophical Society in 1789, Crèvecoeur sent a book, the pages of which he describes as "made of the roots and barks of different plants and trees." (APS Archives. April 1, 1789. St. John de Crèvecoeur to James Hutchinson and others. "Archives" Box 1788–1790.) Crèvecoeur seriously engaged with circulating natural-historical ideas, claiming, for instance—contra Raynal—that "Let us say what we will of [American Indians], of their inferior organs, of their want to bread, etc., they are as stout and well made as the Europeans" (_L_ 215). But even as he disputes Raynal's claim about the robustness of the Indians, his logic agrees with Raynal's that the environment can ultimately make the man. Bauer points out that the dedication's tone mixes both reverence and mockery (_Geography_ 211), as a reader finds Crèvecoeur's overly effusive praise suspect and that Crèvecoeur works to "deconstruct the fiction of authenticity and break through the various levels of scientific authorship to the effect of exposing the imperialist geo-politics of Natural History and its institutionalized geographic division of intellectual labor" (_Geography_ 202). I tend to agree with Christopher Iannini, who characterizes Crèvecoeur as actively working with Raynal's ideas. Iannini describes how Crèvecoeur's "Sketches of Jamaica" engage with Raynal's theories about the Caribbean (_Fatal Revolutions_ 131–76). Jennifer Greeson also argues that Crèvecoeur "invokes and works within conventions of European imperialism," including "scientific theories of climate determinism," particularly those of Raynal; see "Colonial Planter to American Farmer: South, Nation, and Decolonization in Crèvecoeur," in _Messy Beginnings: Postcoloniality_

and Early American Studies, eds. Malini Johar Schueller and Edward Watts [New Brunswick: Rutgers University Press, 2003], 112–13). Yael Ben-Zvi shows how Raynal impacted Crèvecoeur's thoughts on empire ("Mazes" 74–75).

22. For an alternative reading that highlights how James "debunks . . . determinist theories" and "emphasizes the importance of innate differences such as race and culture," see Bauer, *Geography*, 216, 231. I stress a more conflicted and ambiguous sense in *Letters*, which sometimes does characterize race as "indelible," as it also explores a more flexible, environmentally-influenced, transformable sense of race. Leo Lemay also sees a more contradictory Crèvecoeur on these matters, arguing that *Letters* participates in "the change in philosophy of civilization from a belief in degeneration to a belief in progress," partaking at times of both paradigms (194). Lemay claims that Crèvecoeur "attempts to justify both the popular French belief in the *degeneration* of man in America with the nationalistic American belief in man's *regeneration* in America" (209). See Lemay, "Frontiersman." While I am most interested in James' racial articulations in *Letters*, many critics have concerned themselves with the ways that *Letters'* tone shifts dramatically from the beginning to the end of the text. For redactions of this critical debate, see Robert P. Winston, "'Strange Order of Things!': The Journey to Chaos in *Letters from an American Farmer,*" *Early American Literature* 19.3 (1984), 249–67; David M. Robinson, "Community and Utopia in Crèvecoeur's *Sketches,*" *American Literature* 62.1 (1990), 17–31; Holbo, "Imagination;" Iannini, *Fatal Revolutions*, 131–76; and Goddu, *Gothic America*, 26–32. See also Ed White on how Crèvecoeur advances but then examines the limits of what White calls "yeoman seriality" (*Backcountry* 51).

23. For more on the general rhetoric of natural history in *Letters*, see Regis, *Describing*, 106–34.

24. Most literary critics who note *Letters'* belief in the efficacy of the environment to make the man have overlooked its specifically racial components. Seeing Crèvecoeur's thinking as physiocratic, Vernon Parrington reads Crèvecoeur's agrarian language as an economic metaphor (*Main Currents in American Thought: An Interpretation of American Literature from the Beginnings to 1920*, Vol. 1 [New York: Harcourt, Brace and Co., 1930], 142). Jack Babuscio and Albert Stone also cite Crèvecoeur's physiocratic philosophy. See "Crèvecoeur in Charles Town: The Negro in the Cage," *Journal of Historical Studies* 2 (1969), 284; Stone, "Introduction," 18. Mary Rucker expresses a contrary, more pessimistic view in "Crèvecoeur's *Letters* and Enlightenment Doctrine." Leo Marx emphasizes that in Crèvecoeur's America "the relation between mankind and the physical environment is more than usually decisive," in regards to "the new kind of man being formed in the New World" (*The Machine in the Garden: Technology and the Pastoral Ideal in America* [New York: Oxford University Press, 1964], 109–10). D.H. Lawrence famously lambastes Crèvecoeur for his romantic portrayal of nature, what he calls this "Nature-sweet-and-pure business" in *Studies in Classic American Literature* (New York: Penguin Books, 1977), 31. James L. Machor reads Crèvecoeur's environmental determinism in a Lockean sense in "The Garden City in America: Crèvecoeur's *Letters* and the Urban-Pastoral Context," *American Studies* 23.2 (1982), 69–83. See also Lemay, "Frontiersman," on this Lockean view (210). Larzer Ziff notes Crèvecoeur's belief in "the shaping influence of environment" in *Writing in the New Nation: Prose, Print, and Politics in the Early United States* (New Haven: Yale University Press, 1991), 31. See also Kulungian, "Aestheticism" on this point. Elayne Rapping remarks on the general sense in which *Letters* "test(s)" general eighteenth-century thought, including the idea that man "was also a product of his environment" ("Theory" 707).

Edward Cahill analyzes the role of Crèvecoeur's landscape writing in *Letters* in *Liberty*, 130–32.

25. Comte George-Louis Leclerc de Buffon, *A Natural History, General and Particular*, reprt. in *Race and the Enlightenment: A Reader*, ed. Emmanuel Chukwudi Eze, (Malden, MA: Blackwell Publishing, 1997), 27.

26. On the racial aspects of Linnaeus' classification system, see Regis, *Describing*, 22; W. Jordan, *WOB*, 213–22; Dain, *Hideous Monster*, 9–14; Roann Wheeler, *CR*, 25–30; and Smedley and Smedley, *Race*, 218–19.

27. See Regis, *Describing America*, 127–30. Regis also notes how natural-historical thinking underlies James' description of the new American (128–30). For more on natural-historical theories of racialization, see Roxann Wheeler, *CR*, 1–48; Dain, *Hideous Monster*, 1–39; Smedley and Smedley, *Race*, 159–212; Parrish, *American Curiosity*, 77–102; and W. Jordan, *WOB*, 216–565.

28. *Blood* has been used as a metaphor to denote familial, class, or racial distinction since at least the fourteenth century, but in the eighteenth century it was also considered to be part of the human body that was affected by the environment. *Blood* had a still-lingering humoral connotation before the nineteenth century, when scientists and, following them, lawmakers would imagine it to be the physical location of racial "truth." The *OED* (1989) tells us that "blood is popularly treated as the typical part of the body which children inherit from their parents and ancestors; hence that of parents and children, and of the members of a family or race, is spoken of as identical, and as being distinct from that of other families or races." In the eighteenth century, *blood* was used, as Crèvecoeur does here, to denote what one inherits from one's parents and what can be crossed with that of different peoples through interracial sex. As W. Jordan explains, in the first half of the eighteenth century, "the use of 'blood' in connection with miscegenation represented, especially before the advent of knowledge about genetics, much more than a convenient metaphor. For blood was the essence of man, the principle of life. More important, at least from the time of the Greeks it had been intimately and explicitly linked with the concept of human genera-tion . . . Thus the term *blood* implied for the colonists a deep inherency and permanence through the generations, and when they called sexual union between Negroes and whites a mixture of bloods they were expressing a strong sense of radical distinction between the two kinds of peoples" (*WOB* 165-6). Yet, blackness was often explained by "the action of the sun, whether the sun was assumed to have scorched the skin, drawn the bile, or black-ened the blood" (*WOB* 13). As W. Jordan points out, the use of *blood* cut both ways: to denote how God made all men of one blood and to signify the difference among peoples. As W. Jordan says: "It was the old shell game: now you see the identity of all men, now you don't" (*WOB* 197). It is crucial to note, however, that even as blood was simultaneously considered to signal differences among people and to be a racial marker influenced by the environment, it was not until the rise of race science in the nineteenth century that blood was thought to be the ultimate seat of racial "truth." This language of blood was written into law as a way to determine one's racial identity, in the notions of the "one drop rule" of the Jim Crow era and "blood quantum" of the Dawes Act. See also Jack Forbes, *Africans and Native Americans: The Language of Race and the Evolution of Red-Black Peoples* (Urbana: University of Illinois Press, 1993).

29. Immanuel Kant, *On the Different Races of Man*, reprt. in *Race and the Enlighten-ment: A Reader*, ed. Emmanuel Chukwudi Eze, (Malden, MA: Blackwell Publishing, 1997), 43, 48.

30. Ironically, in his reading of Crèvecoeur, W. Jordan stresses Crèvecoeur's mixture of blood, overlooking his environmentalist language. W. Jordan points out that Crèvecoeur's emphasis on the crossing of bloodlines in creating a new American was a minority view. See W. Jordan, *WOB*, 336–37. In contrast, for readings of this passage that note Crève- coeur's environmentalist language, see Russel Nye, "Michel-Guillaume St. Jean De Crève- coeur: *Letters from an American Farmer*," 32–45; and Saar, "Heritage."

31. For how James "explores the central metaphor of American pastoral experience, the metaphor of the land as woman," see Annette Kolodny, *The Lay of the Land: Metaphor as Experience and History in American Life and Letters* (Chapel Hill: University of North Car- olina Press, 1975), 52–66. See also Nelson, *National Manhood*, 48–51 on this passage.

32. Although it is secondary to my point about James' characterization of the "Ameri- can," several scholars have interestingly analyzed Crèvecoeur's vacillating political affilia- tions. See Ed Larkin, "Cosmopolitan;" Paul Downes, *Democracy, Revolution, and Monar- chism in Early American Literature* (Cambridge: Cambridge University Press, 2002); Myra Jehlen, *Readings at the Edge of Literature* (Chicago: University of Chicago Press, 2009), 32–49; Rucker, "Crèvecoeur's *Letters* and Enlightenment Doctrine;" Thomas Philbrick, "Crèvecoeur as New Yorker," *Early American Literature* 11.1 (1976), 22–30; and Traister, "Criminal."

33. Larkin, "Cosmopolitan," 68.

34. Benedict Anderson, *Imagined Communities: Reflections on the Origin and Spread of Nationalism*, 1983, revised ed. (London: Verso, 1991), 58, 60.

35. Ibid.

36. For an important reworking of Anderson's claims based upon a careful historical contextualization of them, see Ed White, "Early American Nations as Imagined Communi- ties," *American Quarterly* 56.1 (2004): 49–81. For White, creoles developed a sense of "nation" less from "being crowded out of the empire" ("Early" 67) and more from seeing themselves as distinct from Native American nations. Although White disagrees with as- pects of Anderson's argument, we both emphasize the development of a national identity rather than the anachronistic presumption of an already-forming one, as White points out, "it is fair to say that with Crèvecoeur we are witnessing a transition to the 'nation' of the United States" ("Early" 72).

37. I tend to agree with Larkin on this point. Despite the way many critics see *Letters* as an American nationalist text, James' connectedness to "our famed mother country" (*LAF* 39) is evident. At several points in *Letters*, James emphasizes his British loyalties while extolling the American continent. In the concluding chapter, James dreads a separation from Great Britain. As the revolution breaks out to establish a mutually-exclusive national identity for the new Americans from the British, James refuses to take sides, planning to withdrawal with his family to the wilderness. Indeed, rather than posit a national subject, the text is quite fraught over a proposed break with England. Published in 1782 before the formal conclusion of the Revolutionary War but set in a somewhat tranquil time period that leads up to the outbreak of the war, *Letters* historically telescopes a recently declared nation-state (post–Declaration of Independence in 1776) back into its British colonial past. The text itself appears melancholic over its loss of ties to its mother country and seems profoundly divided over the issue of political independence. James finds himself "happy in my new situation," that of "an American farmer possessing freedom of action, freedom of thoughts, ruled by a mode of government which requires but little, . . ." which isn't con- tradictory with paying his king "a small tribute" and "loyalty and due respect" (*L* 52).

He attributes many successes in America to the work of Englishmen (*L* 66) and links "our government" with the "crown" (*L* 69). For James, one who relocates from Britain "is now an American, a Pennsylvanian, an English subject" (*L* 83). For how "Europe is something to retain" for James and how cultural identity is linked to the soil, see Behdad, *Forgetful*, 34–41. See also Traister, "Criminal;" Dennis Moore, "Like the Various Pieces of a Mosaick Work Properly Reunited," in *More Letters from the American Farmer: An Edition of the Essays in English Left Unpublished by Crèvecoeur*, ed. Dennis D. Moore (Athens: University of Georgia Press, 1995), xi–lxxvi; and Jehlen, *Edge*, 32–49.

38. Ed White argues for the role of seriality in this scene, *Backcountry*, 38–39.

39. On how Crèvecoeur contradictorily depicts the frontiersman using ideas of both degeneration and progression, see Lemay, "Frontiersman." On the frontiersman's degeneracy, see also Goddu, *Gothic Nation*, 16–17.

40. Crèvecoeur himself claimed to have been an adopted member of the Oneida nation, something fascinating to consider given his changing national affiliations over the course of his life. See Gay Wilson Allen and Roger Asselineau, *St. John de Crèvecoeur* (New York: Viking, 1987), 27–28. Also, in *Journey into Northern Pennsylvania and the State of New York*, Crèvecoeur reproduces an "Indian legend" that he attributes (his biographers Allen and Asseineau claim fictiously) to a Cherokee chief (Allen 215). Also interesting is that although unnamed in *Letters*, the Pennsylvania tribe James speaks of is most likely the Lenni-Lenape, the same tribe Edgar Huntly encounters.

41. Regis also sees a racialized aspect to the change James describes here: "This surrender of identity, of name, of outer shape, and even of the marks of species—a transmutation is the conversion of one species into another—suggests how essential this change would be" (*Describing* 125). She also argues that in the last letter "the natural history that has governed and generated the book threatens James with the loss of his identity, while holding the promise of an orderly outcome to his chaotic situation" (*Describing* 127). See Regis, *Describing*, 123–31. See also Ed White on James's removal, *Backcountry*, 53–55.

42. Indeed, in *Letters*, Indians seem less likely to become European than vice versa. In Nantucket, Indians who come into contact with Europeans "only" suffer disease and possible extinction (*L* 121–23). At Martha's Vineyard, Indians "appeared, by the decency of their manners, their industry, and neatness, to be wholly Europeans" (*L* 133) while still remaining Natives.

43. See note 28 in this chapter regarding the use of *blood*.

44. For an alternate reading that claims the "innate differences of race and culture," see Bauer, *Cultural Geography*, 232.

45. *National Manhood*, 8–9.

46. Additionally, while James leads us to believe that the hot climate has led to the decadence of this Southern slaveholding society (*L* 167), he also intimates that this evil can occur anywhere. James writes that "we often talk of an indulgent nature, a kind parent, who for the benefit of mankind has taken singular pains to vary the genera of plants, fruits, grain, and the different productions of the earth and has spread peculiar blessings in each climate" (*L* 174–75). However, he claims that "even under those mild climates which seem to breathe peace and happiness, the poison of slavery, the fury of despotism, and the rage of superstition are all combined against man!" (*L* 176). Behdad writes that "not surprisingly, Crèvecoeur accounts for this decadence in contradictory terms: his position is both essentialist, blaming the hot 'climate [that] renders excesses of all kinds very dangerous,'

and constructionist, suggesting that commerce and its degenerative effects of greed, luxury, and slothfulness have led to the decline of civilization (152)" (*Forgetful* 43). I use the term *degeneracy* in relationship to its racial aspects, not strictly the moral decay James describes in South Carolina.

47. See Finseth for a great explication of how Crèvecoeur complexly deals with nature, *Shades of Green*, 78–97. Also, while others have noted aspects of slavery's complex relation to Nature in *Letters*, I emphasize its metaphorical linkage to the race-altering Nature in Letter 3. See for instance Finseth; Jeff Osborne, "American Antipathy and the Cruelties of Citizenship in Crèvecoeur's *Letters from an American Farmer*," *Early American Literature* 42.3 (2007), 529–53; Rucker, "Crèvecoeur's *Letters* and Enlightenment Doctrine;" Rapping, "Theory;" Bauer, *Geography*, 230; Parrish, *American Curiosity*, 292–93; Regis, *Describing America*, 117–19; Ruttenberg, *Democratic Personality*, 282–89; Iannini, *Fatal Revolutions*, 131–76; and Babuscio, "Crèvecoeur in Charles Town." Jennifer Greeson emphasizes the importance of the South to Crèvecoeur's national vision in *Our South: Geographic Fantasy and the Rise of National Literature* (Cambridge, MA: Harvard University Press, 2010), 19–32.

48. Nelson, *National Manhood*, 9.

49. As Teresa Goddu has illustrated, this letter truly represents the gothic aspect of the text (17–21), and here, I argue, it reveals the gothic characteristics of what up to this point in *Letters* had been characterized as the rejuvenating natural landscape.

50. See also Ruttenberg on differences between these two "immigrant" experiences, *Democratic Personality*, 283–84.

51. Goddu terms it a "live burial" (*Gothic America* 20), which makes it even more interesting that this burial is above—rather than below—the ground.

52. Angelo Costanzo, *Suprizing Narrative: Olaudah Equiano and the Beginnings of Black Autobiography* (New York: Dover Publications, 1987), 96. Marrant's *Narrative* was produced in conjunction with Reverend William Aldridge, a minister who had previously been associated with the Countess of Huntingdon's Connexion. Most scholars use the fourth edition, over which Marrant had the most editorial control and included scenes omitted from other editions. See Joanna Brooks and John Saillant, Introduction, *"Face Zion Forward": First Writers of the Black Atlantic, 1785–1798*, eds. Joanna Brooks and John Saillant (Boston: Northeastern University Press, 2002), 19. It is worth noting that while Aldridge could have heavily influenced the shaping of the *Narrative*'s typological references, probably only Marrant himself would have had the experiential knowledge to bring Cherokee epistemology to bear on his story. For more on Aldridge, the Huntingdon Connexion, and the *Narrative*, see J. Brooks, *American Lazarus*, 87; Weyler, *Empowering Words*, 97–99; and May, *Evangelism*, 64–82. For more on the narrator-amanuensis relationship, see Gustafson, *Eloquence*, 107–8; Rafia Zafar, *We Wear the Mask: African Americans Write American Literature, 1760–1870* (New York: Columbia University Press, 1997), 53–55; and John Sekora, "Black Message/White Envelope: Genre, Authenticity, and Authority in the Antebellum Slave Narrative," *Callaloo* 10.3 (1987), 482–515.

53. This contrasts with the specificity of tribal names that *Letters* uses in other sections, especially in the description of Nantucket.

54. John Marrant, *A Narrative of the Lord's Wonderful Dealings with John Marrant, a Black*, in *"Face Zion Forward": First Writers of the Black Atlantic, 1785–1798*, London 1785, eds. Joanna Brooks and John Saillant (Boston: Northeastern University Press, 2002), 49. Further references to this edition will be cited parenthetically as *LWD*.

55. See P. Gould for how Marrant reworks the meanings of "mastery" and "liberty" in his narrative, *Barbaric Traffic* 122–41.

56. Tyler Boulware emphasizes the importance of the individual town in organizing Cherokee society in *Deconstructing the Cherokee Nation: Town, Region, and Nation among Eighteenth-Century Cherokee* (Gainesville: University Press of Florida, 2011).

57. For how Marrant revises the notion of the "savage" speaker, see Gustafson, *Eloquence*, 101–10. See Henry Louis Gates, Jr., on Marrant's "curious inversion" of the "trope of the Talking Book" in *Signifying Monkey: A Theory of Afro-American Literary Criticism* (New York: Oxford University Press, 1988), 142–46. Interestingly, among the Cherokee, women often held the power to decide the fate of captives. See Christina Snyder, *Slavery in Indian Country: The Changing Face of Captivity in Early America* (Cambridge, MA: Harvard University Press, 2010), 93.

58. J. Brooks and Saillant, "Introduction," 39.

59. On typology in the *Narrative*, see, for instance, Costanzo, *Suprizing Narrative*, 101–2; Gustafson, *Eloquence*, 102–6; J. Brooks, *American Lazarus*, 98–99; Weyler, *Empowering Words*, 97–113; Zafar, *Mask*, 57–60; Tiya Miles, "'His Kingdom for a Kiss': Indians and Intimacy in the Narrative of John Marrant," in *Haunted by Empire: Geographies of Intimacy in North American History*, ed. Ann Laura Stoler (Durham: Duke University Press, 2006), 175; Benilde Montgomery, "Recapturing John Marrant," in *A Mixed Race: Ethnicity in Early America*, ed. Frank Shuffelton (New York: Oxford University Press, 1993), 107–8; J. Brooks and Saillant, "Introduction," 20; and P. Gould, *Barbaric Traffic*, 130. For readings also emphasizing Marrant's focus on religion, see Elrod, *Piety*, 38–61; and May, *Evangelism*, 64–82.

60. An exception to this critical trend, Tiya Miles insightfully examines Marrant's interaction with the Cherokee. See Miles, "Indians and Intimacy."

61. Indeed, once Marrant arrives in London and is ordained as a minister in Huntingdon's Connexion, he is sent to missionize among blacks *and Natives* in Nova Scotia (Montgomery, "Recapturing John Marrant," 111; J. Brooks, *American Lazarus*, 89). This suggests Marrant's ability to speak and work across cultures. A notice in the sixth edition of Marrant's *Narrative* reads thus: "SINCE Mr. MARRANT's arrival at Nova-Scotia, several letters have been received from him by different persons, and some by Mr. ALDRIDGE, the Editor of this Narrative; from which it appears, that Mr. MARRANT has travelled through that province preaching the Gospel, and not without success; that he has undergone much fatigue, and passed through many dangers; that he has visited the Indians in their Wigwams, who, he relates, were disposed to hear and receive the Gospel.—This is the substance of the letters transmitted by him to the Editor above-mentioned" (qtd. in Carretta, *Unchained Voices*, 132n60).

62. My theorization here of racial transformation along a black-red spectrum relates to but remains distinct from important work on later conceptions of "hybrid" or "mixed" Afro-Native identity. See Tiya Miles and Sharon Holland, "Crossing Waters, Crossing Worlds," in *Crossing Waters, Crossing Worlds: The African Diaspora in Indian Country*, eds. Tiya Miles and Sharon Holland (Durham: Duke University Press, 2006), 1–23; and Jonathan Brennan, "Recognition of the African-Native American Literary Tradition," in *When Brer Rabbit Meets Coyote: African-Native American Literature*, ed. Jonathan Brennan (Urbana: University of Illinois Press, 2003), 1–97. The transformation-causing capacity of Marrant's Indian dress also contrasts with the later performance of black Mardi Gras Indians, so

incisively investigated by Joseph Roach in *Cities of the Dead: Circum-Atlantic Performance* (New York: Columbia University Press, 1996), 192–211. See also Forbes, *Evolution*.

63. The topic of race has played an important role in the Cherokee Nation for quite some time, including up to the present day. Theda Perdue's *Slavery and the Evolution of Cherokee Society, 1540–1866* (Knoxville: University of Tennessee Press, 1979); and *"Mixed Blood" Indians: Racial Construction in the Early South* (Athens: University of Georgia Press, 2003) are foundational studies of Cherokee conceptions of race in the eighteenth century. Further references to this latter edition will be cited parenthetically as *Racial*. See also Shoemaker, *Strange Likeness*, esp. 125–43; Sturm, *Blood Politics*; Celia Naylor, *African Cherokees in Indian Territory: From Chattel to Citizens* (Chapel Hill: University of North Carolina Press, 2008); Tiya Miles, *Ties that Bind: The Story of an Afro-Cherokee Family in Slavery and Freedom* (Berkeley: University of California Press, 2005); and Snyder, *Slavery in Indian Country*, esp. 101–26. Generally speaking, Cherokee conceptions of race and the importance of skin color to those conceptions have changed over time. In the late eighteenth century, while Natives might have noticed differences in pigmentation, these differences did not come to be considered signs of interior, "racial" difference until the nineteenth century. On Cherokee conceptions during the nineteenth century, see Fay A. Yarbrough, *Race and the Cherokee Nation: Sovereignty in the Nineteenth Century* (Philadelphia: University of Pennsylvania Press, 2007). Subsequent to that, Cherokee understandings of tribal membership continued to evolve. Perdue points out that the "blood quantum" rubric that several modern-day tribes use to measure tribal citizenship grew out of late nineteenth-century efforts to dispossess Natives of their land through allotment (Perdue, *Racial*, 98). This in part has led to the "Cherokee Freedmen controversy," wherein the Cherokee Nation has withdrawn citizenship rights previously granted to the descendants of black slaves who were once incorporated into the tribal community, thus showing this topic to be very much a live issue and one that involves the tribe's sovereignty to determine questions of citizenship. Although the Freedmen controversy should not be read backwards onto Marrant's *Narrative*, this earlier text very much forms part of this long history. For academic scholarship on the controversy, see Miles, *Ties that Bind*; Naylor, *African Cherokees*; Sturm, *Blood Politics*; Jodi A. Byrd, *Transit of Empire: Indigenous Critiques of Colonialism* (Minneapolis: University of Minnesota Press, 2011); and Ariela Gross, *What Blood Won't Tell: A History of Race on Trial in America* (Cambridge, MA: Harvard University Press, 2008). On tensions between multiply-identified scholars engaged in cross-racial scholarship, see *Crossing Waters, Crossing Worlds*, including Miles, "Eating Out of the Same Pot?"; Miles and Holland, "Crossing Waters, Crossing Worlds;" and Robert Warrior, "Afterword," in *Crossing Waters, Crossing Worlds: The African Diaspora in Indian Country*, eds. Tiya Miles and Sharon Holland (Durham: Duke University Press, 2006), 321–25. For more on "Red" and "Black" interactions in more contemporary Southern literature, see Melanie Benson Taylor, *Reconstructing the Native South: American Indian Literature and the Lost Cause* (Athens: University of Georgia Press, 2011), 72–117.

64. Snyder, *Slavery in Indian Country*, 55.

65. Ethnohistorian James Axtell writes that white men taken into Native tribes could become Indianized to the point that it could be "difficult to distinguish" between the Native and white man. As Axtell points out, quoting natural historian Samuel Stanhope Smith's *An Essay on the Causes of the Variety of Complexion and Figure in the Human Species*, this "reinforced the environmentalism of the time, which held that white men 'who have

incorporated themselves with any of [the Indian] tribes' soon acquire 'a great resemblance to the savages, not only in their manners, but in their colour and the expression of the countenance.'" See Axtell, "The White Indians," in *Natives and Newcomers: The Cultural Origins of North America* (New York: Oxford University Press, 2001), 195. Elsewhere, Axtell notes a historical incident relevant to our discussion: "When the evangelizing trader Alexander Long told the Cherokees that their religious beliefs were all false, the Indians replied that the fault was not theirs because they did not have the ability to learn from reading and writing. 'If we had,' their spokesman said, perhaps with a hint of sarcasm, 'we should be as wise as you . . . and could do and make all things as you do: [such] as making guns and powder and bullets and cloth . . . and peradventure the great god of the English would cause us to turn white as you are.'" See Axtell, "The Power of Print in the Eastern Woodlands," *William and Mary Quarterly* 44.2 (April 1987), 306. While certainly the Cherokee were poking fun at the Englishman's assumption of superiority, the joke demonstrates a Cherokee awareness of natural-historical theories, and it turns on the idea that one's race—for whatever reason—could possibly undergo change.

66. Naylor, *African Cherokees*, 75–109.

67. Shoemaker, *A Strange Likeness*, 136.

68. Interestingly, this resembles how eighteenth-century Europeans thought of clothing as a crucial "category of difference," what Roxann Wheeler calls a "proto-racial ideology." See Wheeler, *CR*, 14–21. See also Sophie White, *Wild Frenchmen and Frenchified Indians: Material Culture and Race in Colonial Louisiana* (Philadelphia: University of Pennsylvania Press, 2012).

69. Similar to, and intimately related to, the topic of race, slavery has long been a difficult subject in relation to the Cherokee. Perdue argues that the Cherokee adopted European modes of slavery only after becoming involved in the Anglos' capitalist economy, where they were interested in using slave labor to produce surplus wealth. While the Cherokee practiced black slavery in the late eighteenth century, it would come to resemble more closely white plantation slavery during the nineteenth century. For debates about the tenor of Cherokee slaveholding, see Perdue; Naylor, *African Cherokee*; Miles, *Ties that Bind*; and Snyder, *Slavery in Indian Country*. On how slavery and the Civil War ignited a split among the Cherokee tribe, see Perdue, *Slavery and the Evolution of Cherokee Society*.

70. Miles, *Ties that Bind*, 32.

71. See Costanzo who makes a related point about the "ritualized adoption" of non-Natives into Indian tribes and the "transformation procedure" that Marrant undergoes (*Surprizing* 100–1). For other readings of the Indian dressing scene that contextualize it within a triangulated relationship among the red, white, and black races, see Miles, "Indians and Intimacy;" Montgomery, "Recapturing John Marrant;" Weyler, *Empowering Words*, 97–113; and Brennan, "Recognition," 50–52.

72. Reprinted in J. Brooks and Saillant, 54. Also, toward the end of his narrative, Marrant signals his concern for "the salvation of my countrymen," those who are his "kinsmen, according to the flesh" (*LWD* 73). As I argued in Chapter 2 about how Samson Occom uses this phrase, Marrant signals both his inclusion within a metaphysical body of Christ (by drawing upon the Apostle Paul's signature deployment of the phrase) and also his special relationship to his fellow black men located in the body.

73. Adam Potkay and Sandra Burr, "About John Marrant," in *Black Atlantic Writers of the Eighteenth Century: Living the New Exodus in England and the Americas*, eds. Adam Potkay and Sandra Burr (New York: St. Martin's Press, 1995), 68.

74. Simon Schama conjectures that Marrant was one of the musicians playing "God Save the King" when Clinton arrived in Charleston in *Rough Crossings: Britain, the Slaves and the American Revolution* (London: BBC Books, 2005), 107.

75. See Vincent Carretta for a related point about eighteenth-century black authors identifying with the British empire, in Introduction, *Unchained Voices: An Anthology of Black Authors in the English-Speaking World of the Eighteenth Century*, ed. Vincent Carretta (Lexington: University Press of Kentucky, 1996), 6–7.

76. For how Crèvecoeur projects the ill-effects of slavery onto the South, see Greeson, *Our South*, 19–32.

77. For more on black resistance in Charleston, especially efforts to aid British forces, see Cassandra Pybus, *Epic Journeys of Freedom: Runaway Slaves of the American Revolution and Their Global Quest for Liberty.* (Boston: Beacon Press, 2006) 41–42, 57–61; Schama, *Rough Crossings*, 65–91; and Silvia Frey, *Water from the Rock: Black Resistance in a Revolutionary Age* (Princeton: Princeton University Press, 1991), 108–42. On Marrant's itinerant preaching in Birchtown, Nova Scotia, see J. Brooks, *American Lazarus*, 87–113; and Fichtelberg, *Risk Culture*, 121–144.

78. Charles Brockden Brown, *Edgar Huntly; Or, Memoirs of a Sleep-Walker*, ed. Norman S. Grabo, 1799 (New York: Penguin Books, 1988), 87. Further references to this edition will be cited parenthetically as *EH*.

79. For a redaction of this critical debate, see Doolen, *Fugitive Empire*, 41; and Bryan Waterman, "Reading Early America with Charles Brockden Brown," *Early American Literature* 44.2 (2009), 235–42. For connections between Brown's work and Federalist ideology, see Doolen, *Fugitive Empire*, 39–109; and Gardner, *Master Plots*, 52–80. Robert Levine troubles the Federalist/Republican binary, 25–26 in *Dislocating Race and Nation: Episodes in Nineteenth-Century American Literary Nationalism* (Chapel Hill: University of North Carolina Press, 2008). See also Julia Stern, *Plight of Feeling*, 165. Waterman emphasizes the diverse political and religious viewpoints of the members of New York's Friendly Society, which was a profound influence on Brown and his work. See Bryan Waterman, *Republic of Intellect: The Friendly Club of New York City and the Making of American Literature* (Baltimore: Johns Hopkins University Press, 2007). On the novel's competing political preoccupations, see Downes, "Sleep-Walking out of the Revolution: Brown's *Edgar Huntly*," *Eighteenth-Century Studies* 29.4 (1996), 413–31. On Brown's theory of the imagination, see Cahill, *Liberty*, 164–199.

80. For articulations of this reading, see Robert Newman, "Indians and Indian-Hating in *Edgar Huntly* and *The Confidence Man*," *MELUS* 15.3 (1988), 65–74; and Eve Kornfeld, "Encountering the 'Other': American Intellectuals and Indians in the 1790s," *William and Mary Quarterly* 52.2 (1995), 287–314. For a reading of Brown's distance from his narrator, see Levine, *Dislocating*, 51–2; and Philip Barnard and Stephen Shapiro, Introduction, *Edgar Huntly; or, Memoirs of a Sleep-Walker*, eds. Philip Barnard and Stephen Shaprio (Indianapolis: Hackett Publishing Company, Inc., 2006), xix. Critics have also taken different stances on Brown's literary use of Native Americans. Leslie Fielder, Richard Slotkin, and Robert Newman read Brown's Indians mainly as symbols of Edgar's own psychological distress, while later scholars such as John Carlos Rowe, Renee Bergland, Jared Gardner, and Andrew Newman emphasize the actual historical referents of Brown's Indians. Andrew Newman illuminates connections between the novel and the regional history of Indian relations, and he argues that if *Edgar Huntly* invites its readers to feel benevolence toward Native Americans, "it does so in order to squelch it" ("'Light Might Possibly be Requisite':

Edgar Huntly, Regional History, and Historicist Criticism," *Early American Studies* 8.2 [2010], 349). See Leslie Fielder, *Love and Death in the American Novel*, 1960 (Urbana-Champaign: Dalkey Archive Press, 2003), 160; Slotkin, *Regeneration Through Violence: The Mythology of the American Frontier, 1600–1860* (New York: HarperPerennial, 1973), 376; Robert Newman, "Indian Hating," 66; John Carlos Rowe, *Literary Culture and U.S. Imperialism: From the Revolution to World War II* (New York: Oxford University Press, 2000), 25–51; Renée L. Bergland, "Diseased States, Public Minds: Native American Ghosts in Early National Literature," in *The Gothic Other: Racial and Social Constructions in the Literary Imagination*, eds. Ruth Bienstock Anolik and Douglas L. Howard (Jefferson, North Carolina: McFarland & Company, Inc., 2004), 90–103; Gardner, *Master Plots*, 52–80; and Andrew Newman, "Light." The question of whether Brown was an "Indian-hater" may never be settled. Even if Brown maintained critical distance from the perspective of the narrator, he nevertheless chose to paint Native peoples in a negative light. As I will explore in my discussion of Brown's translation of Volney's *View*, he defends them against negative evaluations but also insists that they can and should change their ways.

81. For scholars who understand Brown's novels to depict and endorse the imperial drive to remove Native Americans from their homelands, see Rowe, *Imperialism*, 25–51; Gardner, *Master Plots*, 52–80; Doolen, *Fugitive Empire*, 39–109; Timothy Francis Strode, *The Ethics of Exile: Colonialism in the Fictions of Charles Brockden Brown and J.M. Coetzee* (New York: Routledge, 2005), 47–134; and Kazanjian, *Colonizing*, 139–172. Literary critics who read Brown's fiction to depict, question, and even undermine the colonial project include Sydney Krause, "Penn's Elm and *Edgar Huntly*: Dark 'Instruction to the Heart,'" *American Literature* 66.3 (1994), 463–84; Chad Luck, "Re-Walking the Purchase: *Edgar Huntly*, David Hume, and the Origins of Ownership," *Early American Literature* 44.2 (2009), 271–306; Barnard and Shapiro, "Introduction," xxxix-xlii; and Levine, *Dislocating*, 17–66. See also Janie Hinds on Brown's conflicted "postcolonial desire" in "Deb's Dogs: Animals, Indians, and Postcolonial Desire in Charles Brockden Brown's *Edgar Huntly*," *Early American Literature* 39.2 (2004), 325. Several essays in Barnard, Kamrath, and Shapiro emphasize Brown's questioning—rather than endorsing—various aspects of eighteenth-century ideology and cultural practices. See *Revising Charles Brockden Brown: Culture, Politics, and Sexuality in the Early Republic*, eds. Philip Barnard, Mark L. Kamrath, and Stephen Shapiro (Knoxville: University of Tennessee Press, 2004).

82. Gardner, *Mater Plots*, 72. Gardner also reads *Edgar Huntly* in light of race changes covered in the popular press, but we come to different conclusions about how Edgar's transformation takes place and what it ultimately means.

83. Ibid., 72, 54.

84. Levine has a related reading, wherein he argues that instead of reiterating identity binaries, *Edgar Huntly* collapses binaries such as "virtue/immorality, self/other, civilized/savage" into "dualisms or oneness" (*Dislocating* 46) and that "what collapses stays collapsed and is not reconstituted into some sort of coherent nationalist allegory" (*Dislocating* 47). See also Smith-Rosenberg, who argues that "collapsing white into red, civil into savage, illegitimate land titles into legitimate ones, *Edgar Huntly* confuses the legitimacy of European settlers' claims both to America's land and to a coherent, stable American identity" in *This Violent Empire: The Birth of an American National Identity* (University of North Carolina Press for the Omohundro Institute of Early American History and Culture, 2010), 275. In addition, Janie Hinds brilliantly explores how natural historians' theories about the

divisions between species (for example, between dog and human) informs Brown's depiction of animals and Indians in *Edgar Huntly*. Although Hinds does not dwell on Edgar's transformation into an Indian, her detailed attention to transformations among species and the troubling of natural historical boundaries between them greatly informs my reading here. See Hinds, "Deb's Dogs."

85. Other critics also emphasize Brown's skepticism about the founding of the nation-state. On Brown's *Ormond*, see Stern, *Plight of Feeling*, 153–238; on *Wieland*, see Looby, *Voicing America*, 145–202. For a related argument concerning Brown and geography, see Martin Brückner, *The Geographic Revolution in Early America: Maps, Literacy, and National Identity* (Chapel Hill: University of North Carolina Press for the Omohundro Institute of Early American History and Culture, 2006), 203.

86. See, among others, Waterman, *Republic of Intellect*; Barnard and Shapiro, "Introduction;" and Brückner, *Geographic*, 184–203.

87. On Brown's engagement with these natural historians, see Hinds, "Deb's Dogs," 327–29. See also Goudie on Brown's use of natural historical racial classification schemes in *Arthur Mervyn, Creole*, 175–99. See Justine Murison, "The Tyranny of Sleep: Somnambulism, Moral Citizenship, and Charles Brockden Brown's *Edgar Huntly*," *Early American Literature* 44.2 (2009), 243–70, on Benjamin Rush's influence on Brown, especially in terms of thinking about somnambulism.

88. Hinds, "Deb's Dogs," 328.

89. Stephen Shapiro, *The Culture and Commerce of the Early American Novel: Reading the Atlantic World-System* (University Park, PA: The Pennsylvania State University Press, 2008), 280.

90. On these confluences, see also Catherine O'Donnell Kaplan, *Men of Letters in the Early Republic: Cultivating Forums of Citizenship* (Chapel Hill: University of North Carolina Press for the Omohundro Institute of Early American History and Culture, 2008), 50–9; 87–91. See also Fredrika J. Teute, "The Loves of the Plants; or, the Cross-Fertilization of Science and Desire at the End of the Eighteenth Century," *Huntington Library Quarterly* 63.3 (2000), 319–45, on how Erasmus Darwin's natural historical outlook impacted members of the Friendly Club.

91. D. W., "Account of a singular Change of Colour in a Negro," *Weekly Magazine of Original Essays, Fugitive Pieces, and Interesting Intelligence*, 1:4 (February 24, 1798), 109–111.

92. Jay Fliegelman, "Introduction,"*Wieland and Memoirs of Carwin the Biloquist*, by Charles Brockden Brown, ed. Jay Fliegelman (New York: Penguin Books), xxii.

93. Johann Friedrich Blumenbach, "Observations on the Conformation and Capacity of the Negroes," *Monthly Magazine, and American Review* 1:6 (September–December 1799), 453–6.

94. Johann Friedrich Blumenbach, *On the Natural Variety of Mankind*, in *The Anthropological Treatises of Johann Friedrich Blumenbach*, ed. Thomas Bendyshe (Boston: Milford House, 1973), 113. Doolen reads Brown's inclusion of Blumenbach as evidence of Brown's endorsement of Blumenbach's environmentalist theory, though he claims that Brown's "belief in the biological equivalency of the human species," coupled with a Federalist "retreat from the antislavery movement after 1793," allows the magazine's audience to "profess fraternity with, and sympathy for, the suffering slave, but only to reinforce the logic of white equality and the racial borders of U.S. imperialism" (*Fugitive Empire* 65-7). Robert Levine emphasizes how this and other pieces in the *Monthly Magazine* argue against what

would come to be the dominant scientific racism of the nineteenth century: "The magazines that Brown edited (and mostly wrote) during this period evince a bold antislavery politics and a rejection of the emerging 'scientific' discourse of racial difference (limned in such texts as Jefferson's _Notes on the State of Virginia_ [1785]) in favor of a vision of human oneness" (_Dislocating_ 30). Shapiro also emphasizes "Brown's antiracism" (_Culture and Commerce_ 264).

95. "Reasons for ascribing the colour of negroes to leprosy," from _Transactions of the American Philosophical Society_, rpt. in _Monthly Magazine, and American Review_ 2.4 (April 1800), 298–301. See also Doolen on the implications of Brown's inclusion of Rush's account, _Fugitive Empire_ 71–2. See also Nelson, _National Manhood_, 57–60.

96. Anthony Wallace 113–20.

97. For instance, Levine sees Brown's rejecting Volney's denigrating depiction of Natives (_Dislocating_ 35). See also Hinds on Brown's "rather schizophrenic set of views" revealed in his notes to Volney's text ("Deb's Dogs" 340). On Volney and Brown, see also Slotkin, _Regeneration_, 382–84; Brückner, _Geographic_, 175, 185; and Hsuan L. Hsu, _Geography and the Production of Space in Nineteenth-Century American Literature_ (Cambridge: Cambridge University Press, 2010), 28–29.

98. In one telling instance, Volney claims that American's indigenous tribes should be termed "savages" rather than "Indians," a term more properly used to describe inhabitants of the "great Hindoo peninsula." Brown claims that "savage" "stigmatiz[es] as wicked and cruel, and is given to men in the rudest state of society, only when we allude to their ignorance or ferocity" (352). He thus sees "Indian" as a more proper, because less derogatory, term.

99. Volney, _View of the Soil and Climate of the United States_, 108. Further references to this edition will be cited parenthetically as _View_.

100. See Yokota on the "link between American 'whiteness' and the materiality of civilization" in the theories of these American scientists (_Unbecoming British_ 218).

101. For more on Little Turtle, see Harvey Carter, _The Life and Times of Little Turtle: First Sagamore of the Wabash_ (Urbana: University of Illinois Press, 1986).

102. It is important to note that Little Turtle had once been supportive of the confederation of Native Americans with whom Aupaumut negotiated and, indeed, had fought against Anglo Americans and defeated Harmar and St. Clair before later deciding to cooperate with the United States and its "plan of civilization." See Dowd, _Spirited Resistance_, 131–138. He himself had owned a cow, but it was killed by a fellow Native American because it was seen as a departure from Indian ways of life (_View_ 378).

103. It is worth noting that despite having earlier defended Native Americans from Volney's label of "savage," here Brown uses it, and he does so in an instance in which Volney is clearly invested in the intelligence of his interviewee and Brown wants to discount him. In _Edgar Huntly_, Edgar uses the term to discuss both panthers and Indians.

104. Charles Brockden Brown, "Art. V. [Review of] New Views of the Origin of the Tribes and Nations of America. By Benjamin Smith Barton, M.D. &c.&c. 8vo. pp. 274. Philadelphia. Printed for the Author by John Bioren. 1798," _Monthly Magazine, and American Review_ 1:2 (May 1799), 117–19.

105. Volney and Brown also disagree over whether alterations to one man's body might be inheritable. Disputing those who claim that Indians are beardless, Volney argues that Indians pluck their hair. He claims that "no wonder if this practice, continued for _several generations_, enfeeble the roots of the beard" (_View_ 366–67). Brown is incredulous: "How

should the practice of one man, in this respect, affect the growth of hair in his grandson?" (*View* 367). See also Slotkin on this point: "Brown denies that the Indian is unchangeable, his character fixed by racial inheritance. Habits and conditioning make each man what he is, and the characteristics that develop from conditioning cannot be inherited. Change the education and circumstances of the Indian child, and he will not be a savage like his fathers before him. Volney's remarks, says Brown, are the result of ignorance and prejudice . . ." (*Regeneration* 383).

106. "An Account of the Late Proceedings of the Society of Friends (or Quakers) for the Civilization of the Indian Tribes," *Literary Magazine, and American Register* 4:25 (October 1805), 276–87.

107. This claimed intention may be true, but Brown's "Account" does state that the Quaker efforts were endorsed by the US government. Levine has a less skeptical view, underscoring how Brown "extols his fellow Quakers for regarding Indians as capable of becoming part of the national community. Rather than seeking to convert the Indians, the Quakers he describes accept them on their own terms and wish simply to improve 'their private and domestic condition'" (*Dislocating* 35).

108. A similar argument is made in "On the Consequences of Abolishing the Slave Trade to the West Indian Colonies," *Literary Magazine, and American Register* 4: 26 (November 1805), 375–81. Levine credits Brown as probable author of this piece (*Dislocating* 31). Here Brown argues that slaves develop bad qualities from their time in slavery but that these characteristics are not natural to them. He notes how the "Russians" have "fundamentally improved" and claims that "those who argue about races, and despise the effect of circumstances, would have had the same right to decide upon the fate of all the Russias, from an inspection of the Calmuc skull, as they now have to condemn all Africa to everlasting barbarism, from the craniums, colour, and wool of its inhabitants." Here, Brown takes issue with natural historians who attributed racial difference to some sort of unchanging biology rather than to circumstances. Brown claims that "there is nothing in the physical or moral constitution of the negro, which renders him an exception to the general character of the species, and prevents him from improving in all estimable qualities, when placed in favourable circumstances." These types of statements directly counterpose those of Jefferson who hinted toward separate creations for the races, and they support the natural histories of Samuel Stanhope Smith who purported that external factors caused the differences among the races, after their shared, single creation.

109. Grabo, "Introduction," xviii. See also Gardner, *Master Plots*, 52–80.

110. Krause, "Penn's Elm." In 1682, William Penn famously negotiated a "treaty of friendship" (464) with the Lenni-Lenape under a historic elm. According to Krause, "Penn followed through on his good intentions" (467), but the white-Native relations took a devastating turn in 1737 with the Walking Purchase Treaty. Penn's sons presented the tribe "with a copy of what purported to be a deed paid for in 1686 by treaty with their father's agents for an unspecified tract of Forks land to be measured by as far as a man could walk in a day and a half, or roughly forty miles" (468). After much negotiation, the Lenni-Lenape agreed to fulfill their obligations under the 1686 treaty. On September 19, 1737, the land the colonialists were to claim was "walked off," but the Penn sons had arranged for a professionally-trained runner to traverse the distance. In the end, the whites claimed almost double the area that the tribe assumed would be covered (468). For more on the Walking Purchase Treaty of 1737, see Rowe, *Imperialism*, 41–43.

111. Krause also notes Edgar's citation of this justification ("Penn's Elm" 467).

112. See also Matthew Wynn Sivils, who argues that Deb comes to represent the "dispossessed Indian nations and their fight to retain sovereignty over the land that defines their existence," in "Native American Sovereignty and Old Deb in Charles Brockden Brown's *Edgar Huntly*," *ATQ* 15.4 (2001), 294. See also Hinds on the complexity of Edgar's depiction of Deb in "Deb's Dogs;" and Bergland, "Diseased States," 96.

113. Sivils, "Old Deb," 270, 298.

114. See also Sivils, who calls Old Deb's actions "taxation" ("Old Deb" 296).

115. Critics, starting with Leslie Fielder, frequently note that none of the Indians in *Edgar Huntly* ever get to speak, and while Edgar recounts Deb's words, he never quotes her directly. See also Rowe on Edgar's acquisition of the Lenni-Lenape language (*Imperialism* 43).

116. For a related reading, see Strode, *Ethics*, 122.

117. See Rowe, *Imperialism*, 46, and Barnard and Shapiro, "Introduction," xlii.

118. See also Hinds on this scene, "Deb's Dogs."

119. Several scholars note the importance of this imagery in showing the developing proximity between Edgar and the Indians. See Grabo, "Introduction," xv; Levine, *Dislocating*, 51; and Gardner, *Master Plots*, 72–73. See also Elizabeth Dillon on the "republican body" in this scene in *The Gender of Freedom: Fictions of Liberalism and the Literary Public Sphere* (Stanford: Stanford University Press, 2007), 177–79.

120. On Clithero's descent into savagery, see Gardner, *Master Plots*, 68; Smith-Rosenberg, *Violent*, 277.

121. Gardner does claim that this marks Edgar "as potentially a savage" and that here Edgar's "savage potential is realized" (*Master Plots* 76). However, he simultaneously claims that Edgar has "reentered society" (*Master Plots* 76). Along the lines of my reading, see Levine's emphasis on the ambiguous and unresolved ending to this novel, *Dislocating*, 54–55.

122. Ezra Tawil, "'New Forms of Sublimity': Edgar Huntly and the European Origins of American Exceptionalism," *Novel* 40.1–2 (2006–2007), 114.

123. Gardner, *Master Plots*, 75.

Chapter 4

1. Olaudah Equiano, "To Mr. Gordon Turnbull, Author of 'An Apology for Negro Slavery.'" *Public Advertiser* February 5, 1788, 1–2.

2. Ibid., 2.

3. Olaudah Equiano, *The Interesting Narrative of the Life of Olaudah Equiano*, ed. Vincent Carretta (New York: Penguin Press, 1995), 45. Further references to this edition will be cited parenthetically as *IN*. See Vincent Carretta, *Equiano, the African: Biography of a Self-Made Man* (University of Georgia Press, 2005; New York: Penguin, 2006), 261, for a related point. Further references to this edition will be cited parenthetically as *B*. Also on Equiano's use of monogenesis, see Boulukos, *Grateful Slave*, 184; Finseth, *Shades of Green*, 116; McBride, *Impossible Witness*, 132–33; and Douglas Anderson, "Division Below the Surface: Olaudah Equiano's Interesting Narrative," *Studies in Romanticism* 43.3 (2004), 439–60.

4. Roxann Wheeler emphasizes the "limits to associating anti-slave trade sentiment with an assumption of human equality" (*CR* 236) and the way that "a writer's belief in monogenesis does not ensure that he considers color or national differences inconsequential" (*CR* 253). I want to highlight how Equiano nevertheless stresses the potential of transformable race in order to contrast that sharply with the behavior of many whites toward both black slaves and free blacks.

5. See Gates's argument on the link between literacy, rationality, and humanity for black peoples (*Signifying Monkey* 127–69). For important critiques of Gates's theory on black literacy, see Srinivas Aravamudan, *Tropicopolitans: Colonialism and Agency, 1688–1804* (Durham: Duke University Press, 1999), 233–88; Ronald A. T. Judy, *(Dis)Forming the American Canon*, 1–98 (esp. 85–98); and Langley, *Black Aesthetic*, 126–31. See also Christopher Hager, *Word by Word: Emancipation and the Act of Writing* (Cambridge, MA: Harvard University Press, 2013).

6. While two eighteenth-century newspaper articles alleged that Equiano was not born in Africa as he said, the contemporary scholarly debate centers on Vincent Carretta's claim that Equiano might have been born in South Carolina. Carretta points to a 1759 baptismal certificate and a 1773 ship muster that list Equiano's birthplace as Carolina. While almost all Equiano scholars note or engage in the debate over whether Equiano was born in Africa or America, a few stand out. S. E. Ogude emphasizes how Equiano drew upon several sources in his description of Africa and that a "dominant element in *The Interesting Narrative* is fiction" in *Genius in Bondage: A Study of the Origins of African Literature in English* (Ile-Ife, Nigeria: University of Ife Press Ltd., 1983), 131. Paul E. Lovejoy challenges Carretta's claims in "Autobiography and Memory: Gustavus Vassa, alias Olaudah Equiano, the African," *Slavery and Abolition* 27.3 (2006), 317–47. See also the exchange that follows between Carretta and Lovejoy in the April 2007 *Slavery and Abolition* 28.1 (2007). John Bugg casts doubts on several of Carretta's contentions in "The Other Interesting Narrative: Olaudah Equiano's Public Book Tour," *PMLA* 121.5 (2006), 1424–42. See also the exchange between Bugg and Carretta that follows in the March 2007 *PMLA* (122.2). Cathy Davidson brilliantly enumerates several compelling reasons why Equiano perhaps misrepresented himself not in *The Interesting Narrative* but in the baptismal certificate and the ship muster in "Olaudah Equiano, Written by Himself," *Novel* 40.1/2 (2006), 18–51. In the collection *Olaudah Equiano and the Igbo World: History, Society and Atlantic Diaspora Connections*, scholars such as Chima J. Korieh, Catherine Obianuju Acholonu, and Dorothy Chinwe Ukaegbu exmine links between *The Interesting Narrative* and Igbo culture (ed. Chima J. Korieh [Trenton, NJ: Africa World Press, 2009]). Alexander X. Byrd relates *The Interesting Narrative* to eighteenth-century understandings of Igbo identity in "Eboe, Country, Nation, and Gustavus Vassa's *Interesting Narrative*," *William and Mary Quarterly* 63.1 (2006), 123–48. Other critics who address this debate include Jonathan Elmer, *On Lingering and Being Last: Race and Sovereignty in the New World* (New York: Fordham University Press, 2008), 76–7; Babacar M'Baye, *The Trickster Comes West: Pan-African Influence in Early Black Diasporan Narratives* (Jackson, MS: University Press of Mississippi, 2009), 105–43; Christine Levecq, *Slavery and Sentiment: The Politics of Feeling in Black Atlantic Antislavery Writing, 1770–1850* (Durham, NH: University of New Hampshire Press, 2008), 122–33; and Langley, *Black Aesthetic*, 97–138.

7. On the attribution of these reviews and others to Wollstonecraft, see Janet Todd, "Prefatory Note," in *The Works of Mary Wollstonecraft*, Vol. 7, eds. Janet Todd and Marilyn Butler (New York: New York University Press, 1989), 14–18.

8. Mary Wollstonecraft, Review of *The Interesting Narrative of the Life of Olaudah Equiano, or Gustavus Vassa, the African. Analytical Review*, May 1789, rpt. *The Works of Mary Wollstonecraft*, Vol. 7, eds. Janet Todd and Marilyn Butler (New York: New York University Press, 1989), 100.

9. Ibid.

10. Ibid.

11. Mary Wollstonecraft, Review of *An Essay on the Causes of the Variety of Complexion and Figure in the Human Species* by Samuel Stanhope Smith, *Analytical Review*, December 1788, rpt. in *The Works of Mary Wollstonecraft*, Vol. 7, eds. Janet Todd and Marilyn Butler (New York: New York University Press, 1989), 50. For more on how Wollstonecraft's acceptance of Smith's theories impacted her writings, see Scott Juengel, "Countenancing History: Mary Wollstonecraft, Samuel Stanhope Smith, and Enlightenment Racial Science," *ELH* 68.4 (2001), 897–927.

12. Bell, *Patriot-Improvers*, 138. Bauer points out that Equiano's use of Mitchell directly contradicts claims made by Jefferson in *Notes*, "Hemispheric," 52.

13. See, for instance, Finseth, *Shades of Green*, 102; and Carretta, *Biography*, 5.

14. It is also important that Clarkson's *Essay* specifically uses the example of the Jews to argue for environmentally-produced differences in appearance (207–8). Scholars who also address Equiano's analogy include Roxann Wheeler, who emphasizes the similar organizations of society (*CR* 261–2). Laura Doyle looks at how Equiano "establishes a biblical racial genealogy for the Benin people—and a noble origin for the African liberty story" in *Freedom's Empire: Race and the Rise of the Novel in Atlantic Modernity, 1640–1940* (Durham: Duke University Press, 2008), 199. Elrod stresses that Equiano parallels Africans and Jews because they are "a biblical people chosen and favored by God" (*Piety* 68). Also giving a strictly biblical interpretation, Geraldine Murphy suggests that "a Calvinist, Equiano would be inclined to read his culture in typological terms, spiritually awaiting the good news of the Gospels and materially achieving fulfillment in commercial partnership with the west" in "Olaudah Equiano, Accidental Tourist," *Eighteenth-Century Studies* 27.4 (1994), 563. Elmer writes that "like the Jews, Equiano is structurally included, as it were, while simultaneously remaining an other within. To identify with the Jews is, from the perspective of the Christian West, to find one's identity through a mark of difference that both cannot, and must not, be erased" in *On Lingering*, 70. Paul Gilroy reads the analogy as making a link between two similarly constituted diasporas in *Against Race*, 122. See also Babacar M'Baye, *Trickster Comes West*, 139–40; Potkay and Burr, "Introduction," in *Black Atlantic Writers of the Eighteenth Century: Living the New Exodus in England and the Americas*, eds. Adam Potkay and Sandra Burr (New York: St. Martin's Press, 1995), 11–13; James Sidbury, *Becoming African in America: Race and Nation in the Early Black Republic* (New York: Oxford University Press, 2007), 47–8; Levecq, *Sentiment*, 130; and Tanya Caldwell, "'Talking Too Much English': Languages of Economy and Politics in Equiano's *The Interesting Narrative*," *Early American Literature* 34.3 (1999), 263–82. For two different perspectives on the role of geography and the environment in shaping Equiano's identity, see F. Odun Balogun, "Self and Place in African and African-American Autobiographical Prose: Equiano and Achebe, Soyinka and Gates," in *Sacred Spaces and Public Quarrels: African Cultural and Economic Landscapes*, eds. Ezekiel Kalipeni and Paul Tiyambe Zeleza (Trenton, NJ: Africa World Press, Inc., 1999), 197–232; and Michael Wiley, "Consuming Africa: Geography and Identity in Olaudah Equiano's *Interesting Narrative*," *Studies in Romanticism* 44.2 (2005), 165–79.

15. Equiano's quote does not exactly replicate that in Clarkson's *Essay*, omitting a reference to the impact of intermarriage, and he combines two quotes (one from Mitchell and one from the *Treatise*) that are cited separately in Clarkson's book into one quote in his own text.

16. Bauer, "Hemispheric Genealogies," 51.

17. See also Finseth, *Shades of Green*, 102, on this point.

18. Werner Sollors, "Introduction," in *The Interesting Narrative of Olaudah Equiano, or Gustavus Vassa, the African, Written by Himself, by Olaudah Equiano*, ed. Werner Sollors (New York: Norton, 2001), xxvi.

19. See note 5, this chapter.

20. Bell, *Patriot-Improvers*, 140. For more on Mitchell, see Bell, *Patriot-Improvers* 138–48; and Roxann Wheeler, *CR*, 26–27, 265.

21. Equiano's quote does not exactly replicate that in Clarkson's *Essay*, omitting a reference to the impact of intermarriage, and he combines two quotes (one from Mitchell and one from the *Treatise*) that are cited separately in Clarkson's book into one quote in his own text.

22. See Finseth, *Shades of Green*, 42–3 on a related point.

23. Roxann Wheeler claims that here Equiano "argues for the operation of a reverse European color aesthetic in Africa" (*CR* 268) and that "instead of showing the way aesthetic assumptions operate culturally, Equiano's example tends to support the acceptability of skin color as a sign of belonging to a nation and the universality of color prejudice" (*CR* 269). I, on the other hand, would like to emphasize how profound Equiano's revaluation of whiteness is, especially as it is linked to Mitchell and Clarkson's theories. On Equiano's relationship to whiteness, see also Susan M. Marren, "Between Slavery and Freedom: The Transgressive Self in Olaudah Equiano's Autobiography," *PMLA* 108.1 (1993), 94–105. For another viewpoint, see Caldwell, "Talking."

24. Jefferson, *Notes*, 186–7.

25. See, for example Felicity A. Nussbaum, *The Limits of the Human: Fictions of Anomaly, Race, and Gender in the Long Eighteenth Century* (Cambridge: Cambridge University Press, 2003), 202; Roxann Wheeler, *CR*, 269; M'Baye, *Trickster*, 140; and Elmer, *Lingering*, 71.

26. Equiano here quotes liberally from both Benezet (which Equiano acknowledges) and the Burkes (which he does not). See Carretta, *Biography*, footnotes n307 and n308 (271).

27. Roxann Wheeler argues that this is "possibly Equiano's most successful reference to climate" (*CR* 267).

28. See, for instance, Peter Dorsey, *Common Bondage: Slavery as Metaphor in Revolutionary America* (Knoxville: University of Tennessee Press, 2009).

29. For a brilliant reading of how Equino's *Narrative* characterizes Philadelphia as both "free and unfree, hospitable and inhospitable, and civilized and uncivilized" (34) and demonstrates the importance of the West Indies to early American identity, see Goudie, *Creole America*, 32–36.

30. For a germinal reading of the economics in Equiano's *Narrative*, see Houston Baker, *Blues, Ideology, and Afro-American Literature: A Vernacular Theory* (Chicago: University of Chicago Press, 1984), 15–63. Other key texts that address the discourse of economics in *The Interesting Narrative* include Nahum Dimitri Chandler, "Originary Displacement," *boundary 2* 27.3 (2000), 249–86; Kazanjian, *Colonizing Trick*, 35–88; Gould, *Barbaric Traffic*, 133–88; Joseph Fichtelberg, "Word between Worlds: The Economy of Equiano's Narrative," *American Literary History* 5.3 (1993), 459–80; Ross J. Pudaloff, "No Change without Purchase: Olaudah Equiano and the Economies of Self and Market," *Early American Literature* 40.3 (2005), 499–527; Marion Rust, "The Subaltern as Imperialist: Speaking of

Olaudah Equiano," in *Passing and the Fictions of Identity*, ed. Elaine K. Ginsberg (Durham: Duke University Press, 1996), 21–36; McBride, *Impossible Witness*, 122–26; Zafar, *Mask*, 92–3; Marren, "Between Slavery and Freedom"; Levecq, *Sentiment*, 121–22; and Elizabeth Jane Wall Hinds, "The Spirit of Trade: Olaudah Equiano's Conversion, Legalism, and the Merchant's Life," *African American Review* 32.4 (1998), 635–37.

31. Carretta notes that it would have been advantageous for Equiano to gain his freedom legally rather than by escape; a legally free man could ostensibly choose to stay in the British North American colonies, but an escaped slave would have to journey back to England, where nevertheless his master could attempt to reclaim him. See *Biography* 105.

32. For a related argument about performative speech acts in *The Interesting Narrative*, see Jesse Molesworth, "Equiano's 'Loud Voice': Witnessing the Performance of the *Interesting Narrative*," *Texas Studies in Literature and Language* 48.2 (2006), 123–44. On the relationship between textuality and legality, see Hinds, "Spirit of Trade."

33. *Colonizing Trick* 57.

34. Stressing the precariousness of Equiano's current position as a free black, Carretta points out that his inclusion of the papers "suggests that he kept a copy with him at all times, because the liberty of a free black man was always open to challenge wherever race-based slavery existed" (*B* 114). Baker calls the manumission "an economic sign with competes with and radically qualifies the ethical piousness of its enfolding text. The inscribed document is a token of mastery, signifying its recipient's successful negotiation of a deplorable system of exchange" (*Blues* 36). See also Chandler on the theoretical complexity of Equiano's purchase of his freedom ("Originary" 277–82). Hinds notes that "Equiano's inclusion of the papers here hints at the less-than-protective nature of the original document" ("Spirit of Trade" 643).

35. *Colonizing Trick* 58.

36. Scholars have pointed out numerous episodes where Equiano demonstrates how he was mistreated as both a slave and as a free black man, and here I focus on episodes in which the unreliability of texts is significant. See, for instance, Carretta, *Biography* (189 and passim); Kazanjian, *Colonizing Trick*, 35–88; Doyle, *Freedom's Empire*, 196; Roxann Wheeler, *CR*, 236 and passim; Nussbaum, *Limits*, 200; Bugg, "Other," 1428; Davidson, "Written by Himself," 36; Pudaloff, "No Change;" Rust, "Subaltern;" Hinds, "Spirit of Trade;" Marren, "Between;" and Boulukos, *Grateful Slave*, 173–200. See Elmer on how the "full achievement of an emancipated, sovereign selfhood is always deferred, always only available through the future perfect tense" (*Lingering* 53). For an important reading of these and other documents as a way that Equiano interpellates his readers as "character witness[es]," see Molesworth, "Loud Voice."

37. Murphy, in "Accidental Tourist," argues that given the immediate context of Equiano's time and, of course, his inability to see what would become of the implementation of his suggestion, Equiano's proposal for Britain to establish a "commercial intercourse with Africa" (*IN* 234) makes sense (561). On Equiano's economic proposal, see also Roxann Wheeler, *CR*, 283–85; Baker, *Blues*, 38; Fichtelberg, "Word between Worlds;" Pudaloff, "No Change;" Rust, "Subaltern;" Zafar, *Mask*, 94–95; Caldwell, "Talking;" Gould, *Barbaric Traffic*, 133–88; and Finseth, *Shades of Green*, 110.

38. APS, Violetta Delafield-Benjamin Smith Barton collection. Notes—Scientific, Misc. (3 of 9) 1796 August 5–1813 Sept. 21. For more on Barton, see Yokota, *Unbecoming British*, passim.

39. Barton's interest in the skin colors of humans was long-forming. His uncompleted dissertation at the University of Edinburgh concentrated on albinos among Native Americans and African Americans (APS, Misc. Ms. Collection [ca. 1786]). In addition, in 1789 in his commonplace book, Barton wrote about a "white negress" mentioned by the Abbe Dicquemare (APS, Benjamin Smith Barton journals; Commonplace Book, in Journals, Ann. by W. L. AcAtee. B B284.2 part 1, 10).

40. This is not to say that preliminary notes toward any scientific theory call into question the validity of that theory. However, it is to underscore the process of how natural historians wrote these stories and interpellated these very categories of persons into being in addition to how there was a great deal of uncertainly and disagreement over which theory was correct. Furthermore, this is to say nothing of the issue that Barton did not finish his degree at Edinburgh. As Yokota points out, although Barton received training at the University of Pennsylvania and the University of Edinburgh, he ultimately did not finish his degrees at either institution (197–98). Here, I am less interested in highlighting the veracity of Barton's specific claims or his lack of degree or in parsing out who was right and who was wrong in this debate and more invested in emphasizing the necessarily conjectural nature of these successive natural historical claims about race and the writing—engendered by these debates—through which these racial theories came into being.

41. *Early Proceedings of the American Philosophical Society for the Promotion of Useful Knowledge Compiled by One of the Secretaries from the Manuscript Minutes of its Meetings. 1744–1838* (Philadelphia: Press of McCalla & Staverly, 1884), 241. The published version of Barton's paper, "Account of Henry Moss, a White Negro" in *Philadelphia Medical and Physical Journal* can be found in the American Philosophical Society: APS B P31X#5.

42. For how Brackenridge "delineates the limitations of Enlightenment and republican thought" in relationship to rationality and social order, see Paul Gilmore, "Republican Machines and Brackenridge's Caves: Aesthetics and Models of Machinery in the Early Republic," *Early American Literature* 39.2 (2004), 299–322.

43. Hugh Henry Brackenridge, *Modern Chivalry*, ed. Ed White (Indianapolis: Hackett Publishing Company, Inc., 2009), 240. Further references to this edition will be cited parenthetically as *MC*.

44. Bell begins his analysis with Brackenridge's (then anonymous) "Memoir to the American Philosophical Society," a 1787 piece that I discuss later in this chapter (*Gazette Publications* [Carlisle, PA: Alexander & Phillips, 1806], 256–64). See Bell, "As Others Saw Us: Notes on the Reputation of the American Philosophical Society," *Proceedings of the American Philosophical Society* 116.3 (1972): 269–78.

45. See William Stanton, *The Leopard's Spots: Scientific Attitudes toward Race in America, 1815—59* (Chicago: University of Chicago Press, 1960); W. Jordan, *WOB*; Charles D. Martin, *The White African American Body* (New Brunswick: Rutgers University Press, 2002); Sweet, *BP*.

46. Davidson attributes the novel's ability to avoid taking "a 'position' on any of the various issues adumbrated within the text" while still being able to advance a "social stand" to the text's picaresque form in *Revolution and the Word: The Rise of the Novel in America*, expanded ed. (New York: Oxford University Press, 2004), 248. For Nelson, the political dialogues that the novel illustrates and, indeed, enacts advance a "theory of democratic representation [that] expands the scope of political representation, making literature part

of a cohort of representative practices that are necessary to democratic work" in "'Indications of the Public Will': *Modern Chivalry*'s Theory of Democratic Representation," *ANQ* 15.1 (2002), 24. For Looby, the many voices of *Modern Chivalry* make it the "American dialogic novel par excellence," one that is "overtly a universalizing linguistic project, and covertly (or actually) a pluralizing project" in *Voicing America*, 204, 205.

47. Gilmore, "Republican," 300.

48. Further biographical information on Brackenridge can be found in White, "Introduction," *Modern Chivalry*, ed. Ed White (Indianapolis: Hackett Publishing Company, Inc., 2009), ix–xxviii; Joseph J. Ellis, *After the Revolution: Profiles of Early American Culture* (New York: Norton, 1979), 73–110; and Daniel Marder, *A Hugh Henry Brackenridge Reader: 1770–1815*, ed. Daniel Marder (Pittsburgh: University of Pittsburgh Press, 1970). Further references to this edition will be cited parenthetically as *Reader*. See also Daniel Marder, *Hugh Henry Brackenridge* (New York: Twayne Publishers, 1967). Further references to this edition will be cited parenthetically as *Brackenridge*.

49. See also Marder, *Reader*, 16–20.

50. E. White, "Introduction," xv.

51. Ibid., xvi.

52. On how Brackenridge's support of the Constitution affected his constituency, see Marder, *Reader*, "Introduction," 13–14; and *Brackenridge*, 43–49. See also Marder on his switch from being a Federalist to a Democrat, *Reader*, "Introduction," 20–21; and E. White, "Introduction," xviii-xx.

53. E. White, "Introduction," xvii. For more on Brackenridge's conflicted role in the Whiskey Rebellion, see Marder, *Reader*, "Introduction," 16–20; and *Brackenridge*, 49–54.

54. For more on *The United States Magazine*, see Marder, *Brackenridge*, 73–9.

55. Hugh Henry Brackenridge, "Thoughts on the Enfranchisement of the Negroes," 1779, in *A Hugh Henry Brackenridge Reader: 1770–1815*, ed. Daniel Marder (Pittsburgh: University of Pittsburgh Press, 1970), 104.

56. Ibid., 104.

57. Hugh Henry Brackenridge, "Establishment of These United States—An American Account," 1779, in *Reader*, 100.

58. *Brackenridge* 35–37, 99–105; *Reader*, 9–11.

59. Brackenridge, Henry Hugh, ed. *Narratives of a Late Expedition against the Indians, with An Account of the Barbarous Execution of Col. Crawford; and The Wonderful Escape of Dr. Knight and John Slover from Captivity, in 1782* (Philadelphia: F. Bailey, 1783), 32. Futher references to this edition will be cited parenthetically as *LE*.

60. Marder problematically defends Brackenridge's attitudes towards both Indians and African Americans, and he sees Brackenridge's view on the freeing and immediate colonizing of African Americans as "consistent." See *Reader*, "Introduction," 23.

61. See also Ellis, *After the Revolution*, 89–92; Robert Lawson-Peebles, *Landscape and Written Expression in Revolutionary America: The World Turned Upside Down* (Cambridge: Cambridge University Press, 1988), 130; Edward Watts, *Writing and Postcolonialism in the Early Republic* (Charlottesville: University Press of Virginia, 1998), 49.

62. E. White, "Introduction," x, xxix–xxxi.

63. Parrington, *Main Currents*, 393.

64. Joseph H. Harkey, "The *Don Quixote* of the Frontier: Brackenridge's *Modern Chivalry*," *Early American Literature* 8.2 (1973), 194.

65. John Engell, "Brackenridge, *Modern Chivalry*, and American Humor," *Early American Literature* 22.1 (1987), 43–62.

66. Looby, *Voicing America*, 244.

67. E. White, "Introduction," x–xii; Looby, *Voicing America*, 242–49. Scholars who emphasize the distance between the narrative voice and Brackenridge include Nelson, "Indications," 35; Emory Elliott, *Revolutionary Writers: Literature and Authority in the New Republic, 1725–1810* (New York: Oxford University Press, 1982), 183–84; G. Rice, *Transformation of Authorship*, 134; and Watts, *Postcolonialism*, 28. William W. Hoffa underscores the foolishness not only of the characters but also "in the *narration* as well" in "The Language of Rogues and Fools in Brackenridge's *Modern Chivalry*," *Studies in the Novel* 12.4 (1980), 294. Davidson sees Farrago as the chief protagonist (*Revolution and the Word* 20). Cynthia S. Jordan claims that the "Captain's attempts to maintain order eventually becomes overshadowed by the rival story line of his challengers, whose dissident voices grow in strength as they grow in number" in *Second Stories: The Politics of Language, Form, and Gender in Early American Fictions* (Chapel Hill: University of North Carolina Press, 1989), 60.

68. In the final chapter of the book, entitled "A Key to the Preceding," Brackenridge's narrator declares that when he was serving in the Pennsylvania legislature in 1787, he was approached about being nominated for the APS if he would only "skin a cat-fish, or do something that would save appearances, and justify the society in considering me a man of philosophic search, and resources" (*MC* 533). However, not wanting to be among those nominated for membership, the narrator got the idea to have a candidate like Teague be nominated "for that honour" (*MC* 533).

69. Looby, *Voicing America*, 243.

70. Brackenridge's 1787 (then anonymous) "Memoir." A letter "To Mr. Br—ge" from "Amicus" published in the *Independent Gazetteer* responds to the "Memoir," challenging Brackenridge to deny he is the author of "such a farrago of unmeaning words" (*Independent Gazetteer* February 22, 1787, 6:374: 2). See also Daniel Marder, who sees the "prototypes of Farrago and his ambitious servant in the 'Memoir'" (*Reader* 31), on Brackenridge's satire of the APS. See Marder, "Introduction," *Reader*, 3–46. See Bell, "As Others Saw Us."

71. Other scholars have made similar points. In introducing Teague, the narrator tells us, "the servant that he had at this time, was an Irishman, whose name was Teague Oregan. I shall say nothing of the character of this man, because the very name imports what he was" (*MC* 3). The narrator means both that with his Irish name, Teague would have a certain stereotypical character *and* that "'Teague' itself is "the generic term for footman often used to address an Irish servant in the employment of an English soldier or gentleman;" see Herb Smith, "Hugh Henry Brackenridge's Debt to the Stage-Irish Convention," *Ball State University Forum* 30.1 (1989), 16. Looby emphasizes how "the caricatured 'wild Irishman' was the standard metonym for ethnicity in general" (*Voicing America* 249) and in Pennsylvania at this moment, "the Irish became, synecdochically, the representative group posing the ethnic threat" (*Voicing America* 251). On the connection between Teague and Indians, see Sweet, *BP*, 310; on the link between Teague and African Americans, see E. White, "Introduction," xii; Martin, *White*, 45–6; and Samuel Otter, *Philadelphia Stories: America's Literature of Race and Freedom* (New York: Oxford University Press, 2010), 75–76. For how "the particular physiognomic features of the faces of subordinate groups (such as Teague's) bear a negative relationship to embodying public character" (145), see Christopher Lukasik,

Discerning Characters, 140–52. Although not talking in explicitly racial terms, Mark Patterson emphasizes how Teague serves as "a signifier without a referent, a character who can be made to appear as almost anything in this society" in *Authority, Autonomy, and Representation in American Literature, 1776–1865* (Princeton: Princeton University Press, 1988), 45.

72. Much later in the text, Farrago repeats this association when he says that he "bought him from an Irish vessel, just as a curiosity" (*MC* 242). Scholarship on constructions of Irishness in the antebellum period has shown how the association between Irishness and blackness was made and also challenged. Richard Dyer points out the association between Irish and blacks in the American imaginary in *White*, 52–54. David Roediger and Noel Ignatiev both detail how Irish peoples came to be seen as and represented as white during the nineteenth century; see Roediger, *Abolition of Whiteness*; and Ignatiev, *How the Irish Became White* (New York: Routledge Press, 1995). This work has been crucial in understanding race and racial associations in the nineteenth century, but while Ignatiev, for example, describes how the Irish came to be considered white, I am analyzing a very different type of "becoming"—the eighteenth-century idea that bodies themselves could change and become something different to what they previously were.

73. Martin, *White*, 46.

74. In contrast, although John Mitchell comments directly on the experiments he performed on black peoples in his "Essay," Equiano does not remark upon it.

75. APS Archives VI, 4: Curator's Record Vol. 1, 1769–1818, 35.

76. Ibid., 39.

77. Ibid.

78. Murphy D. Smith claims that the Indian skin must have been part of the otter skin (14). However, both the curator's handwritten records and the printed *Early Proceedings of the American Philosophical Society for the Promotion of Useful Knowledge Compiled by One of the Secretaries from the Manuscript Minutes of its Meetings. 1744–1838* list and count these two items as separate entries. See Smith, *A Museum: The History of the Cabinet of Curiosities of the American Philosophical Society* (Philadelphia: American Philosophical Society, 1996).

79. John Morgan, "Some Account of a Motley Coloured, or Pye Negro Girl and Mulatto Boy, Exhibited before the Society in the Month of May, 1784, for Their Examination, by Dr. John Morgan, from the History Given of Them by Their Owner Mons. Le Vallois, Dentist of the King of France at Guadaloupe in the West Indies," *Transactions of the American Philosophical Society* 2 (1786), 392–95. Further references to this edition will be cited parenthetically as "SA."

80. Winthrop Jordan assumes that Morgan brought the children to the APS meeting. He writes that "Dr. John Morgan had presented two other living specimens before a meeting of the Philosophical Society" (*WOB* 521–22). Charles Martin also writes about what he calls "the exhibition" (*White* 24–26). Sweet mentions a wax anatomical model of Adelaide at the Harvard Medical College (*BP* 276–77). Karl Pearson, et al., surmised that Morgan "brought her before the Philosophical Society" (236), but his *Monograph on Albinism in Man* also includes a picture of the anatomical model of Adelaide that was held at Harvard (Plate TT, Figures 154 and 155). Pearson does not mention a similar model of Jean Pierre; see Karl Pearson, Edward Nettleship, and Charles H. Usher, *A Monograph on Albinism in Man* (Cambridge: Cambridge University Press, 1911). Focusing on the published

account in *Transactions* rather than any presentation, Whitefield Bell views Morgan's explanation for the "streaks of lighter pigmentation" as "embarrassingly naïve" in *John Morgan, Continental Doctor* (Philadelphia: University of Pennsylvania Press, 1965), 253. Although the essay's title claims that the presentation took place in May, 1784, this appears to be incorrect. Neither the *Early Proceedings* nor the manuscript minutes mention anything about this for May 1784. Indeed, both these sources date the presentation in May 1786, "May 5, 1786. 4 present. Morgan's papers on a snake in a horse's eye, and two spotted negro children, read" (*Early Proceedings* 142).

81. APS Archives, 1791 January 31. APS Sales of Dr. Smith's oration. Film 54–60. Frame 162–63.

82. For more on Smith and the role his theory plays in early American thinking on race, see Stanton, *Leopard's*, 1–23; W. Jordan, *WOB*, 486–88, 513–17, passim, and "Introduction;" Dain, *Hideous Monster*, 40–80; Sweet, *BP*, 279–80; Martin, *White*, 37–41; and Yokota, *Unbecoming British*, 220–28.

83. Anon, "Last Wednesday Evening," *Freeman's Journal: or, The North-American Intelligencer* (March 7, 1787), 6:307:3.

84. W. Jordan, "Introduction," xv, in Samuel Stanhop Smith, *An Essay on the Causes*.

85. Ibid., li.

86. For how Cuff upsets the hierarchy of the APS itself, see Martin, *White*, 45–48. Ellis claims that "the content of his speech is no more and no less ridiculous than the observations of educated white members of the society" (*After the Revolution* 99). On the Cuff scene, see also W. Jordan, *WOB*, 524–25; Sweet, *BP*, 310–11; and Otter, *Philadelphia*, 75–76.

87. Looby, *Voicing America*, 223.

88. Ed White agrees, claiming that "one might find in the black servant Cuff's dialectic address to the philosophical society a harsh condemnation of the lax standards of republican institutions, not to mention the usual ridicule of semiliterate African Americans. But we might better read the episode as expressive of the philosophers' Teagueomaniacal desire to have Cuff within their society—Cuff, after all, comes across as the more rational participant" ("Introduction," xiii).

89. W. Jordan, "Introduction," xxx, in Samuel Stanhop Smith, *An Essay on the Causes*.

90. In his 1810 edition, Smith tries to clarify his earlier statements regarding whether the complexion of African Americans and Native Americans would become white. In a footnote, he writes that "I have before assigned reasons why a change in the complexion is less speedily to be expected in the blacks or any discoloured people, than in their features, and persons. Some annotator on the edition of Rees' Cyclopædia now publishing in Philadelphia by Bradford, and others, has been pleased to assert that I have maintained that the black complexion of the American negroes is growing sensibly lighter. Whatever may be the fact, I have, certainly, made no such assertion; but on the other hand, have assigned reasons why no very sensible effect of this kind should yet be expected. But, that time will efface the black complexion in them I think very probable, as it has done in the colony which, according to the testimony of Herodotus, was anciently transferred from Egypt to Colchis" (155). See Samuel Stanhope Smith, *An Essay on the Causes of the Variety of Complexion and Figure in the Human Species*, 1810, ed. Winthrop Jordan (Cambridge, MA: Belknap Press of Harvard University Press, 1965). Dain emphasizes the long time period and even the doubt that blacks would become lighter (*Hideous Monster* 47).

91. W. Jordan, "Introduction," xlvi, xlv, in Samuel Stanhop Smith, *An Essay on the Causes*.

92. Here, the narrator compares black peoples who would have had to die in the great flood to "the Mammoth, whose bones are found on the Ohio, whose bones are found on the Ohio, and other places, which was too big for Noah to get into the ark" (*MC* 75). As E. White notes, this refers to the collection of bones collected along the Ohio River, taken back to France, and discussed by Buffon in his *Histoire Naturelle* (*MC* 75). Clearly, Brackenridge shows how this talk about racial thinking is related to this debate around Buffon and his statements about the New World.

93. Citing how God cursed Ham when he looked upon his father Noah's nakedness, some slave apologists interpreted the curse of Ham to be a justification for slavery. Abolitionists argued that this curse had no link to blackness. For more on Ham, see Curran, *Anatomy*, 76–79; Kidd, *Forging*, 35; Smedley and Smedley, *Race*, 200, 216, 244; Thomas F. Gossett, *Race: The History of an Idea in America* (Dallas: Southern Methodist University Press, 1963), 5; and Dain, *Hideous Monster*, 126–27. For more on the curse of Cain, see Kidd, *Forging*, 33–35.

94. Elliott, *Revolutionary Writers*, 194.

95. Watts argues that Farrago's reasoning on "domination and subjection" echoes Jefferson's *Notes on the State of Virginia*, while the narrator uses the "best language of pamphleteers" (*Postcolonialism* 42–43). On the illogic of Farrago's argument, see also Ulla Haselstein, "Collateral Advantages: Hugh Henry Brackenridge's *Modern Chivalry*," REAL: *The Yearbook of Research in English and American Literature* 19 (2003), 307–23; and Otter, *Philadelphia*, 77–78.

96. Looby, *Voicing America*, 263.

97. As I have mentioned, Brackenridge had already written texts that characterized natives as both savage beasts and also as misunderstood and underappreciated beings. *Narratives of a Late Expedition against the Indians* was written in 1783, and "Trial," while not published until 1806, was written in 1785. Additionally, in Volume 3, both Teague and the narrator have long speeches in which each expounds upon the vices of native tribes and justify the current military action against them (*MC* 152–54). However, given that this pair of speeches follows the two speeches made by Farrago and the narrator defending the institution of slavery, one wonders if the second pair enacts the same parodic tone as the first. As Paul Gilmore attests, the cave scene both characterizes Indians and others as "not human," but yet the scene also, "with its universalization of taste, moves against this logic by gesturing toward an aesthetic faculty as a ground of human commonality" ("Republican" 315). Emory Elliott argues that this scene "balances the criticism of the Indians that Brackenridge had included in the earlier books. While Brackenridge was suspicious of Indian treaties and promises, he recognized the tragedy the whites had wrought on Indian civilizations" (*Revolutionary* 200).

98. See Looby on how this scene laments the Indians' departure but seeks to "preserve the cave and its contents for Euro-American posterity" (*Voicing America* 264). See also Paul Gilmore on how "Brackenridge's determination to eradicate Indians from his scene of primitive artistic achievement" is coupled with this scene's move "toward revealing some underlying, shared human capacity as the basis for a continued faith in democracy" ("Republican" 313–14).

99. For an important reconsideration of this assumed divide between literate cultures and oral cultures, see Birgit Brander Rasmussen, *Queequeg's Coffin*; and Matt Cohen, *Networked Wilderness*.

100. For a reading of the cave as an "aesthetic sphere as an alternative realm to a rationally organized, machinelike republican government [that] suggests the emancipatory potential latent within early American constructions of art as a pre-Wordsworthian retreat into nature" (302), see Paul Gimore, "Republican."

101. Sidney Hart, ed., *The Selected Papers of Charles Willson Peale and His Family, Volume 5, "The Autobiography of Charles Willson Peale,"* by Charles Willson Peale (New Haven: Yale University Press, 2000), 111.

102. Ibid., 221.

103. Ibid., 222.

104. Charles Willson Peale, "An Account of a person born a Negro, or a very dark Mulatto, who afterwards became white," *National Gazette* (October 31, 1791), 1:1:3. For more on Peale's portrait of James, see Martin, *White*, 29–33; W. Jordan, *WOB*, 521; Sweet, *BP*, 279; and Melish, *Gradual Emancipation*, 144. James's portrait remained in the museum until 1854, when it was sold (Hart 186).

105. Charles Willson Peale and A.M.F.J. Beauvois, *A Scientific and Descriptive Catalogue of Peale's Museum* (Philadelphia: Samuel H. Smith, 1796), 3.

106. Peale, "Autobiography." *The Selected Papers of Charles Willson Peale and His Family, Volume 5, "The Autobiography of Charles Willson Peale.,"* by Charles Willson Peale (New Haven: Yale University Press, 2000), 112.

107. Hart, *Selected Papers*, 266.

108. Murphy Smith, *Museum*, 19.

109. See also Ed White on this point, "Introduction," xvii–xviii. Harkey claims the cave scene "suggests a satire on Jefferson's interest in prehistoric animals; the incident from *Don Quixote* was refashioned to ridicule a kind of American quixotism as Brackenridge saw it—the penchant for neglecting larger philosophical ideas in favor of the study of old bones and other oddities" ("Frontier" 195). Sarah Wood also links it to the discourse on degeneration, as she claims that "the spectacle in the cave provides an unnerving glimpse beneath the 'surface' appearance of American progress; it burrows through the patriotic hyperbole and taps into underlying anxieties which petrified the early republic: the inexorable mutability of the American landscape, in socio-political as well as geological terms, and the concomitant fear of New World degeneration, a theory averred by Count Buffon and fiercely rebuffed in Jefferson's *Notes on the State of Virginia*" (*Quixotic* 90).

110. For more on Henry Moss, see Sweet, *BP*, 271–86; W. Jordan, *WOB*, 521–23; Melish, *Gradual Emancipation*, 140–50; Dain, *Hideous Monster*, 25–26; Stanton, *Leopard's*, 5–7; and Martin, *White*, 33–44.

111. Benjamin Smith Barton, "Account of Henry Moss, a White Negro: together with Reflections on the Affection called, by Physiologist, Leucaethiopia humana; Facts and Conjectures relative to the white Colour of the Human Species," *Philadelphia Medical and Physical Journal*: 3–18. APS B P31X #5. 4. Further references will be cited parenthetically as "AHM."

112. Benjamin Rush's Commonplace Book, 1792–1813. APS Archives. B R89c.

113. Benamin Rush, *The Autobiography of Benjamin Rush: His "Travels Through Life" together with his Commonplace Book for 1789–1813*, ed. George W. Corner (Princeton: Princeton University Press for the American Philosophical Society, 1948), 307.

114. Benjamin Rush, "Observations Intended to Favour a Supposition that the Black Color (As It Is Called) of the Negroes is Derived from the Leprosy," *Transactions* 4 (1799), 289–97. Further references to this edition will be cited parenthetically as "Leprosy."

115. Whitfield Bell notes that "In one of the last papers he presented to the Society, on July 14, 1797, Rush argued that the color of Negroes was owing to leprosy. Were this a fact, it might have benevolent consequences: if a cure could be found, Rush concluded, and black become white, the argument for enslaving Negroes because of their color would be destroyed. . . ." (*Patriot-Improvers* 463). See also W. Jordan, *WOB*, 517–21; Dain, *Hideous Monster*, 23–25; Takaki, *Iron Cages*, 28–35; Martin, *White*, 41–43; and Nelson, *National Manhood*, 57–60.

116. Rush, *Autobiography*, 202.

117. Bell, *Patriot-Improvers*, 456. Rush worked over many years with the black community in Philadelphia. In what turned out to be a tragic example, Rush encouraged Absalom Jones and Richard Allen, two influential black ministers, to organize African American volunteers to nurse the sick and bury the dead during the 1793 yellow fever outbreak in Philadelphia in order to increase the white community's respect for them. Rush mistakenly believed that African Americans were immune to the disease, and he lamented this mistaken belief that lead to the loss of lives. For more on Rush and his role in the yellow fever epidemic, see Otter, *Philadelphia*, 26–52; and Gary Nash, *Forging Freedom: The Formation of Philadelphia's Black Community, 1720–1840* (Cambridge: Harvard University Press, 1988), 121–24.

118. Rush records that he owned William Grubber, "a native African whom I bought, and liberated after he had served me 10 years" (*Autobiography* 246).

119. *BP*, 284.

120. *Autobiography*, 269.

121. Ibid., 164.

122. Caldwell even claims that Benjamin Smith Barton essentially took Caldwell's thesis and made it his own (*Autobiography* 164). He also explains that he undertook this examination in order to dispute Smith's claim that the varieties in humankind were due to external factors (*Autobiography* 269–74).

123. Sweet, *BP*, 272.

124. Ibid., 271. For more on the examinations of Moss, see Sweet, *BP*, 271–86; and Melish, *Gradual Emancipation*, 147–48, who also emphasizes "these disturbingly detached explorations of living human bodies" (147).

125. These issues recur again in oblique form in the book's final volume, where a debate erupts over whether to extend suffrage to animals (420, passim). On this scene, see Otter, *Philadelphia*, 78–81.

126. Dugatkin, *Moose*, 81–100.

127. For a reading of Teague as an "American sansculotte," see Caryn Chaden, "Dress and Undress in Brackenridge's *Modern Chivalry*," *Early American Literature* 26.1 (1991), 55–72.

Epilogue

1. See Foucault, *The Order of Things*; Wiegman, *American Anatomies*, especially chapter 1. Drawing on Foucault's *The Order of Things*, Wiegman argues that this change in the understanding of race occurs at the close of the eighteenth century as a part of a larger cultural shift from what Foucault terms classical to modern "epistemes of knowledge." Foucault ascribes "the birth of 'man' as an object of study" to this rise of the human sciences (*American Anatomies* 22). Wiegman writes that "through this reorganization [of knowledge], the human

being acquires for the first time in history an organic body and an interior psychic depth, becoming the primary object of investigation and making possible a host of new technologies, institutions, and disciplines" (*American Anatomies* 22). Wiegman extends this logic to explain why the change in thinking about *race* as an inner phenomenon occurred at this time in the United States: "The move from the visible epidermal terrain to the articulation of the interior structure of human bodies thus extrapolated in both broader and more distinct terms the parameters of white supremacy, giving it a logic lodged fully in the body" (*American Anatomies* 31).

2. See W. Jordan, *WOB*, 537–8; Melish, *Gradual Emancipation*, especially chapter 4. Melish contends that as more African Americans became emancipated in the North in the early nineteenth century, whites increasingly believed race to be "fixed" and "not subject to substantial change by external experience" (*Gradual Emancipation* 161). Melish claims that whites sought a way to assure themselves that blacks fundamentally were different from themselves, even if they became free: "The popular conclusion about the stability of whiteness paralleled the direction of scientific thought, which increasingly turned away from environmental explanations in the early nineteenth century" (*Gradual Emancipation* 161).

3. See Nelson, *National Manhood*, especially chapters 3–4; Tawil, *The Making of Racial Sentiment*; and Boulukos, *The Grateful Slave*.

4. See Dain, *Hideous Monster*.

5. *Gradual Emancipation*, 150.

6. Ed White makes a compelling and related argument regarding slavery, Underhill's aborted abolitionism, and conservative politics in "Divided We Stand: Emergent Conservatism in Royall Tyler's *The Algerine Captive*," *Studies in American Fiction* 37.1 (2010), 5–27. On Underhill's "amnesia" at the novel's conclusion, see Sarah Wood (*Quixotic* 124) and Gesa Mackenthun, "The Transoceanic Emergence of American 'Postcolonial' Identities," in *A Companion to the Literatures of Colonial America*, eds. Susan Castillo and Ivy Schweitzer (Malden, MA: Blackwell Publishing, 2005), 342. On the ending, see also Keri Holt, "'All Parts of the Union I Considered My Home': The Federal Imagination of *the Algerine Captive*," *Early American Literature* 46.3 (2011), 481–515; Edward Larkin, "Nation and Empire in the Early US," *American Literary History* 22.3 (2010), 501–26; Ed Watts, *Postcolonialism*, particularly chapter 3; and Aaron Hanlon, "Unworthy Global Citizens: Quixotic Influence and the Underhill Legacy in *The Algerine Captive*," *Comparative American Studies* 9.2 (2011), 119–30. Cathy Davidson offers an alternate reading of the ending, *Revolution* 303–4. On narration, see William C. Spengemann, *The Adventurous Muse: The Poetics of American Fiction, 1789–1900* (New Haven: Yale University Press, 1977), esp. 119–42; Watts, *Postcolonialism*, 73–94; and Joseph C. Schöpp, "Liberty's Sons and Daughters: Susanna Haswell Rowson's and Royall Tyler's Algerine Captives," in *Early America Re-Explored: New Readings in Colonial, Early National, and Antebellum Culture*, eds. Klaus H. Schmidt and Fritz Fleischmann (New York: Peter Lang, 2000), 291–307. Although Ed Watts sees Tyler himself critiquing the point of view of Underhill as a narrator in order to reveal the problems of colonial thinking, I am more in agreement with William Spengemann's description of the narration, one that is written by the character-*cum*-narrator who has ostensibly developed and changed over the course of the novel. See also Holt, "All Parts" on Underhill's development. Like Watts, Joseph Schöpp, Aaron Hanlon, and John Engell see Underhill maintaining his naiveté throughout. See Engell, "Narrative Irony and National Character in Royall Tyler's *the Algerine Captive*," *Studies in American Fiction* 17.1 (1989), 19–32.

7. See, for instance, Benilde Montgomery, "White Captives, African Slaves: A Drama of Abolition," *Eighteenth-Century Studies* 27.4 (1994), 615–30; Jennifer Margulis, "Spies, Pirates, and White Slaves: Encounters with the Algerines in Three Early American Novels," *Eighteenth-Century Novel* 1 (2001), 1–36; and Sarah F. Wood, *Quixotic.*

8. I am thankful to Susan Ryan for suggesting this to me. See also Hester Blum on important differences between American and Algerian slavery in *The View from the Masthead: Maritime Imagination and Antebellum American Sea Narratives* (Chapel Hill: University of North Carolina Press, 2010), 57.

9. Timothy Marr, *The Cultural Roots of American Islamicism* (Cambridge: Cambridge University Press, 2006) 22. For more on this moment in US–North Africa relations, see Marr, *Cultural Roots*, esp. 26–62. See also Jacob Berman, *American Arabesque: Arabs and Islam in the Nineteenth Century Imaginary* (New York: New York University Press, 2012); Robert J. Allison, *The Crescent Obscured: The United States and the Muslim World, 1776–1815* (New York: Oxford University Press, 1995), esp. 3–34; 87–126; and Lawrence A. Peskin, *Captives and Countrymen: Barbary Slavery and the American Public, 1785–1816* (Baltimore: The Johns Hopkins University Press, 2009), esp. 71–89.

10. Marr, *Cultural Roots*, 32.

11. Allison, *Crescent Obscured*, 87–106.

12. See note 6 on narration.

13. Royall Tyler, *The Algerine Captive, or, The Life and Adventures of Doctor Updike Underhill, Six Years a Prisoner Among the Algerines.* (New York: Modern Library, 2002), 18. Further references to this edition will be cited parenthetically as *AC.*

14. Gossett, *Race*, 5.

15. For more on how the curse of Ham gets linked with African slavery in the Americas, see Curran, *Anatomy*, 76–79; Kidd, *Forging*, 35; Smedley and Smedley, *Race*, 200, 216, 244; Thomas F. Gossett, *Race: The History of an Idea in America* (Dallas: Southern Methodist University Press, 1963), 5; and Dain, *Hideous Monster*, 126–27.

16. Underhill also gestures toward this link when he compares his employment as a schoolteacher to the life of a slave, claiming that "to purchase a school master and a negro was almost synonimous" (*AC* 83).

17. See note 27, Introduction.

18. Gardner links this scene to Underhill's national identity, claiming that "Updike's first moment of patriotism is born out of his anxiety lest Buffon see in the failure of American science the fulfillment of his darkest prophecies for the American race" (*Master Plots* 30).

19. Ada Lou Carson and Herbert L. Carson, *Royall Tyler* (Boston: Twayne Publishers, 1979), 87.

20. Qtd. in Gardner, *Master Plots*, 29.

21. Ibid., 29.

22. For more on Rush, see W. Jordan, *WOB*, 286–87.

23. Gardner, *Master Plots*, 42. Gardner notes, however, that perhaps Tyler conflated him with another John Hunter, one who also wrote on race from an environmentalist point of view (*Master Plots* 194). If so, this further shows how *The Algerine Captive* was drawing upon multiple epistemological frameworks simultaneously.

24. See Wiegman, *American Anatomies*, 51–55.

25. James R. Lewis, "Savages of the Seas: Barbary Captivity Tales and Images of Muslims in the Early Republic," *Journal of American Culture* 13.2 (1990), 80.

26. Ed White, "Emergent Conservatism."

27. One how the novel evokes the morally defunct "Plantation South" in order to locate the United States "on a moral-geographical imaginative world map," see Jennifer Rae Greeson, *Our South*, 82–89.

28. Davidson, *Revolution*, 299.

29. Whether this is truly the "humane" thing to do—attending to sick slaves to ensure their eventual sale—is certainly up for debate. The novel represents an alternative to Underhill's choice. A ship clerk suggests that they "tie [the diseased slaves] up and cast them over the ship side together, and thus, at one dash, to purify the ship. *What signifies, added he, the lives of the black devils; they love to die. You cannot please them better, than by chucking them into the water*" (*AC* 100, emphasis in original).

30. See also Kelly Bezio on how this scene relates to "geohumoral theories of human variation" in "National Inoculations, Immunities, and Identities in Royall Tyler's *the Algerine Captive*," *Symbiosis* 15.1 (2011), 32.

31. See Michele Crescenzo, who argues that Tyler reverses "the trope which for at least two hundred years had associated 'whiteness' with good and 'blackness' with evil" in "'Ernestlie Lookinge for a Better Countre': The Racial Discourse in Royall Tyler's *Algerine Captive*," *Publications of the Mississippi Philological Association* (2005), 21. See also Margulis, "Spies," 21–22.

32. Adam Smith, *The Theory of Moral Sentiments*, 1759, eds. D. D. Raphael and A. C. Macfie (Oxford: Clarendon Press, 1976), 9. Further references to this edition will be cited parenthetically as *TMS*.

33. Stern, *Plight of Feeling*, 24, emphasis added.

34. Ibid.

35. Christopher Castiglia, "Abolition's Racial Interiors and the Making of White Civic Depth," *American Literary History* 14.1 (2002), 34, emphasis added.

36. It is crucial to note, however, as Stern explains, that Smith's theory of sentiment was predicated upon an imperfect exchange between individual's interiors, an idea that usefully illustrates the difficulty of cross-racial sentimental interchange in early America. Castiglia also argues that the black slave sufferer must present his suffering in such a way that allows the white sympathizer to identify with him, but only temporarily. See also Susan M. Ryan on imperfect exchanges of sympathy, especially page 17, in *The Grammar of Good Intentions: Race and the Antebellum Culture of Benevolence* (Ithaca: Cornell University Press, 2003). For more on the epistemology of seeing in Tyler, see Matthew Pangborn, "Royall Tyler's *The Algerine Captive*, America, and the Blind Man of Philosophy," *Arizona Quarterly* 67.3 (2011), 1–27.

37. *American Anatomies*, 22–23. For how Wiegman extends Foucault's insight into the shift from natural history to the human sciences at the close of the eighteenth century to describe this "reorganization" of racial "knowledge," see *American Anatomies*, 21–42.

38. Ibid., 30.

39. Ibid., 31.

40. See Ellison, *Cato's Tears*; Nicole Eustace, *Passion Is the Gale: Emotion, Power, and the Coming of the American Revolution* (Chapel Hill: University of North Carolina Press for the Omohundro Institute of Early American History and Culture, 2008); and Sarah Knott, *Sensibility and the American Revolution* (Chapel Hill: University of North Carolina Press for the Omohundro Institute of Early American History and Culture, 2009).

41. The important work of Tawil and Boulukos on the relationship between race and sentiment has crucially informed my thinking. Boulukos examines how the trope of the grateful slave and the way it suggests meaningful difference in blacks' and whites' capacity for sentiment went hand in hand with developing notions of racial difference. In a related argument, Tawil investigates how American frontier romances of the 1820s imagined the differences between blacks and whites as emotional—rather than physical—differences. See Tawil, *Racial Sentiment*; and Boulukos, *Grateful Slave*.

42. One should note that after the *Sympathy*'s departure, the slaves invite Underhill to return with them to their "native country." Underhill declines, and when he sees a ship that he suspects is the *Sympathy* returning, he "intimate[s] to them that they might conceal themselves in the brush and escape" (*AC* 104). Only one refuses Underhill's offer in order to be reunited with his son aboard the slaver.

43. For more on the dangers of sympathetic over-identification, see Ryan, *Grammar*, 19.

44. Wiegman usefully qualifies the epistemological break that Foucault posits. "The intensification of scientific efforts to ascertain the origin and bodily foundation for race in the nineteenth century, alongside the persistence of environmentalism as a key explanation for racial difference in the United States in the antebellum period, indicates a less emphatic break, a more troubled confusion, between classical and modern apprehensions of race. To a large extent, such an intensification points to the importance of thinking about epistemic organizations as heterogeneous, containing subcultural formations of knowledge that exist in contradiction or tension with each regime's primary features" (*American Anatomies* 34). As Dror Wahrman puts it, "historical change, once again, is surely not all that straightforward. It was to take many more years before rigid, essentialized, racialized, congenital understandigns of human difference . . . were to drive their pre-modern flexible, mutable counterparts to the cultural margins, and even then the triumph would not be complete. The closing decades of the eighteenth century witnessed the beginnings of this historical change: beginnings that were often messy, tentative, halting, replete with dead ends, and in which the new jostled and overlapped with the old" (*Modern Self* 117).

45. *Gradual Emancipation*, 161.

46. For more on "good intentions," race, and benevolence in the nineteenth century, see Susan Ryan, *Grammar*. For more on sentiment and captivity, see Michelle Burnham, *Captivity and Sentiment: Cultural Exchange in American Literature; 1682–1861* (Hanover and London: University Press of New England, 1997).

47. See Gardner for how the Algerine becomes a "composite of all the racial and national destinies he does not want for his country," including Native American (*Master Plots* 27).

48. James Adair, *The History of the American Indians*, ed. Kathryn E. Holland Braund (Tuscaloosa: University of Alabama Press, 2005), 67.

49. Ibid., 66.

50. Jefferson and Smith famously hypothesized about the minutia of colored skin strata. For instance, in *Notes*, Jefferson argues that "the first difference which strikes us is that of colour. Whether the black of the negro resides in the reticular membrane between the skin and scarf-skin, or in the scarf-skin itself; whether it proceeds from the colour of the blood, the colour of the bile, or from that of some other secretion, the difference is fixed in nature, and is as real as if its seat and cause were better known to us. And is this difference of no importance?" (186). In *Essay on the Causes of the Variety of Complexion and Figure in the Human Species* (1810), Smith contends that "the human skin has been discovered by anatomists to consist of three distinct lamellæ or

integuments; the external, or scarf-skin, which is an extremely fine netting, and perfectly transparent in the darkest coloured nations,—the interior, or true skin, which, in people of all the different grades of colour, is white,—and an intermediate membrane, which is cellular in its structure, somewhat like a honeycomb. This membrane is the proper seat of colour, being filled with a delicate mucous, or viscid liquor, which easily receives the lively tinge of the blood when strongly propelled, by any cause, to the surface, or the duller stain of the bile when it enters in any undue quantity into the circulation. The smallest surcharge of this secretion imparts to it a yellow appearance; which, by remaining long in contact with the atmosphere assumes a darker hue, and if exposed, at the same time, to the immediate influence of the sun, approaches, according to the heat of the climate and the degree in which the bile prevails, towards black" (35).

51. Cosmetic creams promising to lighten women's complexions have persisted to the present day. For a discussion of skin-lightening products used in twenty-first century Mexico, see Jamie Winders, John Paul Jones III, and Michael James Higgins, "Making *Güeras*: Selling White Identities on Late-Night Mexican Television," *Gender, Place and Culture* 12.1 (2005), 71–93.

52. P. Gould, *Barbaric Traffic*, 113. See P. Gould, *Barbaric Traffic*, 113–4; Malini Johar Schueller, *U.S. Orientalisms: Race, Nation, and Gender in Literature, 1790–1890* (Ann Arbor: University of Michigan Press, 1998), 53–54; and Jacob Rama Berman, "The Barbarous Voice of Democracy: American Captivity in Barbary and the Multicultural Specter," *American Literature* 79.1 (2007), 19–20. See also Schueller and Berman for how this scene destabilizes Underhill's gender identity as well.

53. The setting of white slavery in North Africa is key. Because of changing understandings of race at the time, Underhill becomes black internally while staying white externally, thereby enabling his capture in this particular type of slavery. Then, once enslaved, he can represent the binary opposite to white citizenship, which, as we shall see, comes to be crucial to the novel's conclusion.

54. See Montgomery, "White Captives."

55. See also Martin Brückner on how Tyler's book, using "the metanarrative design of school geographies" (*Geographic* 179) concludes with unifying rhetoric. On the use of unifying rhetoric, see also Edward Larkin, "Nation and Empire," 515; Schöpp, "Liberty's," 303; and Mackenthun, *Transoceanic*, 341. For an alternative account that emphasizes diversity, see Holt, "All Parts." She argues that Underhill acquires a cosmopolitan and federalist worldview that he puts into service for the nation made up of diverse peoples.

56. Edmund Morgan, *American Slavery, American Freedom: The Ordeal of Colonial Virginia* (New York: Norton, 1975).

57. For an alternative view on how Underhill's composition "keep[s] an earlier promise," see Davidson, *Revolution*, 303.

58. David W. Blight, *Race and Reunion: The Civil War in American Memory* (Cambridge, MA: Belknap Press of Harvard University Press, 2001).

59. Michael Rogin, "'Make My Day!': Spectacle as Amnesia in Imperial Politics," *Representations* 29 (1990), 106.

60. See also Mackenthun on how the novel "dramatizes the emergence of an American national identity through amnesia" ("Transoceanic" 342).

61. Sarah Knott explains how early Americans, and in particular, Federalists, used sentiment to help draw the new US citizenry together, often excluding women and African Americans. See *Sensibility and the American Revolution*, esp. chapter 5.

{ INDEX }